Asia Pacific
Financial Deregulation

D1766459

Recent events in East Asia have highlighted the risks of volatility and contagion in a financially integrated world. Countries in the region had been at the forefront of the movement towards increased integration but the crisis that struck Thailand in July 1997, and the rapidity with which it spread to other East Asian nations, suggested that all was not well. Weaknesses in domestic financial intermediation, poor corporate governance and deficient government responses to large capital inflows all played a role in the build-up of vulnerability. *Asia Pacific Financial Deregulation* provides an insight into financial liberalisation and structural reform in the region generally and as illustrated by a number of countries.

This volume is edited by Gordon de Brouwer, Reserve Bank of Australia, with Wisarn Pupphavesa, National Institute of Development Administration, Thailand, and is based on the papers presented at the Twenty-fourth Pacific Trade and Development (PAFTAD) conference held in Chiangmai, Thailand in May 1998.

Asia Pacific Financial Deregulation

Edited by Gordon de Brouwer
with Wisarn Pupphavesa

London and New York

First published 1999 by Routledge
11 New Fetter Lane, London EC4P 4EE

Simultaneously published in the USA and Canada
by Routledge
29 West 35th Street, New York, NY 10001

Routledge is an imprint of the Taylor & Francis Group

Transferred to Digital Printing 2004

Typeset in Garamond by ANU Graphics, Canberra, Australia

British Library Cataloguing in Publication Data
A catalogue record for this book is available from the British Library

Library of Congress Cataloging in Publication Data
A catalogue record for this book has been requested

ISBN 0-415-20842-4 (hbk)
ISBN 0-415-20843-2 (pbk)

Contents

Figures

Tables

Contributors

Gordon de Brouwer, Chief Manager, International Markets and Relations, International Department, Reserve Bank of Australia

Pedro Alba, Principal Economist, Economic Policy Unit of the Poverty Reduction and Economic Management Network, World Bank

Amar Bhattacharya, Senior Advisor in the Development Economics Vice Presidency, World Bank

Stijn Claessens, Principal Economist, Financial Economics Group of the Financial Sector Practice, World Bank

Kevin Davis, Colonial Professor of Finance and Head of the Department of Accounting and Finance, University of Melbourne

Matthew Field, Goldman Sachs, Hong Kong

Farid Harianto, Deputy Chairman, The Indonesian Bank Restructuring Agency

Swati Ghosh, Senior Economist, East Asia region, World Bank

Don Hanna, Director of Non-Japan Asia Economic Research, Goldman Sachs (Asia) LLC

Leonardo Hernandez, Senior Economist, Research Department, Central Bank of Chile

Akiyoshi Horiuchi, Professor of Economics, University of Tokyo

Masahiro Kawai, Chief Economist, East Asia and the Pacific, World Bank

Manuel F. Montes, Senior Fellow, East-West Center, Honolulu

Mari E. Pangestu, Executive Director, Centre for Strategic and International Studies, Jakarta

Sang Yong Park, Professor of Finance, College of Business and Economics, Yonsei University, Seoul

Wisarn Pupphavesa, Dean, Graduate School of Development Economics, National Institute of Development Administration, Thailand

Chaipat Sahasakul, First Bangkok City Bank

Jia-Dong Shea, Research Fellow, Institute of Economics, Academia Sinica; Professor, Department of Economics, National Taiwan University; Deputy Governor, Central Bank of China; President, Taiwan Economic Association

David C.Y. Sun, Assistant Director General, Central Bank of China, Taiwan

Weiying Zhang, China Centre for Economic Research, Peking University

Abbreviations

ACU	Asian currency unit
ADB	Asian Development Bank
ADM	Asian dollar market
AFIC	Australian Financial Institutions Commission
AFTA	ASEAN Free Trade Agreement
AGPS	Australian Government Publishing Service
APRA	Australian Prudential Regulatory Authority
ASC	Australian Securities Commission
ASEAN	Association of South East Asian Nations
ASEAN-4	Indonesia, Malaysia, the Philippines and Thailand
ASIC	Australian Securities and Investment Commission
BAPEPAM	Badan Pelaksana Pasar Modal
BIBF	Bangkok International Banking Facility
BIS	Bank for International Settlements
BOT	Bank of Thailand
CAR	capital adequacy ratio
CARSEL	Capital adequacy, Asset quality, Regulatory compliance, Strategies and stability, Earnings and Liquidity
CBC	Central Bank of China
CD	certificate of deposit
CDIC	Central Deposit Insurance Corporation
CEO	chief executive officer
CPI	consumer price index
EEF	exchange equalisation fund
EU	European Union
FDI	foreign direct investment
FY	financial year
GDP	gross domestic product

GNP	gross national product
HK	Hong Kong
ICBC	Industrial and Commercial Bank of China
ICOR	incremental capital output ratio
IFC	International Finance Corporation
IMF	International Monetary Fund
IPO	initial public offer
ISC	Insurance and Superannuation Commission
JKSE	Jakarta stock exchange
KLSE	Kuala Lumpur stock exchange
KSE	Korean stock exchange
LGS	liquid and government securities
LIBOR	London interbank offered rate
MOF	Ministry of Finance
MSE	Manila stock exchange
NBFI	non-bank financial institution
NIE	newly industrialising economy
OECD	Organisation for Economic Cooperation and Development
OTC	over-the-counter
PPP	purchasing power parity
PTA	policy target agreement
RBA	Reserve Bank of Australia
RBNZ	Reserve Bank of New Zealand
R&D	research and development
RM	ringgit
Rp	rupiah
RRP	reverse repurchase facility
SBI	Bank Indonesia certificate of deposit
SEHK	Stock Exchange of Hong Kong
SES	Stock Exchange of Singapore
SET	Stock Exchange of Thailand
SOE	state-owned enterprise
SRD	statutory reserve deposit
TBTF	'too big to fail'
TSE	Taiwan stock exchange
US	United States
WPI	wholesale price index
WTO	World Trade Organisation
yoy	year on year

Preface

This book is a compilation of papers presented at the 24th Pacific Trade and Development (PAFTAD) conference on Asia Pacific Financial Liberalisation and Reform, held in Chiangmai, Thailand, on 20 to 22 May 1998. The conference was hosted by the School of Development Economics at the National Institute of Development Administration (NIDA), Bangkok, in cooperation with the PAFTAD International Steering Committee.

PAFTAD is an international forum of senior academic economists in the Asia Pacific region. Its steering committee, chaired by Professor Hugh Patrick of Columbia University, comprises Narongchai Akranasee and Florian Alburo (University of the Philippines), Mohamed Arif (Malaysian Institute of Economic Research), Chia Siow Yue (Institute of Southeast Asian Studies), Wendy Dobson (University of Toronto), Peter Drysdale and Ross Garnaut (Australian National University), Ralph Hueneman (University of Victoria, Canada), Wisarn Pupphavesa (National Institute of Development Administration), Rong-I Wu (Taiwan Institute of Economic Research), and Ippei Yamazawa (Hitotsubashi University). The committee organises an international conference every eighteen months. The PAFTAD internet site provides a comprehensive overview of PAFTAD's objectives and history, conference information and a list of publications <http://sunsite.anu.edu.au/paftad>.

The staff of the National Institute of Development Administration in Bangkok organised an excellent conference, with particular thanks to the host committee of PAFTAD 24: Thammanum Pongsrikul, Klin-Keo Chintakananda, Suchittra Chamnivickorn, Komain Jiranykul, Nada Chunsom, Chanika Charoenwong, Somporn Silpsuwon and the staff at NIDA. Matthew Terpstra, from the PAFTAD secretariat at the Australian National University, also provided valuable assistance. We also thank the Westin Hotel, Chiangmai, for their service and support, and the Ford Foundation (USA), the Institute for Southeast Asian Studies (Singapore), the University of Toronto, the Australian National University, the Taiwan Institute for Economic Research, the Korea Member Committee of the Pacific Basin Economic Council, the National Centre for Development Administration (Thailand), the Centre for Strategic and International Studies (Indonesia), the Foundation for Advanced Information Research (Japan), the Japan Federation of Economic

Organisations (Keidanren), the Kansai Economic Federation (Kankeiren), the Rockefeller Brothers Fund (USA), the Korea Development Institute, the Ministry of Foreign Affairs (Japan), the Asia Foundation (USA) and the Chinese Taipei PECC Secretariat for generous financial support.

This book reflects the work of many people, for which the PAFTAD International Steering Committee and the editor wish to express their deepest appreciation. We would especially like to thank Denise Ryan for her excellent supervision of the publication process, and Raylee Singh for superb editorial work.

Gordon de Brouwer and Wisarn Pupphavesa
November 1998

1   Introduction

Gordon de Brouwer

THE ISSUES

The East Asian financial crisis is one of the defining economic events of the last quarter of the twentieth century. The crisis was sparked by a currency adjustment in Thailand in June 1997, but extended its reach to most of Asia and, indeed, from the second half of 1998, to the world.

The crisis was the result of the interaction of a number of factors. New opportunities to access international finance, combined with weak bank and corporate governance and the expectation of rising regional exchange rates, led to widespread unhedged and short-term foreign currency borrowing by both banks and businesses in East Asia. Access to foreign capital was unprecedented, driven by the steady winding back of capital controls in emerging East Asia and an unparalleled willingness of foreign financial institutions to lend to the rapidly growing economies in the region. While capital flowed to a range of productive sources, expanding the capacity of the economy, there was also excess investment in some of these sectors (like motor vehicles) and in less productive, more speculative sectors (like property). Funds had also been directed – sometimes by government and sometimes by private commercial connections – to projects which did not necessarily have the highest risk-adjusted returns.

The trigger for the collapse happened to be an exchange rate realignment in Thailand which had pegged its currency at a value that was moderately out of line with fundamentals that had deteriorated following the global excess supply in semi-conductors and the rise in the US dollar against Japan and Europe. But the trigger itself could have been almost anything. The event spread to other markets, as lenders re-evaluated their financial investments, and other currencies depreciated. Again, foreign borrowing was short-term and currency exposures were not generally hedged, and domestic financial institutions were fundamentally weak. The scramble to reverse exposures, as currencies started to drop, in turn exacerbated the fall. Financial markets responded as a herd, exiting the markets en masse and pumping up the risk premium on lending to the region without regard to the actual circumstances in particular countries. Political uncertainties, especially in Indonesia in early 1998, compounded the problem. Initial international policy responses were also misguided, interpreting events as a classic balance of payments problem driven by government profligacy, rather than a financial crisis, and focusing on reforms which were not directly relevant to the problems at hand.

The crisis was contained within East Asia until August 1998, when the Russian government defaulted on its debt. Markets again overreacted, losing their appetite for risk and failing to distinguish the very different circumstances of particular countries and borrowers. With this, the Asian financial crisis became a fully fledged emerging market crisis (although the situation in East Asia itself improved at this time).

The next step was for the crisis to spread to the industrialised economies of the world. The loss of appetite for risk was one element by which events in East Asia had spread to industrialised countries, with the risk premium on lower grade corporate borrowing rising substantially. But the more potent force was through the financial institutions of Europe and the United States. The first leg was the exposure of the banks – and Swiss, French and German banks in particular – to emerging markets in Asia, eastern Europe (including Russia) and Latin America. These exposures involved loan write-downs, lower profits and falling share prices, which undermined world share markets (widely thought to be overvalued and vulnerable to a fall), and adversely affected consumer sentiment (especially in the United States). The second leg was bank lending, especially of US banks, to hedge funds, which had taken huge leveraged speculative positions in financial markets around the world and suffered large losses when these positions turned against them. European and, especially, US banks had also taken what turned out to be unprofitable proprietary positions in asset markets. This led to major disorder in world financial markets in October 1998, as market liquidity dried up, bank earnings fell substantially and fears of a credit crunch and weakness in consumer and business sentiment became widespread. The US Federal Reserve responded by lowering interest rates several times. The financial crisis triggered by the baht depreciation in July 1997 became a world financial crisis.

THIS BOOK

This book goes back to analyse the start of it all: Asia Pacific financial deregulation. The argument is set out in five parts in a collection of twelve essays by experts in their field.

Part I: The changing architecture of financial regulation

The first part examines the changing architecture of financial deregulation in East Asia. Chapter 2, written by Pedro Alba, Amar Bhattacharya, Stijn Claessens, Swati Ghosh and Leonardo Hernandez, sets the scene by explaining what happened in East Asia and why. In 'Volatility and Contagion in a Financially Integrated World', Alba and his colleagues provide a detailed analysis of the origin of the East Asian financial crisis. Relying on extensive analysis of the data, the authors argue that the crisis was largely the result of weaknesses in domestic financial intermediation, poor corporate governance and inadequate government policies in dealing with large capital inflows. Weak due diligence by external creditors and ample global liquidity obscured these fundamental weaknesses in the financial system and were more a trigger for the crisis, rather than its cause. The authors also argue that the financial crisis was not inevitable and, for most countries, was triggered by spill-over effects from Thailand's exchange rate crisis. It also sets out some implications of the crisis for dealing with volatile capital flows and the structure of the financial system.

Chapter 3, written by Jia-Dong Shea and David C.Y. Sun, assesses the conditions for the successful prudential regulation of financial institutions in the Asia Pacific region. The authors argue that what happened in East Asia was a failure of the financial system, markets and superintendence. They make the point that maintaining macroeconomic stability, particularly in monetary policy, is generally important for maintaining financial stability. But, more broadly, the preconditions for financial stability also include well-developed banking supervision, effective market discipline, the efficient resolution of problem loans in banks and mechanisms to secure stability of the financial system as a whole. They argue that this task has been complicated by financial innovation and globalisation. They focus their discussion on the experiences of Taiwan.

Part II: Regional financial integration

Part II shifts focus to regional financial integration. Masahiro Kawai, in Chapter 4, provides a comprehensive account of the pattern of capital flows in emerging East Asia, examining foreign direct investment, portfolio investment, banking transactions and foreign exchange transactions before and after the crisis. He analyses the differences in the forces underlying capital flows and regulation in the Asian NIES, ASEAN and China, and considers some ways to restore capital inflows, such as privatisation and guarantees from multilateral institutions. He explores the lessons of the East Asian financial crisis, concluding that it shows the need for sound economic management, financial system resilience (including the need for flexible monetary policy and possible temporary use of capital controls, at least on inflows), solid corporate governance, viable exchange rate regimes and international cooperation. He argues that the crisis does not obviate the importance of financial liberalisation, but it does show that the speed and scope of liberalisation should depend on a country's stage of development.

In Chapter 5, 'The Development of Asian Equity Markets', Matthew Field and Don Hanna trace and explain the reasons behind the growth of East Asian stock markets over the past decade, including providing a handy chronology of developments in individual country share markets. They identify domestic demand and supply factors, and the role of foreign participation, as key factors behind the growth of markets up until the mid-1990s. They analyse the financial crisis and its effects on equity markets and investment in the Asia Pacific region, arguing that recovery in regional stock markets will be slow, reform of laws and practices extensive and foreign ownership substantially expanded. They also expect private equity placements to become more common.

In Chapter 6, Manuel Montes addresses the relative positions of Hong Kong, Singapore and Tokyo as regional financial centres. He presents a taxonomy of financial centres within financial intermediation and identifies the key requirements for a financial centre: market efficiency (including taxation regime), market innovation, human infrastructure, language, concentration of financial institutions, political stability, business infrastructure and quality of life. The relative attributes of Hong Kong, Singapore and Tokyo are discussed with reference to a classification of systems and criteria. Montes argues that Hong Kong has particular advantages as a service centre for China, as Singapore has for Southeast Asia, but that Singapore has the overall advantage because it has strong government support. He believes that Tokyo will decline in relative importance.

Part III: Patterns of corporate governance, finance and reform

Weakness in the corporate governance of banks and businesses was a key factor in the East Asian financial crisis, and is an issue deserving particular focus in analysis of the crisis. Part III looks at the experiences of Indonesia, China and Korea.

Farid Harianto and Mari Pangestu examine developments and the prospects for the Indonesian corporates in Chapter 7, providing a concise insight into corporate structure and behaviour leading into the financial crisis. They trace the shift in corporate governance – or the accountability of company owners and managers to outside investors – over the past few decades, shifting from family-owned enterprises to ones which are professionally managed and have to compete internationally. State-owned enterprises have also been subject to the same forces of change, albeit at a slower pace. Harianto and Pangestu identify the key features of, and differences between, corporate governance and market discipline for state-owned enterprises, Chinese-owned businesses and *pribumi* (indigenous) businesses. The market in Indonesia is characterised by myriad imperfections and government involvement. The authors describe how Chinese businesses, which are family based, have generally used their own commercial networks to supplant imperfections and internalise transactions (including the provision of funds), as well as developing close ties with government in order to protect their vulnerable social position. *Pribumi* businesses, by way of contrast, have lacked effective networks, even though they have had close links with government, and would use alliances with Chinese groups to develop expertise and gain access to capital. Disclosure has typically been poor, and regulation and enforcement weak, although the authors argue that recent changes to bank disclosure and structure and to bankruptcy proceedings should impose more discipline on corporates.

In Chapter 8, Zhang Weiying assesses recent developments in Chinese corporate finance, one of the many interesting dimensions of change in China. In the post-reform period, from 1978 to the present, there has been a substantial shift in the distribution of national income, with households surpassing the state as the main source of finance for investment capital. But while corporate finance has changed, corporate governance has not, with state-owned enterprises still owned by governments which lack sufficient incentive to make these firms efficient. Moreover, households have weak incentives to monitor banks which in turn have weak incentives to monitor firms. Zhang argues that the financial crisis has placed particular stresses on state-owned enterprises and the banks which lend to them. But the crisis has also shown that the problem, and the issue of corporate governance of both firms and banks, have to be addressed by the government.

Sang Yong Park examines financial reform and its impact on corporate governance in Korea in Chapter 9. He argues that the financial crisis and economic contraction in Korea were not accidental, and that recent events point to the need for major reform in product, labour and financial markets and in corporate governance. Park outlines the process of financial reform in Korea during the past decade and how it affected corporate organisation, practices and financing in that country. He thinks that the crisis provides Korea with a once-in-a-lifetime opportunity to reform and hence defeat the normal political tide of opposition to structural reform, but he admits that events have been hugely costly and reform generates enormous uncertainty about the rules of the game, all of which are a major challenge to politicians.

Part IV: Case studies in financial reform

Part IV changes tack, focusing on the experiences of a number of countries in the Asia Pacific region. Chapter 10 starts with Japan. In 'Financial Fragility in Japan', Akiyoshi Horiuchi explains how the broad-ranging failure of governance mechanisms worsened the effect of the banking crisis in that country. Many industrialised countries, including Japan, experienced banking crises in the late 1980s and early 1990s, but Japan's crisis has endured longer than others. Indeed, the problem has become progressively worse. Horiuchi describes the way this crisis evolved and explains how the governance structure of banks has been systematically undermined by the operation of government, including, for example, the appointment of retired government officials into senior positions in financial institutions. He argues that the immunity of the management from market discipline has undermined Japan's banks and delayed necessary structural adjustment.

In a more positive tone, in Chapter 11 Kevin Davis outlines the nature of the successful – but at times also eventful – financial reform undertaken by Australia and New Zealand. He starts off with a summary of the process and pressures for reform in the two countries. While the approach to domestic monetary policy largely converged in the mid-1990s, the approaches to prudential supervision are quite different, with New Zealand taking a 'buyer-beware' market approach and Australia taking a wholistic and active approach to supervision of its financial system. One feature of interest in the New Zealand system is that its banks are largely foreign owned, which can be regarded as an advantage in stabilising the banking system of a small open economy. It also implies that the authorities essentially refer financial supervision to the home country of their banks, which, in New Zealand's case, is Australia.

In Chapter 12, entitled 'Thailand's Financial Reforms', Chaipat Sahasakul provides an example of the depths of the difficulties in financial reform currently facing much of emerging East Asia. Chaipat summarises the process of reform in the 1990s and then explores the reasons for the foreign exchange rate crisis in 1997. He argues that the Bangkok International Banking Facility was a key conduit for volatile short-term capital inflows, with much of the excess capital inflow at this time going into unproductive investment projects. The mix of high Thai interest rates, low foreign interest and the pegged exchange rate was also an important factor underlying the acquisition of large unhedged foreign exposures which left the system highly exposed to a negative 'shock' and reversal of capital inflows. The author provides an assessment of the Thai financial reform package.

Part V: Looking forward

Part V brings the debate together, focusing on the prospects for the future and the implications from the analysis of previous chapters. Chapter 13, by Gordon de Brouwer, comprises two parts. The first considers the recovery and reform process underway in East Asia, examining the likely speed of recovery and what recent experience indicates is the appropriate speed, order and content of reform, especially given domestic political constraints. This also includes an assessment of the lessons for emerging East Asia from Japan's experience, arguing that Japan is a poor role model for emerging economies. The second part analyses, more generally, the evolving debate about the international architecture. It starts by reviewing the reports and outcomes of the G22 (Willard Group) working groups on transparency, financial system reform and managing financial crises. Since the debate has also turned to the role or otherwise of capital controls, de Brouwer provides a summary of the arguments for and against such controls. He also assesses how the IMF position on capital controls has evolved in light of experiences with financial markets in 1998.

Part I

The changing architecture of financial regulation

2 Volatility and contagion in a financially integrated world: lessons from East Asia's recent experience

Pedro Alba, Amar Bhattacharya, Stijn Claessens, Swati Ghosh and Leonardo Hernandez

INTRODUCTION

Recent events in East Asia have highlighted the risks of financial structures in a financially integrated world. The build-up of vulnerabilities in the region was mainly the result of weaknesses in domestic financial intermediation, of poor corporate governance and deficient government policies, including poor macroeconomic policy responses to large capital inflows. Weak due diligence by external creditors, in part fuelled by ample global liquidity, also played a role in increasing vulnerability, but global factors were more important in triggering the crises than in causing them. Nevertheless, for most East Asian countries, a large financial crisis was not 'inevitable' but was mainly triggered by spill-overs from nearby countries. Differences between countries, both in degree of vulnerability and depth of crisis, support this conclusion.

Private capital flows to developing countries increased sixfold over the years 1990–6. These large inflows were not simply an independent and isolated macroeconomic shock for these countries to manage. They were, rather, the manifestation of a structural change in the world economic environment, in the form of a transition by many countries from near financial autarky to fairly close integration with world capital markets. The capital inflow phenomenon, and the associated need to address potential macroeconomic overheating, were the direct products of the transition between these polar financial integration regimes. In the new, more integrated environment, however, capital could potentially flow out as well as in. Key challenges facing newly financially integrated countries concern not just how to manage large inflows, but also how to reduce their vulnerability to the potentially disruptive effects of sudden and massive capital outflows.

Countries in East Asia were at the forefront of the worldwide movement towards increased financial integration (World Bank 1997). They fared quite well during the initial inflow stage of this process, especially in comparison with many countries outside the region. Indeed, in many ways, lessons to be applied elsewhere regarding the appropriate adjustment to large capital inflows have been drawn from the experiences of East Asia. Countries in the region also weathered the storm associated with the Mexican currency crisis of December 1994 in relatively good form, suggesting that the policies they adopted to manage inflows also proved effective in rendering their economies relatively less vulnerable to the financial shock that created serious disruptions elsewhere.

Nonetheless, in mid-1997, it became evident that this view could no longer be sustained. The crisis that struck Thailand, and the rapidity with which it spread to other countries in East Asia, suggested that all was not well. The extent of the subsequent fallout has been surprisingly large and the crisis has also been deeper and more protracted than many had anticipated. What went wrong? What are the policy implications? Was East Asia inevitably doomed to undergo the crisis? Or was it mainly due to its rapid financial integration and the functioning of global financial markets? The answers to these questions matter, of course, not just for the design of future policies in the afflicted countries in East Asia, but also for countries elsewhere that have more recently embarked on the road to financial integration.

OVERVIEW OF CAPITAL FLOWS AND MACROECONOMIC DEVELOPMENTS

Magnitude and composition of capital inflows

East Asia led the developing world in the resurgence of private capital flows in the late 1980s (Table 2.1). It quickly emerged as the most important destination for these flows and its share of total flows to developing countries increased from 12 per cent in the early 1980s to 43 per cent during the 1990s. During this period, the composition of the flows to East Asian countries also changed. In the second half of the 1980s, commercial bank lending was replaced by foreign direct investment (FDI). For the ASEAN-4 (Indonesia, Malaysia, the Philippines and Thailand) in the period 1993–6, portfolio flows (both bond and equity) expanded rapidly (to 3.4 per cent of GDP), as did short-term borrowing (an additional 2.3 per cent of GDP). Whereas the dominant role of FDI distinguished East Asia from Latin America in the late 1980s and early 1990s, more recent borrowing was much more skewed towards short-term flows than was the case in Latin America.

Another important characteristic of private capital flows to East Asia was that, unlike in Latin America, they were preceded rather than followed by a surge in investment (Table 2.2). In the second half of the 1980s and in the early 1990s, the bulk of the increase in investment was financed by a corresponding increase in national savings (Figure 2.1). During the more recent period, however, a much higher fraction of the increase in investment was financed abroad. Nevertheless, the magnitude of private capital flows was much higher than the amount of foreign savings absorbed, leading to substantial reserve accumulation.

Table 2.1 Magnitude and composition of capital inflows, 1985–96 (% of GDP)

	1985–8	1989–92	1993–6	1985–8	1989–92	1993–6
	East Asia			ASEAN-4		
Net long-term capital flows	1.3	1.7	4.3	2.0	4.8	6.9
Net official flows	0.5	0.3	0.0	1.2	1.3	0.4
Net private flows	0.8	1.4	4.4	0.8	3.5	6.6
Bank/trade lending	0.3	0.0	0.5	−0.3	0.9	0.8
Portfolio bond	−0.2	0.2	1.2	0.2	−0.1	1.4
FDI	0.7	0.9	1.6	0.9	2.3	2.4
Portfolio equity	0.0	0.3	1.1	0.1	0.4	2.0
IMF credit	0.0	0.0	0.1	−0.1	−0.1	0.0
Other private flows	−0.7	0.7	−1.0	0.3	2.0	−0.1
of which: short-term debt	−0.1	0.7	0.6	0.1	2.0	2.3
	South Asia			Latin America		
Net long-term capital flows	2.2	1.9	2.6	1.3	1.7	4.3
Net official flows	0.9	1.1	0.4	0.5	0.3	0.0
Net private flows	1.3	0.8	2.1	0.8	1.4	4.4
Bank/trade lending	1.1	0.5	0.4	0.3	0.0	0.5
Portfolio bond	0.1	0.2	0.0	−0.2	0.2	1.2
FDI	0.1	0.1	0.6	0.7	0.9	1.6
Portfolio equity	0.0	0.1	1.1	0.0	0.3	1.1
IMF credit	−0.4	0.2	−0.1	0.0	0.0	0.1
Other private flows	0.0	0.3	0.6	−0.7	0.7	−1.0
of which: short-term debt	0.4	0.1	−0.2	−0.1	0.7	0.6

Table 2.2 Investment, savings and capital flows, 1985–96 (% of GDP)

	Latin America			ASEAN-4		
	1985–8	1989–92	1993–6	1985–8	1989–92	1993–6
Investment	20.5	20.6	20.1	25.7	32.6	35.0
National savings	20.6	19.6	17.6	23.9	27.6	29.3
Private	16.5	16.2	15.1	19.1	19.2	19.4
Public	4.1	3.3	2.5	4.8	8.4	9.9
Current account deficit	1.0	1.1	2.4	1.1	3.8	4.6
Total capital inflows	0.7	2.4	3.5	2.2	6.7	6.8
Reserve accumulation	−0.3	1.3	1.0	1.0	2.9	2.2

Note: ASEAN-4 = Indonesia, Malaysia, the Philipines, Thailand

Figure 2.1 Trends in investment, savings, current accounts, reserve accumulation and private capital inflows, 1980–96 (% of GDP)

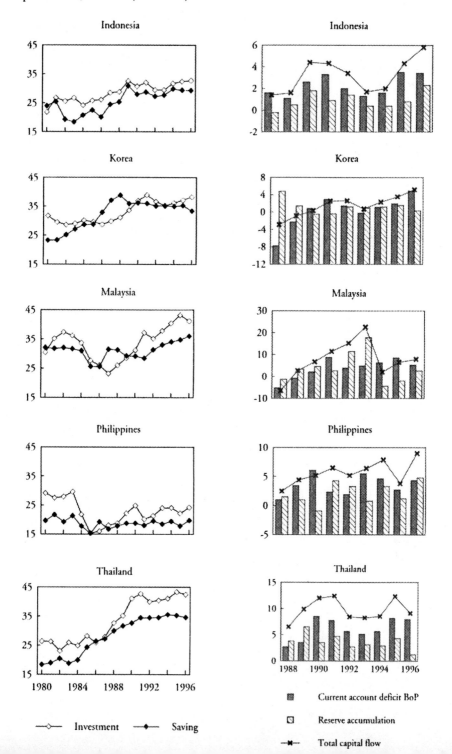

There was considerable variation, however, at the individual country level: Malaysia and Thailand received the largest amount, in excess of 30 per cent of gross domestic product (GDP); the Philippines also received substantial inflows during 1993–6; but Korea did not receive more than 15 per cent of GDP.

Macroeconomic policies during the early inflow period

The macroeconomic strategy in East Asian countries during the early inflow period had two characteristics: first, an exchange rate regime oriented towards enhanced competitiveness, that is, the achievement of a real exchange rate target to complement the outward orientation embodied in structural policies. This policy was implemented through step devaluations in the currencies of several countries in the region during the mid-1980s, followed in some countries by continuous depreciation. In East Asia, therefore, unlike in many countries of South America, nominal exchange rate management during the capital inflow episode was not primarily devoted to the establishment of a nominal anchor. This exchange rate policy indeed seems to have been relatively successful in avoiding currency overvaluation over the mid-1980s to mid-1990s decade.

The second macroeconomic component was the adoption of a tight medium-term stance for fiscal policy. Overall, public sector budgets in the region, which had exhibited deficits not out of line with those which characterised other middle-income developing countries at the time, moved steadily into surplus after the mid-1980s. As the economies grew and the tight fiscal stance restrained, and at times reversed, the growth of public sector debt, public sector debt-to-GDP ratios fell throughout the region. This coincided with the arrival of capital inflows. By the mid-1990s, several of the countries had achieved sizeable fiscal surpluses and ratios of debt to GDP substantially below those of many industrial countries.

Overall, then, the macroeconomic policy mix was one in which the nominal exchange rate was assigned to a competitiveness objective, while fiscal policy was assigned the objective of price level stabilisation. Other policies, of both structural and stabilisation dimensions, that were being pursued simultaneously, however, turned out to have important implications for subsequent events. On the structural side, the economies of East Asia continued the process of liberalisation that had begun in the mid-1980s. Trade liberalisation, capital account liberalisation and, especially, financial sector liberalisation, all proceeded during the inflow period. On the stabilisation side, monetary policy was also usual as a short-run stabilisation instrument, varying the intensity of sterilised intervention in the foreign exchange market in accordance with domestic macroeconomic needs.

This mix of structural and macroeconomic policies proved at once attractive to foreign capital – and thus was associated with large capital inflows – and was initially successful in preventing the emergence of macroeconomic overheating. Most importantly, countries avoided excessive real exchange rate appreciation but oriented aggregate demand towards high yield and risky investment rather than consumption (Table 2.3). This was the outcome of the policy mix undertaken. The effects of tight monetary policy tend to bias investment towards risky activities, such as asset speculation. An outward-oriented strategy in which tight fiscal policy supports a depreciated real exchange rate exerts a systematic effect on the composition of aggregate demand, favouring investment over consumption.

Table 2.3 Disposition of capital inflows during inflow episodes (% of GDP, except for columns 7 and 8 which are in per cent)

(1)	(2)	(3)	(4)	(5)	(6)	(7)	(8)
Country	Inflow period	Net private inflows	Net official inflows	Current account deficit	Reserve accum.	Change in current account	Change in reserve accum.
East Asia							
China	1993–6	2.65	0.35	1.04	1.96	34.7	65.3
India	1992–6	1.03	−0.58	−1.05	1.51	−231.1	331.1
Indonesia	1990–6	2.22	−1.08	0.14	1.00	12.2	87.8
Korea	1991–6	5.10	0.59	6.17	−0.48	108.5	−8.5
Malaysia	1989–96	8.08	0.11	6.05	2.14	73.9	26.1
Pakistan	1992–6	2.60	0.31	1.90	1.00	65.4	34.6
Philippines	1990–6	5.38	−0.65	3.37	1.36	71.3	28.7
Thailand	1988–96	6.72	−1.19	2.81	2.72	50.8	49.2
Other countries							
Argentina	1991–4	2.13	0.11	1.03	1.21	45.9	54.1
Brazil	1992–6	2.65	−0.01	0.80	1.84	30.5	69.5
Chile	1989–96	1.46	−3.38	−4.19	2.28	219.3	−119.3
Colombia	1992–6	5.20	−0.83	4.81	−0.44	110.0	−10.0
Mexico	1989–95	4.93	0.46	5.03	0.37	93.2	6.8
Peru	1990–6	4.75	0.04	2.11	2.68	44.0	56.0

Notes:
Columns 3–6: average during inflow period minus average during the immediately preceding 5-year period
Column 5: a minus sign means an improvement in the current account balance
Column 6: a minus sign means a decrease in reserve accumulation
Column 7: column 5 as a percentage of the sum of columns 3 and 4
Column 8: column 6 as a percentage of the sum of columns 3 and 4
Sources: World Bank data; IMF, *International Financial Statistics*

Reversal in capital flows

The financial crisis has led to a sharp reversal in the net private capital flow to East Asian countries since mid-1997, both on account of foreign lenders and domestic corporations. Whereas new international lending fell sharply in the second half of 1997, the main source of the turnaround in private capital flows was the reluctance of international banks to roll over the large volumes of short-term debt and the push by domestic corporations to cover their unhedged positions. By the fourth quarter of 1997, new international bond issues and loan commitments were 60 per cent lower than in the corresponding period of 1996. Altogether, net private capital flows to the five countries most affected by the crisis – Korea, Indonesia, Malaysia, the Philippines and Thailand – are estimated to have been more than US$100 billion less in 1997 than in 1996, with all of that decline taking place in the second half of 1997 (World Bank 1998).

WHAT CAUSED THE CRISIS?

Why did the crisis occur? Why has it been so protracted? Many explanations have been put forward: Corsetti et al. (1998), Feldstein (1998), IMF (1997), Krugman (1998), Radelet and Sachs (1998a, 1998b), and Sachs et al. (1996), among others, provide typologies of different types of financial crises that may be applicable to East Asia (see Box 2.1 for that of Radelet and Sachs 1998a).

Box 2.1 Types of financial crises

1   *Macroeconomic policy-induced:* basically, the financial crisis is a result of the pursuit of a set of inconsistent macroeconomic policies. This includes the case of a Krugman (1979) type balance of payments crisis, where the exchange rate collapses as domestic credit expansion by the central bank is inconsistent with the exchange rate target, as well as Obstfeld's type of self-fulfilling crisis (1986, 1996). This explanation presumably also includes the presence of some structural weaknesses (e.g. declines in competitiveness as a result of poor labour upgrading or weak financial systems) which make initial macro policies more likely to be inconsistent.

2   *Financial panic:* the country is subject to the equivalent of a run on a bank (Diamond and Dybvig 1983) where creditors, particularly those with short-term claims, suddenly withdraw from the country, leaving it with an acute shortage of foreign exchange liquidity. The withdrawal may be rational for each creditor as there is lack of coordination among creditors, and each individual's incentive is to withdraw first because of fears that others will do so.

3   *Collapse of a bubble:* the collapse of a stochastic speculative bubble, as in Blanchard and Watson (1982), which was itself a rational equilibrium, nevertheless was ex post irrational and always had a positive probability of collapse.

4   *Moral hazard crisis:* excessive, overly risky investment by banks and other financial institutions, which were able to borrow because they had implicit or explicit guarantees from government on their liabilities and were undercapitalised and/or weakly regulated (Akerlof and Romer 1993). Foreign as well as domestic creditors went along with this risky behaviour, as they knew the government or international financial institutions would bail them out. Krugman (1998) applies this model to the East Asian crisis.

5   *Disorderly workouts:* this refers to the equivalent of a grab for assets in the absence of a domestic bankruptcy system to deal with corporate liquidity problems (Miller and Zhang 1997; Sachs 1994a, 1994b). Since there does not exist a means of reorganising claims in the case of an international liquidity problem, a disorderly workout would result, which in turn would destroy value and create a debt overhang.

Conceptually, there is some overlap between these categories and, in practice, there will be elements of each, simultaneously or at different points in time, in causing or triggering financial crises or in making a crisis more severe. And none of these hypotheses is necessarily a complete explanation.[1]

Source: Radelet and Sachs 1998a

Although the causes of the East Asian crisis are complex and multifaceted, and with important differences across countries, two main 'competing' hypotheses have now become the subject of popular debate (e.g. *Economist* 10 April 1998). One is that the underlying structural weaknesses and macroeconomic policies were such that a crisis was inevitable. The other is that, although such weaknesses existed, it was the sudden run on the currency that led to a shift to a worse equilibrium. This distinction is similar to the ones taken by Radelet and Sachs (1998a), who contrast the possibility of a financial panic and disorderly workout with all the other hypotheses, and by Corsetti et al. (1998) who contrast weak fundamentals with financial panic.

Distinguishing between these alternatives is important for the policy agenda. In the case of a bank-type run/disorderly workout, ample and rapid provision of liquidity – by the government of the countries involved, international financial institutions and others – could have helped stabilise the situation and prevent the crisis from worsening (Feldstein 1998). When structural problems are the cause, the provision of liquidity might at best paste over them in the short term, but might actually aggravate them, given the moral hazard problems of easy liquidity in delaying reforms.

We will take the intermediate view, but leaning more towards the financial panic interpretation. In the run-up to the crisis, the most affected East Asian economies did show growing vulnerability, although lack of good information masked some weaknesses, such as the magnitude of unhedged short-term debt. Other weaknesses, for instance in the financial sector and corporate governance, had been well recognised for some time but they did not ring alarm bells in the minds of many investors, except in the last year or so for Thailand and, later, for Korea. An important difference between the East Asian crisis and the debt crisis of the 1980s (when fiscal deficits were the rule, except for Chile), and even the Mexican peso crisis of 1994–5, is that fiscal policy and public sector debt did *not* contribute to the increase in vulnerability or in triggering the crisis.

Indeed, this growing vulnerability was the result of private sector decisions rather than public sector deficits. The vulnerability can be attributed to the private investment boom and surge in capital inflows, which themselves were based on the region's success, particularly its strong economic fundamentals and the structural reforms of the 1980s. But the pace and pattern of investment in recent years, and the way in which it was financed, made some countries susceptible to a loss of investor confidence and a reversal in capital flows. These private sector activities took place, however, in the context of government policies that did not do enough to discourage excessive risk-taking, while providing too little regulatory control and insufficient transparency to allow markets to recognise and correct the problems. At the root of the problem were weak and poorly supervised financial sectors against a backdrop of large capital inflows. Equally, inadequate corporate governance and lack of transparency masked the poor quality and riskiness of investments. In addition, although macroeconomic policies were generally sound, pegged exchange rate regimes and implicit guarantees tilted incentives towards excessive short-term borrowing and capital inflows. These weaknesses in the policy framework were aggravated by undisciplined foreign lending and volatile international flows.

In attempting to provide an explanation for the East Asia crisis, this chapter will distinguish between three aspects: the causes and manifestations of vulnerability; the factors that triggered the crisis; and the factors and dynamics that have led to a more severe downturn than was generally anticipated.

Three major elements led to growing vulnerability: weaknesses in the financial sector, both moral hazard and incentive problems as well as institutional and regulatory shortcomings; weaknesses in corporate governance and transparency; and incentives to borrow and lend imprudently. The main manifestations of these weaknesses, generally known for some time, were: widening deficits and slowdowns in productivity and export growth; increased banking sector fragility, associated with lending and asset booms and rising exposure to risky sectors; high leverage; and currency and maturity mismatches that left some economies highly vulnerable to reversals in capital flows. There were, therefore, three dimensions to this increasing vulnerability: some deterioration in economic fundamentals despite starting from strong initial conditions; growing contingent liabilities that were not adequately recognised before the crisis; and increased risks of an external liquidity crunch, primarily because of a large build-up of external short-term debt, much of which was unhedged.

The magnitude of these weaknesses differed considerably among the countries. They were most pronounced in Thailand, where it was growing perceptions about a misalignment of the exchange rate that led to pressures on the baht, in much the same way as in Mexico in 1994 and the Czech Republic in 1996. There were also similar warning signals in Korea. But in the case of the other Southeast Asian countries, it was the devaluation of the baht that triggered the speculative attacks, thus negating an explanation based only on fundamentals as these would have shown up in more striking country differences than in a general regional slowdown.

The build-up of vulnerabilities and some similarities in financial conditions and structures did leave some East Asian countries exposed to the possibility of a bank run in the face of shocks. Even where they did not trigger the crisis, there was increased focus on structural weaknesses and financial systems in the aftermath of the initial attacks. Together with delayed policy responses, political transition, uncertainty in some countries and the lack of mechanisms for orderly external and domestic debt workouts, there was a sharp erosion in investor confidence. The result was a move to a worse equilibrium, which resulted in a loss of creditworthiness that could not be fully offset by liquidity from official sources.

Weaknesses in financial sectors

Financial system weaknesses were probably the single most important factor contributing to vulnerability in the East Asian economies. Insufficient capital adequacy ratios, inadequate legal lending limits on single borrowers or group of related borrowers, inadequate asset classification systems and poor provisioning for possible losses, poor disclosure and transparency of bank operations, and the lack of provisions for an exit policy for troubled financial institutions all contributed to banking fragility (Claessens and Glaessner 1997). Relative to other developing countries, the limited role of foreign banks in local markets also reduced the ability of banking systems to absorb shocks and, more generally, inhibited the institutional development of banks (Claessens and Glaessner 1998).

Figure 2.2 illustrates these weaknesses, as perceived by the market towards the end of 1997. Each on its own, or even in combination, may not necessarily lead to financial distress. In combination with other vulnerabilities and shocks, however, they can lead to or exacerbate a crisis. There were also considerable differences among the countries in terms of financial fragility, with the Philippines, for example, considerably less fragile than the others, except for Hong Kong and Singapore. At the same time, the financial sector was being liberalised. Domestic and external liberalisation increased competition in the banking system, which reduced the franchise value of banks and induced them to pursue risky investment strategies. Rapidly growing non-bank financial institutions (NBFIs) were an additional important source of competition, especially in Korea and Thailand. Furthermore, as NBFIs were generally less regulated and subject to weaker supervision than banks, their growth directly exacerbated fragility.

Figure 2.2 Contributing factors to financial fragility in Asia, late 1997

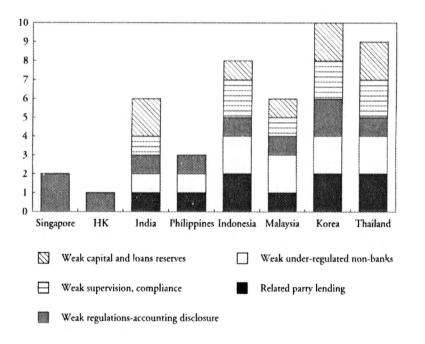

Note: On 0–10 scale, 0 = the most robust and 10 = the most fragile
Source: Ramos 1997a

The lingering effects of past policies dealing with financial distress aggravated the impact of these weaknesses. Specifically, several countries had experienced a financial crisis that was partly resolved through partial or full public bailouts, including Thailand (1983–7), Malaysia (1985–8) and Indonesia (1994). These bailouts reinforced the perception of an implicit deposit, or even wider liability, cover, to the detriment of market discipline. Indeed, in some cases, management of the restructured financial institutions had not even been changed.

Banks and NBFIs became more vulnerable to economic shocks over this period for two main reasons: by lending to sectors or firms whose debt service capacity was particularly susceptible to shocks; and by reducing their own capacity to absorb negative shocks, especially by exacerbating currency and maturity mismatches and by under-provisioning for future potential losses.

Lending booms

Financial liberalisation, through decreasing reserve requirements and surges in foreign capital inflows, led throughout East Asia to increases in monetary aggregates. In turn, increased liquidity and monetisation resulted in a generalised surge in bank and NBFI lending, although the amplitude and duration of these cycles, as well as their apparent relationship with financial liberalisation and the surge in capital inflows, varied from country to country. For example, in Malaysia, the Philippines and Thailand, bank and non-bank credit to the private sector began growing at higher rates and on a sustained basis following the surge. This high growth rate strained banks in their capacity to properly screen borrowers and projects. In Korea and Indonesia, in contrast, the growth in credit to the private sector was lower during the inflow period than in the previous years (Figure 2.3).

The rising fragility was not detected during the lending booms as the growth in bank loan portfolios was accompanied by rising measured profits. In countries in which credit growth was high (with the exception of the Philippines), there was an increase in the profitability of the banking sector, consistently across all indicators (Figure 2.4). Conversely, in countries where the lending boom was smaller – in absolute terms or proportional to GDP – profitability tended to show a small increase, or even a decrease, depending on the profitability indicator used.

Increased exposure to risky sectors

Real estate lending was high and the banking sector exposure to real estate was greater in countries where the growth of credit was larger than proportional to GDP growth (Figure 2.5). It should be noted that data on real estate lending are not comparable across countries and, for several countries, probably underestimate the exposure of the banking system to that sector (since loans to developers are not classified as lending for real estate). But there were significant differences among countries: Korean banks, for example, did not have a large property exposure. Korean banks did, however, increase the share of bonds and other securities in their portfolios to almost 20 per cent (and

Figure 2.3 Credit growth as a ratio of GDP growth (annual averages)

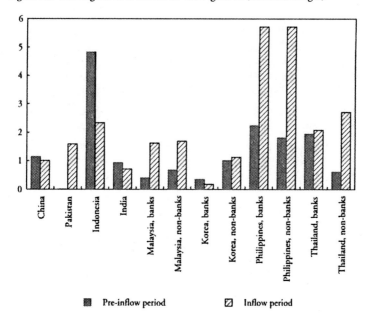

■ Pre-inflow period   ▨ Inflow period

Note: Rates of growth are calculated on an annual basis and in real terms. See Table 2.3 for relevant years
Source: IMF, *International Financial Statistics*

Figure 2.4 Banks' return on average equity, and their net interest margins, 1991–5 (%)

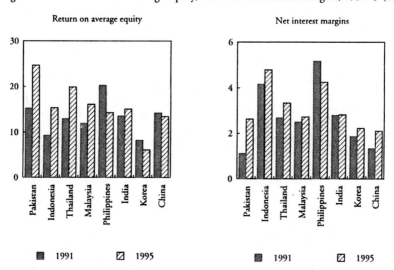

Note: 1994 figures, instead of 1995, are used for Pakistan
Source: IBCA

Figure 2.5 Exposure of the banking system to risk (%)

Propert sector:total loans

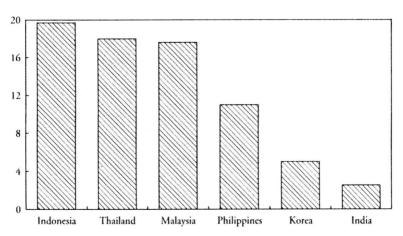

Bonds and other securities as a share of total assets

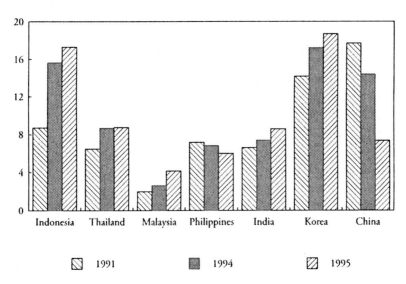

Note: Data for Indonesia start from 1992
Source: Goldman Sachs, *Banking Research*, September 1997

extended large amounts of guarantees on securities issued by corporations). Except for China and the Philippines, countries increased their exposure to bonds and other securities (see Figure 2.5).

Both real estate and securities markets have been very volatile in East Asia. Real estate price fluctuations during the 1990s were the highest in the Philippines and Malaysia, with the ratio of highest to lowest prices of 3 and 2, respectively. Still, in both countries, vacancy rates in 1996 were relatively low, at around 2 per cent (and banking sector exposure to real estate appeared to be low in the Philippines). In Thailand and Indonesia, the variability of real estate prices was lower, with high to low ratios of 1.25 and 1.32, respectively. In both countries, vacancy rates in 1996 were relatively high, at around 14 per cent, and increasing. The space under construction in Southeast Asia at the end of 1996 already suggested a significant oversupply of real estate during 1997–9, especially in Thailand (Figure 2.6).

Increased foreign exchange exposure

Especially in Thailand, Malaysia and the Philippines, there was a significant increase in the foreign exchange exposures of banks in the period 1989–96 (Figure 2.7). For Korea, Thailand and the Philippines, there was also a very rapid increase in the stock of foreign liabilities of NBFIs. In Indonesia, the increase in the exposure of banks was significant up to 1994, and was followed by a small decrease, but the overall exposure was small. Commercial banks in Korea did not show any increase during this period, but merchant banks in Korea did increase their foreign exchange exposures significantly.

Maturity mismatches

Vulnerability also emerged in maturity mismatches, especially on the external financing side. With the exception of Indonesia, initial levels of external debt were low in East Asia by international standards (Figure 2.8). The accumulation of short-term external liabilities over the 1989–96 period, however, was rapid and most of this borrowing went unhedged (Figure 2.9). While the liabilities of Indonesian banks did not increase rapidly, those of corporations did. The crisis itself has revealed that short-term borrowings were even higher than these figures suggest, as much non-bank liabilities and borrowing escaped national and Bank for International Settlements (BIS) coverage.

The most telling indicator of vulnerability was the ratio of short-term external debt to external reserves prior to the crisis (Figure 2.10). In June 1997, short-term debt exceeded external reserves by a large margin for Korea, Thailand and Indonesia, more than for many other developing countries. These high ratios made these countries much more vulnerable to a potential run on their currencies in the face of a loss of investor confidence (see also Radelet and Sachs 1988b; Sachs et al. 1996).

Weaknesses in corporate governance and transparency

While many East Asian countries had made rapid and substantial progress in developing their capital, especially equity, markets during the 1990s, both corporate

Figure 2.6 Real estate office supply and vacancy rates, 1988–99

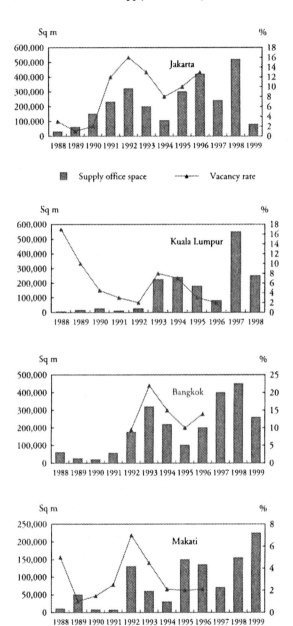

Note: 1997–9 comprises office space under construction
Source: Jones Lang Wootton, *Asian Pacific Property Digest,* January 1997

Figure 2.7 Foreign exchange exposures in banking systems, 1989–96 (ratio (%) of foreign exchange liabilities to foreign exchange assets)

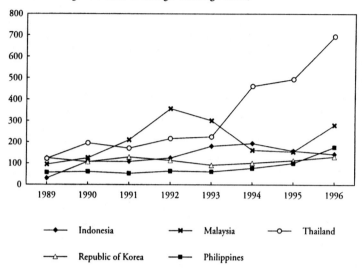

Source: IFS

Figure 2.8 Total external debt-to-export ratios, 1996 (%)

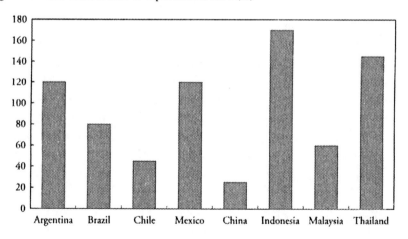

Source: Debt Reporting System, Institutional Investors

Figure 2.9 Short-term debt flows, 1989–92 and 1993–6 (% of GDP)

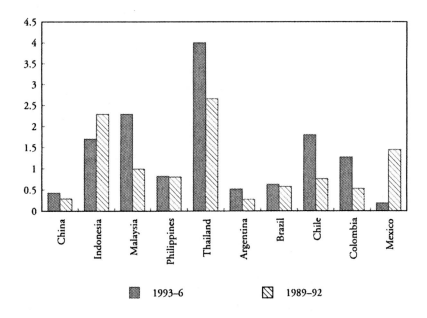

Source: IMF, *World Economic Outlook*, database

Figure 2.10 Short-term debt, June 1997 (% of total reserves)

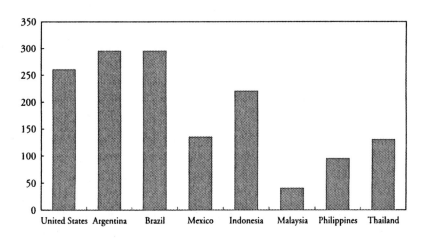

Sources: BIS; IMF, *International Financial Statistics*

governance and disclosure systems were still weak and capital markets played a limited role in the governance of firms. Perverse connections between lenders and borrowers were common and led to insider and poor quality lending (see Figure 2.2), and the financing of prestige projects. There were four related problems in corporate governance: concentrated ownership; weak market incentives; poor protection of minority shareholders; and weak accounting standards and practices. But most of these problems were *not* more severe in East Asia than in many developing countries.

High ownership concentration is typically both a symptom and a cause of weak corporate governance. It is a symptom because, in the face of weak legal and regulatory protection against abuse by corporate insiders, ownership concentration is a means for investors to be better able to monitor and control management. It is a cause because, given high ownership concentration, large and presumably politically powerful shareholders will not be a source of pressure for improvements in disclosure and governance as those may erode their corporate control and inside owner benefits. Reflecting both developments, Asian firms are generally closely held and managed by majority, often family, interests. On average, excluding Korea, the three largest shareholders own some 50 per cent of the shares of the ten largest non-financial private firms, and 46 per cent for the ten largest firms in Asia.[2] While this ownership concentration is not very different from that in Latin America, it does raise the possibility of increased risk-taking.

Market incentives to improve, either at the individual firm or country level, disclosure and governance were limited in many countries. Many firms had comfortable relations with banks and other financial intermediaries and were easily able to raise equity through new stock issues. This lack of market discipline appears to have been due to five factors. First, the interlocking ownership between financial intermediaries and corporations played a role. Korea is a good example of how such interrelationships reduced market discipline. Second, the rapid and large increase in stock prices in the early 1990s throughout emerging Asia may have reduced the sensitivity of equity investors to company disclosure and governance. Third, the requirement in some countries for government approval of new equity issues (and their prices), government ownership and contingent government support (e.g. in large infrastructure projects) may have also comforted investors. Fourth, there are few well-governed domestic institutional investors in the region. Privately managed institutional investors are rare and the large publicly controlled funds and investment banks have been mostly passive players in corporate matters. And, fifth, market institutions that play a key role in facilitating and creating the incentives for market discipline in industrial countries, like credit rating agencies, were not fully developed in the region. The nascent regulatory framework further aggravated this lack of market institutions. While, by 1997, most East Asian countries had built the legal and regulatory basis to move from a merit- to a market-based regulatory system, markets were not yet adequately performing their signalling and monitoring functions.

The legal and regulatory systems of many countries in the region include a relatively wide set of provisions to protect shareholders from abuse by insiders. Shareholder and creditor protection is stronger in Asia than in Latin America (Table 2.4). In the enforcement of property rights, however, the region, especially Indonesia and the Philippines, scores much below Latin America, meaning that shareholders cannot fully use their legal protecting mechanisms. Furthermore, weak disclosure means that shareholders often do not have the information to judge corporate performance and insider behaviour.

Accounting and auditing standards in the region are generally consistent with those issued by the International Accounting Standards Committee.[3] Malaysia and Thailand have strong reporting standards,[4] but those in the Philippines appear weaker. There is strong anecdotal evidence, however, that accounting *practices* in the region were not yet up to international standards. Compliance with accounting rules was further hampered by weaknesses in industry self-regulatory organisations. In Indonesia, for instance, in the absence of strong professional associations, the official capital market regulatory agency licenses legal and accounting professionals to work in the securities areas. An additional problem has been a shortage of well-qualified accountants and auditors, especially in Indonesia, the Philippines and Thailand. The impact of this shortage was compounded by restrictions on the activities of foreign accounting firms in many countries in the region (e.g. Indonesia).

Table 2.4 Investor protection in Asia and Latin America

	Investor protection[a]	*Creditor protection*[b]	*Judicial enforcement*[c]
India	2	4	6.1
Indonesia	2	4	4.4
Malaysia	4	4	7.7
Pakistan	5	4	4.3
Philippines	4	0	4.1
Sri Lanka	2	3	5.0
Thailand	3	3	5.9
Average	**2.2**	**0.8**	**6.1**
Argentina	4	1	5.6
Brazil	4	1	6.5
Chile	4	2	6.8
Colombia	1	0	5.7
Mexico	0	0	6.0
Venezuela	1	n.a.	6.2
Average	**3.1**	**3.1**	**5.4**

Notes:
a An index of how well the legal framework protects equity investors. It will equal six when (1) shareholders are allowed to vote by mail; (2) shareholders are not required to deposit share in advance of a meeting; (3) cumulative voting is allowed; (4) when the minimum percentage of share capital required to call a meeting is less than 10%; (5) an oppressed minority mechanism is in place; and (6) when legislation mandates one vote per share for all shares (or equivalent).
b An index of how well the legal framework protects secured creditors. It will equal four when: (1) there are minimum restrictions, e.g. creditors' consent, for firms to file for reorganisation; (2) there is no automatic stay on collateral; (3) debtor loses control of the firm during a reorganisation; and (4) secured creditors are given priority during a reorganisation.
c An index measuring the quality of judicial enforcement ranging from 1 to 10 (best) equal to the average of five sub-indexes measuring: (1) efficiency of the judicial system; (2) rule of law; (3) corruption; (4) risk of expropriation; and (5) risk of contract repudiation.
Source: La Porta et al. 1997 and 1998

Incentives to borrow abroad

The macroeconomic conditions prevailing in 1994–6, together with the policy mix the authorities chose in response, created incentives for firms to borrow abroad on an unhedged basis. Micro factors further added to this. There were considerable differences, however, between and within countries in the incentives and possibilities facing entities in the financial and corporate sectors to borrow abroad.

Macroeconomic conditions 1994–6

As mentioned earlier, following the structural reforms of the 1980s, Southeast Asian countries saw sharp increases in their investment rates. For example, in Indonesia the investment–GDP ratio rose from an average 25 per cent during 1985–9 to 32 per cent during 1990–6, while in Korea the investment rate rose from an average of 30 per cent to 37 per cent. Malaysia and Thailand saw even larger increases: from 26 per cent to 40 per cent, and 30 per cent to 42 per cent of GDP, respectively.

Against a backdrop of high rates of investment, the four countries that have been hardest hit by the crisis – Indonesia, Korea, Malaysia, and Thailand – all experienced an acceleration in the growth of domestic demand and the emergence of demand pressures during 1994–6. The Philippines has been somewhat different, not only in terms of economic conditions but also in the timing of the economic cycle during 1994–6.

In Korea, the growth of domestic demand picked up very sharply in 1994 and 1995, with its contribution to GDP growth averaging around 9 per cent (from 4 per cent in 1993). In Malaysia, the contribution of domestic demand to GDP growth had already accelerated in 1993, from 3.5 per cent the previous year, to over 9 per cent. During 1994 and 1995, the contribution of domestic demand to GDP growth increased further, to around 13 per cent. Similarly, Thailand, which had already had a two percentage point pick-up in the contribution of domestic demand to GDP growth in 1993, experienced a further increase in 1994 and 1995. Indonesia saw an acceleration in the growth of domestic demand slightly later, in 1994, which was sustained in 1995 and into 1996. In the Philippines, on the other hand, following a period of stagnation during 1991–2, economic activity grew by 2 per cent in 1993 and increased progressively to reach 5.7 per cent in 1996. In all five countries, the acceleration reflected a pick-up in the growth of both investment and consumption, although the relative mix differed. Along with the sharp increase in the contribution of domestic demand, the contribution of the external sector to GDP growth turned negative during the period (see Figure 2.11). Inflows of private capital reinforced these demand pressures (Box 2.2).

The demand pressures were manifested primarily in a sharp widening of current account deficits, although there was also some increase in inflation (Figure 2.12). Malaysia's current account deficit widened by more than two percentage points in 1995, from under 6.3 per cent to 8.5 per cent of GDP. Thailand's, high throughout the 1990s, increased from 5.6 per cent in 1994 to 8 per cent in 1995. Although Korea had run very small current account deficits throughout the 1990s, the change after 1993 was significant: from a small surplus of 0.1 per cent of GDP in 1993 to a deficit of 1.2 per cent in 1994, to 2 per cent in 1995 and then to almost 5 per cent in 1996. In Indonesia, the current account deficit widened from 1.6 per cent of GDP in 1994 to 3.6 per cent in 1996. In the Philippines, demand pressures did not emerge until 1996. Although inflation rose by 1.5 percentage points in 1994, this was largely due to supply shocks, and the widening of the current account deficit to GDP that occurred with the initial pick-up in economic activity in 1993 reversed thereafter.

Macroeconomic policy responses

The policy mix used to deal with overheating and capital inflows stimulated further inflows of private capital, and the accumulation of short-term unhedged external liabilities in particular.

In dealing with demand pressures, greater reliance was placed on monetary policy. The tightening of monetary policy increased domestic interest rates and the differential between domestic and international interest rates. Adding to the pressures on domestic interest rates was the change in fiscal policy stance during 1994–6. It is important to recognise that the Southeast Asian countries had undertaken fiscal reforms and consolidation during the 1980s and had seen very significant improvements in their overall fiscal balances. During the 1990s, their fiscal policy remained conservative, in the medium-term structural sense. However, in light of the cyclical upturn in economic activity in 1994–6, the fiscal positions were not contractionary. Indeed, the fiscal impulse (the change in fiscal stance) turned positive at a time when these economies were experiencing overheating pressures.

Exchange rate systems also played an important role. Concerned with preventing an appreciation of their real exchange rates, the Southeast Asian countries maintained pegged systems, with the authorities intervening in the foreign exchange markets to maintain the peg in the face of the large capital inflows.[5] It could be argued that allowing a greater degree of nominal exchange rate appreciation may have reduced the incentives to borrow abroad, inasmuch as an appreciation of the nominal exchange rate increases expectations of a future depreciation.

The fact that exchange rate policies in these countries implied relatively *predictable* nominal rates, further encouraged the accumulation of these external liabilities in the form of *unhedged obligations.*[6] In particular, by reducing the perceptions of exchange rate risks, the relatively narrow range of nominal exchange rate fluctuations reduced incentives to hedge external borrowing. Moreover, since short-term flows are more affected by fluctuations around the central parity – whereas long-term flows are more affected by movements in the central parity itself – the relatively narrow exchange rate movements meant that even potentially very short-term flows were not deterred from responding to the higher interest rate differentials.

In sum, domestic interest rates (adjusted for actual exchange rate movements) rose and were sustained through sterilisation efforts during 1994–6, which encouraged further inflows of capital.[7] Since short-term capital flows tend to be the most

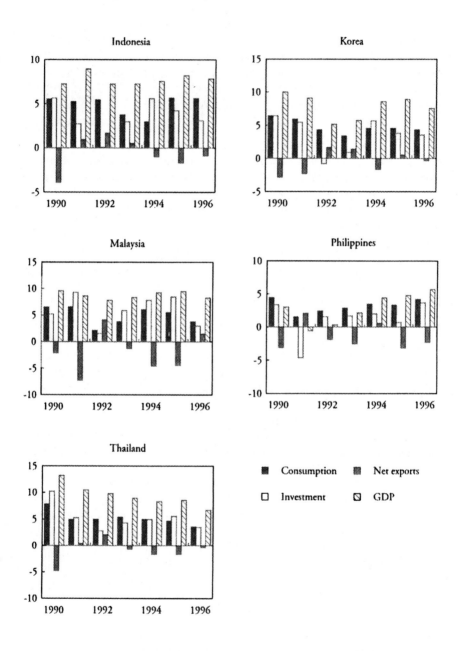

Figure 2.11 GDP growth and its components, 1990–6 (%)

Figure 2.12 Inflation and current account positions, 1990–6 (%)

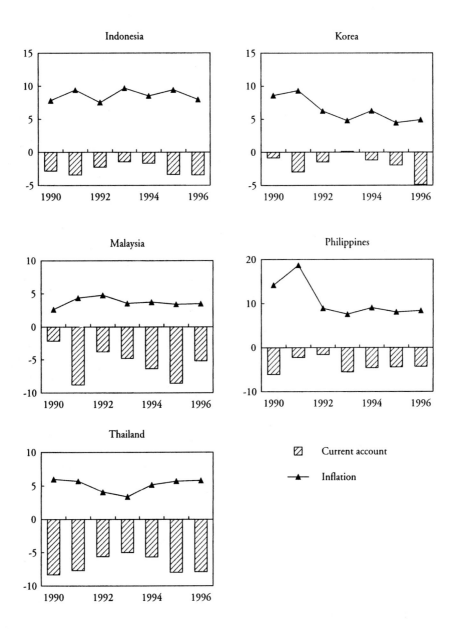

Box 2.2 Private capital flows and domestic macroeconomic cycles

In principle, private capital flows can both generate and exacerbate domestic macroeconomic cycles through various channels.

- Domestic demand pressures can be accommodated by borrowing abroad. If this excess demand falls primarily on the tradables sector, it is likely to be manifested in a widening of the current account deficit, while if it falls on non-tradable goods, it will lead to domestic inflationary pressures.
- A country that has become relatively more attractive to investors will receive inflows of private capital, which, in turn, can lead to problems of domestic absorption and 'overheating' pressures. This can happen even if these flows are financing investments, since there is a lead time before these investments increase productive capacity. Again, this will be manifested in a widening of the current account deficit and/or inflationary pressures.
- To the extent that excess demand falls on domestic assets, it will contribute to *asset price* inflation. In turn, asset price increases and attendant increases in financial wealth can further contribute to a consumption boom.

In fact, capital flows have tended to move very much in tandem with domestic macroeconomic cycles, particularly in Indonesia, Thailand and Korea. In Malaysia there was less of a correspondence between the capital inflows and demand pressures in the early 1990s, but, since the mid-1990s, capital inflows have moved with the domestic macroeconomic cycle.

Figure 2.13 Capital flows and excess demand pressures, 1990–6

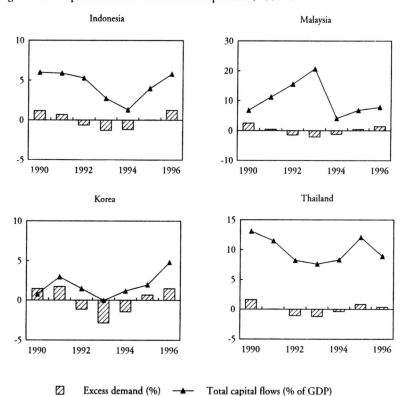

⊿ Excess demand (%)   ▲ Total capital flows (% of GDP)

Note: Excess demand is defined as the percentage deviation of actual GDP from potential GDP. Potential GDP was estimated using the Hodrick Prescott filter

responsive to interest differentials, and nominal exchange rate movements were relatively limited, the composition of external liabilities became more skewed towards short-term unhedged obligations.[8] Moreover, the 1990s has seen a progressive increase in the responsiveness of private capital flows to cross-border investment opportunities.[9] Thus, while most of the Southeast Asian countries had experienced earlier bouts of macroeconomic overheating (for example, Indonesia saw demand pressures emerge in 1990–1, as did Thailand), and, while the macroeconomic policy response had been similar, the speed and magnitude of the accumulation of short-term external liabilities was much greater during 1994–6. Consider the key countries in turn.

Indonesia

While less so than in the 1990–1 overheating, Indonesia relied quite heavily on monetary policy in dealing with demand pressures in 1995–6. Following rapid growth in monetary aggregates in 1994, which had been based on an expansion of domestic credit, monetary policy was tightened significantly by mid-1995. The primary instrument of monetary management was open market operations using SBIs (Bank Indonesia certificates of deposits), but use of discount operations was also made. This was reinforced by measures to control bank credit growth more directly. In particular, Bank Indonesia emphasised 'moral suasion', and banks were required to submit annual business plans and implementation reports, and to set guidelines for credit policy formulation.

Although the exchange rate band had been widened several times during late 1994 and 1996–in an effort to further enhance the effectiveness of monetary policy – Indonesia still had to undertake significant sterilisation, particularly in 1996, as monetary tightening induced further capital inflows.[10] The potential contribution of net foreign assets to reserve money growth of 72 per cent in 1996 was offset by a significant contraction of domestic credit, which resulted in a much lower actual growth in reserve money of 37 per cent (Figure 2.14). Despite large-scale open market operations to sterilise inflows and maintain a tight monetary stance (the stock of outstanding SBIs rose to Rp12 trillion at end 1996, compared with 5 trillion at end 1995), monetary aggregates continued to expand rapidly in 1996. Several additional measures were therefore introduced during the course of the year: increasing banks' reserve requirements from 2 per cent of deposit liabilities to 3 per cent; and resorting to greater moral suasion to limit the growth in domestic credit.[11]

Fiscal management had been a major element in the government's success in adjusting to the large external shocks that the country had experienced in the 1980s, and its fiscal accounts continued to show improvement during the 1990s. In fact, since 1994 Indonesia had recorded fiscal surpluses, generated in part by privatisation, which it had used to prepay external public debt and improve its debt indicators.[12] In 1995 and 1996, the conservative fiscal position allowed a sizeable build-up in government deposits with Bank Indonesia, which served as a moderating influence on reserve money growth. Despite the conservative fiscal position, however, fiscal policy

Figure 2.14 Indonesia: policy responses and incentives to borrow (%)

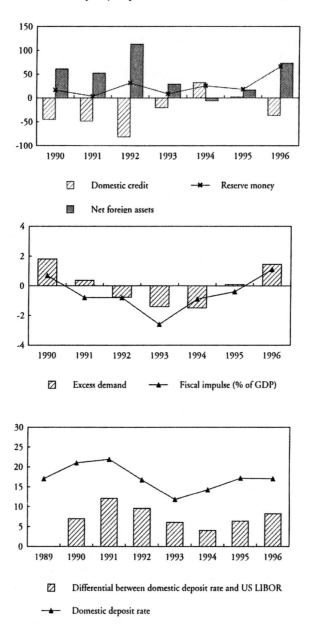

Note: Fiscal impulse estimates based on the non-oil sector

was pro-cyclical in 1996. In particular, while the fiscal stance (which measures the difference between the cyclically neutral balance and the actual balance) remained contractionary, it became less contractionary (i.e. the fiscal impulse was positive) at a time when demand pressures were intensifying.[13]

These factors led to higher domestic interest rates during 1995–6 than in 1994, when interest rates were raised to discourage capital outflows in the aftermath of the Mexico crisis. Three-month deposit rates, for example, increased by almost three percentage points at the end of 1995, compared with the previous year. At the same time, US dollar interest rates were declining. As a result, while the differentials between domestic and international interest rates (adjusted for exchange rate movements) were not as large as they had been in the previous macroeconomic cycle of 1990–1, they nonetheless increased sizeably during 1995–6. The differential between the three-month domestic deposit rate and the three-month US LIBOR (London interbank offered rate), for example, rose from an average of 8 per cent during 1993–4 to over 11 per cent during 1995–6.

At the same time, Indonesia's exchange rate policy played a role in reducing incentives to hedge the external borrowing that was taking place in response to the higher domestic interest rates. Until the exchange rate was floated in August 1997, Indonesia maintained a pegged exchange rate system in which Bank Indonesia set the central rate and intervened in the foreign exchange market at a band around the central rate.[14] While, in principle, the central rate was set against a basket of currencies, in practice, Indonesia attempted to target the real exchange rate by depreciating the rupiah vis-à-vis the US dollar to broadly offset inflation differentials between the two countries.[15] This implied a relatively constant rate of depreciation of the rupiah. Moreover, while Indonesia had been progressively widening the exchange rate band, the existence of a band further helped in creating a relatively predictable nominal exchange rate. In other words, the movement of the central parity was fairly constant and the fluctuations around it were relatively limited. This behaviour is borne out by the fact that the variability of the nominal exchange rate around the trend was less than 0.25 per cent throughout the 1990s.

Korea

With the expansion in economic activity during 1994–5, there was a sizeable increase in the Bank of Korea's net foreign asset position, reflecting both a small current account surplus as well as capital inflows. The bank sterilised inflows through the issuance of large amounts of monetary stabilisation bonds (Figure 2.15).

Fiscal policy in Korea has generally been formulated within a medium-term framework, subject to the constraint that outlays remain broadly in line with revenues. While this has helped maintain a conservative fiscal position, the focus on achieving fiscal balance has meant that fiscal policy has, on occasions, been quite procyclical. In 1994, the fiscal stance, while remaining contractionary, was slightly procyclical, although less so than in previous cycles. With the pick-up in economic activity and the tightening of monetary policy, domestic interest rates rose and the

Figure 2.15 Korea: policy responses and incentives to borrow (%)

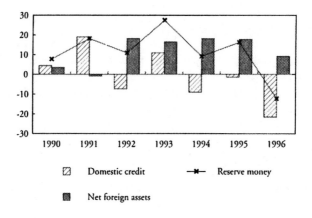

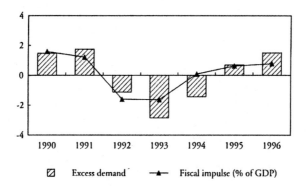

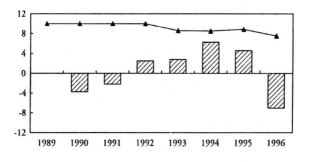

differential between domestic and international rates, adjusted for exchange rate movements, widened significantly during 1994–5 relative to 1993.

Under Korea's 'market average rate' exchange system, the nominal won–US dollar rate was allowed to float in the interbank market within a daily range around the weighted average of the previous day's interbank rates for spot transactions, and the range was widened in late 1993 to plus/minus 1 per cent. Since the Bank of Korea acted to prevent what it considered excessive fluctuations, the system was still a managed float. From the end of 1994 until the first half of 1996, though, Korea did allow the nominal exchange rate to appreciate. This reduced the pressures on domestic inflation, and, by alleviating some of the need to tighten monetary policy, it reduced the impetus for further capital inflows. Moreover, the won varied more around the trend, particularly from early 1994 onwards, than either the Thai baht or the Indonesian rupiah.

Malaysia

In Malaysia, monetary policy played a relatively important role during 1995–6, although, as discussed below, Malaysia also used the nominal exchange rate to a greater extent than Indonesia and Thailand to absorb potential overheating associated with capital inflows. Monetary policy was tightened progressively from late 1995 to mid-1996 (Figure 2.16). In recent years, changes in the statutory reserve requirements, direct borrowing from, or lending to, the banking system, and the transfer of government and Employees Provident Fund deposits to the central bank have been the main instruments of monetary management. These have been supplemented by the sales of government securities and Bank Negara bills. In 1996 the statutory reserve requirements were increased twice in February and March to 13.5 per cent of eligible liabilities. In addition, Malaysia introduced a number of credit control measures, both in order to reduce banks' credit expansion and for prudential reasons.

As in the other Southeast Asian countries, the fiscal restructuring and consolidation that Malaysia implemented resulted in significant improvements in its fiscal balance during the 1990s. In 1995, however, while still achieving a surplus, the federal government position registered a sharp decline, from 3 per cent of GDP in 1994 to 1.3 per cent. (The slower pace in revenue growth was in part due to income tax cuts and reductions in import duties.) The budget surplus declined again marginally, to 1.1 per cent of GDP in 1996, and although, as in Indonesia, the fiscal stance remained contractionary in 1995 and 1996, it became less so.

The policy response reinforced the upward trend in domestic interest rates that had begun with the growing demand pressures in 1995. Domestic interest rates thus rose during 1995–6 in Malaysia as well, albeit to a lesser extent than in Indonesia or Thailand. Three-month fixed deposit rates, for example, increased from 5.3 per cent in 1994, to 6.6 per cent in 1995 and to 7.2 per cent in 1996. Again, this led to a widening of interest rate differentials (adjusted for exchange rate movements) between domestic and international interest rates during 1994–6 relative to 1993.

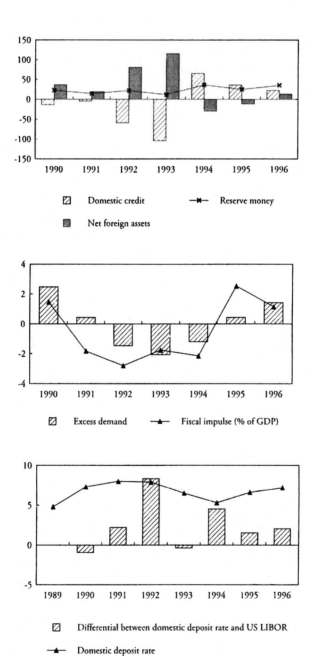

Figure 2.16 Malaysia: policy responses and incentives to borrow (%)

In contrast to Indonesia and Thailand, however, Malaysia's exchange rate policy provided less of an incentive for unhedged external borrowing during the period. In principle, Malaysia allowed the exchange rate to be market-determined, with Bank Negara only intervening to avoid what it considered excessive fluctuations. But since the bank also monitored the exchange rate against a basket of currencies of major trading partners, in practice, Malaysia was also implementing a managed float. However, Malaysia allowed the nominal exchange rate to appreciate by around 6.5 per cent between the beginning of 1994 and mid-1995 (and then depreciate by 4 per cent between mid-1995 and the beginning of 1996). There was also much less predictability associated with the ringgit.

The Philippines

Monetary policy in the Philippines is based largely on a reserve money program which takes into account economic activity, inflation and the balance of payments position. In recent years, monetary management has relied on open market operations and changes in reserve requirements, moving away from direct controls such as credit controls and directed credit. Inflation rose in 1994 and reserve money was tightened somewhat, with the authorities sterilising much of the capital inflows that had picked up since 1992–3. Following some loosening in 1995, monetary policy was tightened again in 1996, in response to emerging demand pressures. In particular, Bangko Sentral intensified open market operations through borrowings under the reverse repurchase facility (RRP) and the sale of its holdings of government securities (Figure 2.17).[16]

On the fiscal front, the 1994–6 period witnessed significant improvements. In particular, revenue-enhancing measures (both to widen the revenue base as well as to improve its buoyancy), combined with privatisation, resulted in a decline in the central government overall deficit, from 1.6 per cent of GDP in 1993 to 0.4 per cent in 1996. Accordingly, the fiscal stance was contractionary from 1994 onwards and fiscal impulse was only marginally expansionary in 1995 – when there was little sign of demand pressures – and almost zero in 1996 when demand pressures began to emerge.[17]

Interest rate differentials widened sharply in 1994 when monetary policy was tightened to deal with the spike in inflation, but they declined during 1995–6. The fact that banks' reserve requirements were also being lowered during 1993–6 as part of a program to bring down intermediation costs and interest rates also helped in exerting downward pressures on domestic interest rates. (Reserve requirements had been reduced six times during 1993–5, from 24 per cent to 15 per cent by May 1995.)

Although the movements in the nominal exchange rate were significantly lower during 1994–6 than had been the case in the past, the rate was still less predictable than in the case of Indonesia or Thailand. The macroeconomic incentive for the accumulation of unhedged short-term external debt during this period was therefore less.[18]

Figure 2.17 Philippines: policy responses and incentives to borrow (%)

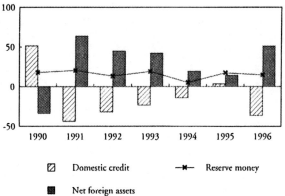

☒	Domestic credit	—✕—	Reserve money
■	Net foreign assets		

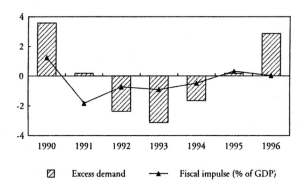

☒	Excess demand	—▲—	Fiscal impulse (% of GDP)

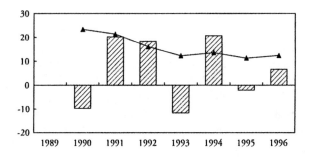

☒	Differential between domestic deposit rate and US LIBOR
—▲—	Domestic deposit rate

Thailand

Like Indonesia, Thailand relied quite heavily on monetary policy and sterilised interventions.[19] It began to experience excess demand pressures in 1995 and monetary policy was tightened progressively during that year. One of the constraints to undertaking open market operations was the scarcity of high grade securities, and an important measure taken in 1995 was the introduction of Bank of Thailand (BOT) bonds. Despite substantial increases in net foreign assets, the contraction in domestic credit extended by the BOT succeeded in containing reserve money growth at 22 per cent a year. In addition, the BOT introduced a series of administrative measures designed to reduce the credit growth of banks and finance companies: extending the credit monitoring scheme to include finance companies with assets over 20 billion baht in late 1994; requiring that reserves for non-resident baht deposits be held entirely as non-remunerated deposits at the central bank in 1995; and tightening the limits on financial institutions' foreign exchange position in 1995. During the first half of 1996, when private capital inflows were sustained, the BOT continued to sterilise through repurchase operations and increased issuance of BOT bonds (Figure 2.18).

Following the fiscal consolidation undertaken during the Sixth Development Plan (1987–91), Thailand had succeeded in eliminating fiscal deficits and its fiscal position remained conservative throughout the 1990s. Although fiscal surpluses had declined during the Seventh Development Plan (1992–6) as the policy focus shifted towards addressing infrastructure bottlenecks, they remained around 2 per cent of GDP during 1992–4. In 1995, the surplus rose to 2.5 per cent of GDP. In 1996, it declined to 1.6 per cent, entailing a strongly expansionary fiscal impulse, although economic growth had also slowed slightly.

Again, as in Indonesia, domestic interest rates rose sizeably. Interest rates on three- to six-month deposits, for example, rose from 8.5 per cent in 1994 to 11.6 per cent in 1995, and the differential with three-month US LIBOR, adjusted for exchange rate movements, was sustained at over 5 per cent during 1994–6. Thailand's exchange rate policy was the one which most encouraged unhedged borrowing, inasmuch as it entailed the least variation with respect to the nominal exchange rate. Since the baht had been devalued in late 1984, it had remained around 25 per US dollar, showing only small changes around this value.[20]

Overall therefore, the policy mix was one which contributed to higher domestic interest rates and entailed relatively limited and predictable exchange rate movements. The latter, in turn, reduced the perceived risk of exchange rate depreciation and of large fluctuations, which, combined with high domestic interest rates, served to increase incentives for unhedged external borrowing. During 1994–6, this policy mix was most pronounced in the case of Indonesia and Thailand.

Reinforcing processes and market imperfections

The process of external financial liberalisation, and the surge in private capital inflows that accompanied it, thus worked as an additional force to reinforce the upswing in the

Figure 2.18 Thailand: policy responses and incentives to borrow (%)

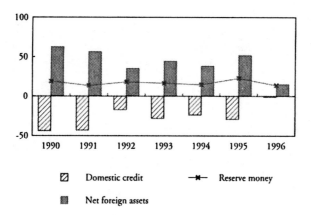

| ▨ | Domestic credit | —✕— | Reserve money |
| ▦ | Net foreign assets | | |

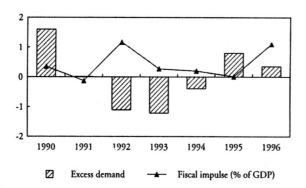

| ▨ | Excess demand | —▲— | Fiscal impulse (% of GDP) |

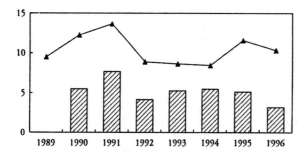

▨ Differential between domestic deposit rate and US LIBOR

—▲— Domestic deposit rate

domestic business cycle. The increase in private capital inflows, which in the case of East Asian countries was motivated mainly for investment purposes, provided the additional liquidity that allowed banks and non-bank financial intermediaries to increase lending, despite efforts to sterilise the inflows. Furthermore, capital flows contributed to increases in asset prices. Finally, the policy response to the inflow surge, which relied primarily on tight monetary policy and heavy sterilisation, provided further impetus to these flows, which added to the process and aggravated the fragility in the corporate (and therefore) banking sector through sustained high interest rates (Figure 2.19).

An important explanation for the failure of aggregate macroeconomic policies to stem capital inflows, alter their composition or adequately minimise their adverse consequences lay in the quality of domestic financial intermediation and the governance of corporations. Those East Asian countries which received foreign capital mostly intermediated through the domestic banking system or lent directly to the corporate sector (in the form of bonds, loans and short-term paper) became more vulnerable than countries which had received flows mostly in the form of FDI.[21] Three factors were important: the implicit insurance provided to financial institutions; high domestic funding costs and market segmentation; and certain specific institutional changes in the 1990s in some of the countries.

Implicit or explicit insurance on liabilities provided by the government to the financial system or the corporate sector is an important factor in motivating excessive risk-taking, including large foreign exchange risks (McKinnon and Pill 1997). As some of the cost of a default of an individual borrower is expected to be passed on to the rest of the domestic economy, risks are underpriced. This happened in Chile in the late 1970s and in Mexico in the early 1990s, and was an important factor in Thailand and Korea.

A decomposition of the nominal lending rate for non-prime borrowers for Thailand over the period 1991–6 shows that domestic financial intermediation costs accounted for a significant part of the nominal baht interest cost: almost 28 per cent of the average nominal interest rate.[22] Individual bank data confirm that overall intermediation costs, as measured by net intermediation margins, were high in East Asia. As a result, domestic costs of funds were significantly higher than offshore costs, even after taking into account exchange rate risks. Typically, however, access to foreign funds is only available to the largest and best credit corporations and financial institutions, with smaller and less creditworthy firms confined to the domestic market. This market segmentation, not uncommon in other countries, made it more difficult to limit offshore borrowings to prudent levels as it, in effect, created a strong constituency favouring a regime with implicit insurance and other distortions.

Specific institutional changes played a role in encouraging foreign inflows. Important among these was the creation of offshore financial markets where local financial institutions were to provide clients in nearby countries with financial services. For example, Malaysia promoted Labuan as a financial centre and the Philippines developed an offshore Euro–peso market. These markets were often given regulatory and tax advantages over domestic markets and substantial external

Figure 2.19 Self-reinforcing dynamics resulted in increased vulnerability

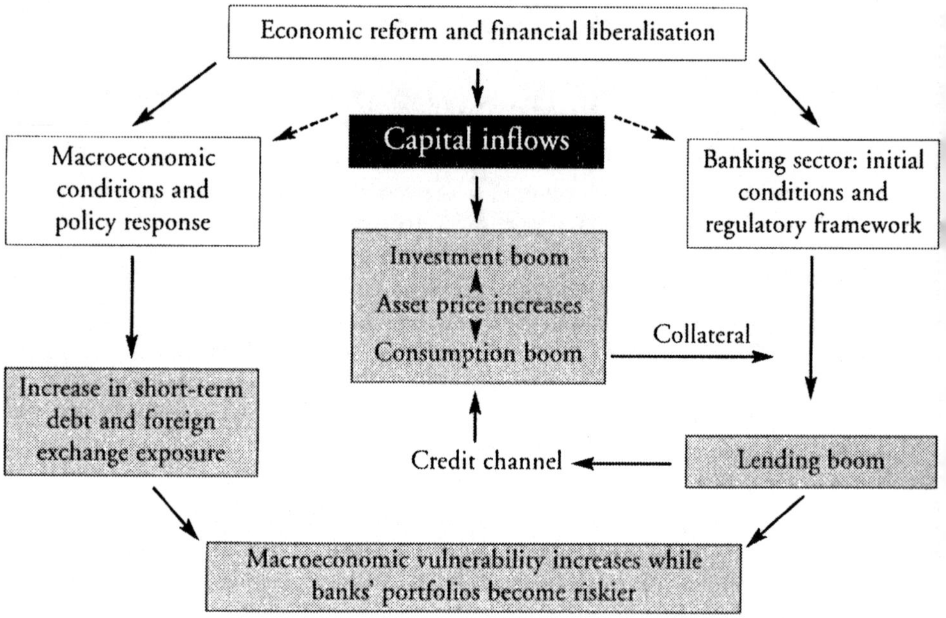

financing was channelled through them.[23] They also generated pressures to reform and deregulate local markets, as firms would otherwise switch to the offshore market. However, these offshore markets became vehicles for funding domestic firms rather than for providing regional financial services, and encouraged more offshore borrowings. This was most severe in Thailand (Box 2.3).[24]

Insufficient risk pricing and due diligence

Foreign investors do not always price risks adequately or perform proper due diligence of countries or individual borrowers. At times, risks appear to be overestimated and spreads react too rapidly to events; at other times, excessive appetite for the assets of emerging markets leads to an underestimation of risks and too low spreads. Eichengreen and Mody (1998), for example, find that changes in observable issuer characteristics do not provide an adequate explanation for changes over time in the volume of new bond issues and launch spreads. Blanket shifts in market sentiment, such as after the Mexican crisis, play the dominant role in increasing spreads. They also note that the first half of 1997 saw a period of large-scale bond issues by emerging market borrowers and dramatic spread compression, with no obvious changes in fundamentals. Similarly, Cline and Barnes (1997) show that spreads for emerging markets after the Mexican peso crisis fell by more than can be explained by the upgrading of emerging markets' economies by rating agencies or improved fundamentals. They find that the unweighted

---

Box 2.3 Offshore centres: Thailand

Thailand's Bangkok International Banking Facility (BIBF) set-up contributed greatly to the crisis. In March 1993, permission was given to 46 domestic and foreign commercial banks to operate international banking business in Bangkok. In 1994, further privileges were granted to BIBF-based banks, including the right to open branches outside Bangkok and to issue negotiable certificates of deposit (CDs). Because of special incentives, the BIBF provided an important channel through which the domestic financial sector could raise short-term funds ('out–in' lending). Bilateral tax treaties between Japan and Thailand meant that Japanese banks could offset withholding taxes levied on foreign exchange borrowings by Thai companies against their other income in Japan. As a result, Japanese banks, which had about one-quarter of the BIBF-market, were willing to absorb the withholding tax and lend at very low spreads to Thai companies.

The supply of funds was further boosted by the incentive for foreign BIBFs to become full bank branches, the approval of which was made dependent on the volume of loans. Historically low international interest rates, especially on Japanese yen, were another factor in the large financing available and low spreads charged. As a result, out–in lending boomed between 1993 and 1996 (from 126 billion baht to 331 billion baht). Reflecting the rapid growth of BIBF out–in lending, Thai commercial banks' foreign currency loans rose at the end of 1996 to US$31.5 billion, or 17 per cent of private sector loans, while their short-term external liabilities surged.

---

spread on sovereign issues of fourteen emerging markets would have been about 245 basis points in the second quarter of 1997 if the statistical relationship between spreads and economic performance had been the same as it was over the 1992–6 period. In fact, the average spread was 130 basis points. By this test, more than half of the decline in spreads in early 1997 was attributable to rising capital supply, including underestimation of risk, rather than improved country fundamentals.[25]

Spreads for non-sovereign borrowers in East Asian countries, which were already lower than for other emerging markets, declined even faster than those for borrowers from other emerging markets during the 1990s. Spreads for many borrowers in East Asian countries in late 1996/early 1997 were only marginally above those for long-maturity loans to US corporations. This increased appetite for Asian emerging markets was accompanied by poor due diligence. As late as May 1997, for example, investors were buying large amounts of short-term paper from Indonesian corporations with only a few days of due diligence.

EVOLUTION OF THE CRISIS AND CONTAGION

Onset and evolution

The reinforcing effects of high and rising – but increasingly risky – investment levels, large private capital inflows and asset booms, combined with underlying weaknesses, led to the build-up of vulnerabilities: widening current account deficits, slowdowns in productivity growth, and increased banking fragility. These effects were reinforced by macroeconomic policies and reinforced each other as well, although there were differences among countries.

The widening of the current account deficits that occurred need not have been unsustainable and, indeed, some countries, such as Chile, Singapore and Thailand itself, have sustained high current account deficits over a long period of time. But these deficits were progressively reflecting investments of uncertain quality. Whereas, in the late 1980s, the surge in investment was directed primarily towards tradables, and in particular the export sector, there was a large shift in the mid-1990s towards non-traded activities, particularly in Thailand and Indonesia. This shift was associated with lower overall productivity, although levels of productivity remained high relative to other regions (Sarel 1997). Incremental capital output ratios (ICORs) rose sharply during the 1990s in all countries following a general pattern of decline in the second half of the 1980s. The rise in ICORs was in part due to the exceptionally high rates of investment, but probably also occurred because many large investments were not subject to market discipline and were supported by explicit or implicit government guarantees. In Korea, where most investments remained largely geared towards tradables, excessive expansion occurred in some sectors, such as automobiles and steel.

Against this backdrop, developments in 1996 and early 1997 led to growing concerns on the part of investors. First, Thailand saw a sharp deterioration in export performance. After having averaged over 14 per cent in real terms during 1990–5, its export growth turned negative in 1996. At the same time, its real exchange rate appreciated by about 10 per cent. The bulk of this appreciation was due to an appreciation in the nominal effective exchange rate, which, in turn, reflected fluctuations between the US dollar (which Thailand was, in effect, targeting) and the currencies of Thailand's other trading partners, notably Japan. Using competitor weights, the appreciation in Thailand's real exchange rate was even larger at 15 per cent. Moreover, the fact that the other East Asian countries also saw an appreciation in their real exchange rates after 1995, and a concurrent slowdown in the growth of their exports, led to investor concerns regarding the region's competitiveness generally.

Export growth, which had been very strong during the 1990s in the other East Asian countries as well, decelerated sizeably in 1996, albeit much less than in Thailand. Malaysia's export growth slowed from an average of 14 per cent a year during 1990–5 to 5 per cent in 1996, and Indonesia's from an average of 8 per cent a year to 5 per cent. In Korea, exports slumped in 1996, in large part because of a decline in terms of trade as a result of a glut in the global electronics markets that resulted in a sharp fall in prices, but were growing at a rate of 15 per cent in mid-1997. Export receipts in the Philippines during the same period increased by about 20 per cent.

Retrospective analysis shows that the slowdown in the region's export growth largely resulted from reduced world demand (Bhattacharya et al. 1998). The slowdown was greatest for Indonesia, at over 6 per cent; Malaysia's export growth slowed by around 5 percentage points; and Thailand's by just over 4 percentage points. In Malaysia and to an even larger extent Thailand, exchange rate appreciation was also a significant factor. Nonetheless, the slowdown in their export performance was greater than would be expected based on slower export market growth and real exchange rate appreciation alone.

Two other factors could have accounted for this difference: the global downturn in demand for some specific products in 1996, such as semiconductors; and growing competition from low-cost producers. In Indonesia, Malaysia and especially Thailand, declines in recent years in market shares in their top ten products have been associated with increases in China's market shares (Bhattacharya et al. 1998). All three countries have, however, increased their share in more skill-intensive products and their world market share in total manufactures exports has continued to grow.

This suggests that the deterioration in the region's export performance and the implications for future competitiveness were not as severe as the market assessed them to be. However, it is likely that exchange rate appreciation and export slowdown were very important in affecting investor perceptions. Increasingly, investors began to focus on the misalignment of the exchange rate in Thailand. Following the prolonged poor policy reaction in that country, the crisis was then triggered. Consider how the crisis evolved country by country.

Thailand

There was a lag of almost a year between the onset of confidence weakening and vigorous policy reaction. Equity investors were the first to withdraw. The stock market, which had peaked in February 1996, had already fallen by 40 per cent by early 1997, with the equity prices of financial institutions falling by even more: a cumulative 60 per cent. Capital flows in 1996 were increasingly in the form of short-term debt as financial institutions and some corporations had difficulty obtaining longer maturity funding. Several large investments ran into difficulty obtaining financing as early as 1996, notably Alphatec, a large (about US$1 billion) semiconductor investment with weak economic prospects. Total private capital flows started to slow down, with bond issues and syndicated loans falling in the first half of 1997 to US$4 billion, from US$6.5 billion in the first half of 1996. Confidence in Thailand was further reduced by the default of Somprasong Land on a eurobond issue.

External factors – the cyclical slowdown in world trade, problems in the world semiconductor market, and the appreciation of the US dollar vis-à-vis the yen – played a role in the build-up of pressure in 1996 and early 1997. The sharp export slump in 1996 slowed the asset price (especially property prices) inflation that had been underway for several years in Thailand. Credit rating agencies issued some warnings as early as mid-1996 and Moody's downgraded Thailand's short-term debt on 4 September 1996. Thailand was put on notice for possible further review in early 1997 and, on 10 April, was downgraded by Moody's from A2 to A3. However, IBCA, a credit rating agency for banks, did not change its ratings of Thai banks throughout this period and, as late as March 1997, said that it was maintaining the rating of the six leading Thai banks. S&P reaffirmed its rating of Thailand as late as July 1997.

After periodic speculative attacks in 1996, the Thai baht came under renewed pressure in late January and early February 1997. As before, the central bank was able to defend the currency through spot and forward sales and increases in interest rates. The market's expectations of an exchange rate devaluation had increased, however, both directly, as export growth was still minimal, and indirectly, as it became less likely that the Bank of Thailand would sustain a prolonged period of high interest rates. The unwillingness or inability to adjust the exchange rate in the face of overwhelming perceptions of overvaluation led, however, to a decline in official foreign exchange reserves and required a hefty increase in interest rates. Similarly, the unwillingness to tackle the weaknesses in the financial system, and the lack of transparency on the extent of the problem, compounded difficulties and led to negative market reaction.

In May, the pressure on the currency re-emerged in full force and the government had to resort to using exchange controls to stem the loss of foreign exchange. Effectively, on 15 May, the authorities segmented resident and non-resident baht borrowings, driving a wedge between the local and offshore markets for baht. However, the measures failed to restore confidence and may actually have led to a greater loss of confidence as weaknesses in the financial sector mounted. These weaknesses ultimately made the attack on the currency successful because they precluded the Bank of Thailand from pursuing a high interest rate policy to defend the currency.

In the meantime, the loan portfolios of banks and other finance companies continued to deteriorate in quality and increase in riskiness as property prices stagnated and asset-liability maturity and currency mismatches grew. Liquidity problems in many finance companies increased and the stock of liquidity support from the Bank of Thailand to finance companies amounted to about 10 per cent of GDP in early August, much of it accumulated during the May–June period. Concerns mounted about the government's delayed and weak policy responses to the financial sector weaknesses. In June and July, the baht again came under sustained pressure. On 27 June, the Bank of Thailand closed sixteen struggling finance companies, but markets considered this 'too little, too late'.

After losing another US$4 billion in foreign exchange reserves (and thus a cumulative loss between January and July of US$12 billion), and incurring a US$23 billion forward position, the Thai authorities finally let the exchange float on 2 July. The misalignment of the exchange rate meant that the real exchange rate had to depreciate. The financial fragility implied that it was the nominal exchange rate that ultimately moved, as the authorities had lost other degrees of freedom. Thailand's large short-term indebtedness meant that, once the exchange rate moved, it had to move substantially to equilibrate demand for foreign and domestic assets. The currency therefore immediately depreciated by about 10 per cent against the US dollar relative to May levels, and fell by another 8 per cent in the following two weeks.

Other Southeast Asian countries

The crisis focused market attention on the vulnerability of other Southeast Asian countries, particularly their macroeconomic conditions, weaknesses in their financial sectors, their political situations and commitment to reform, and their future prospects generally. Large short-term foreign exchange borrowings exposed several of the countries to 'bank-runs', as problems in the financial and real sectors accumulated. Indonesia, Malaysia and the Philippines were soon drawn in, as foreign and domestic investors reassessed their positions. Unlike Thailand, the other countries stopped intervening relatively quickly and abandoned their implicit exchange rate pegs or bands. The Philippines floated its currency on 12 July and, immediately afterwards, Indonesia widened its band from 8 per cent to 12 per cent but then floated its currency on 14 August in the face of some foreign exchange losses. Malaysia stopped defending its exchange rate in mid-July after some losses. Taiwan ceased intervention on 17 October and its currency depreciated by about 7 per cent in the following weeks. Singapore and Hong Kong also came under pressure, with Hong Kong successfully fighting off speculative attacks on its pegged exchange rate while Singapore let its currency depreciate (Table 2.5).

Stock markets fell sharply in all East Asian countries throughout the fall of 1997. Although Thailand posted initially modest gains in the wake of the initial devaluation, its stock market fell further and was at a record low by the end of the year (in dollar terms more than 80 per cent lower than the peak reached in early 1996). The other countries suffered somewhat lower declines in their stock markets, with drops of between 50 and 60 per cent for the Philippines, Indonesia and Malaysia between early 1996 and the end of 1997. Malaysia established a large fund to support the stock market, but it had little effect and was later scaled back substantially.

After moving to floating exchange rates, governments in all countries tightened domestic liquidity. The most stringent response came from Bank Indonesia, which imposed very tight liquidity for several weeks (including by moving about Rp10 trillion – about 10 per cent of reserve money – of state enterprise deposits from commercial banks to the central bank) and closed the discount window. Overnight interest rates were in excess of 100 per cent during the second half of August, but eased later to about 35 per cent, and the discount window was selectively reopened. The increase was less in the Philippines but, when reserve requirements were raised in late August, interest rates went over 25 per cent and then fell again slightly later in the year. In Thailand, rates were around 20 per cent in October/November. Malaysia was the exception; it did not raise interest rates very much and they continued to be in the range of 7.5–8 per cent.

All four countries introduced new restrictions on foreign exchange transactions by attempting to deny speculators the domestic credit needed to establish a net short domestic currency position. As noted, the Thai authorities limited the sale of baht

Table 2.5 Exchange rates and stock prices, 1997 (% changes)

	Stock market (Jan–June)	Stock market (July–Dec)	Exchange rate (July–Dec)
Indonesia	14	–45	–122
Malaysia	–13	–45	–53
Philippines	–11	–34	–50
Thailand	–37	–29	–93
China	36	–17	0
Korea	14	–51	–80

for dollars to non-residents in the spot foreign exchange market for speculative purposes in May. In the Philippines, the central bank prohibited local banks from engaging in forward contracts with offshore banks for a period of three months. Malaysia imposed restrictions on the sale of ringgit to non-residents, other than for commercial reasons. It temporarily prohibited short sales in the stock market, but was forced to lift this restriction in the wake of large sell-offs by foreign investors. Indonesian banks were prohibited from extending credit to non-residents for swap transactions.

Korea and other countries

Spill-over effects were not limited to Southeast Asia. The US stock market and some emerging markets were negatively affected. On 23 October, the Australian dollar fell by 11 per cent, and on 27 October, following weak markets in Hong Kong and the rest of Asia, the Dow Jones industrial average dropped 554 points (7 per cent), its largest absolute point drop ever. Vulnerable emerging markets outside the region, including Argentina, Brazil, Mexico and Russia, also came under pressure and needed to increase local interest rates to support their currency and take steps to reduce risks. In October, Korea was affected by the crisis as it lost market confidence and was no longer able to attract sufficient amounts of new credits and roll over its existing obligations.

This foreign exchange liquidity crunch followed a year in which Korean *chaebol* bankruptcies had mounted, starting with the default of Hanbo in January 1997 and followed by Kia Motors and Sammi Steel. Profit margins had been shrinking for several years, as the *chaebols* ambitiously expanded and diversified without regard for economic profitability (the profit margin for the top 30 *chaebols* in 1996 was only 0.2 per cent). Their activities included numerous overseas investment projects and a concerted drive into the electronic and semiconductor sectors in both domestic markets and in the emerging markets of East Asia, the former Soviet Union and Eastern Europe. The number of overseas projects rose to well over 2,000 a year and Korean outward FDI amounted to about US$2.5 billion in 1996. Low profitability forced the *chaebols* to borrow, from both domestic and foreign sources, in order to maintain operations. Debt obligations in the manufacturing sector, for example, accounted for over 47 per cent of total assets and the average debt to equity ratio for the *chaebols* was over 300 per cent by the end of 1996. Key corporate financial ratios deteriorated further in 1997.

Following the inability of domestic banks to roll over short-term external debts in October, the Korean won depreciated by about 85 per cent in a two-month period and real interest rates rose to around 30 per cent. The country faced an extraordinary liquidity crunch. More than half of Korea's external debt was short-term, of which about US$20 billion fell due in the last two months of 1997. As for the other East Asian countries, the lack of willingness among foreign creditors to extend new credit stemmed from concerns over the health of Korea's financial systems and the strength and competitiveness of its industrial sector. Political uncertainty related to the presidential elections in December increased these concerns.

The extent of the fallout from the Thai baht crisis was surprisingly large, considering the differences among the countries. The size of the current account deficits and the degree of short-term funding varied, with Thailand standing out as having a very skewed funding structure. Reserve cushions and external debt ratios were very different and there were substantial variations in export performance. The degree of financial system weakness also differed, with Thailand more extreme in terms of the size of the lending boom, the currency and maturity mismatch of lending, and the concentration of the banking portfolio in the real estate sector. In other countries, notably the Philippines, the magnitude and duration of the lending boom had been smaller. In Indonesia and Malaysia, there was much less recourse by the financial sector to short-term external borrowing to expand lending, although in Indonesia offshore borrowing by corporations was large. However, increased lending for real estate was a common feature of all the countries. There were also differences in the speed and consistency of policy responses. While the tight liquidity conditions put pressure on many of the region's financial institutions, only Thailand provided extensive liquidity support to ailing banks and finance companies prior to the crisis.

Lack of similarities notwithstanding, there has been considerable co-movement in asset prices across the region. Exchange rates have been under similar pressure in all countries. Between June 1997 and April 1998, Malaysia, the Philippines and Thailand simultaneously experienced large exchange rate depreciations (Figure 2.20). In Indonesia, the decline was even more severe, while the Korean exchange rate decline started in October and was very large by November and December. Taiwan (ROC) and Singapore saw weaker declines, and China and Hong Kong even less. Nevertheless, correlations between the exchange rate movements of the four Southeast Asian countries during the period August–February were very high, and even higher in the period October–early January. Since mid-January, there has been less co-movement, as the Malaysian ringgit, the Korean won and the Thai baht have appreciated while the Indonesian rupiah has further depreciated.

Secondary market spreads on sovereign bonds saw very similar movements for most East Asian countries during this period. Until July, the spreads had been around 100 basis points, with the exception of the Philippines which was closer to 200 basis points (Figure 2.21). From October, they rose simultaneously and sharply: to above

400 basis points in December for the Philippines and Thailand, and to more than 500 basis points for Indonesia. Since then spreads have declined and, by April 1998, were about 300 basis points for Malaysia, the Philippines and Thailand and 350 basis points for Korea. Country differences have also become more pronounced: for Indonesia in April 1998, the spread was about 530 basis points.

Prior to the crisis, East Asian stock markets did not show strong co-movement. As noted, the stock price in Thailand had been experiencing a decline since January 1996, cumulating to a loss of about 65 per cent in real local currency terms by June 1997. Between January and June 1997, the Philippines and Malaysia had also experienced a decline in their stock markets but of a smaller magnitude, while Indonesia and Korea still registered increases of about 10 per cent. Following the 2 July crisis, the Thai stock market rebounded strongly at first, with a 25 per cent increase in July. In the rest of East Asia that month, stock prices declined modestly. Co-movement increased greatly in August, however, as stock prices in the region fell by about 25 per cent and prices in Korea and Hong Kong declined (Figure 2.22). September saw a period of consolidation, with little change across the region. From mid-November to mid-January, stock market declines continued in East Asia, with the exception of China and Taiwan.

Between mid-January and April 1998, markets rebounded strongly in most East Asian countries, with gains in domestic currency between 30 and 43 per cent, and even more in dollar terms. The exception has been Indonesia, where, after an initial gain, prices fell sharply after early February. Cumulative over the period 2 July 1997–mid-February, however, stock markets in East Asia have in local currency terms declined between 23 per cent (the Philippines) and 44 per cent (Korea). The exceptions have been China and Taiwan.

Reflecting the strong co-movement during certain periods, correlations between stock prices in East Asia and in other emerging markets were at times very high. Before 2 July, the average correlation among 22 major emerging markets was about 10 per cent, but during the crisis period to February 1998 it increased to around 20 per cent. In the October–mid-November period, correlations among these markets were on average close to 30 per cent, and within regions correlations among stock prices were even higher. Between the Philippines and Malaysia, for example, the correlation was 16 per cent in the year before the crisis but rose to 29 per cent during the crisis, and was 59 per cent October to mid-November.

Contagion, or similarity in changes in fundamentals?

Whether or not these large co-movements reflect contagion (i.e. pure spill-over), or are in part due to similarities in changes in underlying fundamentals, is difficult to tell (Valdes 1996). Asset prices reflect market expectations of future real returns, which depend on expectations about fundamental economic variables and the market's perception of risks and its willingness to absorb risk. Both expected fundamentals and risks have probably changed in similar ways in all of these countries during this period because of a number of factors: trade linkages meant that declines in demand or imports in one country led to declines in exports in other countries. The competitiveness of one country was affected by the exchange rate depreciations of other countries, thus negatively affecting future exports prospects. Financial linkages, including through FDI, bank lending and capital market activities, meant that events in one country negatively affected another. Countries may have been affected by similar external shocks (e.g. global economic slowdown or events in Japan). And events in one country may have led market participants to revise their model of development more broadly, thus affecting asset prices in a larger group of countries.

Some positive correlation between asset prices can thus be expected and does not 'prove' contagion. One needs to define 'normal' and 'excessive' correlations, where normal is based on some 'model' which relates to fundamentals, risk perceptions and preferences. Many of these fundamentals are difficult to capture, however, particularly in a rapidly changing environment, but there are some indicators where one might expect differences in fundamentals to show up. One is whether declines in aggregate stock markets depend on the sectoral composition of listed stocks. Specifically, one would expect stock markets dominated by firms producing tradables to have declined less than stock markets dominated by non-tradables, particularly stocks of financial institutions, since the currency depreciations should have led to an increased foreign demand for tradables but not for non-tradables. To the degree that this is the case, it would provide some evidence for rational discrimination between markets by investors and thus argue against simple contagion. Likewise, if declines in asset prices can be differentiated by risk factors between countries (e.g. the degree of external indebtedness), some indirect evidence exists that markets act rationally.

A full-fledged analysis still remains to be done (Kaminsky and Schmukler 1998 provide some initial results). Evidence to date suggests, however, that there have been periods of excessive co-movement, particularly in the October–mid-November period. Cline and Barnes (1997) observe, for example, that the run-up in spreads in late October for emerging markets was beyond what could be explained by historical relationships. The average spread for fourteen emerging market economies of around 260 basis points at the end of October was above the level predicted by the 1992–6 statistical relationship of spreads to economic variables. In other periods, it appears that markets did discriminate between countries, depending on risk factors and perceptions about reform commitments. Spreads declined considerably for Korea, for example, following the deepening of its reform program with the International Monetary Fund (IMF) in late December and early January, while they rose for Indonesia.

Trade linkages in the region can explain some, but not all, of the co-movements. Intraregional exports among East Asian countries accounted for almost 40 per cent of total exports in 1996, up from 31.7 per cent in 1990. If Japan is included, the figure rises to 51 per cent. These high levels of intraregional trade may have tended to increase the speed and directness of contagion. While these effects may have been large, their exact magnitude can only be ascertained through a full econometric model of demand and supply of trade. Changes in countries' competitiveness vis-à-vis third

Figure 2.20 Index of exchange rate movements, January–May 1998

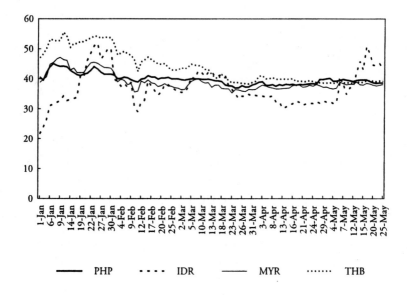

Note: PHP = Philippines peso; IDR = Indonesian rupiah; MYR = Malaysian ringgit; THB = Thai baht

Figure 2.21 Secondary market spreads on sovereign debt, June 1997–February 1998 (basis points)

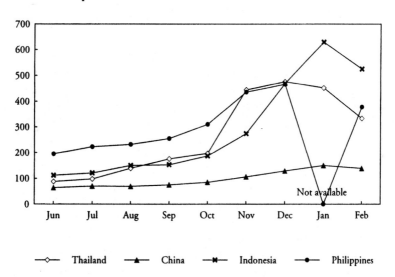

Source: Bloomberg datastream

Figure 2.22 Real local stock prices, July 1997–February 1998

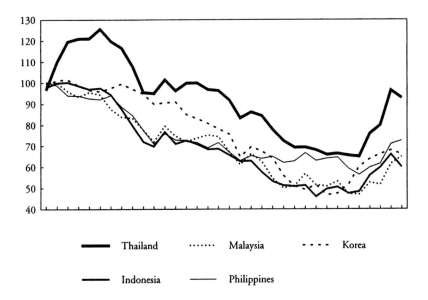

Thailand .... Malaysia - - - - Korea

Indonesia —— Philippines

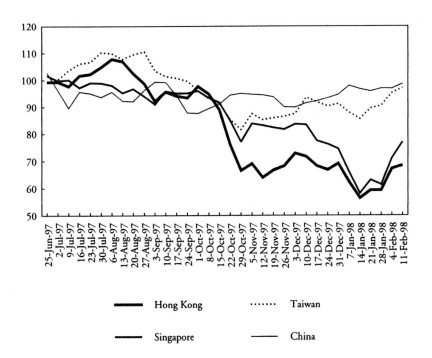

Hong Kong .... Taiwan

Singapore —— China

Note: Stock prices in local currency have been deflated by using CPI indexes. 1 July = 100
Source: IFC, Emerging Markets Database

markets as a result of the depreciations appear, in contrast, less likely to have played a large role in causing contagion (see Box 2.4).

WHY HAS THE CRISIS BEEN SO PROTRACTED?

The crisis has been deeper and wider than many had anticipated. Until it erupted, most observers were predicting relatively robust growth for most of the region. The consensus forecast (the average of monthly economic forecast from 25 economic institutions) until October for GDP growth in developing Southeast Asian countries was still above 5 per cent. Since then, growth forecasts have been drastically lowered: for Korea, for example, falling sharply from 6.2 per cent in October to 1.8 per cent in December and –0.1 per cent in January. Nor did financial markets anticipate events. Credit ratings for almost all sovereign claims on East Asian countries in June 1997 were the same as a year earlier, and Thailand was still able to borrow at 90 basis points over ten-year US Treasuries only a few months before its crisis erupted. On 1 July 1997, spreads for East Asian countries over ten-year US Treasuries varied between 55 basis points (Korea) and 90 basis points (Hong Kong). Credit rating agencies only started to downgrade countries weeks after the crisis had erupted. Korea was downgraded very sharply in a short period of time: rated AA- in October, it was downgraded on 22 December to below investment grade status, a downgrade of five notches in only two months. After July, spreads rose sharply and were, for example, 350 basis points for Thailand in early March 1998, falling to 280 basis points in April.

As confidence in the region fell, foreign investors adopted a wait-and-see approach for most countries, given uncertainties on short-term prospects and lack of conviction on their part on improvements in fundamentals and policy measures. External financing was sharply reduced and foreign lenders were even unwilling to roll over short-term loans for trade financing. The financing gap was partly filled by official financing, but most of the adjustment came from sharp contractions in imports. In Korea, trade deficits turned around sharply, to surpluses of about US$3 billion in each month between December and April, largely due to a sharp contraction in imports. Since many corporations and banks were unhedged, there was an increased demand for foreign exchange as these institutions tried to cover open positions in anticipation of further depreciation and currency volatility. These factors created perceptions of further currency declines, thus increasing incentives for buying foreign exchange sooner rather than later, and validating and aggravating currency declines. Because large declines in currencies and tight liquidity impaired the balance sheets of both corporations and banks, credit risks increased and downward spirals and continued weaknesses in exchange rates and stock prices resulted in almost all countries. In early 1998, the situation stabilised somewhat and most exchange rates recovered from their 1997 lows, reflecting reform progress, especially in Korea and Thailand.

Compared with other recent financial crises, for example, the 1994–5 Mexico crisis, the one in East Asia has been much more protracted. In the case of Mexico,

Box 2.4 Competitive devaluations: an unlikely cause of contagion

If the East Asian countries compete in the same export markets, a devaluation of one currency will put competitive pressure on other currencies, which then may be forced to also devalue in order to restore their competitiveness. Can the successive competitive devaluations explain the sharp depreciation of the currencies? The answer seems to be no. We calculate the realignment of East Asian currencies versus the US dollar that would be necessary to restore the real exchange rate to its June 1995 level, using two scenarios: one, a country devalues alone, and the real competitive exchange rate versus the dollar of all other countries remains unchanged; and, two, all five countries devalue simultaneously. Figure 2.23 presents the results of our calculations. If each country devalues alone, the required depreciations vary between 10 and 20 per cent. If all devalue at the same time, the required depreciations increase only by one-half to one percentage point. The difference between the two scenarios is thus relatively small, and competitive devaluations appear insufficient to explain actual depreciations.

Figure 2.23 Actual depreciation versus US dollar, December 1996–June 1997, and devaluation needed to bring exchange rates back to June 1995 levels under different assumptions (%)

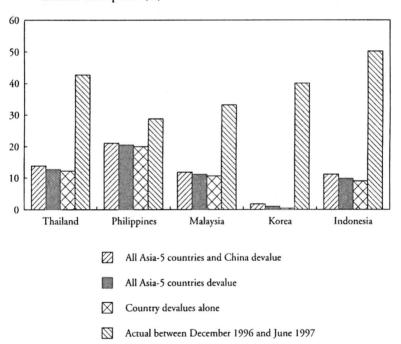

Legend:
- All Asia-5 countries and China devalue
- All Asia-5 countries devalue
- Country devalues alone
- Actual between December 1996 and June 1997

Source: Bloomberg datastream

private flows recovered in six months to about their previous level. This is not the case for any of the East Asian countries. Figures on bond and other capital market instruments show that private flows have virtually come to a standstill. Stock markets have also fallen much deeper than was the case in the Mexico crisis. The amplitude and severity of the East Asian stock markets' boom-and-bust cycle had, in the past, been less than that of emerging markets in Latin America, and only slightly more pronounced that those in G7 countries (Kaminsky and Schmukler 1998). In contrast, the drop in stock prices (in dollar terms) since July 1997 has been much more pronounced than in any previous downturn in East Asia, and even exceeds those in most Latin American countries following the Tequila crisis. This protracted crisis appears to have had two causes: the structural nature of problems and associated coordination issues; and the high leverage of corporations and the associated large external exposures.

Structural problems and coordination issues

The events in East Asia have highlighted the nature of macro-financial crises in a financially integrated world. An important dimension in avoiding financial crisis – and in recovering from it – is the preservation of investor confidence. Investors, in turn, focus not only on sound macroeconomic fundamentals but also on the strength of the financial system, corporate governance and competition policy, and a variety of other structural factors. This has been especially so for East Asia where the difficulties do not stem from poor macroeconomic fundamentals but, rather, from structural deficiencies in the financial and corporate sectors.

One implication of this change is that, in the immediate aftermath of a financial crisis, countries are expected to launch a program comprising both macroeconomic stabilisation and structural reforms. Indeed, in the recent East Asian cases, the structural measures announced in the post-crisis packages, which are expected to be implemented over the next few years, have been as important as traditional macroeconomic elements in efforts to restore market confidence. This emphasis on structural change, compared with only macroeconomic stabilisation, has a number of important implications. First, a set of fully articulated structural reforms is difficult to design in the middle of a financial crisis, and political and economic consensus on such reform may be difficult to gain quickly. Second, the reform agenda will take several years to implement and results may take even more time to emerge. And, third, progress in implementing structural change is difficult to observe and assess.

Thus, while structural issues have been squarely part of the programs to restore external investor confidence from the very start, the market has had great difficulty in assessing government commitment to these measures and in judging the future impact of actual decisions taken, particularly during the first phase of crisis management. When the need for structural change is combined with diversified external financing, the potential for coordination problems among creditors is large. In the case of East Asia, there is much more creditor and debtor diversity than was the case in other situations. During the developing countries' debt servicing problems of the mid-1980s, for example, all creditor banks were linked to each other by cross-default clauses, making coordination among creditors relatively easy. Cross-default clauses are not used for lending to a diverse set of corporations and financial institutions, as was the case in East Asia. Also, whereas in the Mexico crisis creditors had to inform themselves mainly about fiscal and aggregate macroeconomic performance, in the case of the East Asian countries prospects for individual financial institutions and corporations have mattered more.

High leverage

Financial depth is high in East Asia because good macroeconomic fundamentals encouraged household savings, most of which were intermediated through the domestic banking systems. In other financial crises, domestic intermediation was low (Figure 2.24). This meant that declines in asset prices had more severe effects on domestic financial intermediation and business cycles in the East Asian countries than in countries with low levels of intermediation. Furthermore, in other crises, corporations had already adjusted themselves to less external funding from domestic financial institutions. In Mexico, for example, export-oriented firms in particular had developed relationships with foreign capital suppliers and were thus less affected by the problems in Mexico's financial sector after the 1995 crisis. This was generally not the case in East Asia.

Figure 2.24 Domestic credit to GDP, 1996 (%)

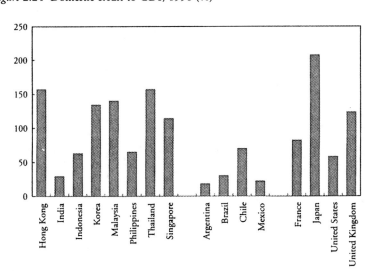

Source: International Financial Statistics

Table 2.6 Comparison of financial ratios of manufacturing companies

	Korea (1996)	Korea (1997)	Germany (1995)	USA (1995)	Japan (1995)	Taiwan (1995)
Debt/equity	332.7	449.4	175	159.7	206.3	85.7

Source: OECD, *Financial Statements of Non-financial Enterprises*

The high level of domestic financial intermediation, combined with biases in the financial systems and culture against equity financing and in favour of debt financing, meant that many firms in East Asia were highly leveraged. The debt to equity ratio of Korean corporations, for example, was almost 450 per cent by the end of 1997, three times the US ratio, and more than five times the Taiwanese ratio (Table 2.6). Correspondingly, interest burdens are very high in East Asian countries. In Korea, the interest-expenses-to-sales ratio of all manufacturing corporations in 1995 was about 6 per cent, compared with 2 per cent in Taiwan and 1 per cent in Japan. Furthermore, and reflective of a high expansion rate, East Asian corporations have relatively few liquid assets. Korean corporations, for example, had a ratio of liquid assets to short-term debts of less than 100 per cent in 1996, compared with 150 per cent in the United States and about 130 per cent in Japan and Taiwan. Liquidity and interest rate shocks thus greatly affect East Asian corporations.

The high leverage means that small shocks to interest rates of operational cash flow greatly affect corporations' ability to service debts. To illustrate, Table 2.7 shows the high leverage of Thai firms and their deteriorating profitability. The number of Thai firms unable to service their debts in full from their operating income rose from 18 in 1994 to 114 in 1997 and the percentage of total loans represented by these firms increased from 1.4 per cent to 36.4 per cent; that is, for about one-third of loans, interest expenses could not be fully covered in 1997 from operating income and had to be rolled over and financed from new loans. With the high leverage, even a small increase in interest rates and a decline in profitability have thus led to a large number of firms running into debt-servicing and liquidity problems, which in turn has negatively affected output.

Table 2.7 Deteriorating corporate performance

Period	Number of firms	Leverage	Profits over liabilities	Profits over interest expenses	No. of firms with profits < interest expenses	Loans of firms with profits < interest expenses (%)
1997:Q4	356	2.95	7.3	1.49	114	36.4
1997:Q3	356	2.95	10.2	2.59	83	30.8
1997:Q2	357	2.12	n.a.	3.18	71	18.4
1997:Q1	353	2.01	n.a.	3.66	54	16.2
1996:Q4	354	1.90	14.9	3.11	49	11.8
1995:Q4	354	1.67	18.1	4.01	34	7.6
1994:Q4	352	1.50	24.0	5.78	18	1.4

Note: Profit is defined as earnings before interest, taxes, and depreciation and amortisation (EBITDA). Leverage is debt over equity.
Source: Stock Exchange of Thailand (SET) database

CONCLUSION

It is clear that the crisis in East Asia has been very different from the debt crisis of the 1980s or even the Mexican peso crisis of 1994–5. While debate on the cause and implications of this crisis will continue, this chapter draws two preliminary conclusions.

First, the crisis occurred because the economies did not have the institutional and regulatory structures to cope with increasingly integrated capital markets. The immediate source of the problems was private sector decisions, both on the part of borrowers in East Asia and on the part of lenders. But these decisions were taken in the context of government policies that created incentives for risky behaviour while simultaneously exerting little regulatory authority and not encouraging enough transparency to allow the market to recognise and correct the problems. Undersupervised financial sectors allowed poorly governed corporations to invest borrowed money in highly inflated or risky assets such as real estate ventures. A lack of transparency – in the form of unreported mutual guarantees, lack of disclosure of companies' and banks' true net positions, and insider relations – masked these poor investments and meant that, once a downturn began, it was difficult to separate good and bad firms. These domestic weaknesses were aggravated by undisciplined foreign lending. The problem was not so much overall indebtedness but the composition of debt, with a build-up of short-term unhedged debt leaving the economies vulnerable to a sudden loss of confidence.

Second, these same underlying factors have meant that the economic and social impact of the crisis has been more severe than some anticipated. The loss of confidence has had an immediate and large impact on private demand, both investment and consumption, which in the short run could not be offset by net external demand. Financial institutions and corporations have been severely affected in East Asia in the aftermath of the crisis because of the very high degree of leverage (two to three times that of Latin America), and the unhedged and short-term nature of foreign liabilities. This, in turn, has resulted in a severe external and domestic liquidity crunch. Political uncertainties have also played a role, but the erosion of confidence has also undermined political stability. Domestic recession, financial and corporate distress, liquidity constraints and political uncertainty have been self-reinforcing, leading to a severe downturn.

Although the situation appears to be stabilising (except in Indonesia), the impact of the crisis will be long-lasting, in part because countries lack the necessary mechanisms for financial and corporate restructuring, including both the legal and institutional underpinnings. Also, social safety nets are lacking, since countries relied on rapid growth and employment to provide social security for its citizens. The social costs of this crisis will be large, therefore, in terms of unemployment and impact on the poor. Despite significant gains in the reduction of absolute poverty, in Thailand, and even to a larger degree in Indonesia, there is a large segment of the population living just above the poverty line. It is this group that is especially vulnerable to the impact.

The crisis has highlighted two important sources of vulnerability in the early stages of financial integration: the rapid build-up of contingent liabilities and the risks of excessive reliance on short-term borrowing. Although their magnitude was not known precisely, contingent liabilities were building up in the system as a result of various weaknesses. Together with other fundamentals, they determine the sustainability of exchange rate regimes. At some time, the market may test the size of this liability by putting pressure on the exchange rate. Vulnerability in the financial position will increase the likelihood of such attacks. If the defence of the exchange rate is not credible, large devaluations and high interest rates could trigger a downward spiral leading potentially to even larger contingent liabilities and, at least temporarily, to a bad equilibrium.

NOTES

This chapter has been a group effort; we would like to thank Jos Jansen and Peter Montiel for very useful contributions, Sergio Schmukler for his insights, Michael Dooley, the discussant, Akira Kohsaka, and seminar participants for comments, and the PAFTAD steering committee for guidance. The chapter draws on and extends the analysis in the joint World Bank–ADB study: 'Managing Global Financial Integration in Asia: Emerging Lessons and Prospective Challenges', 10–12 March 1998. The opinions expressed do not necessarily reflect those of the World Bank or of the Central Bank of Chile.

1   For example, the financial panic explanation requires that there be significant real effects that trigger a move to a worse equilibrium. Since most East Asian countries had low public external debt, however, it is not obvious why their governments could not have prevented the occurrence of crisis by taking over or guaranteeing those private sector liabilities which were subject to a bank run, that is, not being rolled over. Moral hazard was certainly a concern, but this was in the end often not avoided anyway and, besides, the cost was often so high that it could well have been a better policy. There is not yet a complete model that includes the trade-offs between public and private debt.

2   Not corrected for shareholder affiliation and cross-shareholding between firms (see La Porta et al. 1998).

3   Malaysia, for instance, has adopted 24 of the 31 international accounting standards without alteration, while the others are generally consistent with international standards (World Bank 1997).

4   The Center for International Analysis and Research is an investment advisor located in the United States. The index is based on the reporting practices of major domestic corporations with regard to 85 disclosure variables.

5   As discussed below, however, pegging did not in fact prevent their real exchange rates from appreciating. This is because these countries were, de facto, pegging to the US dollar and there were large cross-currency movements between the US dollar and the currencies of their other trading partners, notably Japan, during 1995–6.

6   The predictable nature of the nominal exchange rate is borne out, for example, in the fact that the standard deviations of the error term from a regression of the nominal exchange rate on a constant and a time trend during 1990–6 are very low for all four countries. Malaysia's nominal exchange rate was the least predictable.

7   Theoretically, the actual depreciation of the exchange rate is the best unbiased estimate of the expected depreciation only in the absence of a 'peso problem' (and with constant risk premia). It is difficult to argue that a peso problem existed in the Southeast Asian countries prior to early 1997.

8   This is also borne out empirically in cross-country analysis. Montiel and Reinhart (forthcoming), for example, find that an intensification of monetary tightening and sterilisation is associated with an increase in the volume of short-term capital.

9   One indication of the fact that capital flows have become more responsive to expected rates of return and that the Southeast Asian countries have become more financially integrated is the increase in the 'offset' coefficient – the degree to which a contraction in domestic credit is offset by inflows of capital – during the 1990s. In Indonesia, for example, the offset coefficient increased from 0.47 (i.e. 47 per cent of domestic credit is offset by capital inflows within the quarter) during 1988–93, to 0.64 during 1990–6. Another indication of greater accessibility is the fact that, in the early 1990s, of the firms that were rated, only those rated A or above had access to international bond issuance. During 1994–6, 35 per cent of rated corporations from the Southeast Asian countries (Indonesia, Malaysia, Philippines, Korea and Thailand) that issued international bonds were rated below A grade.

10 The exchange rate band was widened several times, from 1 per cent in January 1994 up to 8 per cent in September 1996.

11 Before February 1996, the reserve requirements of commercial banks consisted of cash in vault and demand deposits with BI. After February 1996, however, cash in vault no longer counted as a component of reserve requirements. Minimum reserve requirements are set at a certain percentage of commercial bank funds, defined as demand deposits, time deposits, savings deposits and other current liabilities. Since February 1996, the coverage has been expanded to include the above liabilities, regardless of maturity. Reserve requirements were further increased, to 5 per cent of deposit liabilities, in April 1997.

12 Prepayment was also used as a means of reducing the net inflows of capital and domestic overheating problems.

13 The fiscal impulse is analysed in terms of the respect to non-oil fiscal balance and demand pressures in the non-oil sector.

14 Indonesia instituted a managed float on 15 November 1978 and replaced the US dollar as its external anchor with an undisclosed basket of major currencies. Since 14 August 1997, Indonesia has had a 'dirty' float, in which the exchange rate is essentially market-determined, with sporadic interventions by the authorities.

15 This is corroborated in the results of a regression of the rupiah–US dollar nominal exchange rate on the inflation differential between Indonesia and the United States, specified in the following form:

$$\log(nexch)_t = 7.55 + 0.67 \log(idncpi - uscpi)_{t-1}$$

$$adjR^2 = 0.98$$

where *nexch* is the nominal exchange rate (defined as rupiah to 1 US dollar), *idncpi* is the Indonesian consumer price index and *uscpi* the US consumer price index. This suggests that a 1 percentage point increase in the differential between the domestic price level and the US price level led to a depreciation of the nominal rupiah–dollar exchange rate of 0.68 percentage points the following quarter. (Figures in parenthesis indicate t-statistics; *indicates significance at the 1 per cent level.)

16 RRPs involve the sale by Bangko Sentral of a financial instrument or asset with the commitment to reverse the transaction in the future. These are considered Bangko Sentral's borrowings from banks.

17 The fiscal impulse has been calculated excluding the privatisation proceeds.

18 In 1992–3, when differentials in interest rates were larger, due to monetary tightening and declines in global rates, the Philippines allowed the exchange rate to appreciate. At the

same time, the authorities implemented measures to reduce the potential loss of export competitiveness, including measures to reduce domestic costs for exporters.

19 Although 'sterilised' interventions are often taken to refer solely to open market operations, here we are referring to the tightening of monetary policy in response to an accumulation of net foreign assets in the central bank, whether through open market operations or by other means.

20 Since late 1986 until mid-1997, the baht fluctuated within a narrow band of plus/minus 3 per cent around its mean of 24.5 baht per US dollar.

21 Kaminsky and Reinhart (1996) confirm this finding for a wider set of countries.

22 Macro and currency risk factors constituted 16 per cent of the total of the average nominal interest rate of 16 per cent over this period, while the base US risk-free rate represented on average 28 per cent of the nominal interest costs.

23 The net financing gain in unclear, however, as it depends on the degree of substitutability: if foreign or domestic investment simply moves from the domestic market to the offshore market, there will be no net financing gain and only a loss of tax and regulatory coverage.

24 See also Kawai and Iwatsubo (1998).

25 Comparing the evolution of the difference between the average spread on emerging markets' Brady bonds with that on high-yield corporate bonds in the United States confirms this. While the difference had been as high as 300 basis points, in 1997 it declined sharply and in mid-July the Brady bond spread even fell below that on high-yield corporate bonds.

REFERENCES

Akerlof, G. and P. Romer (1993) 'Looting the economic underworld of bankruptcy for profit', *Brookings Papers on Economic Activity 2*, Washington DC: Brookings Institution, 1–73.

Bhattacharya, A., S. Ghosh and J. Jansen (1998) 'Has the emergence of China hurt Asian exports?', mimeo, Washington DC: World Bank.

Blanchard, O. and M. Watson (1982) 'Bubbles, rational expectations and financial markets', in P. Wachtel (ed.) *Crises in the Economic and Financial Structure*, USA: Lexington Books.

Claessens, S. and T. Glaessner (1997) 'Are financial sector weaknesses undermining the East Asian miracle', *Directions in Development*, Washington DC: World Bank, September.

—— (1998) 'Internationalization of financial services in Asia', *Working Paper 1911*, Washington DC: World Bank.

Cline, W.R. and K.J.S. Barnes (1997) 'Spreads and risks in emergency market lending', *Research Paper 97-1*, Washington DC: Institute for International Finance.

Corsetti, G., P. Pesenti and N. Roubini (1998) 'What caused the Asian currency and financial crisis?', mimeo, New York University.

Diamond, D.W. and P.H. Dybvig (1983) 'Bank runs, deposit insurance, and liquidity', *Journal of Political Economy* 91, June, 401–19.

Eichengreen, B. and A. Mody (1998) 'What explains changing spreads on emerging-market debt: fundamentals or market sentiment?', *NBER Working Paper W6408*, Washington DC: NBER, February.

Feldstein, M. (1998) 'Refocusing the IMF', *Foreign Affairs* 77, March/April, 20–33.

International Monetary Fund (IMF) (1997) *World Economic Outlook*, December, Washington DC: IMF.

Kaminsky, G. and C. Reinhart (1996) 'The twin crises: the causes of banking and balance of payments problems', unpublished paper, USA: Federal Reserve Board.

Kaminsky, G. and S. Schmukler (1998) 'On booms and crashes: is Asia different?', mimeo, Washington DC: World Bank and Board of Governors of the Federal Reserve System.

Kawai, M. and K. Iwatsubo (1998) 'The Thai financial system and the baht crisis: processes, causes and lessons', mimeo, Institute of Social Science, University of Tokyo.

Krugman, P. (1979) 'A model of balance of payments crises', *Journal of Money, Credit and Banking* 4(11): 311–25.

—— (1998) 'Fire-sale FDI', mimeo, Massachusetts Institute of Technology (paper prepared for NBER Capital Inflows to Emerging Markets conference).

La Porta, R., F. Lopez-de-Silanes, A. Shleifer and R.W. Vishny (1997) 'Legal determinants of external finance', *Journal of Finance* 52:1131–50, July.

—— (1998) 'Law and finance', *Journal of Political Economy* (forthcoming).

McKinnon, R.I. and H. Pill (1997) 'Credible liberalizations and international capital flows: the over-borrowing syndrome', *American Economic Review Papers and Proceedings* 87(2), May, 189–93.

Miller, M. and L. Zhang (1997) 'Sovereign liquidity crises: the strategic case for a payments standstill', mimeo, University of Warwick, November.

Montiel, P. and C. Reinhart (forthcoming) 'Do capital controls influence the volume and composition of capital flows? Evidence from the 1990s', *Journal of International Money and Finance*. .

Montes, M.F. (1998) *The Currency Crisis in South East Asia*, Singapore: Institute of Southeast Asian Studies.

Obstfeld, M. (1986) 'Rational and self-fulfilling balance of payments crises', *American Economic Review* 4(76): 72–81.

—— (1996) 'Models of currency crises with self-fulfilling features', *European Economic Review* 40(3–5): 1037–47, April.

Radelet, S. and J. Sachs (1998a) 'The onset of the East Asian financial crisis', No. 6680, Cambridge, Mass.: National Bureau of Economic Research, August.

—— (1998b) 'The East Asian financial crisis: diagnosis, remedies, prospects', *Brookings Papers on Economic Activity*, Washington DC: Brookings Institution, 26–7 March.

Ramos, R. (1997a) 'Asian banks at risk: solidity, fragility', *Banking Research*, Hong Kong: Goldman Sachs, September.

—— (1997b) '1998: issues and outlook: cyclical slowdowns, structural ills and the odds for recovery', *Banking Research*, Hong Kong: Goldman Sachs, December.

Sachs, J. (1994a) 'Russia's struggle with stabilization: conceptual issues and evidence', in M. Bruno and B. Pleskovic (eds) *Proceedings of the Annual Conference on Development Economics*, Washington DC: World Bank, 57–80.

—— (1994b) 'Beyond Bretton Woods: a new blueprint', *The Economist* 333, 1–7 October, 23, 25, 27.

Sachs, J., A. Tornell and A. Velasco (1996) 'Financial crises in emerging markets: the lessons from 1995', *Brookings Papers in Economic Activity*, Washington DC: Brookings Institution, 147–215.

Sarel, M. (1997) 'Growth and productivity in ASEAN countries', *IMF Working Paper 97/97*. August.

Valdés, R. (1996) 'Emerging market contagion: evidence and theory', mimeo, Cambridge, Mass.: MIT.

World Bank (1997) *Private Capital Flows to Developing Countries*, Washington DC: World Bank.

—— (1998) *Global Development Finance*, Washington DC: World Bank.

3 Financial crises and the prudential regulation of financial institutions

Jia-Dong Shea and David C.Y. Sun

INTRODUCTION

It is generally agreed that both macroeconomic instability and unsound financial sectors have been concrete reasons for the recent financial turmoil in the Asian region. A sound financial system is a prerequisite for sustained growth; a weak financial system is both a standing invitation to crisis and a guarantee of its severity (Camdessus 1998). This chapter emphasises the role of financial supervision in preventing such crises and outlines possible directions for supervisory reform.

From a macroeconomic point of view, the turmoil in Asia resulted from a failure to oversee imbalanced capital inflows as well as overheating asset markets. Many studies describe in detail the causes of the crisis and it is generally agreed that the prospects of high returns on investments attracted foreign capital inflows, most of which consisted of short-term debt. These large inflows led to boom–bust investments in the local real estate and securities markets, which had a negative impact on productivity, while a decline in the growth rate of exports resulted in current account deficits. The pegged or quasi-fixed exchange rate systems prevailing in many of the affected countries provided incentives for speculators, as well as the local financial and corporate sectors, to have huge foreign exchange exposures. Once that fuse was lit, information asymmetry resulted in heavy capital outflows and currency markets suffered badly.

From a supervisory point of view, a key factor in the crisis was the lack of effective financial supervision, which led to volatility in the banking system and poor asset quality. Since the crisis broke out, the question of what kinds of improvements the governing authorities need to make to prevent such a crisis from happening again has often been raised. The appropriateness of monetary and exchange rate policies, which depend on both general assumptions and each country's specific conditions, is a controversial issue, while the financial supervisory function is a more concrete target. In regard to the 1997 currency turmoil, supervisory shortcomings include:

- neglect of the accumulated foreign debt and its usage by the affected countries' financial sectors;

- failure to regulate financial institutions from the standpoint of credit concentration risk, connected lending and imprudent management; and

- unsatisfactory endeavours to improve structural problems such as a lack of information transparency, imprudent standards for bad debts and insolvent institutions, and poor governance of financial institutions.

MACROECONOMIC CONDITIONS AND THE FINANCIAL SECTOR

Generally speaking, macroeconomic instability would certainly weaken the financial sector. An unsound financial sector, based on the perception that individual institutions could hedge their exposure but that the net position of the whole financial system could not be hedged, would undermine both macroeconomic performance and the economy to some extent.

First of all, the quality of loans would deteriorate due to any sharp decline in asset prices or to a cyclical downturn, so that the whole financial sector would become more fragile. Inappropriate monetary policy measures would result in financial institutions making blunted portfolio adjustments that might reduce their profitability. A loose monetary policy might then lead to an asset price bubble that would lay the basis for future problems. The directing or allocating of credit within a planned economy, for the sake of fiscal objectives, might contribute to the unsoundness of the financial sector. Exchange rate instability, together with the lax regulation of foreign exchange risk exposure, might often exert a negative effect on the private sector, especially privately owned financial institutions. Prolonged macroeconomic instability would therefore distort financial operations and erode the capital adequacy of the financial sector.

The manner in which the macroeconomic framework would be affected by an unsound financial sector would be more complicated. An unsound financial system is usually evidenced by a wide interest rate spread, high interest rates and high-risk portfolios, which would deter financial intermediation and eventually impede economic recovery. The monetary policy process would be affected because market indicators such as interest rates and related data, distorted by unsound operations, would not represent real market changes. Monetary policy instruments, direct or indirect, would be less efficient because the transmission mechanism would become less price-elastic. An unsound financial sector, given its low-level profitability and proneness to failure, would have a negative fiscal impact and the effectiveness of the foreign exchange system would also be hampered (Lindgren et al. 1996).

With regard to the foreign exchange system, which would serve as one of the direct causes of financial turmoil, it would be interesting to apply the 'unholy trinity' theorem provided by Robert Parry, president of the Federal Reserve Bank of San

Francisco. The essence of his theorem is that the three conditions required to stabilise a domestic economy – namely, free capital flows, fixed exchange rates and the use of monetary policy – cannot exist simultaneously in a country (Hadjimichalakis 1998). The recent turmoil has been characterised by a lack of coordination between monetary policy and exchange rate policy in certain respects.

Given the above, the macroeconomic policies and the financial sectors of any economy should be reviewed jointly to ensure continued stability and growth. The soundness of the financial sector is basically determined by the operations of financial institutions. The architects of a sound financial system must of necessity, therefore, consider how best to supervise them.

A BROAD FINANCIAL SAFETY NETWORK

Given the importance of strengthening financial supervision, it is necessary to review the broad financial safety network as well as the coverage of the supervisory framework. There is a popular notion that the challenges faced by financial businesses in a crisis are cross-border by nature, while financial supervisory challenges remain mainly national in scope. In fact, financial stability is a basic prerequisite for a sound financial sector in every country. According to the 'Core Principles for Effective Banking Supervision' established by the Basle Committee on Banking Supervision (BCBS 1997), the arrangements needed to promote stability in financial markets include: sound and sustainable macroeconomic policies; a well-developed public infrastructure; effective market discipline; procedures for the efficient resolution of problems in banks; and mechanisms for providing an appropriate level of systemic protection (or a public safety net).

Banking supervisors have a responsibility in regard to each of these. While the introduction of sound and sustainable macroeconomic policies does not fall within the scope of their duties, supervisors should react to inappropriate policies. The BCBS includes 'effective banking supervision' in the 'public infrastructure' category. Furthermore, the supervisory agency should bear responsibility for enhancing the development of the market discipline function, identify and implement solutions with regard to problem financial institutions, and play an active role with regard to the financial safety net.

Financial sector instability, regardless of whether it occurs in emerging markets or industrial economies, can be traced to weaknesses and failings in the areas of corporate governance and management; the incentive structure provided by the financial and institutional frameworks; market discipline; and the regulatory and supervisory structures (Working Party on Financial Stability in Emerging Market Economies 1997). Figure 3.1 shows that every phase of the financial network should be connected with financial safety and soundness. Supervisory agencies are responsible for regulatory discipline, while market discipline would be promoted by market participants who make decisions based on publicly disclosed information. A well-defined deposit protection scheme can enhance market discipline, although excessive insurance coverage may induce adverse selection and lead to moral hazards, which might diminish the market discipline function. In addition, external auditors and self-regulatory organisations (SROs) should play their part in external governance to some extent. Ideally, every financial institution is required to employ a certified public accountancy (CPA) firm to conduct a periodical review, after which the external auditor submits recommendations to the institution. On the other hand, bankers' associations should issue standards which contribute to fair competition and stability in the market. Overall, however, the most important role in governance is that played by the financial institutions themselves.

The primary functions of a supervisory framework are regulation, supervision, examination and enforcement (Figure 3.2).

Figure 3.1 Financial safety networks

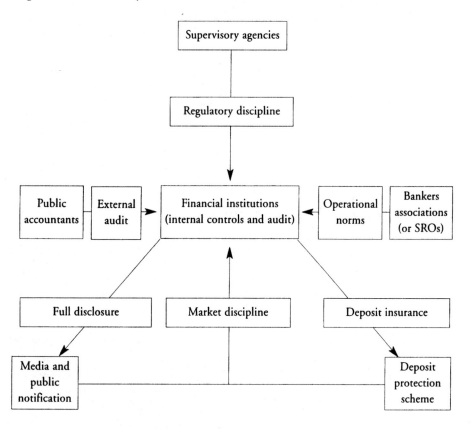

Figure 3.2 Regulatory discipline

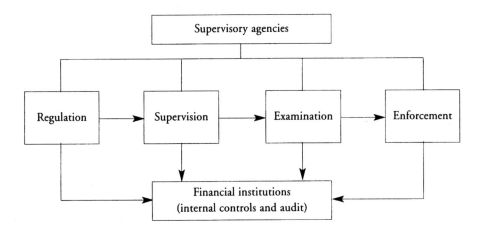

THE CHALLENGES FACING SUPERVISORY AGENCIES

Financial supervisory agencies must now deal with a changing financial environment and so with the need to develop appropriate responses to supervising it.

A new financial environment

From an international perspective, there are two prominent trends towards a new financial environment: increased innovation, and globalisation. Because of technological advances in the payment system, there is a vast array of new financial products, particularly those relating to the growth of derivatives. These new products have changed both the risk profile and the risk management methodology of financial institutions, making them increasingly complex. The progress in information technology, together with the liberalisation of capital movements, has also permitted financial institutions to engage in cross-border activities around the clock. Thus, domestic financial markets have become increasingly exposed to external disturbances which alter not only the nature of systemic risk but also the volatilities and vulnerabilities of these markets.

From a regional or national perspective, the changes in the financial environment are of three kinds: market entry deregulation, financial services liberalisation, and pricing deregulation.

Many developing countries have gradually relaxed their restrictions relating to the establishment of an increasingly wide range of new financial institutions, in order to meet the rapidly expanding demand for financial services. On the other hand, they have also had to open up their domestic markets in varying degrees to entry from abroad, or to create a level playing field for financial institutions from different countries. Subsequently, market competition and the associated risks have quickly increased.

In the pursuit of profits and improved performance, different kinds of financial institutions have tried to engage in more varied activities. Recently, the prospect of 'universal banking' and 'financial conglomerates' has become a controversial issue in some developing countries. The homogeneous evolution of different financial institutions has had a dramatic impact on legal frameworks, business operations, risk management, and systems of supervision.

The deregulation of interest rates and the foreign exchange rate may well be the most critical part of the entire financial liberalisation program. At the initial stage, interest and exchange rate control measures should be lifted or diminished. Financial resources should be allocated through the market mechanism. However, during the transition, financial institutions which lack experience in managing credit and foreign exchange risks are often exposed to price disturbances. Therefore, both the supervisory framework and financial institutions' internal governance should be strengthened in parallel with any liberalisation.

The need for a new response

As a result of these changes, supervisory agencies now face a number of challenges: reregulating rather than deregulating; adopting a macro rather than a micro approach; being dynamic rather than static; and taking anticipatory rather than retrospective action.

Regulation, the first step in regulatory discipline, is concerned with setting up the 'rules of the game', which serve as the cornerstone of the whole supervisory system. At the outset of liberalisation, it is necessary to remove any intrusive, outdated or inadequately implemented regulations in order to facilitate the continued evolution of the financial services industry. As liberalisation progresses, the supervisory agency should actively work to formulate new regulations in parallel with the changing financial environment. 'Minimum Standards for the Supervision of International Banking Groups and Their Cross-Border Establishments' (1992) and 'Risk Management Guidelines for Derivatives' (1994), issued by the BCBS, were good examples of past reregulation. In the case of a national financial supervisor, reviewing and setting up appropriate regulations and the accompanying framework would be definitely the mission of first importance.

Strengthening the system of financial supervision should be looked at comprehensively. Each part of the system – regulation, supervision, examination, enforcement – involves the application of sophisticated philosophies, procedures and practices. The pertinent coordination of these four parts is also a decisive factor in an efficient system. Supervisory agencies should not resort to stopgap measures to patch up specific phenomena. For instance, the whole system would not function properly if supervisors were to emphasise field examination practices while neglecting the improvement of enforcement actions. On the other hand, supervisors should be aware that market discipline and the internal governance of financial institutions also play significant roles within broad financial safety networks. Regulatory discipline and market discipline must be complementary if the supervisory infrastructure is to be most effective. In other words, a successful supervisory agency should keep its eyes on the trees but still have a vision of the whole forest.

Along with liberalisation and innovation, the greater volume of transactions and rapidly growing competition have increased the degree of volatility in financial markets. For financial supervisors to merely scrutinise periodical reports or conduct regular examinations would not be an adequate means of responding to the rapidly changing markets. In this regard, supervisors should place emphasis on the financial institution's ongoing system for managing risk, rather than solely engaging in point-in-time transactions testing (Phillips 1997b). The related supervisory structure and procedures should be shifted from conventional balance sheet auditing to an evaluation of the internal risk management process (Greenspan 1997). In other words, supervisors should take the initiative to oversee and analyse financial phenomena in a more active manner.

There is a broad consensus that effective enforcement actions to prevent the occurrence of serious financial accidents need to be taken in advance, but an overprotected financial market would give rise to moral hazard problems. A suitable compromise can be reached through cost–benefit analysis. Financial supervisors, with the help of an early warning system, should take 'prompt corrective actions' to resolve potential problems at an early stage. In such cases, the social cost can be minimised and moral hazard mitigated. On the other hand, the supervisory system should be adjusted in line with environmental changes in order to avoid regulatory gaps. For instance, financial supervisors in emerging countries should be familiar with risk management concepts and techniques so that they can adapt to the developments taking place in investment banking. They should establish an adequate legal system in advance to resolve potential problems arising from universal banking and Internet banking. It would be more risky for supervisors to simply follow the financial services industry as it evolved. However, responding to these challenges is easier said than done.

FINANCIAL SUPERVISION IN TAIWAN

If we combine the change rates of the exchange rate and the stock market index into an indicator of the effect of the financial crisis, we find that Taiwan experienced a decline of 30.65 per cent between June 1997 and May 1998, much less than that of neighbouring countries.

Some basic observations explain why Taiwan has been affected relatively lightly by the turmoil. It has enjoyed stable economic growth as well as the absence of a financial bubble phenomenon in its asset markets. Successive current account surpluses indicate that it has not relied excessively upon foreign capital in the process of its economic development. It has adequate foreign exchange reserves but limited foreign debt. An ordered and gradual approach to liberalising foreign capital movements has lessened the impact of external shocks on domestic markets. The upgraded private sector, with its improved financial structure, can adapt to changing conditions. Finally, as explored in more detail below, Taiwan has improved both its financial system and its supervisory framework.

Supervisory structure and practice

Under the current system, the agencies which are entitled by law to carry out financial examination work include the Ministry of Finance (MOF), the Central Bank of China (CBC) and the Central Deposit Insurance Corporation (CDIC). These agencies divide their duties roughly according to type of financial institution. The CBC examines all but three of the domestic banks established before 1991, as well as the local branches of European, American and African banks, and all bills finance companies. The MOF examines all banks established since 1991, the three old banks, two development (and trust) corporations, and all securities finance companies and insurance companies. The CDIC examines insured financial institutions, community financial institutions (including credit cooperative associations and the credit departments of farmers and fishermen's associations), and the rest. As of 31 December 1997, there were a total of 4,473 financial units which were subject to examination: 1,291 by the CBC; 856 by the MOF; and 2,326 by the CDIC. Copies of the reports made by the CBC and the CDIC are required to be sent both to the examined institutions and to the MOF. Recommendations must also be made to the MOF if they involve administrative sanctions or legal action. In order to integrate these supervisory activities and to efficiently utilise examination resources, a financial examination committee, composed of the representatives of supervisory agencies and related institutions, has been established. Its major function is to enhance supervisory coordination and review related issues, including improvement of the financial supervisory system.

Besides on-site examination, the MOF, CBC and CDIC also undertake off-site monitoring. The mechanisms used for this include: the CARSEL monitoring system; enhancement of the internal auditing function; the review of other call reports; and interviews with the management of financial institutions.

Because of the shortage of examination resources and in order to fully understand the financial and operational conditions of financial institutions, the CBC developed and implemented in 1990 the 'financial institution CARSEL analysing and warning system'. This monitoring system utilises financial analysis and management accounting techniques to screen periodical call report data. The CBC can evaluate every institution's performance by analysing its capital adequacy (C), asset quality (A), regulatory compliance (R), strategies and stability (S), earnings (E) and liquidity (L). The institutions whose warning codes receive high marks have to be identified and followed up with specific supervisory actions.

The internal auditing function has been enhanced in four significant ways. First, supervisory agencies have stipulated the qualifications and training requirements for internal auditors and prescribed a minimum standard for the scope and frequency of internal auditing. Second, operating branches, custodian departments and the electronic data processing units of financial institutions have been asked to engage in self-inspection (by means of crosschecking by their own staff) every month. Third, supervisory agencies may now assemble the senior managers of the operations and auditing departments of financial institutions to discuss the problems they are confronting, so as to exchange views and promote safe and sound operations. Finally, agencies may now periodically rate the internal audit functions of financial institutions in accordance with prescribed criteria.

Supervisory agencies may also review the minutes of meetings of the boards of directors and supervisors of financial institutions in order to monitor important policies and screen irregularities (especially abnormal loans with large exposures). In addition, they may review the internal audit reports submitted by financial institutions, to monitor operational conditions and any deficiencies. If the supervisory information indicates unsound practices or exceptional facilities in financial institutions, supervisors will interview the management of those institutions to establish the facts and to discuss appropriate measures.

Recent supervisory experience

During the last decade, the financial sector in Taiwan has expanded tremendously. Many new financial institutions have begun to participate in the domestic market. All financial institutions are subject to prudential regulations relating to accounting principles, capital adequacy, limits on related party lending, the diversification of credit allocation, risk management and internal governance. The supervisory agencies oversee financial institutions by means of periodical inspection and an ongoing off-site monitoring system. Financial institutions that violate regulations or engage in risky activities are identified and required to take corrective action immediately.

In 1995, there were several instances in which community financial institutions experienced panic runs. However, none of these was particularly large and, since there was a sound deposit insurance system already in place, the government was able to respond in a timely manner and, at the same time, calm depositors' fears. The supervisory agencies subsequently encouraged these community institutions either to merge with other financial institutions or else convert themselves into commercial banks. Consequently, the health of financial institutions significantly improved.

Furthermore, financial institutions in Taiwan have adopted a cautious attitude towards loans backed by either real estate or equity securities. For instance, they finance only up to 60 per cent of the value of company stocks, and loans backed by shares account for only 2 per cent of total bank lending. Similarly, banks in general extend mortgages for only about 70 per cent of the purchase price of a house, and all real estate loans are fully secured. For these reasons, even though share prices fell significantly between September and early December 1997, the quality of loans extended by local financial institutions has not been much affected.

Assuming that the financial market was stable, the community financial institutions' problems mentioned above were mostly the result of poor loan portfolio management. Some of these institutions with high overdue loan ratios were perceived as unsound and, once such rumours spread, depositors lined up to withdraw their money. The news media would treat such a reaction as a financial crisis, while the institutions were in fact experiencing a problem of liquidity rather than solvency. The other aspect was that these institutions were not all exposed to the public at the same time, so the financial supervisors were able to resolve the problems on a case-by-case basis and protect them from contagion. Besides, the supervisory agencies have paid close attention to every problem institution and have taken appropriate action to prevent their operations from getting worse.

Financial supervisory reform

The government authorities in Taiwan have stressed the necessity of strengthening financial supervision. The supervisory agencies, including the MOF, CBC and CDIC, have been jointly engaged on a 'bank supervision improvement project' since 1996. They have been required to work together to a detailed timetable which was set up to monitor progress on the project's 52 items. Work on most items has been completed, except for a few legislative issues. In broad outline, the project covers:

• enhancement of the internal governance of financial institutions;
• promotion of market discipline;
• improvement of the examination function;
• revision of the deposit insurance system;
• establishment of a crisis administration system; and
• enhancement of external auditing.

For the purpose of increasing internal audit independence, every institution must appoint an executive officer as general auditor who reports directly to the board of directors. Internal auditors must be categorised according to three levels: department head, auditor-in-charge and staff auditor. For each level, the auditor's qualifications are prescribed by regulations. Every financial institution must reinforce the evaluation of its internal controls and risk management system. At the end of each fiscal year, the president of the institution must submit a statement to the supervisory agency to confirm the effectiveness of the institution's internal controls. Self-regulatory organisations, such as bankers associations, are to be encouraged to issue related standards which will promote fair competition in financial markets.

A number of public disclosure practices have been set up to increase financial information transparency, while supervisory agencies have encouraged the establishment of a credit rating agency and have advised financial institutions to avail themselves of the rating information.

Supervisory agencies have applied management-oriented examination procedures which include the determination and evaluation of operational policies and the functions of directors; and coordination between different management departments, the reporting system, internal controls, internal audit, and the risk management system. The agencies have increased the frequency of target examinations specifically aimed at the crucial areas of financial institutions, as well as strengthening their follow-up procedures and enforcement measures to fulfil the examination objectives. The qualification standards, training requirements and working principles for each level of examiners have been regulated. The timeframes and accuracy of submitted information have been improved in order to enhance the effectiveness of off-site monitoring.

Legislation has been drafted to change the status of deposit insurance from being voluntary to being compulsory. In addition, the deposit insurance agency has been given greater responsibility with regard to enforcement and administration practices.

Every related government department is required to set up a crisis administration unit and to determine relevant practices and procedures in advance. Financial institutions whose situations are deteriorating are monitored constantly by means of a computerised system.

According to the revised Banking Law, a set of guidelines governing the participation of CPA firms in bank examination has been prescribed. In order to enhance the accountability of financial statements, an evaluation regarding the mandatory review by CPA firms of all financial institutions, instead of only a part of them, is being processed.

In addition to the bank supervision improvement project, the MOF and the CBC have jointly proposed a reform program to integrate the financial examination system. Under this program, the MOF will be responsible for the examination of all financial institutions, while the CBC will continue to exercise the right to examine monetary, credit and foreign exchange policies and the national payment system.

DIRECTIONS FOR FUTURE REFORM

Given the close interaction between the macroeconomic environment and financial intermediation, supervisory agencies should restructure their systems on a broader basis instead of merely confining themselves to the role of 'watchdog' or 'fire brigade'. Each element of financial supervision, be it regulation, supervision, examination or enforcement, should be initiated, implemented and reviewed from a macro perspective. Some observations on the directions for future supervisory reform are provided below.

Risk management

A crucial part of financial supervision is risk management. Supervisors should not stifle market efficiency while they seek to maintain financial stability. Such a situation tends to be treated as a cost–benefit opportunity rather than as a 'trade-off'. The market functions on the basis of every financial institution seeking to maximise its profits. Whenever risky activities might get financial institutions into trouble and hence damage the market, financial supervision comes in. The 'best practice' for both financial supervisors and institutions rests with the risk management function. Supervisors should assure institutions that regulatory restrictions do not constitute a barrier preventing them from seeking profit, while the institutions should avail themselves of improved risk management methods and related tools to increase their risk-adjusted rate of return (Greenspan 1996).

There are three sections within the BCBS's core principles (1997) that specifically ask financial supervisors to focus on country risk, transfer risk, market risk and all other material risks. Some experimental changes have also moved in the same direction. In 1997, the Federal Financial Institutions Examination Council in the United States, a coordinated body for federal supervisory agencies, announced that it would be adding 'sensitivity to market risk' to its original CAMEL (capital adequacy, asset quality, management, earnings, liquidity) rating model, renaming it 'CAMELS' as a result. Since then, the Bank of England (1997) has prescribed a risk-based supervisory structure called 'RATE' which focuses on risk assessment, the tools of supervision, and evaluation. Coincidentally, the Bank of Japan revised its 'Checklist for Risk Management' and placed 'management and internal controls' at the top of the new checklist in May 1997.

During the process of reform, financial supervisors should place more emphasis on the risk management systems within the financial services industry. To begin with, supervisors should issue directives for financial institutions to formulate strategic business plans, draw up internal operational policies, and establish management information systems as well as internal control and auditing systems. The most critical part is that supervisors should evaluate, by means of on-site inspection or off-site monitoring, the efficiency of the system in terms of identifying, measuring, monitoring and controlling risk.

Internal governance

The cornerstone of financial soundness is internal governance. The primary responsibility for keeping individual financial institutions sound rests with their owners, directors and managers. Poor internal governance was a factor in virtually all instances where financial institutions were found to be unsound (Lindgren et al. 1996). The 'Framework for the Evaluation of Internal Control Systems', drafted by the BCBS in January 1998, grouped the different types of bank control failures into five categories:

- lack of adequate management oversight and accountability, and failure to develop a strong control culture within the bank;

- inadequate assessment of the risk of certain banking activities, whether on- or off-balance sheet;

- the absence or failure of key control activities, such as segregation of duties, approvals, verifications, reconciliations, and reviews of operating performance;

- inadequate communication of information between levels of management, especially in the upward communication of problems; and

- inadequate or ineffective audit programs and other monitoring activities.

The US financial regulators also pointed out that supervisory and regulatory policies should be more 'incentive-compatible'. The performance incentives of financial institution owners and managers are regarded as being particularly important (Phillips 1997a).

Usually, the owners and their appointed directors will approve strategies and policies, and ensure that the senior management monitors the effectiveness of the system of internal controls. The management is responsible for implementing the strategies and policies so that the financial institution operates in a safe and sound manner. On the other hand, the above incentives would not exist once the owners, directors and managers failed to perform their duties, especially in the case of a conflict of interest.

In this regard, enhancing the internal governance of financial institutions should be the primary concern of supervisory reform. Internal governance begins with the owners and directors. For the purpose of enforceability, both the diversification of share ownership and the specific qualifications of directors and senior managers should be regulated by law. Supervisors should continue to monitor these, regardless of whether the business licence is at the approval stage or after it. In addition, they should issue directives regarding internal governance which would cover: the responsibilities of directors and management; risk assessment and the management mechanism; internal control activities; effective information and communications systems; and independent and comprehensive internal audit functions, among others. What is most important is that supervisors should conduct effective evaluations with regard to the adequacy and efficiency of financial institutions' internal governance. In the event of any detected shortcomings, supervisors should take appropriate action and require that the institution improve them immediately.

Market discipline

Supervisors should assist with the promotion of market discipline. The creditors of financial institutions, including depositors, interbank lenders and securities investors, should be encouraged to choose their business counterparts or clients on the basis of publicly disclosed information relating to the soundness of the institutions. Subsequently, weaker or more poorly performing financial institutions would be less competitive in the market. The depositors might then withdraw their deposits and the interbank lenders would add a premium to the lending rate. This is an example of the 'reward the better and penalise the bad' approach. In the case of the less well-performing economies, such adverse situations would be exacerbated and the worst performers would be forced to exit. Through such market discipline, the incentives for financial institutions to attach greater importance to maintaining a safe and sound status would be enhanced. Examples of past financial crises have revealed an almost total absence of market discipline (Lindgren et al. 1996). However, market discipline serves as a critical factor within a more incentive-compatible supervisory environment (Phillips 1997a).

Faced with the objective of reforming the supervisory system, it is now a suitable time for developing countries to promote market discipline by taking the following steps:

- Related laws and regulations should be reviewed and revised to embody principles such as submitting information to authorities in a timely and correct manner, employing external auditors to oversee such information flows, and publicly disclosing appropriate information.

- A set of generally accepted accounting standards for the financial services industry should be developed and adhered to.

- The appropriate amount of disclosure needs to be determined, which is rather complicated in practice. There are many kinds of information disclosure. US financial regulators use the sophisticated 'uniform banking performance report' (UBPR). Supervisors in Taiwan have applied the same techniques as those included in the UBPR. Other ways in which information can be made more transparent include disclosing it in newspapers or government publications, and making it available at every operating unit of financial institutions.

- Finally, supervisors should encourage financial institutions to use the information disclosed by rating agencies as one of the pricing factors.

The supervisory system

It is important that the financial supervisory system be strengthened. The system serves several functions: regulation; supervision; examination; and enforcement.

Regulation: the essential element of a prudential level playing field

Five years ago, a famous leader of the US supervisory system mentioned that the most serious banking problems had grown out of old-fashioned difficulties with bad loans and excessive concentrations (Corrigan 1992). The situation does not appear to have changed. There are certain key prudential regulations, such as capital adequacy ratios, single lending limits, connected lending limits, liquidity ratios, and foreign exchange exposure limits. However, the most critical factor that can damage a financial sector is credit (Lindgren et al. 1996). Very often, huge credit losses are discovered to be associated with the phenomenon referred to as 'credit under false pretences'. It may be that related parties are using unrelated entities to borrow funds. A bank manager may permit delinquent clients to repay the principal and interest on an old loan with funds from a new loan under another borrower's name. Both cases reveal that violations of prudential regulations may lie just under the surface of what appears to be legitimate activity.

Laws and regulations may not cover every aspect of financial operations, especially when the financial industry has evolved rapidly and become complicated. For instance, the main objective behind limiting a single customer's lending is to reduce the risk of credit concentration. In the case where a borrower wishes to obtain a huge bank loan which exceeds the single lending limit, the borrower may split the loan into a few smaller ones using different borrowers' names.

How can supervisors wipe out such irregularities and use the regulations to achieve desired results? One possible approach is to vest supervisors with the authority to pass judgment relating to the implementation of prudential regulations. Whenever supervisors are confronted with a case that is legal on the surface but a violation in essence, they could, with the force of law, regard it as imprudent and ask the financial institution to take the necessary corrective action.

Supervision: an ongoing surveillance system

Financial supervisors should oversee market conditions and assess trends by means of timely and correct information. Any institutions with operational irregularities should be identified and followed up with appropriate supervisory action. Furthermore, supervisors should develop a nationwide surveillance system to monitor potential risk on a macro basis (Sheng 1997). Although supervisory agencies would not focus on the coordination between the financial sector and other sectors, a key issue in most emerging countries would be to strengthen financial sector risk management.

A surveillance system relies on some early warning indicators which point out the riskier activities or fragilities of certain institutions, such that supervisors can take appropriate and timely action to prevent their getting into difficulty. Whether or not the warning indicators function properly and specifically disclose risky institutions is the crucial part of the whole surveillance system.

Some developed countries have applied the CAMEL system. A recent empirical study on Latin American crises concluded that CAMEL variables do not perform effectively in such circumstances because of the less developed state of capital markets, legal systems and supervisory frameworks. The study applied four other indicators – the interest rate on deposits, the bank spread, the rate of growth of loans, and the interbank debt ratio – to the same Latin American data and obtained a more satisfactory result (Rojas-Suarez 1998). These conclusions may not be applicable to other developing countries because of different financial environments. However, they serve as a reminder that early warning indicators should be selected and reviewed for their effectiveness.

Whether or not the information derived from an early warning system can be transmitted directly to policy decisionmakers in a timely manner is an equally important element. Financial supervisors should establish a set of comprehensive procedures to facilitate the analysis of information and related follow-up operations.

Examination: evaluation and verification

Financial examination, regardless of whether it takes the form of on-site inspection or off-site monitoring, plays an active part in the supervisory framework (Figure 3.3). In general, examiners should oversee how the examined financial institutions are complying with applicable laws, regulations and prudential management principles. The examination philosophy remains the same as before, but the financial environment and the challenges faced have changed dramatically as the financial services industry has evolved. An examiner today would deal with both the old-fashioned financial scenario and a new type of risk profile.

Figure 3.3 Financial examination structure

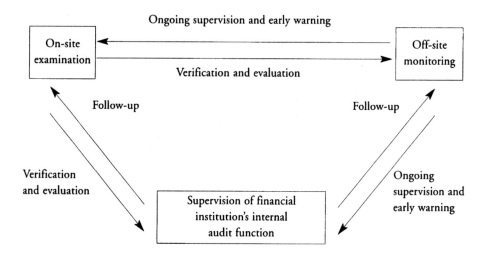

It is generally recognised that an effective supervisory system should be associated with highly qualified, experienced and dedicated examiners. However, many developing countries have been faced with a shortage of capable examiners, given the rapid development of the financial sector. Given the limitations of government budgets, it would not be practical to expect extra increments of examination personnel. There are three possible alternatives:

- Specialists could be invited to participate in examination activities. The advantages of this approach are that highly specialised examiners, who may include public accountants, lawyers and computer engineers, can deal with a variety of onerous financial issues. Nevertheless, it is necessary but also difficult to demarcate responsibility between the public authorities whose work is conducted by government examiners and the private firms which provide technical assistance. Should the private specialists be paid by the institutions they inspect, the situation becomes even more complicated.

- The off-site monitoring system could be promoted. This system complements on-site inspections. Efficient off-site monitoring requires a sophisticated computer system, qualified analysts, maintenance facilities, good coordination with on-site inspections, follow-up procedures and proper information submission systems.

- Training programs for examiners could be improved. According to a recent assessment (Sullivan and Chang 1998), there are significant unmet training needs for bank supervisors in many Asia Pacific Economic Cooperation (APEC) forum member economies. Supervisory agencies in those countries should improve training programs and encourage examiners to upgrade their skills so that the examination function can be enhanced.

Enforcement: resolution of the defects

Enforcement actions constitute the crux of the supervisory framework. Any detected shortcomings should be rectified thoroughly; otherwise, the problems will remain and will probably get worse. In the US Federal Deposit Insurance Corporation Improvement Act of 1991, both 'early intervention' and 'prompt corrective actions' are regarded as primary guides in the field of enforcement, since supervisory failure usually takes the form of forbearance (Lindgren et al. 1996). The reasons for the forbearance mostly come from political interference and insufficient legislation. Supervisors may sometimes adopt a 'wait and see' attitude, and thereby transfer a hot potato into another's hands. By the time enforcement actions can no longer be postponed, handling costs will have increased significantly.

To prevent such circumstances, the best arrangements would be to issue specific regulations prescribing the necessary enforcement action in every respect, so that supervisors no longer exercise any discretion, and to review and revise the related legal framework, particularly regarding mergers, conservatorship, bankruptcy and the like.

Regional supervision

It is important that regional supervision be coordinated. Traditionally, the consolidated supervision of cross-border financial establishments has been the focus of international supervisory cooperation. The growing prevalence in world markets of financial conglomerates presents a new challenge for supervisory cooperation. Consultative documents related to the supervision of financial conglomerates have been drafted.

Today, conglomerates are arising from both 'horizontal consolidation', such as mergers between banks and non-bank financial institutions to form financial supermarkets, and 'vertical consolidation', such as consolidation of the relationship between a holding company and its subsidiaries. Comprehensive legislation should be designed to address both. The supervisory framework should also be adapted to suit the changing environment and international standards. Once cross-border investments and ventures become a concern, coordination between supervisors in related countries is required.

The recent crisis has also made regional supervisory coordination increasingly necessary. Because of the high degree of interaction between regional financial markets, supervisors should pay close attention not only to the domestic financial sector but also to the significant impact of external factors. Organising an active group of regional financial supervisors would be a practical way to enhance information exchange.

CONCLUSION

The financial turmoil in Asia is not unique. A worldwide survey of financial problems indicated that, of 181 International Monetary Fund (IMF) member countries, 133 had suffered financial sector problems between 1980 and early 1996 (Lindgren et al. 1996). The task is to learn from such experiences if we are to avoid some of the problems that might arise should another crisis occur. The sharp acceleration in structural changes may well increase the vulnerability of global financial markets, while many developing countries are still at a stage of financial transition. It would therefore be too optimistic to expect that the worst is behind us and that smooth sailing lies ahead. In that sense, strengthening the supervisory system in order to maintain a safe and sound financial sector is definitely the most important and urgent task facing all developing countries.

REFERENCES

Bank of England (1997) 'A risk-based approach to supervision (the RATE framework)', consultative paper, London, March.

Bank of Japan (1997) 'Checklist for risk management', revised edn, *Bank of Japan Quarterly Bulletin*, May.

Basle Committee on Banking Supervision (BCBS) (1997) *Core Principles for Effective Banking Supervision*, Basle, September.

—— (1998) *Framework for the Evaluation of Internal Control Systems*, Basle, January.

Camdessus, M. (1998) 'Reflections on the crisis in Asia', remarks at extraordinary ministerial meeting of Group of 24, Caracas, 24 February.

Corrigan, E.G. (1992) Remarks at 7th International Conference of Banking Supervisors, Cannes, 8 October.

Greenspan, A. (1996) Remarks at Annual Convention of American Bankers Association, 5 October, in Federal Reserve Board, *Speeches of Federal Reserve Board Members*.

—— (1997) Testimony before Subcommittee on Capital Markets, Securities and Government-Sponsored Enterprises of Committee on Banking and Financial Services of US House of Representatives, 26 March, Basle: BIS Review.

Hadjimichalakis, K.G. (1998) 'The currency crisis in East Asia: will it be the pause that refreshes?', *Alumni News*, Pacific Rim Bankers Program & Pacific Rim Executive Bankers Seminars, February.

Lindgren, C.-J., G. Garcia and M.I. Saal (1996) *Bank Soundness and Macroeconomic Policy*, Washington DC: International Monetary Fund.

Phillips, S.M. (1997a) Remarks at Derivative and Risk Management Symposium of Fordham University School of Law, 19 September, in Federal Reserve Board, *Speeches of Federal Reserve Board Members*.

—— (1997b) Remarks at Exchequer Club, Washington DC, June, Basle: BIS Review.

Rojas-Suarez, L. (1998) 'Early warning indicators of banking crises: what works for emerging markets?: with applications to Latin America', draft paper, Inter-American Development Bank, January.

Sheng, A. (1997) 'Financial stability in emerging market economies', paper presented at APEC Working Level Symposium, Federal Reserve Bank of San Francisco, September.

Sheu, Yuan-Dong (1998) 'SEACEN country report: recent economic and financial developments in the Republic of China', Taipei: Central Bank of China, February.

Sullivan, T.M. and Shaw-Tai Chang (1998) 'Assessment of training needs for bank supervisors in the Asia Pacific Economic Cooperation (APEC) forum member economies', unpublished report to APEC Bank Supervisors Training Consultative Group, January.

Working Party on Financial Stability in Emerging Market Economies (1997) *Financial Stability in Emerging Market Economies: A Strategy for the Formulation, Adoption and Implementation of Sound Principles and Practices To Strengthen Financial Systems*, Basle: BIS, April.

Part II
Regional financial integration

4 Evolving patterns of capital flows and the East Asian economic crisis

Masahiro Kawai

INTRODUCTION

It is often claimed that one of the most important triggers of the recent currency crisis in East Asia was the large inflows and subsequent outflows of private short-term capital. In the pre-crisis period, many affected economies in East Asia pursued financial deregulation, cross-border capital flow liberalisation, and financial market opening in an aggressive manner. This has, no doubt, brought economic benefits in the form of greater financial resource mobilisation for domestic investment and remarkable economic growth to all the economies in the region. The crisis casts some doubts, however, on the virtue of unfettered capital mobility in an increasingly globalised world economy.[1]

Prior to the crisis, it was often argued that East Asia was fundamentally different and therefore would not experience a currency crisis of the type experienced by Mexico in 1994–5. The alleged reasons for this difference were that: (a) the economic fundamentals of the East Asian countries were strong, as reflected in persistently high growth performance, high rates of savings and investment, investment in education and human resources, strong fiscal conditions and controlled inflation; and (b) current account deficits were financed by long-term capital inflows, such as foreign direct investment and bank loans with long-term commitments. The 'East Asian miracle' was believed to be a never-ending success story until the currency crisis broke out and evolved into a serious financial and economic crisis.

The currency crisis and the subsequent financial and economic difficulties in East Asia since July 1997 (see Figure 4.1) have proved that the region's economies can be as vulnerable as any other emerging economy. No emerging economy is immune to large-scale currency speculation and the subsequent financial and economic distress. It is not surprising, therefore, to see that Malaysia has resorted to capital controls and that China has decided to enforce tight restrictions on current account transactions.

There are some important lessons for capital account liberalisation to be learned from the East Asian currency crisis. Capital account liberalisation in emerging economies must be accompanied by sound macroeconomic policies, viable foreign exchange rate policies, a resilient domestic financial system, a financially prudent corporate sector, and an effective framework of international coordination in order to minimise the risks of currency crises once they occur.[2]

Figure 4.1a Exchange rate movements, January 1997–September 1998

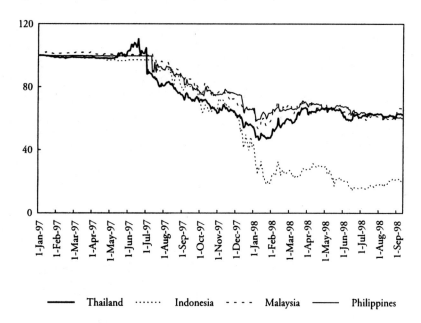

Thailand ⋯⋯ Indonesia - - - - Malaysia ——— Philippines

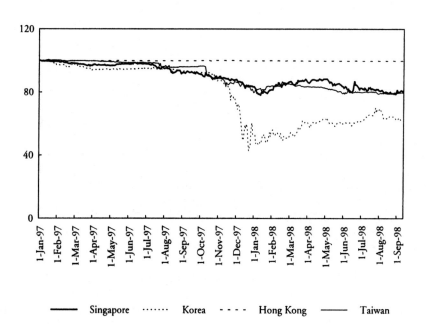

Singapore ⋯⋯ Korea - - - - Hong Kong ——— Taiwan

Figure 4.1b Stock price movements, January 1997–October 1998

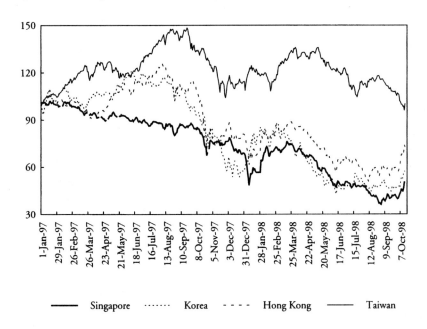

Singapore .... Korea - - - - Hong Kong —— Taiwan

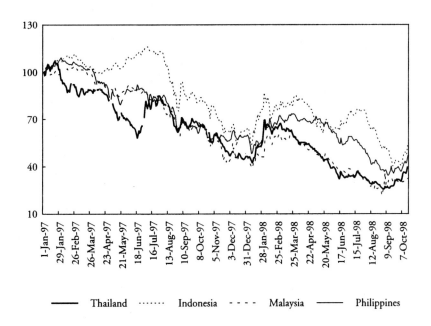

—— Thailand .... Indonesia - - - - Malaysia —— Philippines

FINANCIAL AND CAPITAL ACCOUNT LIBERALISATION

Overall review

A common trend of the East Asian economies in the pre-crisis years was to adopt measures to encourage cross-border capital flows (both inflows and outflows), to open their financial markets and to relax exchange controls.[3] The timing, speed and scope, however, varied significantly across economies. The respective economies took different approaches towards capital flow liberalisation and financial market opening, reflecting differences in stages of economic development, industrial structures, competitiveness of the financial industry and broad institutional frameworks (Table 4.1).

Hong Kong and Singapore have long allowed free mobility of capital and maintained unregulated financial and foreign exchange markets. Indonesia has also maintained free mobility of capital since 1982. Korea, Taiwan, Malaysia and Thailand began to adopt liberal policies of encouraging financial capital flows in the 1990s, after having liberalised foreign direct investment (FDI) inflows in the 1980s. The Philippines alone among the core ASEAN countries did not grow dynamically in the 1980s and was late in achieving current-account convertibility of the currency (September 1995). To catch up with the Asian dynamism, the Philippines embarked on substantial liberalisation in the 1990s to integrate the domestic real and financial sectors with the rest of the world. The transition economies, such as China and Vietnam, have pursued policies to promote inward investment but still maintain various restrictions on the capital account.

In the wake of the economic crisis in East Asia, however, there emerges a clear distinction among countries in policy stances towards international capital flows. While countries under the International Monetary Fund (IMF) program (Korea, Thailand) lifted capital account restrictions in an aggressive manner, those not under the program adopted more restrictive policy measures on the capital account (Malaysia) or the current account (China). Table 4.2 summarises current restrictions on FDI, portfolio investment, banking sector flows and foreign exchange transactions.

Foreign direct investment

In the 1980s, many emerging economies in East Asia began to focus on policies to promote investment by domestic as well as foreign firms. This was particularly pronounced in the Asian newly industrialising economies (NIEs) in the first half of the 1980s and in the ASEAN countries in the second half. They adopted laws to encourage manufacturing sector investment and implemented several measures favouring FDI inflows.[4] As a result of these measures, most of the economies in the region had introduced liberal policies with regard to FDI inflows in manufacturing by the beginning of the 1990s. At the same time, however, these economies often restricted FDI in sensitive non-manufacturing sectors, such as banking and finance, mass media and broadcasting, airlines, real estate acquisition and sectors affecting national security.[5] Many economies either prohibited such FDI or limited foreign ownership by including them on the negative list or by passing specific laws.

Table 4.1 Economic size of emerging East Asia in comparison with US, EU and Japan, 1997

Countries and regions	GDP (US$m)	Population (million)	GDP/Pop. (US$)	International trade		Foreign exchange reserves (US$m)	Stock market capitalisations (US$m)
				Exports (US$m)	Imports (US$m)		
United States	8,083,400	267.9	30,173	688,697	899,020	58,907	11,308,779
European Union-15	8,093,912	373.3	21,684	2,106,905 (823,600)	1,997,616 (802,300)	398,970	5,343,262
Japan	4,190,240	125.7	33,338	420,957	338,754	219,648	2,216,699
Emerging East Asia	2,501,579	1,747.8	1,431	978,547	974,492	489,713	1,233,312
Asian NIEs	1,003,445	77.7	12,917	571,747	600,114	267,963	849,334
Singapore	98,400	3.4	28,599	124,986	132,437	71,289	106,317
Hong Kong	172,297	6.5	26,316	188,063	208,616	92,804	413,323
Taiwan	285,355	21.7	13,148	122,081	114,425	83,502	287,813
Korea, Republic of	447,393	46.0	9,728	136,617	144,636	20,368	41,881
ASEAN-4	550,182	367.0	1,499	214,973	221,876	77,270	177,612
Malaysia	98,472	20.5	4,806	78,904	79,046	21,101	93,608
Thailand	153,907	60.6	2,540	57,538	62,859	32,317	23,538
Philippines	83,208	76.1	1,093	25,088	38,277	7,266	31,361
Indonesia	214,595	209.8	1,023	53,443	41,694	16,587	29,105
China	923,070	1,226.3	753	182,877	142,189	142,762	206,366
Vietnam	24,881	76.8	324	8,950	10,313	1,718	–

Note: Export and import figures in parentheses indicate figures excluding intra-EU trade, based on IMF DOT data
Sources: IMF, International Financial Statistics, October 1998, and Direction of Trade, 1998; IFC, Emerging Stock Markets Factbook, 1998

Table 4.2 Restrictions on cross-border capital flows

	Foreign direct investment	Foreign securities investment	Banking transactions	Foreign exchange transactions (date of acceptance of Article VIII)
Japan	Prior notification required for some outward FDI and inward FDI. Inward and outward FDI in certain industries restricted.	No significant restriction. Upper limits on Japanese institutional investors' foreign securities holdings.	No restriction on bank loans. Foreign bank entry liberalised but under administrative guidance.	April 1964. No significant restriction.
Singapore	Foreign ownership in certain sectors limited. No controls on direct investment or liquidation of direct investment.	Foreign acquisition of stocks in certain sectors limited. Dual listing of shares and cross-trading of securities in SES and Taiwan stock exchange. Plans to further liberalise Central Provident Fund unit trust scheme, rewrite investment guidelines, raise disclosure standards.	Approval for large loans for use outside Singapore. Restrictions on loans for foreign purchase of residential properties. Foreign bank entry relatively limited. Resident limit on offshore banks raised (to S$300m).	November 1968. Relatively restrictive system of capital controls but some liberalisation to relax restrictions on use of Singapore dollar-denominated instruments by non-residents, to deepen the domestic bond market, and to ease foreign stock listing on the SES.
Hong Kong	No restriction (except broadcasting).	No restriction.	No restriction on bank loans. Foreign bank entry relatively free. Regulation for prudential purposes.	No capital restrictions. Government intervention in stock and futures markets (August 1998), acquiring large volumes of blue chip stocks.
Taiwan	A negative list for inward FDI. Outward FDI not fully liberalised. Limit to amount of money that can be moved abroad (US$5m/person and US$50m/company).	A limit on foreign investors' direct acquisition of securities (15% limit in a company's shares for each investor and 30% overall limit for all investors; US$600m for individual QFIIs, US$50m for corporations and US$5m for individuals).	A limit on New Taiwan dollar lending by foreign banks.	Not an IMF member. Central bank approval required for large outward/inward remittances. Non-delivery forward market transactions limited to foreign business.

Table 4.2 (continued)

	Foreign direct investment	Foreign securities investment	Banking transactions	Foreign exchange transactions (date of acceptance of Article VIII)
Korea	Direct investment through mergers and acquisitions permitted. The negative list reduced to 1.5% of all industries listed in the Korean standards industrial classification. Industries in manufacturing no longer on the negative list. Outward FDI permitted without notification to the FX bank except for investments exceeding US$50m.	The ceiling on individual foreign ownership of a listed Korean company raised to 50% (December 1997). The aggregate ceiling on foreign investment in Korean equities eliminated (May 1998). Foreign investment fully liberalised indomestic money market instruments issued by non-financial institutions (February 1998), and by financial institutions (May 1998).	Restrictions lifted on: foreign borrowing (over 3 year maturity in December 1997; 1–3 year maturity by end-98; venture companies up to US$2m); loan usage regulations with maturities greater than 5 years brought in by foreign manufacturing companies.	November 1988. FX banks: allowed to conduct forward futures, swap and option transactions; and limits on open FX positions. Capital account almost completely liberalised.
Malaysia	100% foreign ownership allowed if export-oriented (more than 80% of products exported). Profit repatriation and remittance from FDI limited. FDI outflows restricted.	Foreign firms' membership in the stock exchange not permitted. Foreign M&A requires approval. Foreign ownership limited. Residents' offshore investment allowed without restriction below RM100,000.	Central bank approval required for large amount bank loans. The central bank has allowed external borrowing to only those firms with foreign exchange earnings. Residents with no domestic borrowing allowed to open foreign currency accounts overseas. Residents with domestic borrowing require prior approval. A limit on foreign ownership of banks, unless fully incorporated.	November 1968. Selective capital controls imposed in September 1998: controls on non-resident repatriation of proceeds from sales of portfolio investment for 12 months; limits on dividends taken out of Malaysia by FDIs; prohibition of ringgit-denominated offshore transactions; limits on ringgit exports and imports by non-residents; limits on exports of foreign currencies by residents; and limits on outflows of Malaysian investments abroad.

Table 4.2 (continued)

	Foreign direct investment	Foreign securities investment	Banking transactions	Foreign exchange transactions (date of acceptance of Article VIII)
Thailand	100% foreign ownership allowed if export-oriented (more than 80% of products exported).	An upper limit on foreign acquisition of stocks (49%). Alien board for foreigners if an upper limit is reached. Portfolio investments abroad require approval of BOT.	Upper limit on foreign ownership of banks and finance companies (25%) lifted on a case-by-case basis for a period of 10 years (June 1997). Commercial banks required to maintain minimum of foreign exchange deposits at BOT, government and other eligible securities.	May 1990. FX bank system. Foreign currency receipts need to be surrendered to FX banks. Approvals required (at the FX bank) for inward remittances. Separation of onshore and offshore FX markets (introduced February 1997) abolished in January 1998.
Philippines	100% foreign ownership allowed if not on the negative list (40% if on the list). No restrictions on BSP-registered FDI for repatriation of capital and remittance of profit, dividends and other earnings. Prior approval from BSP required for outward FDI by residents of more than US$6m (per investor/year); and effective 11 September 1997, applicant's income tax return required to support application to purchase foreign exchange under the US$6m limit.	100% foreign acquisition of stocks allowed if not on the negative list (40% if on the list). Only B-shares available to foreign investors if subject to the 40% limit. Non-residents required to register with BSP if the source of FX needed for capital repatriation and remittance of dividends, profits and earnings.	Upper limit on foreign ownership of banks (30%). Residents and non-residents allowed to hold FCDU. BSP approval not needed for FCDU in the case of (a) short-term loans to financial institutions, (b) short-term loans to commodity and producers or manufacturers, and (c) private sector loans serviced from outside the banking system. Long foreign exchange positions limited.	September 1995. FX bank system: limits on FX positions monitored by BSP and subject to sanctions; long FX positions limited to the lesser of 5% of unimpaired capital or US$10m; short FX positions limited to 2% of unimpaired capital. Central bank permission required for borrowing from abroad. Few capital account restrictions. Recent tightening of prudential regulations on foreign exchange transactions.

Table 4.2 (continued)

	Foreign direct investment	Foreign securities investment	Banking transactions	Foreign exchange transactions (date of acceptance of Article VIII)
Indonesia	A negative list exists but entry restriction substantially reduced. Foreign ownership of 100% allowed on almost all non-bank FDI, with minimal divestment requirements. No control on capital inflows, but each investment subject to approval by the Investment Board, BKPM.	No limitation on foreign acquisition of non-bank shares, as at September 1997 (previously 49% limit). Foreign purchase of commercial bank shares limited to 49%. No restriction of outward securities investment, except for those by insurance companies, etc.	Banks permitted to lend locally in FX. Ceilings on foreign borrowing by state-owned enterprises and banks. Foreign bank activity: (a) entry allowed as a joint venture; (b) equity participation in a joint bank limited to 85%; and (c) one branch per city and confined to 6 cities.	May 1988. No foreign exchange controls since 1982. FX bank system: control on the net open position of FX banks (25% of capital); banks' forward selling of foreign exchange currency to non-residents limited to US$5m in August 1997. Capital flow monitoring mechanism in preparation.
China	Tight control: prohibited or restricted in certain sectors. Preferential tax policies abolished in 1996. Recent measures to stimulate FDI: preferential treatment, simplified procedures, opening up of sectors, regulations to eradicate random local government fees, and more pilot projects to be launched.	Only B-shares available to foreigners. Domestic fixed-income security markets closed to overseas investors. Outward investment prohibited. Recent announcement that issuance of international investment trust (including A-shares) for foreign investors abroad will be allowed.	Tight controls on bank loans. Foreign bank activity: (a) entry tightly controlled; and (b) branches not allowed to deal RMB.	December 1996. FX bank system. Current account convertible, but August –September 1998 measures: to curb illegal FX transactions; to strengthen monitoring of FX payments; and to discourage outflows of foreign exchange. Remittances overseas require customs certification and contracts.
Vietnam	A 10% tax imposed on repatriated profits on FDI. New measures to encourage FDI inflows adopted (January 1998).	No equity or bond markets currently available. Restriction on investment in government treasury bills.	Approval required from SBV for bank borrowing abroad, offshore accounts, or lending to non-residents. Foreign banks restricted to small dong-deposit mobilisation.	Current account inconvertible. Tighter controls on FX adopted (September 1998): all enterprises subject to FX surrender requirements.

Sources: IMF, Exchange Arrangements and Exchange Restrictions: Annual Report, 1998; World Bank staff assessments

In response to the reduced FDI inflows following the outbreak of the Asian crisis, policymakers have pressed ahead on further FDI liberalisation and relaxed the restrictions still in place. Policies have included raising or eliminating foreign ownership limits (Thailand, Korea, Malaysia), shortening the negative list (the Philippines, Indonesia, Korea, China), and introducing preferential policies and simplified procedures for FDI (China, Vietnam).

Outward FDI used to be highly regulated in many East Asian economies, but authorities in these countries have taken many steps towards liberalisation. Korea and Taiwan, in particular, pursued liberalisation of FDI outflows as a result of large current account surpluses in the 1980s and the early 1990s.

Portfolio investment

Many East Asian economies began liberalisation of foreign investment in their stock markets in the 1980s or early 1990s. Until the mid-1990s, foreigners' investment in fixed income instruments had been small on average because of underdeveloped domestic debt markets.[6] As a result, these economies began developing domestic debt markets, providing greater opportunities for domestic and international portfolio investors.

Korea and Taiwan took a cautious, step-by-step approach, by first offering international investment trusts (Korea Fund and Taiwan Fund) to foreigners abroad and then allowing foreign institutional investors, non-institutional firms and individuals to directly acquire domestic shares and stocks. These two economies set upper limits on foreign investors' holdings of domestic stocks, which were relaxed gradually over time. Thailand and Indonesia (firms on the negative list) also set an upper limit (49 per cent), although Indonesia relaxed its limit in 1997. Despite the lack of formal regulatory limits on the foreign acquisition of stocks, other policies make it difficult for foreigners to hold significant numbers of shares. Examples include Malaysia's *bumiputera* policy, and in several countries self-imposed clauses in the articles of association of firms.

Several countries maintain partly separate (Thailand, Singapore, the Philippines) or fully separate (China) stock markets for foreigners. Thailand's Foreign Board is a stock market for foreigners, in which they may trade stocks that have reached the 50 per cent foreign ownership limit. Philippines' firms on the negative list often issue two separate shares for residents and non-residents: A-shares, with more than 60 per cent of the total, for residents only; and B-shares, with less than 40 per cent of the total, for domestic and foreign investors.[7] Some Chinese firms issue A-shares (denominated and settled in the renminbi) for Chinese investors, and B-shares (denominated in the renminbi but settled in a foreign currency, that is the US dollar in Shanghai and the Hong Kong dollar in Shenzhen) for foreign investors. Several other Chinese firms issue shares in Hong Kong, called H-shares (settled in the Hong Kong dollar).[8] China's bond markets are closed to overseas investors.

Restrictions on the listing of foreign firms on domestic exchanges vary from country to country. In Singapore, the government allows foreigners to have access to

University of Glasgow
Adam Smith Library

Customer name: Lin, Yuan

Title: Asia Pacific financial deregulation / edited
by Gordon de Brouwer with Wisarn
Pupphavesa.
ID: 30114013492080
Due: 10-10-13

Total items: 1
23/05/2013 12:39
Checked out: 4

Please retain this receipt for your record.
All books are subject to recall, which may mean
earlier due dates.

the domestic bond and stock markets for greater foreign participation. In September 1996, foreign firms in Singapore were permitted to list on the stock market and to issue bonds in domestic currency. In Korea, restrictions on foreign portfolio investment – both shares and bonds – were almost completely liberalised between end-1997 and mid-1998 under the IMF program. Foreigners are now allowed to invest in domestic money market instruments issued by financial and non-financial institutions without any limitation. The regime on foreigners' portfolio investment has also been liberalised in Taiwan, but only slightly; the limit on foreign investment in a single local company in relation to total shares outstanding is now 30 per cent.

In contrast to these countries, Malaysia continues to retain strict rules on portfolio investment by foreigners as well as overseas portfolio investment by residents, and these rules were tightened further in September 1998 as part of its controversial capital controls. The restrictions include: deposit requirements of ringgit securities with authorised depositories; transaction requirements of ringgit securities held by non-residents through an authorised depository for good delivery; and prohibition of conversion of all proceeds from sales of Malaysian securities by non-residents into foreign exchange for a year. Also, limits are imposed on the amount residents are allowed to invest overseas (RM10,000 or its equivalent in foreign currency per transaction); beyond this requires the approval of the authorities.

Banking transactions

Long-term bank loans have been a major vehicle of capital transfers between industrialised and emerging economies, and short-term bank loans were frequently used to finance trade credits and firms' operations.

In East Asia, cross-border bank lending and borrowing was active until 1997. East Asian financial centres—Tokyo, Hong Kong and Singapore—intermediate cross-border banking flows. Hong Kong is unique in that it allows complete integration of the domestic and international banking markets. Singapore has an offshore banking centre (with an Asian Currency Unit account) which is separated from the domestic banking market (denominated in the Singapore dollar). Other East Asian economies have also encouraged inflows of cross-border bank loans by establishing offshore banking facilities (Taiwan, Malaysia, Thailand, the Philippines) which are separated from domestic retail banking markets. This reflects a strategy of attracting cross-border banking flows and foreign banks with advanced financial technologies, while protecting domestic commercial banks from direct international competition.[9]

Regulations concerning cross-border banking transactions are still in place in most of the emerging East Asian economies, although they were loosened considerably in the post-crisis period (particularly in Korea). The regulations either require the central bank's approval – which is not always transparent for cross-border banking transactions with large amounts (Singapore, Malaysia, Indonesia, China) – or the imposition of an upper limit on the volumes of such transactions (Singapore, Taiwan, Korea). Indeed, Indonesia and Thailand had very liberal policies with regard to short-term cross-border borrowing through banks and corporations, as evidenced by the large exposures domestic banks and corporations accumulated prior to the currency crisis. Even Korean banks, which were supposed to be subject to tight restrictions on foreign financing, borrowed heavily externally.

With regard to foreign banks' entry into the domestic retail market, many economies took a cautious approach. The authorities almost always require licences for new entry, whether by a domestic or foreign institution, and often discriminate against foreign banks by maintaining tighter entry restrictions to protect or to avoid excessive competition faced by domestic banks. The restrictions have taken various forms, including prohibiting new foreign bank entry (Malaysia); limiting the form of entry (Korea as a branch or a joint venture, Indonesia and the Philippines as a joint venture); imposing upper limits on foreign equity ownership (25 per cent for Thailand, 40 per cent for the Philippines and 49 per cent for Indonesia); restricting the location and number of branches (Singapore, Malaysia, Thailand, Indonesia, China); and regulating the types of businesses (Singapore, Korea, Malaysia, Thailand, the Philippines, China). In countries with offshore banking facilities, foreign entry into full banking is often restricted while entry into offshore banking is easier (Singapore, Malaysia, Thailand, the Philippines).

Even before the crisis, some of these economies had begun to introduce increasingly open policies; for example, Thailand announced in November 1996 that it had decided to grant full branch licences to seven specific foreign banks in operation in the Bangkok International Banking Facility (BIBF). In the midst of the crisis, the three countries under the IMF program (Thailand, Indonesia and Korea) began to allow, or have decided to allow, 100 per cent foreign ownership of banks. This liberalisation was motivated by the need for private funds to recapitalise distressed commercial banks.

Foreign exchange transactions

Liberalisation of foreign exchange control is an important element of cross-border capital flow liberalisation because tight controls restrict the growth of cross-border flows. However, in the wake of the deepening crisis, some countries decided to adopt restrictive measures (Malaysia, Hong Kong and China, while Indonesia started monitoring), given extraordinary market conditions brought about by massive speculative capital movements.

Recent developments contrast with the situation in the late 1980s. Many emerging East Asian economies began to liberalise foreign exchange transactions alongside the cross-border capital flows. Most economies accepted their obligations under Article VIII of the IMF Agreements by establishing current account convertibility of currencies (Table 4.3).[10] Hong Kong and Singapore had long liberalised all types of foreign exchange transactions, including those on capital accounts. Indonesia had relatively lax exchange controls on capital account-related activities, while Malaysia required central bank approval for large inflows of foreign currency. Korea had maintained one of the most restrictive exchange control systems, and Taiwan, Thailand, the Philippines and China had several explicit restrictions on payments for capital account activities. Many Indochina economies (such as Vietnam) have yet to establish currency convertibility on current account transactions.[11]

However, the policy stances that have emerged during the crisis are not uniform across the region. While the IMF program countries (Thailand and Korea) shifted to a liberal foreign exchange policy, others decided to adopt restrictive measures to counteract the volatile foreign exchange markets.[12] The most notable example of the latter group is Malaysia. In September 1998, the Malaysian government announced its intention to impose extensive capital (outflow) controls, in effect closing its capital account. These controls include limits on the following transactions: ringgit-denominated onshore and offshore transactions; outflows of short-term capital (one-year holding period); import and export of ringgit by foreigners; exports of foreign currencies by residents; and outflows of Malaysian investment abroad (see Table 4.2). Furthermore, the exchange rate of the ringgit was fixed at RM3.8 per US dollar. Hong Kong also resorted to unprecedented measures by intervening in the stock and futures markets (August 1998), as well as introducing measures to reduce interest rate volatility (September 1998). Indonesia, which has had no foreign exchange control since 1982, introduced a capital flow monitoring mechanism in October 1998.

CAPITAL FLOW LIBERALISATION AND ITS CONSEQUENCES

Asian NIEs

Capital flow liberalisation and financial market opening in the East Asian economies, except Hong Kong and Singapore, did not begin until the 1980s. The process started with the liberalisation of inward FDI, followed by liberalisation of portfolio investment and financial market opening.

By the early 1980s, the Asian NIEs (Korea, Taiwan and Singapore) had completed their shift away from import substitution to outward-oriented economic development strategies. The trade, industrialisation and foreign investment policies of these NIEs were formulated with an eye towards export promotion. As part of these export-oriented policies, these countries started to reduce restrictions on inward FDI. By the mid-1980s, the ASEAN countries, prompted by the success of the NIEs, also shifted from inward- to outward-oriented strategies and liberalised their trade and FDI regimes. The result was a rise in FDI flows in East Asia and a mutually reinforcing expansion of FDI and trade.

Next, the East Asian economies started to focus on policies to stimulate capital inflows in various forms. The ASEAN countries have particularly emphasised the role of equity markets. Korea and Taiwan took a cautious approach by gradually opening the domestic equity markets to foreigners, first by offering international investment trusts for foreign investors abroad and then by allowing qualified foreign institutional investors and individuals to purchase directly listed stocks within prescribed upper limits. These two countries had also taken a conservative approach with regard to opening the domestic financial services industry to foreign financial institutions.

Table 4.3 Exchange arrangements and regulatory frameworks for current and capital transactions (end-1997)

	Japan	Singapore	Hong Kong	Korea	Malaysia	Thailand	Indonesia	Philippines	China	Vietnam
IMF status										
Date of joining the IMF	13 Aug 52	3 Aug 66	Accepted by UK	26 Aug 55	7 Mar 58	3 May 49	21 Feb 67	27 Dec 45	27 Dec 45	21 Sep 56
Article VIII status	1 Apr 64	9 Nov 68	Article VIII	1 Nov 88	11 Nov 68	4 May 90	7 May 88	8 Sep 95	1 Dec 96	Article XIV
Exchange rate arrangement	Ind. float	Man. float	Man. float	Ind. float	Man. float	Man. float	Ind. float	Ind. float	Man. float	Man. float
Arrangements for payments and receipts										
Bilateral payment arrangements	–	–	–	–	yes	–	–	–	–	–
Payment arrears	–	–	–	–	–	–	–	–	–	yes
Control on payments for invisible transactions and current transfers	–	yes	–	yes	–	–	–	yes	yes	yes
Proceeds from exports and/or invisible transactions										
Repatriation requirements	–	–	–	yes	yes	yes	–	–	yes	yes
Surrender requirements	–	–	–	–	yes	yes	–	–	yes	yes
Capital transactions										
Controls on:										
Capital market securities	yes	yes	–	yes	yes	yes	yes	yes	yes	yes
Money market instruments	–	–	–	yes	yes	yes	yes	yes	yes	yes
Collective investment securities	–	–	–	yes	yes	yes	yes	yes	yes	yes
Derivatives and other instruments	–	–	–	yes	yes	yes	yes	yes	yes	n.a.
Commercial credits	–	–	–	yes	yes	–	yes	yes	yes	yes
Financial credits	yes	–	–	yes	yes	yes	yes	yes	yes	yes

Table 4.3 (continued)

	Japan	Singapore	Hong Kong	Korea	Malaysia	Thailand	Indonesia	Philippines	China	Vietnam
Guarantees, sureties, and financial backup facilities	–	–	–	yes	yes	–	yes	yes	yes	n.a
Direct investment	yes	–	–	yes	yes	yes	yes	yes	yes	yes
Liquidation of direct investments	–	–	–	yes	yes	yes	yes	yes	yes	n.a.
Real estate transactions	–	yes	–	yes	yes	yes	yes	yes	yes	yes
Personal capital movements	n.a.	–	–	yes	yes	yes	yes	yes	yes	n.a.
Provisions specific to:										
Commercial banks and other credit institutions	yes	yes	yes	yes	yes	yes	yes	yes	yes	yes
Institutional investors	yes	–	–	yes	yes	yes	yes	yes	–	n.a.

Notes: Ind. float = independently floating; Man. float = other managed floating. The notation 'yes' indicates that the specified practice is a feature of the exchange arrangement; 'n.a.' indicates that data were not available at time of publication.

Sources: IMF, *Exchange Arrangements and Exchange Restrictions: Annual Report*, 1997; *International Financial Statistics*, October 1998

Effective financial opening in these two countries did not begin until the start of the 1990s.

Pre-crisis liberalisation of cross-border capital flows was accompanied by measures to open the domestic financial markets to foreign investors and institutions. To attract more FDI and portfolio investment in the domestic stock markets, Korea and Taiwan liberalised foreign financial institutions' access to these markets, because foreign firms and investors would require their own institutions in the host economies. In addition, international pressure to open domestic markets and financial services to the rest of the world was mounting. To prepare for OECD membership and its capital liberalisation code, for example, Korea had to demonstrate that it was engaged in liberalisation of cross-border capital transactions and the opening of the financial market and had established full convertibility of currency on capital accounts, thus being ready for membership. Since December 1997, Korea, under the IMF program, has accelerated its efforts in order to signal its commitment to capital account liberalisation to world capital markets, thereby restoring foreign investors' confidence. Taiwan, aiming to join the World Trade Organisation (WTO), also tried to convince the international community that it was liberalising cross-border capital flows and deregulating and opening the domestic financial services industry to foreign investors and institutions.

Korea and Taiwan also liberalised cross-border capital outflows. The accumulation of large current account surpluses and the consequent upward pressure on their exchange rates in the latter half of the 1980s were major factors leading to capital outflow liberalisation. First, capital outflows were encouraged in the face of large current account surpluses, upward pressure on exchange rates, the accumulation of foreign exchange reserves due to the lack of private capital outflows, and the resulting inflationary pressure. Second, the pace of capital outflow liberalisation was accelerated when the United States insisted that Korea and Taiwan revalue their currencies vis-à-vis the US dollar in the second half of the 1980s. Relaxation of controls on capital outflows was considered necessary to eliminate domestic inflation and to ease upward pressure on the external value of the currency.

ASEAN: competitive liberalisation

The situation in the ASEAN countries and in China had been quite different. Liberalisation of capital flows and foreign exchange transactions in these countries was motivated by competitive pressure and, hence, was autonomous and unilateral. This process may be called 'competitive liberalisation'.[13]

Most of the ASEAN countries completed their shift from inward-oriented to outward-oriented strategies by the mid-1980s and then embarked on unilateral liberalisation of trade and FDI inflows. These regime changes were prompted by the earlier success of outward-oriented policies in the NIEs. The result was a massive inflow of FDI in the late 1980s and early 1990s, not only from developed countries but also from the Asian NIEs. The Asian NIEs were the largest sources of FDI in ASEAN and China during this period.

However, the trend varied greatly. For example, the Philippines was never a big recipient of FDI inflows, mainly because of its political and social unrest and its external debt problem, although the situation improved in the 1990s. Thailand, which received large amounts of foreign FDI, had a shortage of industrial infrastructure and local middle managers, thereby deterring a further expansion of foreign firms' operations. Malaysia also experienced a similar bottleneck. These two countries greatly needed to develop industrial infrastructure and regional business activities and to train highly skilled managers and human resources. FDI inflows into Indonesia faced these problems, albeit to a lesser extent, and competition with China was forcing Indonesia to take an increasingly liberal attitude towards FDI inflows.

These trends implied that the ASEAN countries had to diversify their sources and forms of foreign capital inflows. Financing of industrial infrastructure was a matter of increasing urgency, which domestic sources alone were unable to cover. Competition for the pool of world savings was intensifying and the ASEAN countries had the incentive to attract various forms of foreign capital. They all adopted liberal equity market policies, allowing relatively free entry and exit without much restriction on repatriation of income and capital, although Indonesia imposed certain restrictions on repatriation. They also shifted to a more flexible policy with respect to foreign banks' entry into their domestic markets. Thailand decided to give full branch licences to several foreign banks operating in the Bangkok offshore banking centre. Although too rapid an opening of domestic financial markets and services could cause a backlash, a commitment to capital inflow liberalisation and financial market opening, particularly in banking, was deemed a prerequisite for sustained economic growth in an integrated world economic system. An open financial market was believed to be an important element of the institutional infrastructure necessary to attract various types of foreign capital. Up until the currency crisis broke out, competitive liberalisation in the ASEAN countries was expected to continue to attract foreign capital.

China

FDI inflows into China had grown quickly since the late 1980s because of its gradual but persistent economic reforms, open-door liberalisation policy and political and social stability despite the Tiananmen Square incident in 1989. In 1993, China became one of the world's largest recipients of FDI. Its coastal areas attracted investment not only from Japan, Europe, the United States, Hong Kong and Taiwan but also from ASEAN countries, and had more rapid economic growth than any other area in the world. FDI inflows have been the vehicle of China's economic transformation, upgrading its trade patterns as well as its entire industrial structure. Again, openness to foreign capital was considered vital to China's economic development.

As in other East Asian economies, China also attracted foreign capital to the equity market. Its intention to offer international investment trusts, including A-shares, to foreign investors reflected the desire to raise capital for large-scale enterprises with strong prospects. Listing privatised enterprises abroad would also encourage China's integration into international capital markets. However, the authorities still maintain tight restrictions on capital inflows, foreign entry into domestic financial services and foreign exchange transactions; they have taken a cautious approach to capital flow liberalisation, financial market deregulation and opening, and relaxation of foreign exchange control.

Recent capital control measures: Malaysia and China

In response to the crisis, Malaysia moved towards closing capital accounts and China decided to strictly enforce regulations on current account transactions. The primary objectives of the Malaysian controls are to limit capital outflows and to close the offshore ringgit market in Singapore, thereby reducing the downward pressure on exchange rates. The authorities attempt to regain monetary policy independence under fixed exchange rates by imposing capital controls. By delinking monetary policy from exchange rate movements, the authorities intend to pursue a more expansionary monetary policy without inducing further capital flight and a sharp decline in the ringgit. Prime Minister Mahathir maintains that the controls will be removed once stability returns to financial markets and an appropriate global regulatory framework governing international capital flows is in place. Along with the aggressive fiscal thrust, the authorities appear to be trying to boost the economy by stimulating domestic demand rather than relying on external demand.

In August and September 1998, the Chinese authorities (State Administration of Foreign Exchange) announced new measures and strengthened enforcement of existing regulations aimed at curbing illegal foreign exchange transactions by residents. The reason for such measures was a concern over renminbi devaluation that intensified along with the deepening of the crisis. The unchanged level of foreign exchange reserves, despite persistent trade surpluses and FDI inflows, has invited worries about capital flight. Though the 'leakage' of foreign exchange reserves can be partly explained by the tripling of foreign currency holdings of mainland residents and enterprises, the authorities also attributed it to firms' keeping export proceeds abroad instead of sending them back, as required under regulations. The authorities were also aware of the rising trend that more companies began to borrow renminbi for early repayment of foreign currency loans. The new current account measures are to ensure validity of transactions, while other measures aim at strengthening control on capital account management.

CAPITAL FLOWS IN EAST ASIA

The changing pattern of capital flows prior to the crisis

Total net capital flows into East Asia jumped from around US$16 billion a year in the second half of the 1980s to US$65 billion in the 1990s until the outbreak of the currency crisis. A substantial part of the increase was private capital inflows, jumping from US$10 billion to US$56 billion. In 1996, one year before the crisis, private capital flows to the region stood at US$101 billion (Table 4.4). What is important also is the fact that these inflows in the 1990s often exceeded the size of current account deficits. This implies that there was a large inflow of foreign exchange reserves in many East Asian countries during the period.

While net private capital inflows expanded, the composition of capital flows changed over time. In the 1980s, syndicated commercial bank loans were a dominant component of the inflow, while FDI also rose in the second half of the decade (see Table 4.4; Kohsaka 1996; World Bank 1993). By the early 1990s, FDI had become the most important investment vehicle, and towards the mid-1990s portfolio investment and short-term banking flows began to rise (Table 4.5). Countries such as Thailand, Korea and Indonesia saw a rapid rise in unhedged short-term capital inflows in the few years before the start of the crisis. Essentially, financial sector deregulation and capital account liberalisation in the 1990s facilitated large inflows of capital, in the form of portfolio investment and short-term banking funds, and thereby changed their nature and composition. Relatively stable long-term FDI was replaced by short-term volatile portfolio investment.

Figure 4.2 illustrates clearly the changing composition of capital inflows in East Asia. The composition shifted from FDI up until the early 1990s to portfolio investment and bank loans in the mid-1990s. This pattern is clearly observed in Thailand, Indonesia and the Philippines, while in Korea portfolio investment was a dominant form of capital inflows throughout the 1990s. It is interesting to observe that in non-crisis countries, such as Singapore and China (not shown in the figure), FDI has always been a dominant form of capital inflows.

One common feature of the affected East Asian economies prior to the crisis is that they all faced increasing exposure to international banks, especially with short-term maturity. When large quantities of bank loans began to flow into these countries, the maturity structure was also changing. The share of short-term loans rose at an alarming rate. At the end of June 1997, a night before the devaluation of the Thai baht, about 66 per cent of banking loans in Thailand, 68 per cent in Korea and 59 per cent in Indonesia were loans with a maturity of up to and including one year (Table 4.6). The sheer size of these short-term loans was also huge: US$70 billion for Korea, US$46 billion for Thailand and US$35 billion for Indonesia – or 206 per cent, 145 per cent and 170 per cent of foreign exchange reserves, respectively.[14] All these countries had accumulated short-term bank loans far exceeding foreign exchange reserves, thus placing them in financially vulnerable situations: once confidence in the currency value is in doubt, withdrawal of international bank loans from these countries could lead to an instantaneous liquidity crisis.

With respect to the sectoral distribution of loans, domestic banks were major borrowers from international banks in the case of Korea (the share of bank borrowing was 65 per cent) and Taiwan (62 per cent). In the ASEAN-4, the non-bank private sectors were the major borrowers, particularly in the case of Indonesia (68 per cent), Thailand (60 per cent) and Malaysia (57 per cent). Essentially, the banking sector was a large debtor in the case of Korea, while the non-bank sector was a large debtor in the case of Indonesia and Thailand.

Table 4.4 Capital flows to all developing countries and to East Asia and Pacific, 1970–97 (US$b)

	1970	1975	1980	1985	1990	1991	1992	1993	1994	1995	1996	1997
All developing countries												
Official development finance[a]	5.4	18.3	34.3	36.0	56.4	62.7	53.8	53.6	45.6	54.2	34.7	44.2
Private flows	5.5	24.8	49.7	27.8	41.9	53.6	90.1	154.6	160.6	189.1	246.9	256.0
Private loans	3.4	17.5	45.3	17.1	15.0	13.5	33.8	44.0	41.1	55.1	82.2	103.2
Commercial banks	2.3	13.8	29.5	5.4	3.8	3.4	13.1	2.8	8.9	29.3	34.2	41.1
Bonds	0.0	0.2	2.6	3.7	0.1	7.4	8.3	31.8	27.5	23.8	45.7	53.8
Other	1.1	3.5	13.1	8.0	11.1	2.7	12.4	9.4	4.7	2.0	2.3	8.3
Foreign direct investment[b]	2.2	7.3	4.4	10.7	23.7	32.9	45.3	65.6	86.9	101.5	119.0	120.4
Portfolio equity flows	0.0	0.0	0.0	0.0	3.2	7.2	11.0	45.0	32.6	32.5	45.8	32.4
Total net flows, all developing countries	10.9	43.1	84.0	63.7	98.3	116.3	143.9	208.1	206.3	243.2	281.6	300.3
East Asia and Pacific												
Official development finance[a]	1.2	1.9	3.5	4.6	7.9	8.8	8.6	10.2	8.4	12.6	6.2	14.3
Private flows	0.6	3.8	7.1	8.1	18.4	21.2	37.5	63.5	70.5	82.9	101.3	89.1
Private loans	0.4	2.8	5.8	5.1	6.3	7.4	13.9	10.4	16.1	18.0	28.2	34.4
Commercial banks	0.4	2.5	3.6	-0.7	5.8	5.6	7.8	2.0	2.7	8.1	10.4	13.1
Bonds	0.0	0.0	0.2	3.3	-1.0	0.6	0.3	4.9	9.4	8.2	13.1	15.3
Other	0.0	0.3	2.0	2.5	1.5	1.2	5.9	3.5	4.0	1.7	4.7	5.9
Foreign direct investment[b]	0.2	1.0	1.3	2.9	10.3	13.1	21.5	38.5	44.3	50.2	58.7	53.2
Portfolio equity flows	0.0	0.0	0.0	0.0	1.7	0.7	2.1	14.6	10.1	14.7	14.4	1.5
Total net flows, East Asia and Pacific	1.8	5.7	10.7	12.6	26.4	30.0	46.1	73.7	78.9	95.5	107.4	103.4

Notes:
a Excludes technical cooperation grants
b IMF data
Sources: World Bank, Data Reporting Systems; IMF, International Financial Statistics; OECD

Table 4.5 Composition of capital flows, 1990–7 (US$m)

Asian NIEs and China	1990	1991	1992	1993	1994	1995	1996	1997
Singapore								
Current account	3,119	4,918	5,958	4,272	11,453	14,361	14,723	14,803
Financial account	3,947	2,346	1,793	−1,212	−11,690	−654	−2,438	−4,536
Direct investment (net)	3,541	4,361	887	2,534	4,360	2,949	3,298	4,661
Portfolio investment (net)	−1,037	−907	2,489	−4,966	−9,996	−8,206	−8,614	−10,869
Equity securities	105	−766	1,563	−4,796	−7,842	−7,342	−8,465	−11,431
Debt securities	−1,142	−141	926	−170	−2,154	−864	−149	562
Banks (net)	1,680	−967	−720	2,718	1,118	5,577	4,532	6,634
Other sectors	−199	−127	−855	−1,615	−7,167	−969	−1,655	−4;960
Net errors and omissions	−1,613	−3,032	−1,613	4,589	5,058	−5,037	−4,751	−2,154
Reserve assets	−5,431	−4,197	−6,100	−7,578	−4,736	−8,599	−7,396	−7,940
Korea								
Current account	−1,745	−8,317	−3,944	990	−3,867	−8,507	−23,006	−8,167
Financial account	2,866	6,741	6,994	3,216	10,732	17,273	23,924	−9,195
Direct investment (net)	−268	−309	−434	−752	−1,652	−1,776	−2,345	−1,605
Portfolio investment (net)	322	3,053	5,802	10,015	6,121	11,591	15,185	14,295
Equity securities	310	210	2,490	6,411	3,332	3,981	5,301	2,205
Debt securities	12	2,845	3,313	3,604	2,888	7,610	9,883	12,090
Banks (net)	−302	1,648	−1,471	−3,273	2,307	2,190	1,779	−18,121
Other sectors	4,023	2,636	4,026	−280	4,660	6,064	10,372	−8,222
Net errors and omissions	−1,998	758	1,080	−722	−1,815	−1,240	1,095	−5,010
Reserve assets	1,208	1,147	−3,724	−3,009	−4,614	−7,039	−1,415	11,875
Taiwan								
Current account	10,925	12,468	8,550	7,042	6,498	5,474	11,027	7,776
Financial account	−15,150	−2,228	−6,910	−4,629	−1,397	−8,190	−8,802	−8,154
Direct investment (net)	−3,919	−784	−1,088	−1,694	−1,265	−1,424	−1,979	−2,974
Portfolio investment (net)	−1,006	45	444	1,067	905	493	−1,112	−8,283
Equity securities	−622	35	41	1,112	−63	−48	−1,054	−6,882
Debt securities	−384	10	403	−45	968	541	−58	−1,401
Banks (net)	−4,218	2,732	1,698	200	734	−1,709	−3,185	947
Other sectors	−6,009	−4,152	−7,909	−4,178	−1,730	−5,491	−2,472	2,111
Net errors and omissions	463	−138	120	−544	−135	−565	−470	−36
Reserve assets	3,918	−9,659	−1,367	−1,541	−4,622	3,931	−1,102	728
China								
Current account	11,997	13,272	6,401	−11,609	6,908	1,618	7,243	29,718
Financial account	3,255	8,032	−250	23,474	32,645	38,674	39,966	22,978
Direct investment (net)	2,657	3,453	7,156	23,151	31,787	33,849	38,066	41,673
Portfolio investment (net)	−241	235	−57	3,049	3,543	631	1,744	6,804
Equity securities	0	0	0	0	0	0	0	5,657
Debt securities	−241	235	−57	3,049	3,543	631	1,744	1,147
Banks (net)	−2,315	1,655	−786	−415	−5,222	−4,045	−5,959	−12,572
Other sectors	256	453	−3,334	−2,476	−2,509	1,272	966	−6,623
Net errors and omissions	−3,205	−6,767	−8,211	−10,096	−9,100	−17,823	−15,504	−16,818
Reserve assets	−11,555	−14,083	2,060	−1,769	−30,453	−22,469	−31,705	−35,857
Hong Kong								
Trade balance	49,303	44,117	41,600	63,123	12,187	−38,233	−16,937	−57,146

Table 4.5 (continued)

ASEAN countries	1990	1991	1992	1993	1994	1995	1996	19
Malaysia								
Current account	−870	−4,183	−2,167	−2,991	−4,520	−7,362	−12,252	−13,4
Financial account	1,784	5,621	8,746	10,805	1,288	7,422	18,597	2,5
Direct investment (net)	2,332	3,998	5,183	5,006	4,342	4,132	–	
Portfolio investment (net)	−255	170	−1,122	−709	−1,649	−440	–	
Equity securities	0	0	0	0	0	0	–	
Debt securities	−255	170	−1,122	−709	−1,649	−440	–	
Banks (net)	847	1,312	3,631	4,225	−5,070	91	–	
Other sectors	−1,107	287	1,216	2,849	3,884	3,850	–	
Net errors and omissions	1,085	−151	79	3,624	154	−1,724	–	
Reserve assets	−1,951	−1,236	−6,618	−11,350	3,160	1,765	–	
Thailand								
Current account	−7,281	−7,571	−6,303	−6,364	−8,085	−13,554	−14,691	−2,9
Financial account	9,098	11,759	9,475	10,500	12,167	21,909	19,486	−15,4
Direct investment (net)	2,304	1,847	1,966	1,571	873	1,182	1,405	2,4
Portfolio investment (net)	−38	−81	924	5,455	2,481	4,081	3,544	3,8
Equity securities	440	37	455	2,679	−394	2,121	1,123	2,9
Debt securities	−478	−118	469	2,776	2,875	1,960	2,421	8
Banks (net)	1,027	213	1,862	3,324	13,268	10,481	5,650	−4,8
Other sectors	6,912	9,525	5,333	614	−3,751	6,117	8,945	−7,9
Net errors and omissions	1,419	431	−142	−230	87	−1,196	−2,627	1
Reserve assets	−2,961	−4,618	−3,029	−3,907	−4,169	−7,159	−2,167	9,9
Philippines								
Current account	−2,695	−1,034	−1,000	−3,016	−2,950	−1,980	−3,953	−4,3
Financial account	2,057	2,927	3,208	3,267	5,120	5,309	11,277	6,3
Direct investment (net)	530	544	228	864	1,289	1,079	1,335	1,1
Portfolio investment (net)	−50	110	40	−52	269	1,190	5,317	5
Equity securities	0	0	0	0	0	0	2,122	−3
Debt securities	−50	110	40	−52	269	1,190	3,195	9
Banks (net)	307	473	1,921	−229	1,694	1,648	3,291	2,0
Other sectors	395	1,425	−1,712	1,619	2,989	1,800	1,943	3,4
Net errors and omissions	593	−138	−520	85	157	−2,094	−2,986	−5,1
Reserve assets	388	−1,937	−1,746	−447	−2,107	−873	−4,037	2,6
Indonesia								
Current account	−2,988	−4,260	−2,780	−2,106	−2,792	−6,431	−7,663	−4,8
Financial account	4,495	5,697	6,129	5,632	3,839	10,259	10,847	1,4
Direct investment (net)	1,093	1,482	1,777	1,648	1,500	3,743	5,594	4,4
Portfolio investment (net)	−93	−12	−88	1,805	3,877	4,100	5,005	−2,6
Equity securities	0	0	0	1,805	1,900	1,493	1,819	−4,9
Debt securities	−93	−12	−88	0	1,977	2,607	3,186	2,3

Table 4.6 Outstanding loans from BIS-reporting banks, June 1997 (US$m)

| | Distribution by maturity | | Distribution by sector | | | | Distribution by country | | | | | | Grand total |
| | | | | | | | | | | Western Europe | | | |
	Up to and incl. 1 year	Over 1 year	Banks	Foreign Banks	Non-bank private sector	Public sector	Japan	US	France	Germany	UK	Total (incl. others)	
Singapore	196,600	11,537	174,874	115,529	35,085	1,031	65,035	5,215	15,339	38,351	25,245	113,307	211,192
Hong Kong	183,115	29,391	143,974	101,854	75,291	1,215	87,354	8,847	12,777	32,204	30,063	99,454	222,289
Taiwan	21,966	2,834	15,497	2,610	9,251	398	3,008	2,507	5,150	3,001	3,161	14,439	25,163
Korea	70,182	20,505	67,290	4,756	31,680	4,390	23,732	9,964	10,070	10,794	6,064	36,324	103,432
Malaysia	16,268	8,863	10,486	2,694	16,460	1,851	10,489	2,400	2,934	5,716	2,011	12,672	28,820
Thailand	45,567	21,083	26,069	12,246	41,262	1,968	37,749	4,008	5,089	7,557	2,818	19,804	69,382
Philippines	8,293	4,327	5,485	1,027	6,772	1,855	2,109	2,816	1,678	1,991	1,076	6,795	14,115
Indonesia	34,661	20,549	12,393	1,373	39,742	6,506	23,153	4,591	4,787	5,610	4,332	22,481	58,726
China	30,137	23,174	24,700	2,775	25,562	7,656	18,731	2,932	7,299	7,278	6,906	28,066	57,922
Vietnam	855	571	579	65	756	112	241	101	373	316	130	980	1,456
East Asia total	607,644	142,834	481,347	244,929	281,861	26,982	271,601	43,381	65,496	112,818	81,806	354,322	792,497
Asia total (incl. others)	849,917	258,978	652,643	274,320	470,697	55,963	395,428	75,672	105,882	159,999	111,491	513,005	1,181,938

Percentage of grand total

	Up to and incl. 1 year	Over 1 year	Banks	Foreign Banks	Non-bank private sector	Public sector	Japan	US	France	Germany	UK	Total (incl. others)	Grand total
Singapore	93.1	5.5	82.8	54.7	16.6	0.5	30.8	2.5	7.3	18.2	12.0	53.7	100.0
Hong Kong	82.4	13.2	64.8	45.8	33.9	0.5	39.3	4.0	5.7	14.5	13.5	44.7	100.0
Taiwan	87.3	11.3	61.6	10.4	36.8	1.6	12.0	10.0	20.5	11.9	12.6	57.4	100.0
Korea	67.9	19.8	65.1	4.6	30.6	4.2	22.9	9.6	9.7	10.4	5.9	35.1	100.0
Malaysia	56.4	30.8	36.4	9.3	57.1	6.4	36.4	8.3	10.2	19.8	7.0	44.0	100.0
Thailand	65.7	30.4	37.6	17.7	59.5	2.8	54.4	5.8	7.3	10.9	4.1	28.5	100.0
Philippines	58.8	30.7	38.9	7.3	48.0	13.1	14.9	20.0	11.9	14.1	7.6	48.1	100.0
Indonesia	59.0	35.0	21.1	2.3	67.7	11.1	39.4	7.8	8.2	9.6	7.4	38.3	100.0
China	52.0	40.0	42.6	4.8	44.1	13.2	32.3	5.1	12.6	12.6	11.9	48.5	100.0
Vietnam	58.7	39.2	39.8	4.5	51.9	7.7	16.6	6.9	25.6	21.7	8.9	67.3	100.0
East Asia total	76.7	18.0	60.7	30.9	35.6	3.4	34.3	5.5	8.3	14.2	10.3	44.7	100.0
Asia total (incl. others)	71.9	21.9	55.2	23.2	39.8	4.7	33.5	6.4	9.0	13.5	9.4	43.8	100.0

Source: BIS, The Maturity, Sectoral and Nationality Distribution of International Lending, First Half 1997, January 1998

Figure 4.2 Current account deficits, financial accounts and major components of net capital inflows, 1980–97 (%)

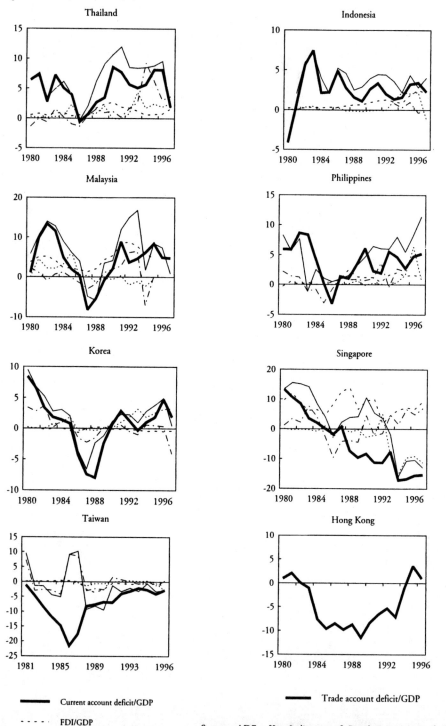

Sources: ADB, *Key Indicators of Developing Asia and Pacific Countries*, 1997; Central Bank of China, *Financial Statistics*, Taiwan, various issues; IMF, *International Financial Statistics*,

Japan, European countries and the United States are the major bank lenders to East Asia. Japan is the biggest single country lender to the region, though the European Union (EU) is the largest lender group (see Table 4.6). Compared with these lender countries' FDI flows into the region, there exists a positive correlation between their FDI and bank loans. In fact, this pattern has a logical explanation. When multinational firms from these countries advanced to East Asia in the 1980s, their banks at home followed them and began to extend loans to these multinationals. With financial market deregulation and capital account opening, these international banks began to lend to local customers as well. This was especially the case in Thailand, for instance. The establishment of the BIBF in 1993 facilitated lending by foreign banks to Thai banks and firms. Indeed, the authorities encouraged this type of activity (see Note 9).

The pattern of foreign capital flows into the emerging East Asian economies prior to the onset of the currency crisis can be summarised as follows:

- Net capital inflows into East Asia expanded in the 1990s, often exceeding the size of current account deficits. Private capital inflows were a major form of net inflows.

- Over time there was a shift in the composition of private capital inflows away from syndicated bank loans in the 1980s towards FDI inflows and portfolio investment inflows by the early 1990s.

- More recently, there was a further shift, from FDI towards short-term banking flows in addition to portfolio investment. Large inflows and rapid outflows of short-term capital were a direct trigger of the currency crisis in Thailand, Indonesia and Korea.

Factors affecting capital flows in East Asia

Under increasingly open capital accounts, macroeconomic factors, both in the respective countries in East Asia and outside the region, have had a large impact on capital flows. In their exchange rate stabilisation to currency baskets, many emerging East Asian economies gave a disproportionately large weight to the US dollar relative to the existing trade and investment pattern in the region (Table 4.7).[15] Although, on average, about 20 per cent of East Asian exports went to the United States, the Japanese and EU markets were equally important (Table 4.8). With the appreciation of the US dollar against the yen since mid-1995 and the relatively high inflation rates in the East Asian economies vis-à-vis the industrialised world, their currencies had also appreciated in real effective terms. Compounded with the falling prices of electronics goods and other major export commodities in 1996, their current accounts deteriorated sharply. The rising current account deficits were largely financed by short-term capital inflows in Thailand, Indonesia and Korea. Large capital inflows generated upward pressure on domestic demand and inflation. Rather than tightening fiscal policy, the authorities decided to use tight monetary policy to contain domestic demand and inflationary pressure. Tight monetary policy, however, maintained domestic interest rates at high

Table 4.7 Regression results for Asian currencies, January 1990–December 1996 (estimated implicit weights assigned to foreign currencies in exchange rate policies)

	Constant	US dollar	Yen	Deutsch-mark	French franc	Pound sterling	SDR	Singapore dollar	Australian dollar	NZ dollar	R-Square adjusted	Std error residuals	DW statistics	Number obs.
Singapore	−0.003**	0.420**	0.021	0.036	–	–	0.600**	–	–	–	0.959	0.005039	1.937	84/0
Hong Kong	0.000	1.003*	−0.002	−0.003	0.006	−0.006	–	–	–	–	0.999	0.001159	1.967	84/0
Taiwan	0.001	0.797**	0.106**	0.068	0.174	0.002	–	–	–	–	0.909	0.008802	1.334	84/0
Korea	0.003**	0.941**	0.088**	0.069	−0.063	−0.067	–	–	–	–	0.958	0.006118	1.364	84/0
Malaysia	0.001	0.589**	0.044	0.018	0.200	−0.006	–	0.340	–	–	0.876	0.010692	1.327	84/0
Thailand	0.000	0.789**	0.104**	0.028	0.017	0.017**	–	0.040*	–	–	0.999	0.000897	1.430	84/0
Philippines	0.002	1.087**	−0.094	−0.106	0.337	−0.022	–	–	–	–	0.798	0.016862	1.236	84/0
Indonesia	0.003**	0.966**	0.014	−0.038	0.058	0.013	–	–	–	–	0.992	0.002713	1.637	84/0
China	0.002*	0.921**	0.042	−0.357	0.253	0.075	–	–	–	–	0.911	0.009206	1.244	82/2
Vietnam	0.005*	0.964**	−0.029	0.087	0.342	−0.222*	–	–	–	–	0.776	0.016823	1.242	69/2
Myanmar	0.000	−0.123	−0.010	–	–	−0.038	1.208**	–	–	–	0.816	0.008948	3.005	84/0
Fiji	0.000	0.270**	0.147**	0.030	0.000	0.146**	–	0.039	0.285**	0.111**	0.989	0.002766	2.578	84/0
Papua New Guinea	0.004*	0.593**	0.074	0.318	−0.236	−0.039	–	–	0.373**	–	0.777	0.016713	0.951	83/1
Solomon Islands	0.006**	0.690**	0.081	−0.237	−0.187	0.068	–	0.327	0.045	−0.056	0.833	0.012653	2.471	84/0
Tonga	−0.001	0.435**	0.017	0.080	−0.041	−0.011	–	−0.187	0.469**	0.215**	0.976	0.004828	1.786	84/0
Western Samoa	0.002	0.372	0.057	−0.152	0.113	0.059	–	0.148	0.336**	0.025	0.778	0.014982	2.675	84/0

Note: Double asterisk (**) and single asterisk (*) denote, respectively, that coefficients are statistically significant at 1% and 5% levels.

Table 4.8 US, EU, Japan and East Asia shares in total international transactions of East Asian economies, 1996 (%)

	Exports					Imports				
	United States	European Union	Japan	East Asia	Total	United States	European Union	Japan	East Asia	Total
Singapore	18.4	13.0	8.2	46.8	100.0	16.4	14.5	18.2	37.9	100.0
Hong Kong	21.3	14.9	6.6	45.1	100.0	7.9	11.1	13.6	60.4	100.0
Taiwan	26.8	13.6	12.9	45.0	100.0	18.2	15.3	25.7	23.0	100.0
Korea	16.7	10.8	12.3	35.9	100.0	22.1	14.1	20.9	15.9	100.0
Malaysia	18.2	13.7	13.4	43.2	100.0	15.6	14.5	24.7	32.6	100.0
Thailand	18.0	16.0	16.8	32.7	100.0	12.6	14.5	27.8	24.3	100.0
Philippines	33.9	15.9	17.9	25.3	100.0	19.7	9.4	21.8	28.3	100.0
Indonesia	16.4	16.6	28.5	29.7	100.0	10.2	22.2	23.2	29.4	100.0
China	17.7	13.1	20.4	35.0	100.0	11.7	14.3	21.0	34.0	100.0
Vietnam	4.5	24.3	26.4	24.1	100.0	5.0	13.0	9.2	57.1	100.0
East Asia	**19.8**	**13.7**	**13.5**	**40.0**	**100.0**	**14.3**	**14.0**	**20.3**	**35.1**	**100.0**

	Foreign direct investment inflows					Outstanding loans from BIS-reporting banks				
	United States	European Union	Japan	East Asia	Total	United States	European Union	Japan	East Asia	Total
Singapore	39.6	23.1	34.3	n.a.	100.0	3.0	54.3	31.1	n.a.	100.0
Hong Kong	9.8	18.1	45.4	22.7	100.0	4.2	41.6	42.2	n.a.	100.0
Taiwan	19.3	5.0	22.2	18.6	100.0	12.4	56.6	12.0	n.a.	100.0
Korea	27.4	27.9	7.9	29.9	100.0	9.4	33.8	24.3	n.a.	100.0
Malaysia	17.0	5.1	27.0	36.8	100.0	10.5	41.4	36.9	n.a.	100.0
Thailand	21.1	16.3	47.2	44.3	100.0	7.2	27.3	53.5	n.a.	100.0
Philippines	3.4	17.5	6.0	41.0	100.0	29.4	47.6	11.7	n.a.	100.0
Indonesia	2.1	16.8	25.6	30.2	100.0	9.5	37.8	39.7	n.a.	100.0
China	8.3	6.6	8.8	68.7	100.0	4.9	47.4	32.3	n.a.	100.0
Vietnam	8.1	16.8	17.3	35.3	100.0	12.0	62.7	16.3	n.a.	100.0
East Asia	**10.7**	**12.1**	**21.2**	**46.7**	**100.0**	**6.2**	**43.2**	**35.4**	**n.a.**	**100.0**

Sources: IMF, *Direction of Trade Yearbook,* 1997; Japan External Trade Organisation, *White Papers on Foreign Direct Investment,* 1997; BIS, *The Maturity, Sectoral and Nationality Distribution of International Bank Lending, First Half 1997,* January 1998

levels, thereby inducing further capital inflows to the country. With easy access to foreign bank loans, domestic banks and firms borrowed increasingly from foreign financial institutions without due attention to the exchange risks involved. Foreign financial institutions, on the other hand, held the expectation of the region's sustained economic growth and stable exchange rates and, hence, were equally willing to lend to local banks and firms without fully assessing the risks entailed.

The lack of efficient bond markets in East Asia was a structural factor behind the large exposure to international banks and maturity mismatches of external borrowing through international banks. Because of the small size of the bond markets, firms were overly dependent on bank loans for their financing needs.[16] This is perhaps why, despite the region's need for longer term capital investment, private capital inflows were predominantly short-term. The very nature of banks (i.e. that they borrow short and lend long) left the East Asian banking sector subject to the risk of maturity mismatch.

With deregulation, competition for market share in the banking sector in East Asia was intensified. As a result, the franchise value of existing banks decreased. To maintain market share and profitability, banks often engaged in aggressive, risky lending behaviour. They extended loans on easy terms because foreign funds were readily available to potential borrowers. This increased bank exposure to non-productive sectors of the economy and also to foreign currency risk because they expanded foreign currency denominated liabilities. Commercial banks in many of the region's economies were already quite vulnerable even before the currency crisis.

The two important structural factors behind the surge in banking flows from abroad can be summarised as follows:

• Premature financial deregulation and capital account greatly facilitated external borrowing in the form of bank loans (and portfolio investment) with an increasingly short maturity structure.

• Easy access to external financing, with inadequate financial supervision and risk assessment, allowed domestic banks to overborrow from abroad. With potential currency and maturity mismatch, this heightened exchange risks should unfavourable external shocks occur.

Capital flows after the onset of the crisis and prospects for the future

The currency crisis originated in Thailand, where the financial sector was already fragile and confidence in the currency value in doubt in the first half of 1997. With the expectation of baht devaluation, domestic borrowers of foreign currency attempted to accelerate foreign currency repayment or to engage in forward selling of baht, portfolio investors tried to pull out of baht-denominated assets and capital flight began to take place. A sudden curtailment of short-term capital inflows and a shift to capital outflows were the major pressures on the baht, culminating in its devaluation in July 1997. Subsequently, international banks' unwillingness to roll over their short-term loans exacerbated the crisis, which quickly spread to other parts of East Asia, such as Indonesia, Malaysia, the Philippines and Korea.

A steep currency depreciation and a hike in interest rates in these countries had an immediate impact on both the corporate and the financial sector. Domestic currency depreciation suddenly inflated the size of external debt (measured in local currency) and the debt servicing obligations of externally indebted corporations. High interest rates increased the interest servicing obligations of domestically indebted corporations. Essentially, the high leverage of corporations made them unable to meet interest payments to domestic or foreign creditors. The resulting rise in non-performing loans aggravated the already weak portfolios of commercial banks, which were forced to stop providing new loans to the borrowers with overdue interest and were even forced to recall some existing loans. In addition, corporations began to experience a cash flow squeeze and a profitability decline due to the shrinking aggregate demand largely brought about by the steep currency depreciation (debt deflation and adverse terms-of-trade shocks) and the contractionary monetary and fiscal policy. Despite large currency depreciations, exports failed to make a positive response. Deterioration of banks' balance sheets and corporate performance led banks to take a cautious lending policy, limiting new commercial loans. The lack of bank credit exacerbated corporate sector distress and contributed to further depression of real economic activity. All East Asian economies in crisis were trapped in this vicious circle, thereby worsening a surprisingly deep and rapid economic contraction.[17]

With confidence in the region's economies at a historic low point, restoration of capital flows in the forms of banking flows and portfolio investment was not imminent in 1998. International bond issues were an option. However, with the downgrading of sovereign risks in all crisis countries in the region, the potential costs due to increased risk premia were high. Indeed, because of the sharply increased risk premia, debt inflows in the region slowed, with the ASEAN-4 suffering most of the decline. In the first half of 1998, only Korea had moderate success in its international bond placement efforts. Other countries, including some of the non-crisis countries, had a disappointing record. Compared with their bond placement just one or two years ago, the bonds subscribed were only a fraction of their previous international bond issuance.

There are several ways to restore capital flows into the region, especially in the crisis countries. One method is through rapid privatisation. Compared with Latin American and East European countries, the East Asian region is lagging behind on this front. In the past, heavy government influence in private sectors may have handicapped foreign investment in certain 'key' or 'strategic' industries. In the midst of the crisis, the restrictions on entry into these sectors were relaxed or even abolished in all crisis countries. This will facilitate FDI flows into a wide array of sectors in these economies. In addition, with the removal of ownership restrictions and strengthened bankruptcy codes, fire sales of FDI are becoming possible. This may also help foreign capital to flow into the crisis countries.

In light of reduced confidence in the region, bilateral donors and international multilateral institutions could also play an active role in encouraging capital flows back into East Asia. Through enhanced investment guarantees or interest subsidies, private sectors and other agencies could provide loans requested by the countries in the region. This policy would be gradually phased out as the economies returned to normalcy.

LESSONS FOR CAPITAL FLOW LIBERALISATION

The East Asian crisis proves that, in a world of free mobility of capital, even a supposedly dynamic economy can come under serious currency attack once confidence in the economy and currency is lost. From this episode, we can learn five lessons for capital flow liberalisation.

Sound management of the macroeconomy and the external account

The East Asian economies had large net capital inflows, often exceeding the size of current account deficits. Some capital inflows were autonomous, attracted by the domestic economic boom, while others were the result of high domestic interest rates and expectations of continued stable exchange rates. The problem was that capital inflows to East Asian economies increasingly took the form of unhedged short-term capital; these inflows were through commercial banks, non-bank financial institutions (NBFIs) and corporations. This made current account financing vulnerable to sudden shifts in market sentiment because short-term capital flows could easily be reversed once confidence in the economy and currency was lost. In fact, when confidence in the value of the currency came into doubt, capital inflows began to decline and net outflows of capital began to occur. In addition, borrowers of foreign currency started to unwind their unhedged foreign exchange positions by selling domestic currency for foreign currency to be repaid (or going short through forward and swap transactions). All of these factors combined to put large downward pressure on the currency.

The first lesson is a reconfirmation that any emerging economy must maintain sound macroeconomic policies and sustainable capital inflows in order to prevent a currency crisis from occurring in the first place. In the case of the affected East Asian economies, while fiscal policy was disciplined and monetary policy was non-inflationary, the authorities failed to achieve both internal balance (full employment and low inflation) and external balance (sustainable current accounts) simultaneously.[18] In view of this, macroeconomic policies must be geared to avoid excessive credit expansion in the domestic economy, large capital inflows, overvaluation of the currency and unsustainable current account deficits.

Financial system resilience

The most important lesson is that, in order to maintain a stable currency in a world of high capital mobility, a sound financial system is necessary. The traditional literature on 'sequencing' emphasises that capital account liberalisation must be preceded by stable macroeconomic conditions, current account liberalisation and domestic financial market deregulation. The experience of the East Asian currency crisis shows that, in addition to these traditional sequencing steps, a country must establish a resilient and robust domestic financial system.[19] That is, domestic financial institutions should be sufficiently capitalised with adequate loan loss provisions and must have the capability and expertise to prudently manage assets and liabilities. The authorities should maintain an effective regulatory and supervisory framework over banks and NBFIs, and strong disclosure and accounting requirements. They should also protect overall financial market integrity without providing guarantees to individual financial institutions, so as to avoid the risk of moral hazard. With a resilient financial system in place, banks and NBFIs should be able to weather macroeconomic shocks and asset price gyrations. A combination of large capital inflows and rapid capital outflows should be less likely to exert an adverse systemic impact on domestic financial institutions and economic activity in general.

Once large-scale inflows and outflows occur and create speculative pressure on the exchange rate, appropriate macroeconomic policy responses are necessary. They include intervention in the foreign exchange market, changes in monetary policy and the use of exchange rate flexibility as options. The introduction of greater flexibility in the exchange rate in Thailand in 1995–6, for example, would have allowed baht appreciation and would have reduced capital inflows by raising exchange risk. Temporary introduction of a Chilean-style capital control in the form of imposing high liquidity or reserve requirements on short-term capital inflows to financial institutions could also be effective in avoiding undesirable exchange rate fluctuations, though they should not be used as a permanent instrument to control capital flows.

Controls on capital outflows are more difficult and less effective than controls on inflows, particularly in the midst of a currency crisis. In general, controls on outflows to pursue an expansionary monetary policy is a recipe for disaster, and this is particularly so if they are used as a substitute for needed structural reform. If applied in the context of a credible economic program, however, temporary controls on outflows may give governments some time in which to put their house in order and may help reduce the real cost of resolving the crisis. Key to the success of temporary outflow controls are credible announcements of a policy program and exit from controls. However, this is very difficult to achieve.

Corporate governance and external debt

One of the most important reasons for the deepening economic crisis in East Asia is a systemic collapse of the corporate sector, which was highly leveraged and vulnerable to a large-scale currency depreciation and a hike in the interest rate. In the face of a crisis, abrupt currency depreciation sharply increased the domestic currency value of external debt and the high interest rates sharply increased debt service obligations of domestic corporates. This worsened corporate balance sheets, which consequently made their banks extremely distressed. In addition, the deepening recession and the consequent shrinkage of aggregate demand further aggravated the already difficult financial positions of corporations. With highly leveraged corporations, a currency crisis and the policy response to it can create serious difficulties for the corporate and financial sectors.

An important lesson, therefore, is that, in a world of free access to international capital, a financially disciplined corporate sector is required so as to maintain sustainable debt to equity ratios. This requires a transparent governance structure on the part of the corporate sector and a prudent management of loan portfolios on the part of banks. Essentially, banks have to know what their clients do, thereby disciplining corporate financial activity, particularly in the area of external debt financing.

A viable exchange rate regime

With free mobility of capital, exchange rate management is not an easy task, particularly for emerging economies. Once investors are convinced that the exchange rate is out of a perceived 'equilibrium' value, massive one-way speculation can take place. To avoid such speculation, the exchange rate must be maintained at a level consistent with an 'equilibrium' level.

Many affected East Asian economies had long attempted to maintain relatively stable exchange rates vis-à-vis the US dollar. For example, Thailand used a basket peg system, until 1 July 1997, which required the Bank of Thailand to stabilise the baht with respect to a basket of foreign currencies where the weight of the US dollar was large. Similarly, other countries de facto stabilised their exchange rates against the US dollar (see Note 15).

However, with high domestic inflation and the US dollar's appreciation since mid-1995 vis-à-vis the major industrialised countries' currencies, particularly the Japanese yen and the deutschmark, the large weight on the US dollar in the East Asian countries' exchange rate policies resulted in currency overvaluation on a real, effective basis. Sustained real overvaluation of the currency was an important factor behind not only a slowdown in exports and sustained current account deficits, but also mounting speculative pressure in the foreign exchange market.

The fact that the East Asian economies have diverse linkages with the rest of the world in trade and FDI implies that exchange rate stabilisation vis-à-vis the US dollar is not an appropriate exchange rate arrangement. It was noted earlier that, for many of these economies, the United States is not the single most dominant trade partner or FDI source (see Table 4.8). Japan and the EU are equally important, and other East Asian economies as a group are often more important. It is therefore appropriate for any East Asian economy to stabilise its exchange rate with respect to a certain basket of currencies consisting of not only the US dollar but also the Japanese yen, the euro (after 1 January 1999), and some regional currencies. This suggests that the economies in the region should increase the role of the yen and the euro as nominal anchor currencies.[20]

The rising degree of intraregional trade and investment interdependence means that economies in East Asia are expected to benefit from avoiding large fluctuations in intraregional exchange rates. This is particularly the case for ASEAN countries, which are expected to complete the ASEAN Free Trade Agreement (AFTA) by the year 2003 through lowering tariffs on manufactured products below 5 per cent.

Essentially, large swings in exchange rates among these countries would be counterproductive because they would alter international price competitiveness suddenly and make the prospective free trade agreement unsustainable. To maintain stable currencies with one another, the ASEAN countries should adopt similar currency baskets, reflecting the degree of economic linkages with the United States, Japan and the EU.

International cooperative frameworks for crisis management

The deepening of financial integration with the rest of the world implies that any emerging economy faces increasing risks of sudden capital inflows and outflows, the consequent pressure on its exchange rate and undesirable effects on local financial institutions and corporations. In a world of greater financial linkages, a currency crisis in one country spreads easily to neighbouring countries. Because of the potentially global nature of the crisis, a multilateral cooperative framework for crisis management is required. At the same time, because of geographically concentrated economic contagion, a regional arrangement for financial coordination is also logical. An efficient cooperative framework for international and regional crisis management is highly recommended to cope with volatile capital flows, currency crisis and contagion.

At the international level, coordinated intervention to provide liquidity for crisis countries can be justified. First, it is important to prevent a crisis in a particular country from becoming unnecessarily severe. When a country has a large amount of short-term foreign currency-denominated debt, the capacity of its central bank to act as a lender of last resort is limited; there will then be a strong case for international assistance to provide lender-of-last-resort services. Provision of international liquidity can thereby help cushion the inevitable adjustment process that would require redirection of a nation's productive resources from the non-traded to the traded goods sector, as is typically the case for an emerging market when foreign capital inflows are interrupted and a large current account deficit has to be reduced. The second rationale for international intervention is to limit the contagious spread of problems to other countries that compete with the crisis country in international markets or share similar macroeconomic and financial characteristics that lead investors to suspect similar problems.

The usual objection to such international intervention is a moral hazard problem. The alleged argument is that international support packages may both encourage emerging economies' governments to run excessively risky policies and induce international investors to rush to emerging markets without adequate assessment of the underlying risks. While the first type of moral hazard may not be negated, the second type is more important. Minimising the risk of moral hazard requires that international support should not be used to bail out international investors, and that transparency should be improved in the form of adequate and timely disclosure of both emerging economies' financial information and international investors' cross-border transactions.

In addition, a collective framework of orderly debt workout in conjunction with international liquidity support at times of a crisis is useful. The purpose of introducing such a framework is to promote debtor–creditor negotiations for debt workout so as to suspend payments on foreign debt during the 'standstill' period and to reach restructuring agreements allowing rollover, extension of maturities and possibly debt reductions. The mechanisms for such collective action by creditors and debtors can help minimise the risk of moral hazard by requiring both private creditors and debtors to share the burden of losses.

With regard to regional arrangements, some already exist in East Asia.[21] In addition to the existing ones, a framework of regional financial cooperation that supplements the financing by international financial institutions (the IMF, the World Bank and the Asian Development Bank) has emerged spontaneously following the crisis. Finance ministers' deputies in the Asia Pacific region agreed in Manila in November 1997 to establish such a framework (a regional facility of the kind developed in response to the Indonesian rupiah crisis) supplemented by regional surveillance, in a way consistent with the multilateral (IMF–World Bank–WTO) framework. In addition, ASEAN countries embarked on regional economic monitoring, again in a way consistent with the multilateral framework.

Regional surveillance and economic monitoring should include exchange of macroeconomic and structural information, such as fiscal positions, monetary and exchange rate positions (domestic and foreign assets and liabilities of the central banks), capital flows, external debt, financial system conditions and corporate sector developments. With an effective surveillance/monitoring mechanism in place, each economy in the region is expected to be under peer pressure so that it is forced to pursue disciplined macroeconomic and structural policies that are conducive to stable external accounts and currencies.

CONCLUSION

The East Asian turmoil revealed that no emerging economy is immune to a currency crisis. This is particularly so once an economy has achieved a certain degree of financial deregulation and capital account liberalisation. Such an economy faces greater risks of sudden capital inflows and outflows and a consequent instability in its financial system and exchange rates caused by these flows. Its impact on the corporate sector and real economic activity can be far greater than expected. Any economy must be prepared to cope with these risks.

That Thailand, Indonesia and Korea, which pursued financial deregulation and capital flow liberalisation, underwent severe currency and financial crisis need not suggest that the liberalisation process in emerging economies be substantially delayed. Instead, each should continue to aim at capital account liberalisation but only based upon the specific conditions of the economy. There is no general rule, but the speed and scope of liberalisation should depend on the specific stage of development of financial institutions in the country in question, its overall financial infrastructure, the scope of available policy instruments, and policymakers' ability to respond with flexibility to macroeconomic and financial shocks. Any liberalisation attempts must be accompanied by effective preventive measures as well as a framework to minimise the risks that such crises may entail once they occur. Preventive measures include pursuit of sound macroeconomic policies, establishment of a resilient and robust financial system (with prudent management of financial institutions and effective regulatory and supervisory mechanisms), operation of financially prudent corporations, maintenance of a viable exchange rate arrangement and improved transparency in the form of adequate and timely disclosure of financial information. A framework to minimise the risk of currency crisis must include effective monetary policy instruments to counteract currency speculation and its contagion effects, as well as international financial cooperation supplemented by effective surveillance mechanisms. An international cooperative framework must be developed to expedite orderly external debt workout, once a balance-of-payments or currency crisis occurs.

NOTES

The author is grateful to Naoko Kojo and Li-gang Liu for their contributions, to Yun-peng Chu and Gordon de Brouwer for constructive comments on an earlier version of the chapter and to David Bisbee and Dana Liu for their research assistance. The views expressed here do not necessarily represent those of the World Bank.

1   There was always some concern that too rapid liberalisation of a nation's capital account could be detrimental because it could easily generate sudden capital inflows and outflows and consequent exchange rate instability. The previous worst scenario was the currency crisis observed in Mexico in 1994–5.
2   This chapter is an update of Kawai (1997), which discussed the East Asian economies' progress in capital account liberalisation in the pre-crisis period.
3   East Asia in this paper includes the Asian NIEs (Singapore, Hong Kong, Taiwan, Korea), the ASEAN-4 (Malaysia, Thailand, the Philippines, Indonesia), China and Vietnam.
4   The first type of measure encouraged FDI inflows by offering tax and tariff incentives to foreign firms; typical examples included the establishment of export processing zones (Korea, Taiwan, the Philippines), free trade zones (Malaysia) and special economic zones (China), though other economies such as Thailand offered similar incentives without setting up formal economic zones. As tariffs were increasingly liberalised, however, the advantage of tariff exemptions began to disappear. The second type liberalised sectors open to foreign investors by introducing a negative list system and reducing the number of prohibited or restricted sectors on the list (Taiwan, Korea, Indonesia, the Philippines). Many manufacturing sectors are now open to FDI in almost all the East Asian economies, unless specifically prohibited. The third type encouraged manufacturing FDI which would contribute to the national economy by allowing substantial foreign ownership. The strategy was to set a maximum limit on the foreign ownership of firms and to relax the foreign ownership limitation, depending on the firm's contribution to the national economy measured through export, employment and regional development (Malaysia, Thailand, Indonesia). Many East Asian economies, except China and Vietnam, now allow 100 per cent foreign ownership in export-oriented manufacturing sectors, such as those exporting more than 80 per cent of the products.

5 Even the OECD capital liberalisation code approves restricting inward FDI in sectors related to national security. Identification of such sectors is left to each member's discretion. Though the OECD initiated the process of reaching a Multilateral Agreement on Investment which is expected to be more liberal than the existing code or any other international obligation, its prospect is uncertain.

6 This underdevelopment partly reflected the lack of large-scale issues of government bonds due to 'balanced budget' policies, the lack of large institutional investors (such as life insurance companies and pension funds), and the inadequacy of basic market infrastructure (such as transparent disclosure systems, effective accounting principles, credible rating agencies and efficient payment systems).

7 Thailand and the Philippines issue international investment trust funds (Thai Fund and Manila Fund), including those shares restricted to foreigners in London and New York, to allow foreign investors to invest indirectly in the restricted shares.

8 It is widely observed that, when the foreign share ownership limit is effective and binding, foreign-owned shares that carry voting rights and rights to dividends, cash flows and assets that are identical to the domestically owned shares of the same firm would trade at price premia.

9 Thailand established the Bangkok International Banking Facility (BIBF) for several purposes: to encourage foreign currency-denominated bank loans (called 'out–in loans') to meet the funding needs of Thai firms and to finance infrastructure development; to attract foreign banks with international reputations, technology and know-how to Bangkok so as to introduce more competition into the banking system and to improve the efficiency of Thai commercial banks; and to encourage foreign banks to extend loans (called 'out–out loans'), via Bangkok, to the greater Indochina area, including Laos, Myanmar, Vietnam and Cambodia (see Kawai and Iwatsubo 1998).

10 As Taiwan has not been a member of the IMF since April 1980, the nature of its exchange restrictions is not readily available from IMF publications and, therefore, it cannot be compared with other economies in the region. From 1 July 1996, before establishing current-account convertibility of the renminbi, China allowed foreign-affiliated firms to buy or sell foreign exchange for current account purposes through foreign exchange banks.

11 Many East Asian economies maintain the so-called 'foreign exchange bank' system in which specialised banks or dealers are authorised to deal in foreign exchange (Korea, Malaysia, Thailand, Indonesia, the Philippines, China). Some of these economies retain a foreign exchange concentration system by requiring export proceeds to be sold to the authorities or deposited at the authorised foreign exchange bank (Korea, Malaysia, China), and some impose position management control on the banks (Korea, Indonesia, China).

12 After repeated speculative attack on the then-fixed baht exchange rate in mid-May 1997, the Thai government imposed restrictions to prohibit residents' (in particular, banks') lending of baht to non-residents for which there was no underlying trade or investment transaction. This created a spread between offshore and onshore rates. In late January 1998, the controls were abolished and the two-tier foreign exchange market was unified.

13 Various papers in Ramstetter (1991), including that of Mari Pangestu, emphasise the importance of the 'unilateral liberalisation' that many ASEAN countries have pursued.

14 The countries not facing an immediate currency crisis had much smaller short-term banking sector exposure relative to foreign exchange reserves: 25 per cent for Taiwan, 61 per cent for Malaysia and 85 per cent for the Philippines. The much larger exposure faced by Singapore (244 per cent) and Hong Kong (291 per cent) is a result of their functions

as international financial centres. One surprising observation derived from Table 4.6 is the size of China's short-term banking loan exposure (US\$30 billion). Although China officially maintains strict control on its capital account, its short-term external debt accumulated by domestic banks and non-bank sectors is nevertheless considerable, though still small relative to its foreign exchange reserves (25 per cent). The share of its short-term bank loans was 52 per cent of its total exposure to international banks.

15 Although weights of currencies in the basket peg system were never disclosed, regression analyses of the kind explored by Frankel and Wei (1993, 1994) and Kawai and Akiyama (1998) suggest that, in the 1990s, many East Asian economies adopted a de facto US dollar peg or a currency basket system with a very large weight of the US dollar. The implied weights attached to the dollar were 59 per cent in Malaysia, 80 per cent in Taiwan, 82 per cent in Thailand, 92 per cent in China, 96 per cent in Vietnam, 97 per cent in Indonesia, 100 per cent in Hong Kong and 110 per cent in the Philippines (a weight exceeding 100 per cent must be interpreted with caution). The estimated weights attached to the Japanese yen were 11 per cent in Thailand and Taiwan and 9 per cent in Korea (see Table 4.7).

16 Compared with other emerging markets, total bonds issues in East Asia as a share of gross domestic product (GDP) were among the lowest (World Bank 1995).

17 For analyses of the development of the East Asian crisis, see ADB (1998), IMF (1997) and World Bank (1998).

18 On fiscal policy, most East Asian economies have maintained budget surpluses for some time and fiscal policy was not a direct cause of the large current account deficit immediately before the crisis. Private sector investment was an important factor behind that deficit, although pre-crisis fiscal contraction would have helped offset the domestic boom, thereby contributing to a smaller current account deficit.

19 See also McKinnon (1992).

20 Though the role of the East Asian currencies is potentially important, the G-3 currencies (the US dollar, the yen and the euro) are the only realistic candidates for inclusion in a basket.

21 The East Asian economies have developed a network of bilateral repurchase agreements and several fora – the EMEAP (Executives Meeting of East Asia and Pacific Central Banks), the Six Markets Meeting and the APEC Finance Ministers Meeting – for cooperation among finance ministers and central bankers. One of the objectives is to establish a cooperative framework to cope with possible currency and financial crises through frequent exchanges of information and the network of repurchase arrangements involving US dollar-denominated foreign exchange reserves.

REFERENCES

Asian Development Bank (ADB) (1998) *Asian Development Outlook*, New York: Oxford University Press.

Frankel, J.A. and S.-J. Wei (1993) 'Is there a currency bloc in the Pacific?', in A. Blundell-Wingnall and S. Grenville (eds) *Exchange Rates, International Trade and Monetary Policy*, Sydney: Reserve Bank of Australia, 275–307.

—— (1994) 'Yen bloc or dollar bloc?: exchange rate policies of the East Asian economies', in T. Ito and A. Krueger (eds) *Macroeconomic Linkage: Savings, Exchange Rates, and Capital Flows*, Chicago: University of Chicago Press, 295–329.

International Monetary Fund (IMF) (1997) *World Economic Outlook: Interim Assessment*, World Economic and Financial Surveys, Washington DC: IMF, December.

Kawai, M. (1997) 'Capital flow liberalization and financial market opening in Asia-Pacific economies', in Y.-S. Kim, I. Yamazawa and W.-H. Park (eds) *Economics of the Triad: Conflict and Cooperation among the United States, Japan and Korea*, Seoul: Korea Institute for International Economic Policy, 247–67.

Kawai, M. and S. Akiyama (1998) 'The role of nominal anchor currencies in exchange rate arrangements', *Journal of the Japanese and International Economies* (forthcoming). [A detailed version: Discussion Paper Series No. F-78, Institute of Social Science, University of Tokyo, October.]

Kawai, M. and K. Iwatsubo (1998) 'The Thai financial system and the baht crisis: processes, causes, and lessons', unpublished ms, Institute of Social Science, University of Tokyo, April.

Kohsaka, A. (1996) 'Interdependence through capital flows in Pacific Asia and the role of Japan', in T. Ito and A.O. Krueger (eds) *Financial Deregulation and Integration in East Asia*, Chicago: Chicago University Press, 107–42.

McKinnon, R.I. (1992) *The Order of Economic Liberalization*, Baltimore: Johns Hopkins University Press.

Ramstetter, E.D. (ed.) (1991) *Direct Foreign Investment in Asia's Developing Economies and Structural Change in the Asia-Pacific Region*, Boulder, Colorado: Westview Press.

World Bank (1993) *The East Asian Miracle: Economic Growth and Public Policy*, New York: Oxford University Press.

—— (1995) *The Emerging Asian Bond Market*, Washington DC: World Bank.

—— (1998) *East Asia: The Road to Recovery*, Washington DC: World Bank.

5 The development of Asian equity markets

Matthew Field and Don Hanna

INTRODUCTION

While Asian securities have been around since the late 1700s, the most dynamic growth in these markets has occurred only in the last ten to fifteen years with the increase in the importance of Asian stock markets and the issuance of domestic and international bonds. This chapter focuses on the development of equity markets in the non-Japan Asia region, as they remain the dominant form of raising funds outside of bank lending. Domestic bond markets, while they exist, remain largely undeveloped and are not widely accessed by enterprises, governments or investors.

REGIONAL OVERVIEW

Growth in Asia from the 1970s through to the mid-1990s outstripped growth rates seen elsewhere in the world. The first group of countries where growth took hold were the newly industrialised economies (NIEs – Hong Kong, Korea, Singapore and Taiwan), where export expansion in the 1970s and 1980s led to a dramatic surge in real gross domestic product (GDP). The late 1980s and 1990s saw growth in the ASEAN-4 (Indonesia, Malaysia, the Philippines and Thailand) region, as lower value-added export production shifted to it from the NIEs (Figure 5.1). As the pace of economic growth increased, new sources of funds were required by companies to finance continued expansion, as investment rates remained high (Figure 5.2). Bank lending served as the primary source of funds, even though many of these countries had had stock markets since the early 1900s. However, these security markets were poorly equipped to take advantage of initial capital requirements. Stock markets in many countries were plagued with unclear or insufficient ownership rights and reporting requirements, so were unable to directly tap into the high saving rates in the region (Figure 5.3). As Modigliani and Perotti (1991) point out, in a country without clear enforceable contractual rights for investors, the ability to raise long-term capital is impaired. Therefore, bank lending comes to dominate funding choices as banks have longstanding relationships with large domestic corporations and maintain the ability to enforce their claims. This characterisation certainly applied to developing Asia.

Figure 5.1 Real GDP growth, 1980–97 (% yoy change)

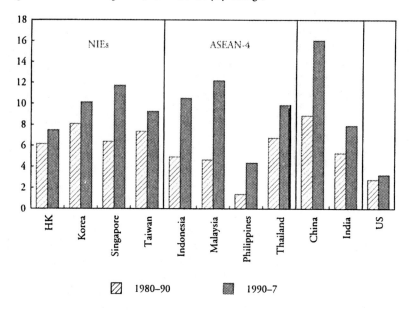

Note: Malaysia data 1982–90, not 1980–90
Sources: CEIC; IMF

Figure 5.2 Gross domestic investment, 1970–97 (% of GDP)

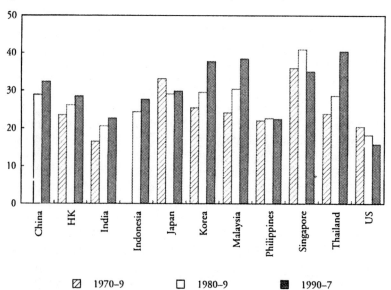

Sources: CEIC; World Bank

Figure 5.3 Gross domestic savings, 1970–97 (% of GDP)

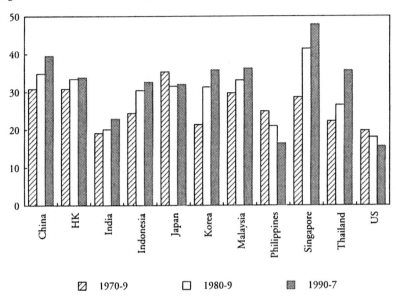

☑ 1970-9　　　□ 1980-9　　　▨ 1990-7

Sources: CEIC; World Bank

As a result of these many factors, stock issuance largely served as a secondary source of finance (Figure 5.4) and is small relative to new bank lending. While bank lending certainly dominates company balance sheets, the aggregate bank loan figures are skewed by lending for mortgages and property which is more likely to use bank financing in favour of stock issuance. Singapore stands out as an exception, but the relatively small size of its economy and the large role the finance sector plays within it makes Singapore different from most other countries. Even though stock issuance remains a secondary source of funds, the prominence of regional markets has risen dramatically. Market capitalisation as a percentage of the world over the period 1987–97 (Figure 5.5) shows the heightened importance of Asian stock markets, as more companies were listed and as increased funds (from locals as well as foreigners) pushed up stock prices. As a percentage of the world, Asian market capitalisation (excluding Japan) quadrupled from 1987 to 1993 before falling back on a weakening of regional currencies and general share-price declines.

Aggregate figures mask a sea-change in Asian markets, however, as the relative importance of different stock markets has changed significantly since 1987 (Table 5.1). For instance, the rapid growth of China's economy and the increased international presence of the country has led to both the development of the Shanghai and Shenzhen stock markets as well as the build-up of Chinese-based but Hong Kong-listed H-shares on the Hong Kong stock exchange. As a result, this has led to an increase in the importance of the stock exchanges of both Hong Kong and

Figure 5.4 New bank lending and stock issuance, 1990 and 1997 (% of GDP)

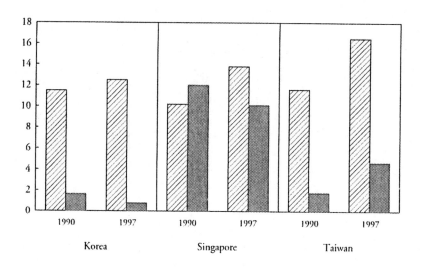

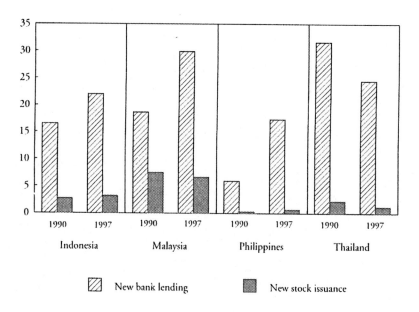

Sources: CEIC; IMF

China, relative to other stock markets such as those of India, Malaysia and Korea. Similarly, the development of the Jakarta stock exchange (see Appendix) increased Indonesia's weighting from 0 per cent in 1987 to 8 per cent in 1996, before falling back to 2 per cent in 1997. The number of corporate listings in Indonesia has also been dramatic, climbing from only 24 in 1987 to 287 as of April 1998. The smaller

Figure 5.5 Asian market capitalisation, 1987–97 (% of world)

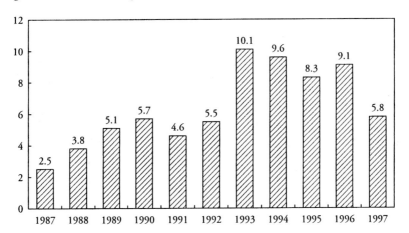

Sources: IFC; Goldman Sachs estimate

weightings on Indonesia, Malaysia and Korea in 1997 are a result of the severe depreciations of these countries' currencies, decreasing their market capitalisation in US dollar terms.

THE RISE OF DOMESTIC FORCES

The greater importance of Asian markets has been a function of many factors. The *initial* surge in these markets was a result of domestic, not outside, pressures. These pressures arose from a desire to increase the supply of stocks (to maintain levels of investment) as well as from increased demand from holders of wealth looking to invest their moneys in higher-yielding investments.

On the supply side, the rapid growth in Asia beginning after the oil shock of the mid-1970s meant an increased need for funds to finance further expansion, and the issuance of equity provided a fairly untapped source of capital. The desire to privatise state-owned enterprises as countries made an effort to streamline bureaucracies also led to further expansion of stock markets from the supply side, especially in the 1990s. On the demand side, the amount of domestic savings rose with GDP growth, as workers had greater income to spend and invest. The stock market served as a good place to put funds, with the hope of garnering a higher return than bank deposits offered. In addition, as some governments had in place forced savings schemes (e.g. the Central Provident Fund in Singapore and the Employee Provident Fund in Malaysia), higher individual incomes boosted the balances in these funds. Much like large pension and mutual funds in other countries, these accounts were also looking for sizeable and liquid investment opportunities.

At the same time, governments realised that fully functioning securities markets were crucial for continued growth in the years ahead. Consequently, nearly every country pushed companies to list on domestic exchanges through various incentive schemes, often ahead of sufficient regulation. As a result, stock market issuance grew

Table 5.1 Non-Japan Asia market capitalisation (%)

	1987	1996	1997	
China	0.0	6.2	15.2	
Hong Kong	27.4	24.6	30.4	
India	8.6	6.7	9.4	
Indonesia	0.0	5.0	2.1	
Korea	16.6	7.6	3.1	
Malaysia	9.4	16.8	6.9	
Philippines	1.5	4.4	2.3	
Singapore	9.1	8.2	7.8	
Taiwan	24.6	15.0	21.1	
Thailand	2.8	5.5	1.7	
Total	100.0	100.0	100.0	

Sources: IFC 1997; Goldman Sachs estimate

rapidly during times of economic growth. For Korea and Taiwan, the first surge in new equity issuance was in the 1970s and 1980s (Figure 5.6). For Indonesia and Malaysia, the surge generally came later, in the 1990s, as economic growth picked up in tandem with accelerated growth throughout the region.

FOREIGN PARTICIPATION IN EQUITY MARKETS

With economic performance so strong, beginning in the 1970s, and Asian markets more established as a result of the build-up domestically, restrictions on foreign ownership were gradually eased. This allowed companies to tap into greater financing than was available domestically. The timing of these openings was fortuitous, as interest in investing abroad increased dramatically in the 1980s.

James Van Horne (1990) points to a number of reasons leading to the surge in funds from developed countries looking to invest in emerging markets (and Asia, in particular). First, the low inflation environment in the mid- to late-1980s, following the high rates seen at the end of the 1970s, made financial assets (equities and bonds) more attractive than 'hard' assets such as real estate and commodities. Second, deregulation in the financial services industry globally led to a reduction of barriers for foreign capital and the creation of many more financial products. Third, volatility in interest and exchange rates increased dramatically, leading investors to look to diversify their portfolios and to reduce risk exposure. On top of these developments, rapid technological advances increased the rate of information flow, streamlined and simplified the settlement process, and reduced costs per transaction. To these factors can be added a greater interest in taking part in the high growth rates seen in Asia, as developed nations were deluged with information painting Asia as the paragon of rapid growth and development.

These developments in the 1980s became even more important in investment decisions in the 1990s, as is evident in figures for the purchase of foreign equities.

Figure 5.6 New capital raised (% of GDP)

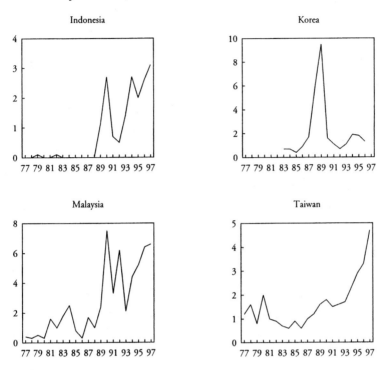

Sources: CEIC; IMF, *International Financial Statistics*

While the flow of funds abroad in the 1980s appeared large relative to historical standards, it became a tidal wave in the 1990s as global investing really came to the fore. Figure 5.7 shows aggregate net flows into foreign stocks from the United States and Japan. In the United States, the net purchase of stocks has steadily increased, with the most notable exceptions being the third quarter of 1987, when the US stock market crash led to a net liquidation of foreign positions, and the fourth quarter of 1997 in the wake of the Asian crisis. Net flows from Japan have been more volatile, as the economy has suffered a greater number of domestic shocks in the 1990s, ranging from Bank of Japan Governor Mieno's increase in interest rates in 1990, to the 1995 Kobe earthquake and the current banking crisis. In both countries, the volume of net purchases has more than doubled in the last ten years.

In theory, increased foreign inflows would be associated with rising stock market returns. To test this hypothesis, a comparison was made between quarterly international flows and stock market returns. As international flow data are lacking across countries, data on quarterly net flows into the Asian countries from the United States were used as a proxy. Stock market returns were calculated as the percentage change in the index share price over the quarter (i.e. the change from the 31 March index level over the 31 December level). This calculation excludes dividend payments, which reduces returns, but with dividends generally low this should not substantively alter our findings. The results (Figure 5.8) prove inconclusive, however. Only in Hong Kong, Singapore, Thailand and Malaysia have greater foreign inflows been associated with increased returns. To more accurately quantify the impacts of foreign investment, the quarterly returns on the US net flows were regressed and the interest rate spread over the London interbank offered rate (LIBOR, which is used to control for the opportunity cost of investing in the domestic stock market).

The fund flows were found to be significant only for Hong Kong, Malaysia and Thailand (Table 5.2). The coefficients are marked in bold, with their t-statistics displayed just below. The coefficient on US flows represents the impact on quarterly stock returns of an inflow of US$1 billion of foreign funds, and the coefficient on the interest spread shows the impact on quarterly returns of a 100 basis point increase in the interest spread over three-month LIBOR. The high coefficients on US flows for Malaysia and Thailand demonstrate the lower importance foreign flows play in these markets and the smaller market capitalisation for them as well (US$1 billion represents 0.2 per cent of Hong Kong's market capitalisation as of February 1998, 0.8 per cent of Malaysia's and 2.6 per cent of Thailand's). The larger negative effect of an increase in the interest rate spreads for Hong Kong versus Thailand (in Malaysia, this coefficient is not significant) reflects the greater interest rate sensitivity of Hong Kong's market, mainly because of the larger importance of the property and banking sector in the stock index but it is also a function of the linked-exchange rate system for the Hong Kong dollar. The low R-squared values demonstrate that interest rates and foreign inflows do not fully explain stock market returns, but this comes as no surprise. The lack of any marked correlation for the other markets is likely to be the result of greater limitations on foreign participation. The Hong Kong, Malaysia and Thailand markets tend to have greater capital account openness and greater liquidity, which attract a greater share of foreign investments. Our inability to find any quantifiable relationship in Singapore is curious and may be the result of a greater importance of regional flows rather than ones from developed markets, as proxied by the United States.

RECENT EXPERIENCES AND OUTLOOK

By the mid-1990s, Asian stock markets all had opened up to some degree to allow foreign participation (see Appendix). Many of the stock markets were privatised and all countries had regulatory bodies in place to ensure fair dealings in the market. The various regulations that governed market activity had come about largely in the aftermath of domestic crashes, and 'up' appeared to be the only direction in which stocks could go. This market buoyancy fuelled a rapid expansion of both their formal and informal financial sectors. In Hong Kong and Thailand, for example, some people quit their full-time jobs to follow stocks, and informal stock brokers with a briefcase and portable computer could be found on street corners to serve the masses. Starting in 1994, however, the Thai and Korean markets began to turn south without looking back.

Figure 5.7 New purchase of foreign stocks, 1977–97

United States

US$ billion

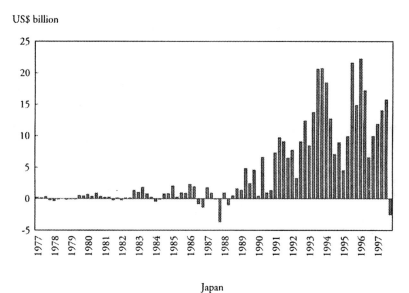

Japan

US$ million

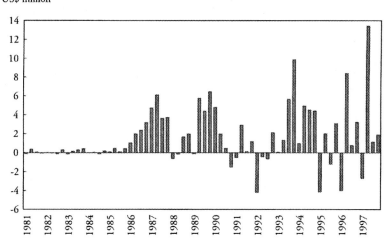

Sources: US Department of Treasury; Bank of Japan

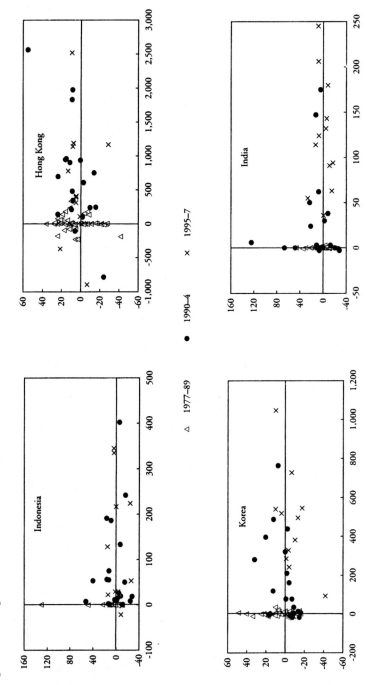

Figure 5.8 Change in stock indices, 1977–97 (%)

Figure 5.8 (continued)

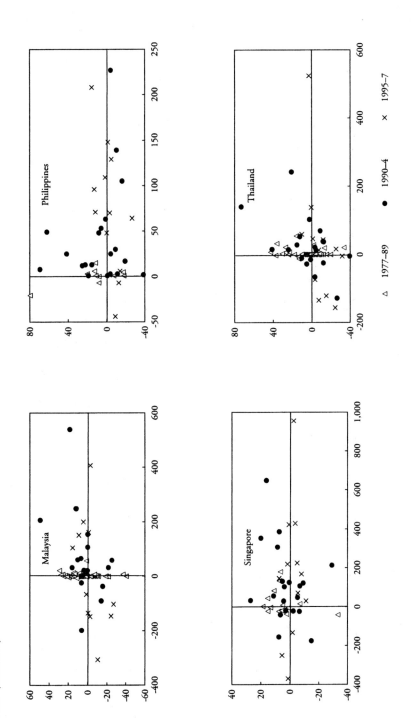

Note: y axis=US net purchases (US$)
Sources: US Department of Treasury; CEIC

Table 5.2 Regression results

	US flows	Interest spread	R-squared
Hong Kong	**9.2**	**−3.4**	10.2
	3.53	−2.06	
Malaysia	**42.8**	**−0.7**	11.7
	2.83	−0.98	
Thailand	**77.3**	**−1.1**	11.8
	2.98	−2.29	

Note: Coefficients are in bold; t-statistics below
Source: Goldman Sachs estimate

While the absolute peak for Singapore and Malaysia is also in 1994, both these countries rebounded with a second peak in February 1996 and 1997, respectively, that was just shy of the 1994 high (see Figures 29 and 30 in the Appendix). All other markets have fallen as well, following the trail blazed by Thailand and Korea. The largest decline from its peak in both local currency and US dollar terms, as of 30 April 1998, is Thailand (Table 5.3). The rupiah's depreciation makes Indonesia the next most affected market in US dollar terms, while Korea is next on a local currency basis.

These market downturns reflected a number of factors, not the least of which was slower growth prospects. As markets are forward-looking, a decrease in the expectation of GDP growth will lead to a decline in the stock market as prospects for corporate growth are reduced. This is especially true for foreign investors who are chasing ever-higher returns. To examine the changing perceptions of growth prospects in the region, current and next-year forecasts from Consensus Economics beginning in 1995 were examined for four of the hardest-hit Asian nations: Korea, Indonesia, Malaysia and Thailand (Figure 5.9). For every country, it appears that stock market declines are accompanied by downward forecast revisions.

Given reduced growth prospects in the coming years, Asian stock markets are likely to post lacklustre performances. This is supported by a study on market crashes by Sandeep Patel and Asani Sarkar (1998) who found that emerging stock markets tend to have quick and steep crises, followed by long recovery periods. On average, they found that it takes emerging markets three years to recover from a crash and that Asian markets tend to take longer than Latin American markets. As per returns during the recovery period, they found a median return of −9 per cent (in US dollar terms, on an annual basis) over the three recovery years. During this period, we have seen and expect to continue to see dramatic changes in Asian markets. In an effort to recapitalise companies and attract foreign currency, many countries have revamped foreign ownership restrictions; Korea, for example, fully removed the limit on foreign ownership. Even more reforms can be expected: revamped regulations on accounting standards, disclosure requirements and transaction transparency are all likely.

Another outgrowth of the current equity market downturn will be the continued rise of other methods of raising capital, especially equity. Mergers and acquisitions,

Table 5.3 Stock market returns

	Peak since 1992		30 April 1998		
	Date	*Index value*	*Index value*	*% change (local currency)*	*% change (US$)*
Bangkok SET	4-Jan-94	1,753.7	412.1	−76.5	−84.5
Singapore DBS50	4-Jan-94	634.0	420.5	−33.7	−32.8
Kuala Lumpur Composite	5-Jan-94	1,314.5	626.0	−52.4	−66.6
KOSPI	8-Nov-94	1,138.8	421.2	−63.0	−77.9
Philippines Composite	3-Feb-97	3,447.6	2,181.3	−36.7	−58.4
China: Shanghai	12-May-97	1,500.4	1,343.4	−10.5	−10.0
China: Shenzhen	12-May-97	518.1	413.3	−20.2	−19.8
Jakarta Composite	8-Jul-97	740.8	460.1	−37.9	−81.7
India	5-Aug-97	4,458.0	4,006.8	−11.9	−20.8
Hang Seng	7-Aug-97	16,673.3	10,383.7	−37.7	−37.7
TWSE	26-Aug-97	10,116.8	8,304.2	−17.9	−28.5

Note: On 5 February 1996, the Singapore DBS50 reached 618.6, and on 25 February 1997 the Kuala Lumpur Composite Index rose to 12,171.6, both just below their 1994 highs
Sources: CEIC; IMF

debt–equity swaps and private equity placement are all areas that are underdeveloped and underutilised. However, with market liberalisation, activity in these three areas has expanded. While much of the evidence for this is colloquial, data for private placements show a rise in funds under management in Asia and a dramatic shift towards funds in non-Japan Asia, as the Japanese economy has remained stagnant (see Figure 5.10). Total funds under management in Asia increased from US$21,925 million in 1991 to US$38,375 million by September 1997, a compounded annual increase of nearly 10 per cent.

The desire of a company to attract funds for growth through channels other than public debt or equity markets has increased over the years. Initially, underdeveloped capital markets led to thin markets in which to raise money, so attracting private funds without going to public markets was an easier way to tap into funds. Listing requirements may also sometimes prohibit equity issuance for medium-sized firms in newly developed businesses, especially in Asia where private companies might not have the resources to meet requirements generally set for larger, government-sponsored companies. Another attraction for a company is outside expertise. As companies grow and compete more in the global marketplace, having a partner who has greater experience or good networks can prove to be an advantage. Finally, the very structure of many businesses in Asia – closely held and family-built – lends itself to private equity placement. This form of investment tends to leave the existing management intact and is less disruptive to current business practices. All of these factors are even more enticing in times of an economic downturn, like now, as equity

Figure 5.9 Consensus GDP and the stock index

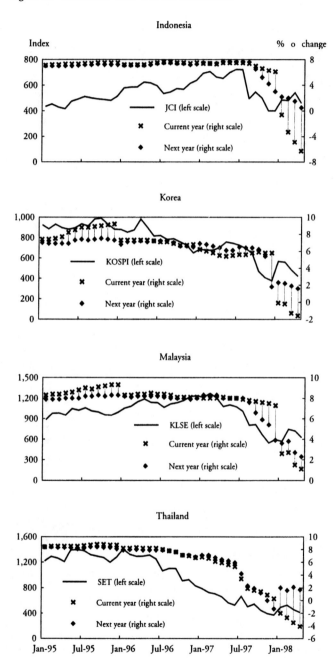

Sources: Consensus Economics; CEIC

Figure 5.10 Asian venture capital pool, 1991–7 (US$m)

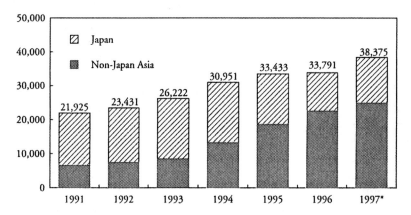

Note: * = All-Asia data for September 1997; shares from June 1997
Source: Asian Venture Capital Journal

prices are low and markets tend to be less liquid, so public equity or debt issuance tends to be more difficult.

For investors, private placement or other means of investing in a company other than buying stock or bonds can be very advantageous as well. As detailed information is sometimes difficult to find on publicly available companies, it may be easier to perform due diligence and easier to make learned investments through direct investment. Once discussions are underway about investment, more data and information can be provided than might be available to an individual investor in public equity markets. This is especially true if the investment can be made through a longstanding personal or family contact. Traditionally, this was how a lot of business was done in Asia. Already knowing somebody from a company allows, in many ways, an investor to sidestep some of the difficulties that Modigliani and Perotti (1991) mention, since the investor has better information than other market participants and knows whether agreements will be upheld.

The development of public markets, itself, has also fed the growth in private equity placement. This is especially true for venture capital, as the purpose of this type of investment is to invest for a few years and then divest, usually through an initial public offering or debt issuance. Consequently, having more established and liquid markets as well as a wider array of financial instruments opens up many more 'exit strategies' to investors. This is further enhanced with the reduction of barriers on foreign investing, which not only allows foreign participation in domestic markets, thus adding liquidity, but also broadens the possible investor base when selling equity.

The raising of funds for private equity placement in Asia has continued through the fray of 1997 into 1998. As of March 1998, there were 51 venture capital funds in the market, attempting to raise a total of US$9,557 million. This amount is 14 per cent higher than one year earlier, when 43 funds were trying to raise US$8,402 million. These figures show that the pace of investment activity has not slackened, even though market and exchange rate volatility have risen. The little data available on mergers and acquisitions also point to vigorous activity. In the ten months January to October 1997, there were 430 merger and acquisition deals within the Asian region, compared with 212 during the same period in 1996 (*Asian Venture Capital Journal*).

The growth of private direct investment should continue even as markets tumble further, since investors in these out-of-market mediums have longer investment horizons and barriers to foreign ownership are likely to continue to fall. These factors will lead to many investment opportunities that appear profitable only when looking ahead to a return of high growth rates.

CONCLUSION

In the development of Asian security markets, equity markets have played an increasingly important role for financing as the economies grew. They have also become an important means through which foreigners can directly participate in the economic growth of the region. While our quantitative work fails to show a definitive positive correlation between net foreign flows and stock returns in the same quarter, many international investors are taking advantage of historic lows in both currencies and stock markets to make long-term investments in Asia. As the region emerges from its current crisis and expectations of growth pick up, stock markets will once again turn around, with additional domestic and foreign inflows as well as increased equity issuance. In the meantime, private equity placement is likely to take a greater role as companies as well as investors find this method of raising/investing funds more advantageous than turning to public markets. At the same time, countries are taking, and should continue to take, this opportunity to reform their financial markets to increase regulatory transparency and corporate disclosure. These steps during the current downturn will lead to stronger and more liquid markets at the end of these tough times.

APPENDIX: A BRIEF HISTORY OF ASIAN EQUITY MARKETS

Stock markets in Asia have a very long history. India is Asia's oldest stock exchange, where capital market transactions outside of a formal exchange date back to when stocks of the East India Company were traded at the end of the eighteenth century. In 1850 the Companies Act led to a build-up in securities that culminated in the dramatic rise in share prices between 1860 and 1865 when the US Civil War disrupted the supply of cotton to Europe (George 1991). The reduced supply ballooned Indian company share prices. With the end of hostilities in the United States, share prices came tumbling down, leading to what may have been Asia's first crash in securities prices. While not all countries have had such long histories with securities trading, the nature and regulation of stock markets have changed dramatically over time, with the most rapid changes occurring in the last ten years.

The timing, pace and nature of the development of the different regional stock exchanges has varied by country, as the demand for equity capital markets has arisen for disparate reasons. In former colonies of Great Britain, stock markets usually developed earliest, arising out of the informal trading of foreign shares, while for other countries the markets emerged out of a need for new venues for raising capital. The different paths to stock market development have been associated with varying rules for foreign participation. To delineate the different approaches to stock market development, the countries are examined in three categories: markets of former British colonies, markets influenced by foreigners, and indigenous stock markets. Markets in the first group of countries (India, Hong Kong, Singapore and Malaysia) mostly grew out of informal trading associations and became incorporated and regulated between 1950 and 1980. Markets in the second group, which comprises Indonesia and the Philippines, have their roots in the Dutch and US markets, respectively. They have developed very differently since their inception, however. Finally, what we term 'indigenous' stock markets (Korea, Thailand, Taiwan and China) tended to develop later, generally to be less open to foreign participation and to be less regulated, as well as remaining government-run for much longer.

Markets of former British colonies

India

As already mentioned, India was the first stock market in Asia (excluding Australia) to develop. The first government move to establish a stock market came in 1850 with the passage of the Companies Act, which led to increased interest in and issuance of corporate securities. In 1887, the Native Shares and Stock Brokers Association was created and this became the forerunner of the Bombay stock exchange. As security investment progressed, stock exchanges sprang up throughout India, until 1956 when the Securities Contracts (Regulation) Act allowed only exchanges recognised by the government to operate. This legislation led to the government adopting broad oversight responsibilities. The Foreign Exchange Regulation Act of 1973 capped foreign ownership at 40 per cent of companies and required foreign ownership levels to be reduced to this maximum where they were in excess. India accounts for the majority of listed domestic companies in Asia, with the combined number of listings from the 20-plus exchanges totalling about 9,000 companies in 1997.

Hong Kong

The first Companies Ordinance for Hong Kong came in 1866, with a stock exchange established in 1891. It was not until 1914, however, that the name was changed to the Hong Kong stock exchange. Little attention was paid to Hong Kong until the 1960s, however, when domestic interest in stocks rapidly expanded and share prices ran up in 1969–73. The dramatic increase in demand for stocks and shares prompted the establishment of the Far East stock exchange in 1969, the Kam Ngan stock exchange in 1971, and the Kowloon stock exchange in 1972. The expansion of equity issuance and the creation of stock exchanges outpaced the development of regulations. At the time, there were no regulations about even the establishment of stock exchanges. The stock market crash of 1973 led to the passage of the Securities Ordinance and Protection of Investors Ordinance in February 1974. This created the first Securities Commission in Hong Kong to regulate the markets. In 1986, the four stock exchanges were unified into the Stock Exchange of Hong Kong Limited (SEHK), which remains the sole stock exchange. In the following year, the stock market crash of 1987 and the subsequent closing of the SEHK for four days led to the creation of the Securities Review Committee to look over the stock market structure. The outgrowth of this committee was the Securities and Futures Ordinance that created the Securities and Futures Commission, the regulatory body for Hong Kong. This body is modelled after and similar to the Securities and Exchange Commission in the United States and has regulatory power over those companies listed on the SEHK. There are no regulations limiting the foreign ownership of shares.

Singapore

Again, the informal trading of shares in companies predates the establishment of a formal stock exchange. In Singapore, European traders bought and sold shares in European stocks back in the 1920s. However, it was not until June 1973 that the Stock Exchange of Singapore (SES) was established out of the dissolution of the Stock Exchange of Malaysia and Singapore (see below). Until 1 January 1990, Malay and Singaporean companies were still cross-listed on each other's exchanges. From that time, Malaysian shares could no longer be listed on the SES, and vice versa. Foreign shares, however, would be allowed to trade on the Central Limit Order Book (CLOB), which was established at about the same time, and Malay shares dominate this market. As far as foreign ownership goes, there are no specific legal restrictions. However, for companies in industries classified as sensitive, company by-laws incorporate foreign ownership restrictions ranging from 20 per cent to 49 per cent.

Malaysia

The history of equity markets in Malaysia starts in Singapore, with Europeans trading shares with each other. Following independence in 1957 and until 1973, the Stock Exchange of Malaysia and Singapore served as the equity market for both countries. In 1973, the Kuala Lumpur stock exchange (KLSE) was created. Again, like the SES, shares were no longer allowed to be cross-listed after 1 January 1990. Regulations on foreign participation in the KLSE allow for holdings of 30 per cent of Malaysian companies. Ownership of some utilities is not allowed and companies can restrict foreign ownership in their by-laws (Harrison 1997).

Markets influenced by foreigners

Indonesia

The Dutch established a stock exchange in Jakarta in 1912 and in Semarang and Surabaya in 1925. Mostly, shares of Dutch companies were traded on the exchanges until 1958 (except during World War II when the exchanges were closed), when the stock exchanges nearly ceased operation with the nationalisation and delisting of Dutch businesses. Equity markets largely lay fallow until 1976, when the Indonesian government provided tax incentives for the listing of companies on the Jakarta stock exchange (JKSE).

In the same year, the Capital Markets Executive Agency, Badan Pelaksana Pasar Modal (BAPEPAM), was established to regulate and manage the JKSE. Unlike those in former British colonies, the stock exchanges were operated by governments, not by exchange members. In 1987–8, the government adopted many reforms to the JKSE that were targeted at building up the equity market. Reforms also allowed foreign participation in the stock market, with foreigners able to hold up to 49 per cent of listed shares. Further reforms led to a rash of corporate listings in 1990 (see Figure 5.11). However, in an effort to get firms listed, the BAPEPAM did not stringently enforce listing requirements or monitor company claims. As a result, prospectuses were often unreliable as indicators of a company's financial position and investors pulled funds from the market, leading to the stock market crash in late 1990. In 1991, the JKSE was privatised, passing into the hands of its members. BAPEPAM continues to regulate but is no longer involved in day-to-day management of the JKSE. In 1997, amid the economic crisis, restrictions on share ownership were set to be removed as of 30 June 1998.

Figure 5.11 Shares listed on Jakarta stock exchange (listed companies)

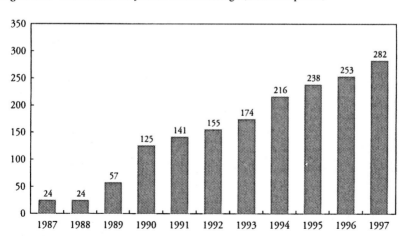

Source: CEIC

Philippines

Following closely behind the creation of stock markets in Indonesia, the Manila stock exchange (MSE) was incorporated in 1927. The Philippines created one of the earliest regulatory bodies for equity markets: the Securities and Exchange Commission in 1936. In 1956, a rival was created: the Makati stock exchange. In 1992, the Philippine stock exchange was established, linking the two exchanges electronically, with all shares traded simultaneously at both locations. Foreign participation is generally limited to 40 per cent and has been allowed since 1973.

Indigenous equity markets

Korea

The Japanese established a securities market in Korea in 1911; this market closed following World War II. While the current market's development has its early roots in that Japanese market, its growth and development has been largely independent of strong outside influences. The Korean stock exchange (KSE) opened in 1956 (originally called the Chosun stock exchange, it was renamed the KSE in 1962). However, it remained largely controlled by the government until it was privatised in 1988. The regulatory body for the KSE, the Security and Exchange Commission, as well as the Securities Supervisory Board which is the enforcement arm of the SEC, were established in 1977. In 1981, foreign participation in the KSE was allowed through international investment trusts. Restrictions on foreign participation have been gradually removed in the 1990s. In 1991, foreign securities' firms could establish branch offices and could get KSE membership. Direct investment by foreign investors was allowed in 1992, and ownership limits were gradually shifted from 10 per cent at that time to 55 per cent for private companies (25 per cent for public ones) by December 1997. There is currently talk of removing the 55 per cent limit altogether in a greater effort to attract foreign capital.

Thailand

The Bangkok stock exchange was founded in 1962 as a private entity. While this incarnation of Thailand's equity market closed in the early 1970s, the Securities Exchange of Thailand Act in 1974 created the Stock Exchange of Thailand under the ownership of the government. The Ministry of Finance was designated as the regulatory body. In 1992, the new Securities and Exchange Act renamed the stock market the Stock Exchange of Thailand (SET) and the Securities and Exchange Commission was created to take over the Ministry of Finance's regulatory role. The Aliens Business Act passed in 1972 limited foreign ownership to 49 per cent for general stocks, and to 25 per cent for commercial banks and finance companies. The turmoil of 1997 has brought with it no change to the written rules regarding ownership restrictions, but the Bank of Thailand appears to be granting exceptions. For instance, foreigners were allowed to hold up to 49 per cent of the Thai Farmers Bank, even though it is a commercial bank. The privatisation of the SET does not appear to be under discussion, however, making Thailand one of the few remaining countries where the stock exchange remains under government control.

Taiwan

The Taiwan stock exchange (TSE) has its roots in the 'land-to-tiller' programs in 1953. This program offered wealthy landowners government bonds and shares in state-owned enterprises (SOEs) in return for the transfer of land to tenant farmers. The trading of these bonds and shares was the beginning of the securities market for Taiwan. More formal steps were taken with the creation of the Securities and Exchange Commission in 1960, one year before the creation of the TSE (Chou and Johnson 1990). As in Korea, steps to allowing foreign participation have been gradual. In 1983, the market was first opened up to very limited foreign investment and, in September 1990, it was opened to foreign institutional investors. Since then, participation has been increasingly allowed. Foreign ownership is limited to 20 per cent. Unlike Korea, where the KSE was fully privatised, the Taiwan government still owns 39 per cent of the TSE, with the remainder held by members of the exchange and corporations.

China

While stock exchanges were established in China in the early 1900s, all of these were closed with the Communist victory and establishment of the People's Republic of China in 1949. It was not until 1990 that formal stock exchanges were once again established in Shanghai and Shenzhen. Initially, both exchanges operated under their own local company and security rules, but, in May 1992, the Standard Opinion of Joint Stock Limited Companies was issued to fill the regulatory void. In 1994, the Company Law superseded the two-year-old legislation. The China Securities Regulatory Commission was established in 1992 as a regulatory body and has attempted to standardise security rules in both Shanghai and Shenzhen. Both stock exchanges are owned by the government. The foreign ownership of shares was allowed in 1991, with the designation of A and B shares. A shares are renminbi-denominated stocks which can be held only by Chinese citizens, while B shares can only be purchased by foreigners and are denominated in US dollars. Another method through which foreigners can access the Chinese market is through H shares. These are stocks issued by Chinese companies but listed on the Hong Kong stock exchange; therefore, they fall under the liberal Hong Kong regulatory framework.

Figure 5.12 Asian stock indices

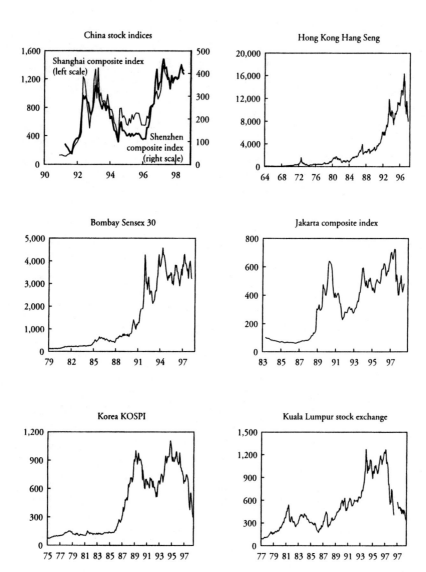

Figure 5.12 (Continued)

Philippines composite index

Singapore DBS50

Taiwan SE weighted

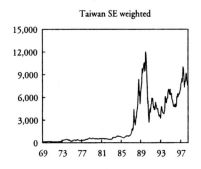

Bangkok SET

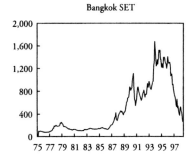

Sources: CEIC; Datastream

REFERENCES

Asian Venture Capital Journal (January 1997–April 1998) Hong Kong: AVCJ Holdings Ltd.
AVCJ Holdings (1997) *The 1998 Guide to Venture Capital in Asia*, Hong Kong: AVCJ Holdings Ltd.
Chou, Shyan-Rong and K.H. Johnson (1990) 'An empirical analysis of stock market anomalies: evidence from the Republic of China in Taiwan', in S.G. Rhee and R.P. Chang (eds) *Pacific-Basin Capital Markets Research*, Amsterdam: Elsevier Science Publishers, 283–312.
George, R.L. (1991) *A Guide to Asian Stock Markets*, Hong Kong: Longman Group (Far East) Ltd.
Harrison, M. (1997) *Asia-Pacific Securities Markets*, 3rd edn, Hong Kong: FT Financial Publishing Asia Pacific.
International Finance Corporation (1997) *Emerging Stock Markets Factbook 1997*, Washington DC: International Finance Corporation.
Korean stock exchange website: <http://www.kse.or.kr>.
Kuala Lumpur stock exchange website: <http://www.klse.com.my>.
Modigliani, F. and E. Perotti (1991) 'The rules of the game and the development of securities markets', in S.G. Rhee and R.P. Chang (eds) *Pacific-Basin Capital Markets Research*, Amsterdam: Elsevier Science Publishers, vol. 2: 49–63.
Patel, S. and A. Sarkar (1998) 'Stock market crises in developed and emerging markets', unpublished working paper.
Stock Exchange of Thailand website: <http://www.set.or.th>.
Van Horne, J. (1990) 'Changing world and Asian financial markets', in S.G. Rhee and R.P. Chang (eds) *Pacific-Basin Capital Markets Research*, Amsterdam: Elsevier Science Publishers, 65–80.

6 Tokyo, Hong Kong and Singapore as competing financial centres

Manuel F. Montes

INTRODUCTION

In the 1990s, Asia's share of international capital flows increased dramatically. Most of this rapid increase was, of course, due to the increase in the capture by Asia's developing countries of these flows. In the 1990s, it is also notable that private flows overwhelmingly explain this dramatic increase. Total net capital flows to East Asia and the Pacific increased from US$26.5 billion in 1990 to US$105.3 billion in 1995 (Reidel 1997). In the same period, net official flows barely increased, from US$6.1 billion to US$7.2 billion, while private flows increased four times, from US$20.4 billion to US$90.3 billion (Table 6.1). Of these private capital flows, portfolio flows increased five times in the same period (from US$2.2 billion to US$12.2 billion).

The emergence of international financial centres is highly reflected in the extent to which Asian flows have become heavily weighted by portfolio and bond flows. Table 6.2 indicates that, for China, portfolio flows increased by six times between 1991 and 1994 (US$653 million to US$3.9 billion). For the Asian economies, 1993 was a particularly strong year of inflow, being the year before the Mexican crisis. South Korea received portfolio flows of US$6 billion in 1993 alone. For six countries in East Asia, (net) bond flows increased from US$1.5 billion in 1991 to US$13 billion in 1994 (Table 6.3). The inflow of net bond flows to Thailand between 1992 and 1994 is particularly striking, increasing 6.8 times, from US$548 million to US$3.8 billion. During this period, Thailand was rapidly expanding its activities as an international financial centre. Its subsequent crisis in 1997 points to the perils that often accompany rapid development in the finance industry.

The emergence of international centres is an unavoidable consequence of these dramatic increases in capital flows to and within the region. Tokyo emerged first as an international financial centre, buoyed by Japan's abundance of domestic savings and, in the 1980s, the rising international value of the yen. Tokyo made its initial mark with the flotation of 'samurai' bonds, first by international financial institutions such as the

World Bank. Hong Kong had served as a regional headquarters for many international companies since the mid-1960s. Its emergence as a financial centre, especially in the 1970s, was due to this early development as a multinational headquarters location and to its relatively unregulated stance, drastically revised in the 1980s, in regard to financial activities. Singapore's efforts began in 1972, with the establishment of rules for setting up Asian currency units (ACUs) and, with state encouragement and support, it has experienced steady growth and development.

This chapter considers the issues attendant on this emergence of three international financial centres in Asia. It investigates their status and evaluates their possible evolution.

Table 6.1 Net long-term capital flows, 1970–95 (US$m)

	1970	1980	1990	1991	1992	1993	1994	1995
All LDCs								
Net capital flows	9,160	75,137	72,540	89,504	123,365	177,929	174,932	198,580
Official flows	3,334	21,848	28,523	27,920	23,980	23,944	16,144	31,417
Private flows	5,768	53,288	44,107	81,514	109,275	154,285	158,788	167,164
Bonds	n.a.	n.a.	2,980	12,833	13,178	38,342	32,163	n.a.
Comm. banks	2,344	34,827	1,721	2,475	13,757	–4,867	9,167	33,391
FDI	2,268	5,098	25,009	34,978	46,510	68,261	60,120	90,346
Portfolio equity	0	0	3,743	7,552	14,957	45,616	34,894	22,001
Other private	1,154	13,363	10,584	3,676	12,673	6,933	2,444	212,426
East Asia & Pacific								
Net capital flows	1,444	11,957	26,529	32,434	51,035	70,889	82,308	105,343
Official flows	614	3,040	6,103	6,238	6,349	8,011	5,019	7,254
Private flows	830	8,917	20,427	26,135	44,586	62,878	80,120	90,346
Bonds	n.a.	n.a.	243	3,312	2,832	8,485	13,200	n.a.
Comm. banks	447	5,249	4,666	5,951	8,808	–3,895	3,385	23,203
FDI	267	1,318	10,968	13,890	21,988	27,872	43,037	53,703
Portfolio equity	0	0	2,268	1,049	5,102	18,107	12,613	12,230
Other private	116	2,350	2,282	1,933	6,276	2,309	5,054	8,953

Notes: 1995 is preliminary. Net capital flows are defined as net resource flows less grants. Regional aggregates of the World Bank rather than the selected East and South Asian countries which appear in the tables below
Sources: Reidel 1997, table 1; World Bank, *World Debt Tables*, 1996

Table 6.2 Portfolio equity flows, 1990–4 (US$m)

	1990	*1991*	*1992*	*1993*	*1994*
East Asia (6)	1,572	1,039	5,080	18,042	2,301
South Korea	518	345	3,045	6,029	2,525
China	0	653	1,194	2,278	3,915
Indonesia	312	0	119	1,836	3,672
Malaysia	293	0	385	3,700	1,320
Philippines	0	0	333	1,082	1,407
Thailand	449	41	4	3,117	−538

Sources: Reidel 1997, table 4; World Bank, *World Debt Tables*, 1996

Table 6.3 Net bond flows, 1990–4 (US$m)

	1990	*1991*	*1992*	*1993*	*1994*
East Asia (6)	−372	1,460	2,047	8,679	12,981
South Korea	168	2,722	2,560	3,694	4,157
China	−48	24	−3	2,238	2,876
Indonesia	−588	−1,475	−632	197	269
Malaysia	−212	143	−374	44	976
Philippines	395	124	−52	734	927
Thailand	−87	−78	548	1,772	3,776

Note: Net bond flows are from private creditors and include both publicly guaranteed and non-guaranteed flows
Sources: Reidel 1997, table 6; World Bank, *World Debt Tables*, 1996

NATURE OF AND REQUIREMENTS FOR INTERNATIONAL FINANCIAL CENTRES

The emergence of an international financial centre usually depends on locational, infrastructural and human resource advantages.

Types of financial markets

Financial markets can be summarised as being of four types, according to the kinds of intermediation provided:

- type 1 (D→D): intermediates between domestic providers of capital and domestic users of capital;

- type 2 (F→D): intermediates between foreign providers of capital and domestic users of capital;

- type 3 (D→F): intermediates between domestic providers of capital and foreign users of capital; and

- type 4 (F→F): intermediates between foreign providers of capital and foreign users of capital.

Type 1 comprises purely domestic intermediation. To be an international financial centre, one has to exhibit expanded participation in types 2 to 4. The most elementary provision of trade credits is in type 2, which says that all financial markets share some of the features of an international financial centre. It is the wideness and the richness of intermediation activities in types 2 to 4 that identify an international financial centre.

In the subsequent discussion, the nature of financial centres will be considered in terms of the three levels in increasing sophistication in intermediation activities: bank lending, bond finance and equity finance. Bank lending relies heavily on project finance and the direct involvement of providers of capital in developing and financing projects. In bond finance, project financing can be sold to capital providers that are not necessarily specialised in providing finance. Potentially, the most 'arms-length' relationship between capital provider and user is in equity finance.

Historically, and in the case of developing countries, it is not necessarily the case that financial intermediation has naturally progressed from bank finance to equity finance. In the most informal and localised economic systems, equity finance is the most convenient, as long as the interest of equity owners can be reliably enforced. Bond markets have had difficulty emerging when national governments have not incurred fiscal deficits, as in the case of Thailand and Singapore. In developing countries, bank finance has traditionally grown out of providing credits for international trade or through the establishment of development finance institutions (using public resources). Consequently, the privatisation of bank finance and its movement out of traditional lending for trade activities is often a large step forward, requiring not only expanded financial resources but capabilities on the part of banking staff to evaluate and monitor loan projects. It is these kinds of evaluation and monitoring capabilities that are critical in the emergence of modern bond and equity markets.

The international financial centres in London and New York evolved from the large domestic financial base and the international involvement of companies based there. This is the progression that Hong Kong seems to following. So a large domestic financial base provides a strong predisposition to the development of a financial centre. For the set of international financial markets to thrive in a location, a regulatory framework and a supporting legal system are required.

Elements of absolute advantage

Discussions regarding the basic requirements for the emergence of international financial centres usually revolve around: locational advantages; human resource capabilities; and business and physical infrastructure. While many countries and cities might have a large domestic financial base and many companies operating internationally, the establishment of activities which are by their nature of an international financial character requires some infrastructural underpinnings. In evaluating financial centres with regard to these basic preconditions, the following criteria seem to be important:

1 Market efficiency

- low transactions costs (including taxes and commissions)
- no excessive restrictions on transactions

2 Market innovation

- high level of activity in basic research on financial instruments
- high level of activity in introduction of new products and services

3 Human infrastructure

- accounting and legal services
- fund managers and people with skills in financial and securities business

4 Language

- English as key language in international financial transactions

5 Concentration of financial institutions

- large number of institutions located in a relatively small area, providing ease of information exchange and meetings

6 Political stability

7 Business infrastructure

- low office rent and other business expenses
- low corporate taxes
- well-developed communications and information networks
- well-developed transportation and urban infrastructure

8 Quality of life

- low cost of living
- good schools, ready access to cultural events and entertainment

The advance of technology implies that financial services do not necessarily have to be located where their sources or users of capital are. Given an adequate communications infrastructure, financial services will seek to be located where the human input into the service activity can be provided at lowest cost and at maximum productivity (see *Economist* 1998 for an excellent discussion of the basic preconditions for financial centres). 'Lowest cost' depends on tax rates and incentives, the cost of living, and the availability of family amenities for the highly educated personnel required by these centres. 'Maximum productivity' depends on convenient and comfortable conditions of work but, more importantly, on the access to information and interaction among the participants in international financial markets. Competition and the imperative to respond to financing problems provoke innovation in financial products in the industry. The accessibility of interaction is important to raise competitive pressures and to identify financing problems that might be responded to through new products and arrangements.

Considering comparative advantage

Analysis of these considerations has tended to focus on the elements of absolute advantage of different cities as opposed to those of comparative advantage. Because our interest is in predicting the location of an economic good that is internationally traded, comparative advantage provides a firmer basis for such an analysis. Comparative advantage necessitates consideration of the relative cost of economic activities within a location, calling upon the possibility that the steepness of internal trade-offs could make trade between different locations in these activities beneficial for each of these trading locations.

In applying such a theory to international trade in financial services, one first runs into problems of determining the level of aggregation or product definition. Should comparative advantage considerations emphasise the internal trade-offs between financial services versus, say, manufacturing or other services? Probably not, since the most important competing input for this industry would be labour. If the type of labour used in financial services is specialised enough not to be an important input to manufacturing or other services, and if the type of labour required to carry out international financial services does not have to be obtained from the domestic labour force and could be competitively sourced from world markets, then the importance of domestic trade-offs at this level of aggregation is not that important.

This suggests that it is more useful to think about comparative advantage in terms of the different activities within the financial services area. One could think in terms of the various market segments in financial services, the different stages of production of the financial services, and the different kinds of instruments. It is beyond the scope of this chapter to comprehensively discuss these comparative advantage considerations, but the following elements suggest themselves as important in this regard:

• One key consideration is the cost trade-off between providing domestic financial services and providing international financial services. The cost of providing domestic services depends on the fierceness of internal competition and on the impact of domestic prudential and tax regulations. For example, a highly oligopolised domestic banking system with high fees for domestic customers could encourage 'trade' which encourages domestic residents to transfer some of their normally domestic banking activities overseas.

• The cost of registering bond and equity placements could differ between locations and encourage the transfer of one segment to overseas providers. One recent example is that of Thailand before its 1997 crisis. Rules of equity placements tended to be extremely strict, and the costs of corporate bond offering relatively smaller; this drew a lot of foreign capital into the latter.

• The design and negotiation of loan and underwriting projects is a stage in the provision of financial services. The initial marketing of the financial instruments from this project could be thought of as another stage, even while accepting that there is a lot of coordination between these two activities. Participation in the secondary markets for these instruments is still another stage. The steepness in cost differences between these 'stages' of production can encourage an external 'trade' in these services.

• The level of aggregation could even be finer and it would be possible for more than one or two financial centres to be providing international services based on differences in domestic cost advantages. For those locations with the ambition of becoming a large international financial centre, these cost differences will exert significant pressure on tax structures and regulatory practices.

Brief surveys of the specific conditions in three financial centres – Tokyo, Hong Kong and Singapore – follow.

TOKYO

Tokyo is the largest financial market in the region. Table 6.4 indicates that the amount of base plus quasi-money circulating in Japan is 14 times that in Hong Kong and 63 times that in Singapore; the Japanese economy is 28 times that of Hong Kong and 46 times that of Singapore. In the 1980s, Tokyo had been expected to naturally progress into the world's third most important international financial centre (along with New York and London). That this presumption is now subject to doubt and that Hong Kong and Singapore are challenging Tokyo's pre-eminence speaks to the failure of Japan to take advantage of its early lead in the region.

The principal reason for Tokyo's stumble was the heavy regulation of its financial markets, even after it attained its international standing. Japan's domestic financial system was characterised by strict differentiation among specialisations, and rules about what kinds of activities each type of financial institution could engage in. These characteristics constituted excessive restrictions on transactions, which in the

Table 6.4 Key comparative statistics, 1996 (US$b)

	Singapore	Hong Kong	Tokyo
Domestic economy (GDP)	94.7	154.5	4,313.0
Base money level	18.5	28.1	1,621.9
As ratio of GDP (%)	20.4	18.2	37.7
Base money+quasi-money level	76.6	327.4	4,841.8
As ratio of GDP (%)	84.4	211.8	112.3
Stock markets			
Capitalisation	215.5	449.4	2,996.4
Turnover	63.5	182.6	837.0

Sources: IMF, *International Financial Statistics*; Bank of Japan Research and Statistics Department, *Economic Statistics Monthly*; Hong Kong Monetary Authority, *Hong Kong Monthly Digest of Statistics*; Monetary Authority of Singapore, *Monthly Statistical Bulletin*

financial area always involved some form of transformation from one type of financial asset to another. Brokers fees and commissions were set by regulation, making the cost of transactions rather high. Restrictions on interest rates created rigidities in the kinds of projects that could be financed by the banking system. Restrictions on foreign exchange transactions (through taxes and transaction fees that discouraged foreigners from holding Japanese bonds, and through restrictions on which banks could engage in exchange transactions) also raised the cost of transformation into and out of yen-denominated financial assets.

These kinds of regulations would be consistent with development-oriented finance. In such an approach, the financial system supports industrial development and is a handmaiden to industry. The development of the financial system itself is not important and the capacity of the financial system to identify and develop capital projects is not critical since this function is carried out in the sphere of industrial policy.

In terms of the typology described above, this stance towards the financial system focuses mainly on type 1 (domestic-to-domestic) intermediation; because of Japan's high savings rate, it did not really require type 2 activities. The approach was thus not conducive to the development of an international financial centre, even though the savings rate was so high that type 3 activities (domestic savers financing external users) could occur, providing Tokyo with its first claim as an international centre.

The result has been that, in the 1980s, even bond flotations by Japanese companies were increasingly being undertaken outside of Tokyo. In 1980, Japan's stock markets represented 17 per cent of total world market capitalisation. This peaked at 46 per cent in 1988 but has since declined, to about 17 per cent in 1997. The recent decline is also attributed to the losses experienced in the financial system as a result of the bursting of the bubble economy created by the initial attempts at financial regulation in the mid-1980s.

As part of its so-called 'big bang' reforms, Japan intends to carry out a thorough deregulation of its financial services industry by 2001. It has been steadily liberalising its financial sector since the late 1980s (Taniuchi 1997). It gradually deregulated interest rates after 1984 in line with the Japan–US agreement of that year. Securities companies are allowed to provide banking services. Commercial banks can offer long-term deposits (up to three years in 1991, five years in 1994, and no limit in 1995).

Reforms in 1994 focused on relaxing the separation of activities between different types of financial institutions, allowing them to enter other industries by setting up subsidiaries (Taniuchi 1997). Securities companies, 100 per cent subsidiaries of major banks, have begun to operate. Because of their smaller size, regional banks and other small institutions are permitted to enter the trust business without setting up subsidiaries. In turn, major securities companies and banks have started trust bank subsidiaries. Subsequent reforms will have to:

- remove controls on brokerage fees and restrict cartel price setting in insurance premia;

- remove composition restrictions on the investments of insurance companies and pension funds;

- ease restrictions on the relationship between parent and subsidiary, retaining only those directly concerned with removing conflicts of interest;

- liberalise restrictions on holding companies; and

- rely more on risk-based capital adequacy measures in monitoring bank operations.

In 1997, it became legal to establish non-financial holding companies in Japan. In April 1998, entry into foreign exchange transactions was liberalised and regulations on cross-border transactions removed. Banks are now also allowed to sell mutual funds. Fees on stock trading of 50 million yen or more have been deregulated. The system of prior approval and licensing in the introduction of new financial products has been replaced by simple registration. In 1999, all regulations on commissions in stock trades will be abolished.

What are Tokyo's prospects for becoming an international financial centre? Using the four-type classification presented earlier, it will probably become one in the next decade, but the scope of its international financial intermediation will be relatively small.

The major reforms are expected to result in a noticeable increase in Japanese domestic savings being invested overseas, especially with the relaxation of foreign exchange rules and the reduction of fund management costs. However, this will mean, in actuality, that the fund management of savings will stay in Japan, so that the overwhelming effect will be in the growth of domestic-to-domestic (type 1) markets in Japan. The fund management business will probably place these funds in other international markets, including in Hong Kong and Singapore. The actual value-added of the financial activities, including the creation of new instruments to soak up the savings, will be in Tokyo. An intensification of the activities of international financial companies in Tokyo has already begun and will accelerate in the future. For Japan, therefore, the ample supply of domestic savings will be overwhelmingly intermediated within its own domestic financial system, albeit with the strong participation of international companies.

Historically, Japanese savings financed required development projects. Logically, liberalisation of the financial sector should permit this subservient relationship to be weakened and savers' demands for higher returns should enjoy a larger influence over the kinds of investments financed. Competition from external investment outlets and the ageing of the Japanese population will exert pressures in this regard.

HONG KONG

Until 1964, almost anyone who could pay the licence fee and the annual fee could set up a bank in Hong Kong, that is, accept money deposits and offer any interest rate deemed suitable. Between 1954 and 1964, the unregulated banking sector experienced rapid growth, with deposits growing 5.1 times and loans increasing by a factor of 8.99 times (Chen and Ng 1998: 12). Equity markets were very rudimentary, even though anyone could also set up a stock exchange. Banks provided 32–39 per cent of investment expenditure, the rest being raised from personal savings. A revised banking ordinance issued in 1964 increased supervision over banks, just a year before a major banking crisis which proved that the 1964 restrictions were inadequate. The 1967 regulations instituted a moratorium on the issuance of new bank licences (which lasted until 1981, except for some eighteen months after March 1978) in order to dampen excessive competition in the banking industry. It called for the doubling of minimum paid-up capital from HK$5 million to HK$10 million and of the annual licence fee for banks from HK$7,500 to HK$15,000.

After 1964, banks agreed among themselves to set maximum interest rates for deposits. This spurred the rapid growth of finance companies, which served also as a means by which international banks could enter the Hong Kong market in the face of the moratorium on banking licences. The regulation of finance companies was instituted in 1976. Out of the 2,000 in existence in 1973, only 200 could meet the registration requirements (Chen and Ng 1998: 14). A more comprehensive regulatory framework was put in place in 1981 (two years before the major economic crisis in 1983). The new rules rationalised the differentiation between types of financial institutions and the different regulations that applied to them. In 1983, restrictions on lending to insiders and directors were introduced. Between 1983 and 1986, four major banks, including one international bank, became insolvent and a new regulatory framework had to be put in place in 1986. At the end of 1989, capital adequacy requirements were imposed.

These developments have been reviewed in order to identify the key elements in Hong Kong's financial development, which play similar roles in its emergence as an international financial centre: the strong lead of the private sector, with regulatory institutions playing catch-up; and the rapid growth punctuated by systemic crises. In the 1980s alone, there were two large events in the financial sector: the banking failures in the early 1980s led to a large revision of banking regulation; and the stock market crash of 1987 and closure for one week of the exchange led not only to criminal convictions but also to a thoroughgoing reform of stock market practices. While its competitors have been deregulating to improve their prospects in carrying out international financial activities, Hong Kong has been regulating.

Compared with Singapore, Hong Kong is clearly a larger financial centre (see Table 6.4); for example, the size of base money plus quasi-money is four times that of Singapore, and the amount of domestic output is 212 per cent, compared with Singapore's 84 per cent. Unlike Singapore, Hong Kong does not require its financial units to separate their domestic and international operations. The extent of international business carried out by Hong Kong-based banks is significant. In 1997, for example, 46 per cent of loans and advances by authorised institutions were for financing trade 'not touching Hong Kong', for loans and advances for 'use outside Hong Kong' or for 'other loans and advances where the place of use is not known' (calculated from Table 7.6 of the *Hong Kong Monthly Digest of Statistics,* February 1998).

Hong Kong has chosen the approach of relying heavily on professional management in setting up its monetary authority and depoliticisation of regulators. In the 1980s, capital adequacy ratios have been raised and regulations on restricting property lending have been put in place. In the 1990s, the deposit rate cartel was broken up (Granitsas 1998).

China's transition to the market has seen the rapid development of Hong Kong's role in providing external trade and financial services for China. China cannot but have a tremendous impact on international capital markets. Its fast growth has permanently raised its demand for foreign investment, including the simple financing of domestic enterprises, and for foreign technology. It has also led to a large domestic savings pool that is seeking effective avenues of investment.

It is expected that Shanghai will recover some of its importance as a financial centre as long as China continues to develop. Shanghai has some cost advantage in certain areas but is at a disadvantage in terms of human skills and international reach. Its growth will depend quite strongly on spill-over from Hong Kong and its fund management will find opportunities for the placement of investment into Hong Kong. For a significant time to come, Shanghai will be at a distinct disadvantage with regard to legal infrastructure, so Hong Kong will continue to dominate, especially in regard to internationally related transactions.

Hong Kong authorities have positioned Hong Kong as the key market for the issue of bonds by the Chinese government and for Chinese companies. The recent growth in this market has been rapid, with Hong Kong itself being able to absorb the new securities being issued by various Chinese entities. In 1992, there were 32 foreign bonds issued in Hong Kong; this increased to 46 in 1993 and to 76 in 1994 (Fujita and Osaki 1995).

In a recently completed review of the financial sector, Hong Kong authorities have announced further efforts at improving the regulatory infrastructure of their stock market (*Wall Street Journal* 1998). This effort is critical, since the demand for new listing and additional capital raising has been, and in the near future will be, much larger than in other stock markets (including those in industrial economies) and threatens to outstrip discretionary regulatory oversight.

In considering Hong Kong's prospects as a financial centre, there is an ambiguity in how to treat the mainland Chinese economy. Hong Kong has a strong comparative advantage in servicing China's international financial requirements. But is China really a 'foreign market' from the point of view of Hong Kong? For now, perhaps, but in the future this will increasingly be unjustified.

Hong Kong will clearly find type 3 markets (intermediating between foreign users of capital – China – and domestic providers of capital) the most dynamic part of its international financing activities. However, as per capita incomes in China continue to rise, savers there will look for more sophisticated investment instruments and Hong Kong can serve this demand. This will mean that type 2 and type 4 markets will show steady growth in the near future, though, by the time these become significant, it will probably be increasingly difficult to treat China transactions as foreign.

In the region, Hong Kong has a long-held advantage in personal finance: the management of assets of individuals (while Singapore has an advantage in the corporate finance market). Growth in this segment from China alone could be quite robust.

SINGAPORE

Since the 1970s, Singapore has pursued a two-track strategy with regard to its financial sector. First, it has sought to have its financial sector play a key supporting role in its development efforts. Second, it has also considered the sector itself as a key industry to develop. As has recently become prominent with the Thai financial crisis, these two aspirations can be at cross-purposes with each other. If the financial sector is to play a supporting role, it needs only to keep pace with the scale and sophistication of the financing requirements required by the growth of the real economy. If the financial sector is an industry to be developed in its own right, then it can be allowed to grow using external resources and provide services that go beyond the requirements of the domestic economy (Montes and Tan 1998).

With regard to the first track, Singapore has placed strong emphasis in maintaining a sound financial system and has progressively improved public oversight and supervisory capability over the system. As far as the second track is concerned, since 1972, as indicated by the granting of incentives for the development of ACUs, Singapore has pursued the independent development of its financial sector. These incentives began as exemptions from required reserve requirements and were subsequently expanded to include tax concessions. Similar incentives were granted to income from offshore insurance business (1979) and to income earned from transactions with non-residents in non-Singapore dollar securities (1987) (see Tan Chwee Huat 1997: 4–6).

Singapore is a financial centre dominated by a large offshore banking sector known as the Asian dollar market (ADM), with neither exchange control nor restrictions on foreign direct investment flows. As of 1997, assets for ADM denominated largely in US dollars stood at approximately US$479 billion, twice the size of the onshore domestic banking system of approximately S$225 billion (Montes and Tan 1998). There exists free convertibility of deposits between local and foreign currencies and swift capital mobility to exploit covered interest arbitrage due to rate differentials, the policy implications being that domestic interest rates are largely determined both by foreign rates and expectations of the future strength of the Singapore dollar.

Nevertheless, in quantitative terms, Singapore has the smallest financial market of the three (see Table 6.4). The capitalisation of its equity market is only 48 per cent of that in Hong Kong and 7 per cent of that of Tokyo. In November 1997, Deputy Prime Minister Lee Hsien Loong outlined future directions in government strategy with regard to the industry as part of the ongoing work of the Singapore government's financial sector review group. In early December, three more committees were formed to work with the group. The Stock Exchange of Singapore review committee has responsibility for proposing a conceptual framework for making the domestic capital markets more 'international, competitive and robust' (*Straits Times* 1997). The corporate financing issues committee is to generate recommendations with regard to regulations, framework of rules, and administrative guidelines applicable to corporate debt markets in order to expand corporate fund-raising activity in Singapore. The banking disclosure standards committee will evaluate standards and practices in developed and other Asia Pacific countries and recommend appropriate changes in disclosure practices.

In February 1998, the bulk of the recommendations of the second committee was accepted by the government. These changes include easing restrictions on how publicly accumulated funds, especially its pension funds, can be invested. About US$76 billion in funds are managed in Singapore: public sector funds account for about 5 per cent of the total. With the reforms, private individuals and companies will have greater leeway to decide how the part of their savings not already committed elsewhere will be invested and what kind of risks to take. This will provide the fund management companies with new resources for their activities. It is expected that this will serve as a spur to the expansion of the range of financial products that will also be of interest to investors from outside Singapore.

Some of the recommendations were also directed at creating a more dynamic bond market, which would also serve regional investors. It is a measure of the conservatism that underlies Singapore's financial management that these recommendations included encouragement to government-linked corporations and statutory boards to begin to borrow from Singapore's debt market so that a market for longer maturity bonds can emerge.

With government support and tax incentives, Singapore has been making great strides in establishing a wide range of financial markets and services. These include commodity trading, futures contracts on goods and financial indices, and derivatives.

There are two issues, inherently related to each other, that Singapore must address in further developing itself as an international financial centre: the internationalisation of the Singapore dollar; and the strict operational firewall between offshore banking (ACUs) and domestic banking. Singapore has successfully resisted the internationalisation of its dollar and one of its tools for doing this has been the effective implementation of firewall regulations. It is expected that the internationalisation of the dollar will be a gradual process (Montes and Tan 1998). At the present time, Singapore investors have access to international financing directly via the Asian bond market (ABM) or the Stock Exchange of Singapore (SES) by selling claims such as straight bond issues, floating rate notes, equities or commercial papers to lenders. Indirect international financing can also be conducted in the Asian dollar market through the ACUs, which deal with all major currencies except the Singapore dollar.

Singapore has therefore attained a very strong position in type 4 markets (intermediating between foreign users and foreign providers of capital). In the region, it has a dominant position in the foreign exchange market. Assuming that it will maintain its high savings rate, its deregulation process should see growth in type 3 markets as a greater proportion of its savings finances projects overseas.

COMPETITION AND COMPLEMENTATION

Summaries of the key elements of each centre – according to the four types of markets and the three major types of financing (bank lending, bond finance and equity) – are provided in Tables 6.5–6.7.

Hong Kong leads Singapore in the 'higher-end' elements: mergers and acquisitions, and syndicated loan offerings. It has also more experience in arranging swaps. Singapore has been providing incentives to encourage the relocation of higher-end activities to Singapore and it has been relaxing its restrictions on domestic bond offering to help develop the derivatives markets which are important in the swap business.

Hong Kong has a clear advantage in dominating China-related business, and Tokyo will be indispensable in serving Japanese financial activities. Singapore has the advantage in providing financial services to the Southeast Asian region and can be expected to serve as an alternative (and a competitor) to Hong Kong in China-related businesses. For example, Singapore has been wooing Chinese companies to list their stocks in Singapore. However, Hong Kong's China advantage will never be lost and it has the clear capacity for becoming the largest financial market in the region as China continues to grow. The growth of Hong Kong's China business can actually strengthen Singapore's role as a financial centre for the other economies in the region. In the case of regional business, however, Kuala Lumpur can be expected to compete with Singapore, even though Singapore's lead is quite substantial. Before the economic crisis, Bangkok had sought to become a competing financial centre, but the crisis has set this effort back at least by half a decade.

What is emerging is a situation of contestability between Hong Kong and Singapore but with the strong possibility of a division of labour, with Hong Kong serving the China market and Singapore providing services for all the other economies. Considerations of comparative advantage suggest the remoteness of a 'knockout punch' in which there would be only one or two financial centres in the region. The size of the elements of comparative advantage will encourage multinational finance companies to internalise these activities to capture the cost advantages that exist. As appears to be happening in the electronics industry in the region, a trend towards the multi-location production of financial services is emerging, which will ensure that other locations (and not just Singapore, Hong Kong and Tokyo) will be participating in providing international financial services.

Where Singapore and Hong Kong will compete most hotly is in the fund management business, which is global in nature and in which Hong Kong has a lead. It has pulled far ahead of Singapore since the late 1980s mainly because of its China-related business. In the future, we can expect Singapore to have the capacity to compete strenuously with Hong Kong in fund management. It has the advantage of a more flexible government with the capacity to focus on the development of the industry by providing incentives and infrastructural support. Another Singaporean advantage is the legal infrastructure, which is increasing its capacity to deal with issues of international business. However, at the present time, with regard to corporate disclosure standards, Hong Kong has a clear lead over Singapore.

Singapore will also seek to capture an increasing proportion of Japanese savings invested overseas in order to increase the size of its fund management activities. In the same manner, we can expect it to put effort into persuading fund management activities now based on London and New York to move to Singapore. It will continue to attempt to improve its infrastructure and support services for these activities.

Fund management for Japanese savings will take place mostly in Tokyo. A major proportion of these funds will be invested overseas. It remains to be seen whether the Tokyo financial markets will establish sufficient dynamism to shed their domestic orientation.

The best judgment that can be made at this point is that the Singapore and Hong Kong markets, while being smaller than Tokyo in terms of transactions volume, will be the keenest competitors as financial centres in the next few years. Hong Kong's volume will grow and its biggest advantage is the China market; Singapore's advantage derives from government support, but in the next few years its growth will be inhibited by the region's financial difficulties, most particularly those stemming from Indonesia. Competition will be accompanied by a large dose of complementation: Tokyo as a stable fund source; Hong Kong with its focus on China and Northeast Asia; and Singapore with its focus on Southeast Asia and international-to-international financial transactions.

There will certainly be other cities providing international financial services in the region. Shanghai, to the extent that China's economy is industrialising, will see notable growth and will take away the simpler markets from Hong Kong. Since the 1980s, because of its accumulated international assets, Taipei has become an important source of international finance. Conservative supervision and uncertainty over the status of Taiwan will, however, hamper the growth of Taipei as an international financial centre, even though as a source of finance it will be important in the years ahead. Sydney's base is the international businesses out of Australia but its growth is stymied by distance from Southeast Asia. Kuala Lumpur is also expected to make a bid as a financial centre; it will have Singapore as a fierce competitor but will have some advantages in terms of lower cost for basing businesses there.

The emergence of dominant centres will depend on government intervention, luck, first-mover advantages and the impact of cumulating agglomeration. With advances in information technology, what prevents a situation in which there is only one world centre, operating 24 hours a day is the fact that liquidity is an indispensable feature of financial markets. During the time when most of the holders of assets in a time zone are asleep, the liquidity of these markets is severely limited.

If Asia is to have an important financial centre, it (or they) must offer advantages beyond the fact that business in the region is carried on in a distinct time zone. The relatively recent emergence of Hong Kong and Singapore (and the declining influence of Tokyo) points to the role these four factors play in the rise of new financial centres. Beyond the fixed costs of investment management and informational (including language) limitations, savers and capital users will utilise the market that provides them with the best and the widest possible risk-return choices. These choices are created by private actors, responding to opportunities and attempting to overcome obstacles to investment. The ultimate arena of competition is therefore that over the basing of large financial companies (and their best personnel) in their centre. Tax incentives will help, but agglomeration economies are also important. That other companies are basing their operations in the same place, plus the relative availability of intellectual capital, is important. Singapore, with a focused government approach to the matter, appears to have an advantage. But there is nothing to prevent Hong Kong, or another city, from succeeding in this effort.

Table 6.5 Tokyo as a financial centre

Type	Bank lending	Bond finance	Equity
1 (D→D)	Dominant portion of the domestic financial market.	High fees and unspectacular returns stifled growth; 'big bang' reforms could resuscitate market, but probably slowly.	Bank lending has been dependent on shares of stock as collateral. Tradition of cross-holdings did not provide the basis for a dynamic, price-sensitive market.
2 (F→D)	High domestic savings rate did not generate much demand for bank borrowing from abroad.	Low domestic returns exert a dampening effect foreign financing through bonds.	Impact of foreign brokerages and funds will increase after reforms.
3 (D→F)	After recovery from the 1997 financial crisis, the reforms will increase the already significant rate of bank lending abroad.	In search of higher returns in the context of the ageing of the population, Japanese savers are expected to increase their holdings of foreign bonds.	In search of higher returns in the context of the ageing of the population, Japanese savers are expected to increase their holdings of foreign equities.
4 (F→F)	Hobbled by language and domestic infrastructure constraints and competition from other markets, this sector will not see significant growth.	Foreign bonds have long been floated in Tokyo but the question is whether foreign sources of funds will use Tokyo as the market site. This segment will probably not see a significant increase.	Eventually (with a appreciable time lag), foreign listing of shares and depository receipts will become significant.

Note: D = domestic; F = foreign

Table 6.6 Hong Kong as a financial centre

Type	Bank lending	Bond finance	Equity
1 (D→D)	Improvement in regulatory framework and legal system critical to the future. The interaction between China and Hong Kong's regulatory and legal system will also be critical	Improvement in regulatory and rating system will be critical to the further growth of corporate bond floating, which will be dominated by companies from China. As Hong Kong and China's middle class grows, the demand for retail bond-holding will increase.	Raising of funds through equity floating of China corporations will remain as the most dynamic part of the market.
2 (F→D)	As long as China's growth is strong, Chinese companies and Hong Kong businessmen would be able to absorb some bank lending from foreign sources.	As fund management activities increase in the region, Hong Kong and China bonds should find buyers from overseas.	The Hong Kong market already has significant foreign participation and this will increase with increased participation from China and from the region. China's own equity markets will have limited foreign participation in the medium term.
3 (D→F)	Bank lending 'abroad' will be dominated by lending by Hong Kong-based banks to clients in China. Project financing for China's enormous and growing infrastructure requirements will constitute a significant part of this business.	As the number of wealthy in China continues to increase and the investment management requirements of Chinese companies become more complicated, demand for holding foreign bonds will increase.	The increase in the listing of foreign shares in Hong Kong will be dominated by equity financing by China companies and by growth in China's domestic equity markets.
4 (F→F)	Hong Kong is competitive as an international banking centre, but the volume of China-related lending will dominate activities. In fact, China-related requirements are expected to be so large that fund raising will spill over into other regional markets.	China-related business will dominate this segment.	China-related business will dominate this segment.

Note: D = domestic; F = foreign

Table 6.7 Singapore as a financial centre

Type	Bank lending	Bond finance	Equity
1 (D→D)	Domestic banking is dominated by Singaporean banks. Foreign banks welcome to compete domestically but local banks have competitive edge in access to domestic savings.	Absence of government bonds (due to consistent public sector surpluses) to provide benchmark returns limits the growth of the market.	Lively and strongly regulated equity market with strong interest in initial public offering activities.
2 (F→D)	Like Japan, activities are limited since domestic savings provide adequate financing for domestic investment.	Like Japan, activities are limited since domestic savings provide adequate financing for domestic investment. However, the conservatism of domestic financiers has provided some openings for venture financing by domestic entrepreneurs.	Foreigners participate actively in domestic stock activities.
3 (D→F)	Singaporean companies have been investing regionally and Singapore-based banks have followed. Since the crisis, there has been greater interest by Singaporean banks in investment in regional banks. Limits on lending to non-residents limit the growth of this market.	Asian dollar bond market based in Singapore has seen strong growth. As Singaporean per capita incomes increase and liberalisation of use of domestic savings proceeds, demand by Singaporeans for foreign bonds, derivatives and other sophisticated instruments will increase.	Singapore is gradually liberalising the listing of foreign shares in domestic markets.
4 (F→F)	All major international banks have offices in Singapore and participate actively in project financing, corporate finance and personal finance, for clients in Southeast Asia, especially from Indonesia, Thailand and Malaysia.	Asian dollar bond market based in Singapore has seen strong growth. In the financial futures market (Singapore International Monetary Exchange, SIMEX), major contracts are traded, such as the ten-year Japanese government bond, Nikkei 225 stock average, and Taiwan stock index.	Singapore's advantage in telecommunications infrastructure and increase in domestically based international fund management activities could increase the incidence of foreign to foreign stock transactions.

Note: D = domestic; F = foreign

REFERENCES

Chen, E.K.Y. and R.C.W. Ng (1998) 'Financial sector development and economic development in Hong Kong: implications for developing countries', paper presented at Evolution of Financial Systems in Asia conference, Tokyo Club Foundation, Tokyo, 26–7 February.

Economist (1998) 'Capitals of capital: a survey of financial centers', 9 May (special section).

Fujita, Y. and S. Osaki (1995) 'Asia's securities markets in the 21st century', *NRI Quarterly,* Autumn.

Granitsas, A. (1998) 'Going for gold: Hong Kong sees a unique chance to jump ahead of the pack to become Asia's premier financial centre', *Far Eastern Economic Review,* 2 April.

Montes, M.F. and Tan Khee Giap (1998) 'Developing the financial services industry in Singapore', paper prepared for AT10 Research Meeting organised by Tokyo Club Foundation for Global Studies, 26–7 February, Tokyo.

Reidel, J. (1997) 'Capital market integration in developing Asia', *Asian Development Review* 15: 1–19.

Tan Chwee Huat (1997) *Singapore Financial Sourcebook,* Singapore University Press.

Taniuchi, M. (1997) 'Recent developments in Japan's financial sector', manuscript, Tokyo: Economic Research Institute, Government of Japan.

Wall Street Journal (1998) 'Hong Kong market regulator to gain power after review', 24 April.

Part III

Patterns of corporate governance, finance and reform

7   Changes in corporate governance structure in Indonesia

Farid Harianto and Mari E. Pangestu

INTRODUCTION: THE SETTING

The Indonesian economy has undergone significant changes in the past fifteen years. Ever since the fall of oil prices in the early 1980s, and especially their plummeting in 1986, there has been a shift from an import-substitution and government-led economic development strategy to an outward-oriented and private sector-led one. As with other developing countries, Indonesia has participated in the Uruguay Round of GATT (General Agreement on Tariffs and Trade) negotiations since 1986, and has had to undertake various policy changes since January 1995 to comply with the agreements. The opening up of its economy, in turn, has provided the confidence needed for Indonesia to support the ASEAN Free Trade Agreement (AFTA) to be achieved in ten years, and to take the lead in establishing the Bogor goals of free trade and investment in the Asia Pacific region by 2010 for developed economies, and 2020 for developing economies, under APEC (Asia Pacific Economic Cooperation).

The shift towards more competition and market-based strategies has induced fundamental changes in the corporate governance of Indonesian companies. Managing corporations in open and more competitive markets is certainly different from managing them in closed and protected markets. Indonesian companies are at the beginning of transforming themselves from family-owned businesses to professionally managed ones which have to compete internationally. Inefficient state-owned companies are also being subjected to the same waves of change, although at a slower pace.

Corporate governance refers to the behaviour of company owners and managers, and their accountability to outside investors, which is influenced by external and internal incentives, rules and norms. Increased competition in products, services, labour and financial sectors is an important external source of discipline for all corporations in a market economy which encourages efficiency and innovation and maximises consumer welfare (Stone et al. 1998). This is in turn achieved through deregulation of trade barriers, opening up sectors previously closed to investment (both domestic and foreign) and simplifying investment procedures, deregulating and strengthening the financial sector to mobilise domestic funds, privatising state-owned enterprises and encouraging export growth and technological progress.

The shift in economic development strategy in response to the oil price decline meant that, during the mid-1980s to early 1990s, Indonesia embarked on deregulation and privatisation. The strategy delivered high growth, averaging 8 per cent per annum, increased non-oil exports and greater diversification of its industrial structure. The financial sector and capital markets were also liberalised dramatically, much more so than in the other Asian countries. The result was an increase in the number of banks, including foreign joint venture banks, and an increase in domestic credit. At the same time, there was increased capitalisation in Indonesian capital markets. Given the decline in oil revenues, the government also gradually phased out subsidies to state-owned enterprises and subsidised credit schemes, thus putting pressure on state-owned enterprises to restructure and improve their performance.

Whereas the internal set of incentives influences corporate behaviour, such behaviour is also shaped by the presence of external and foreign creditors. For corporations wanting to get credit or capital, the disclosure and performance requirements imposed by banks, creditors and capital markets should put pressure on companies for better information disclosure and efficient performance. The behaviour of managers is, in turn, controlled by rules governing the relationship between managers and owners and investors.

How has the external environment affected major companies in Indonesia as they begin to transform themselves from family businesses or inefficient state-owned enterprises into competitive and international institutions?

KEY PLAYERS IN THE CORPORATE SECTOR

The key players in the Indonesian economy have been state-owned enterprises (SOEs), Indonesian Chinese conglomerates and, increasingly, *pribumi* (indigenous) and *pribumi*–Chinese joint ventures. Public enterprises have played a significant, albeit declining, role in the economy since early 1970. In 1995, there were 180 SOEs across all economic sectors, including agriculture (35 SOEs), manufacturing (38), transportation (17), public works (19), finance (30) and others (41). As a group, they produced 15 per cent of gross domestic product (GDP) and employed 1.4 per cent of the total labour force. In addition, there are quasi-governmental institutions, like the central bank and the logistic agency (Bulog), as well as local government-owned enterprises (mainly water utilities).

Many SOEs have a strong presence in their respective sectors, to some extent by virtue of a monopolistic position granted by the government (e.g. PLN in the electricity industry, Telkom in domestic telecommunications, Pertamina in the oil business, PN Gas, and Garuda and Merpati in domestic airlines). In the financial sector, the seven state banks still control about 50 per cent of total banking assets and about 45 per cent of total deposits, while in the insurance industry SOEs such as

Jiwasraya, Jasindo and Astek dominate the markets. Generally speaking, however, SOEs have not been able to match the performance of their private counterparts. The noted exceptions are Indosat, Perumtel and Tambang Timah (world's largest tin producer), all of which have gone public.

In the past two decades, the role of SOEs has declined and been replaced by the private sector. Statistics on investment indicate that public investment represented 36.8 per cent of total investment in the period 1974–9, compared with 34.9 per cent for domestic private and 28.9 per cent for foreign investment. The public share, however, declined to 25 per cent in the period 1989–94, compared with 67 per cent for private domestic and 8 per cent for foreign investment (Booth 1989: 7; Booth 1994: 10; Hill 1996: 108). Such a shift reflects the strengthening of private capital formation, the limiting capacity of the public sector, as well as improvement in the investment environment in general.

The second key player is the Indonesian Chinese conglomerates. In a survey on Asia's emerging economies (16 November 1991), the *Economist* noted that the 5 per cent Indonesian Chinese minority controlled about 75 per cent of corporate assets. A survey by *Pusat Data Business Indonesia* of Indonesia's top 300 companies (1993) indicates that 204 of them (80.1 per cent) are Indonesian Chinese businesses. Similarly, data from the Jakarta Stock Exchange show that, as of August 1994, eight out of the ten biggest raisers of capital were Indonesian Chinese, and only two of them were *pribumi*. These Indonesian Chinese are major players in the petrochemical, automotive, plantation, pulp and paper, food and financial sectors. The largest Indonesian Chinese enterprise in Indonesia is the Salim Group, which has diverse interests in finance, plantation, food, chemicals and cement. The second largest conglomerate is the Astra Group, with 200 or more subsidiaries across various sectors in the economy. In its development, though, Astra has become a true publicly listed company, with diverse ownership and run by professionals employing modern management tools. The third largest Indonesian Chinese conglomerate, Sinar Mas, is more focused on pulp and paper, plantation, finance and property sectors. Of the three, Sinar Mas is the most advanced in terms of competing in international markets, particularly its pulp and paper businesses, and of institutionalising its businesses through the capital markets.

The third key player, the *pribumi* businesses, has become increasingly important in the past decade. Data on changes in the ranking of Indonesia's major business groups (Pangestu and Harianto 1998, forthcoming) indicate that two of them, the Bakrie and Tirtamas Groups, grew very rapidly in the period 1992–7: the Tirtamas Group ranking jumped from 41 in 1992 to 8 in 1997, while that of the Bakrie Group went from 25 to 9. Together with the Soeharto family empire, these companies represented, as a whole, about 3 per cent of Indonesian GDP in 1997. These *pribumi* businesses have been able to grow rapidly largely through their access to the power circle within the government and to the various business privileges granted to them. The *pribumi* are noted for their entry into government-related businesses, such as infrastructure (toll roads, telecommunications, electricity, ports) and other government-related contracts. With a few exceptions, their businesses are largely confined to the non-tradable sectors.

These key players in the Indonesian corporate sectors have both similarities and differences with regards to their corporate governance.

THE PATTERN OF CORPORATE GOVERNANCE

The main features of corporate governance across the key players are compared in Table 7.1. The table covers the internal characteristics of business organisation (decision-making orientation, incentive structure), as well as relevant market disciplines.

Table 7.1 Characteristics of corporate governance of Indonesian Chinese, *Pribumi* and SOEs

	Chinese	Pribumi	SOEs
Key features	Networks supplement markets; close relation with government; strong loyalty.	Close government relationships.	Focused business; conservative growth; mixed business and social mandates.
Overriding concerns	Cost and finance; opportunistic expansions; trust.	Opportunistic expansion; trust.	Play safe; career advancement; political gain.
Organisation/ decision making	Simple organisation; paternalistic family-centred; overlap ownership-management.	Simple organisation paternalistic; family-centred; overlap ownership-management.	Elaborate, hierarchical; paternalistic; bureaucratic; multiple bosses; prone to state interventions.
Incentive structure	Relatively low wage; high bonus.	High fixed salary; high performance-related bonus.	Status-oriented; pay goes with hierarchy.
Market disciplines:			
Product market	Many exporting; some government protection.	No major players in exports; some government protection.	Captive market or monopolistic.
Debt market	Highly leveraged; bank loans and foreign debts.	Highly leveraged; bank loans and foreign debts.	Less leveraged; mainly state banks; controlled foreign debts.
Capital market	Major players in capital markets.	Latecomers and minor players in capital markets.	Minor players in capital markets, but increasing.
Transition in corporate governance	Some successes; some in progress.	No clear success; still in progress.	Some successes.

Pertinent features

Indonesia, as with other developing economies, has two significant and interrelated features: the prevalence of market imperfections and the central (although declining) role of the government in economic and business affairs. Economically speaking, the market imperfections, such as unavailability of market information and weak market institutions, and infrastructure, engendered non-trivial transactions costs. In the absence of such market information, the Chinese commercial networks have, in the past, been able to supplant the functioning of the (imperfect) markets and internalised the transactions, as access to information (about prices, material sources and trading partners) was readily made available through the network. As Indonesian Chinese, like overseas Chinese in general, have experienced bitter social threats and executions under different government regimes throughout their entire history, they constructed defence mechanisms to protect themselves. Close relationships were forged with power-holders in the government, while trust and loyalty were the prevailing norms imposed and reinforced for the members of their family and business organisations.

The deep involvement of the government in economic development also gave Indonesian Chinese ample opportunity to rapidly accumulate capital by way of their close relationships with the power-holder (e.g. Bulog and Pertamina in the early Soeharto era). Building upon these business–government relations in tandem with the accumulated capital, Indonesian Chinese businesspeople expanded their businesses as opportunities arose. The typical expansion pattern involved a transition from trading activities to raw material supplies to manufacturers and to other sectors as well. Effectively, the opportunistic expansion paths covered both vertical as well as horizontal expansion and, hence, the genesis for conglomeration. The driver for such expansions was to economise the economies of information and of capital raising, the two basic strengths of Indonesian Chinese businesses in general.

The trading mentality of traditional Chinese businesspeople also put strong emphasis on the value of time and of money: cash today would always be better than cash tomorrow. After all, trading was conceived as 'arbitraging time and place'. As a result, there was an acceptance of the importance of cash flows and a willingness to favour 'small margin, high turnover' over 'high margin, small volume' business.

Like the Indonesian Chinese, the *pribumi* also took advantage of their close relations with the government to gain access to business opportunities and to rapidly build their capital base. Unlike their Chinese counterparts, however, the *pribumi* were not endowed with a strong base of business and ethnic networks. The *pribumi* were not particularly known for the strong cash-flow mentality nor the frugality of cost-consciousness of their Chinese counterparts. On the other hand, they enjoyed an affirmative-type policy since the 1980s, particularly under the so-called 'buy domestic' drive under Soeharto. Also like Indonesian Chinese, *pribumi* businesses expanded opportunistically, capitalising on their cozy relationships with the government. In many cases, a number of *pribumi*, including the Soeharto family in particular, developed their businesses jointly with Chinese partners. For the Chinese, such a joint venture could be viewed not only as a vehicle to share commercial risk, but also as insurance against social and political risk. For the *pribumi*, such an alliance could be seen as a way to tap into Chinese expertise and capital to speed up the accumulation of their own capital.

State-owned enterprises usually had a very specific mandate in their by-laws, which limited their business activity. Any business diversification was normally difficult to undertake, as it required approval from both their technical ministry as well as from the finance minister. Capacity expansion was easier to achieve, yet needed to go through a lengthy bureaucratic process, which, in tandem with a strong risk-adverse mentality, resulted in conservative attitudes towards growth. In the past, an SOE was seen not only as a business entity but also as a vehicle to carry out a certain social mission. As a result, there was no strong culture for profit-maximising behaviour: any performance shortfall could always be attributed to their social role.

Organisation and decision-making processes

The internal structure of Chinese family businesses, shaped by personal trust and by suspicion towards outsiders, inherently limited their size. A large bureaucratic structure was unusual and complex integration avoided as much as possible. When the business grew, it was subdivided into a federation of small organisational units. These various units were coordinated largely through the trusted personnel assigned to head each unit. At the top, key positions were entrusted to family and a small number of long-time employees and friends. Thus, strong overlaps among control, management and ownership prevailed, with the head of the family at the centre.

The paternalistic organisation of Chinese businesses, with inner circle personnel, provided stability; the inner circle oversaw old retainers in wide-ranging positions, such as cashier, chief accountant, managers and even mundane jobs such as personal driver and security guards. Such an arrangement also provided a sense of security on both sides. A combination of a low fixed salary compensated by a large annual bonus of 9–12 months of salary was typical for Chinese businesses. For key and trusted personnel, family-oriented protection and unexpected gratuity were also standard features of their incentive scheme, to further bond their relationships. For the key people, this scheme provided an 'extra mile' of resources to fall back upon; when specific labour or sacrifice was needed, there was always somebody to rely on.

Similarly, the *pribumi* business organisations were also marked by a paternalistic orientation. The founder was always the centre, surrounded by an inner circle of trusted friends and employees. In contrast to the Chinese, however, many large *pribumi* organisations hired senior staff from other companies for expansion. In addition to the market rate remuneration, they were also offered performance-linked incentives as well as other perks.

In the case of SOEs, organisation was highly hierarchical and bureaucratic, with a strong paternalistic orientation. SOEs had to report to various government agencies, including their respective technical ministry and the ministry of finance. To make life more complicated, they are now to report to a newly formed department, the ministry of SOEs. Such multiple bosses and reporting lines made the management of

SOEs prone to government intervention. Some, like PLN, Pertamina and Garuda, for example, were known to have difficulty in safeguarding themselves from the vested interests of various government officials. Procurement of input materials, equipment and subcontractors were subject to those influences. As a result, SOE management needed to possess not only business acumen but also, and maybe more importantly, political skill. SOE managers were highly preoccupied with managing their career advancement amidst those multiple influences. Often, playing safe became their guiding principle, as opposed to performance-driven behaviour. For managers of a status-driven organisation, their pay and perks increased with their hierarchical advancement.

Market disciplines

As indicated earlier, the behaviour of company owners and managers is shaped by external incentives and disciplines. In a nutshell, it can be argued that the more competitive the market in which a company operates, the more disciplined the company is and the less discretionary the behaviour of the owner and manager. According to the same argument, the more actively a company engages in competitive debt and capital markets, the more it will be subject to the discipline of external markets.

Leveraging upon their trading activity, many Chinese businesses entered into exports which led them to being subject to the harsh discipline of international markets. Some companies had also further diversified their businesses into various regions and built their production bases there, which in effect reduced their risk in one particular country (e.g. Sinar Mas Group; Raja Garuda Mas). Other parts of the Chinese conglomerates, however, may remain in the domestic-oriented sector as in the past – with strong links to government – with a function to accumulate capital as quickly as possible. In contrast, SOEs and *pribumi* businesses are largely not known as major players in world markets (the few exceptions include Pertamina and Tambang Timah). Many SOEs and *pribumi* are in fact still enjoying various forms of government protection, which eliminate the incentive to perform well.

A World Bank survey in 1996 indicates that Indonesian corporations are relatively highly leveraged with a debt-equity ratio of about 90 per cent, the fourth highest after Thailand (155 per cent), Japan (135 per cent) and South Korea (130 per cent). Domestic bank loans are still the dominant source of funding, but increasingly supplanted by cross-border borrowing, particularly since 1994. High domestic interest rates and predictable exchange rate depreciation had, in the past, induced Indonesian corporations to tap cross-border financing. Unfortunately, such cross-border financing had not necessarily been supported by full disclosures. The quality of disclosures and market information of Indonesian corporations was reflected by higher premia. For example, in the US market in 1996, Indonesian entities with double-B rating from S&P's were charged 200–400 basis points premium over T-bills, compared with 130–200 basis points premium for US entities with similar ratings. Increasingly, however, foreign creditors imposed more stringent disclosure requirements on Indonesian entities, in line with the rapid increase in cross-border borrowings by Indonesian corporations.

Among the three players, SOEs have the lowest debt-equity ratio, with state banks as their main creditors. The close relationships between SOEs and state banks in essence reduced the effectiveness of the expected external discipline from the banking sector. Between Indonesian Chinese and *pribumi*, it appears that Chinese firms are more leveraged than the *pribumi*. In 1997, the debt-equity ratio for Chinese businesses ranged from as low as 20 per cent for Sampoerna and 80 per cent for Nusamba, to as high as 280 per cent for the Salim Group, 370 per cent for Astra, 340 per cent for Lippo and Gajah Tungal, and 540 per cent for Sinar Mas (the highest). The *pribumi*, on the other hand, had debt-equity ratios of, for example, 150 per cent for Bimantara, 170 per cent for the Tirtamas Group, 190 per cent for Citra Lamtoto Gung and 210 per cent for the Bakrie Group (the highest). Judging from these ratios, one can argue that the Chinese businesses are relatively more leveraged than *pribumi* and SOEs, and hence are more subject to the scrutiny of creditors, both domestic and foreign.

Another market discipline comes from the capital market. Data from the Jakarta Stock Exchange in 1994 indicated that, of the ten largest raisers of capital on the exchange, eight were Indonesian Chinese and two were *pribumi* (and none were SOEs). Several companies, including two Chinese (Sinar Mas, Indorayon) and four SOEs (Indosat, Telkom, BNI Bank, Tambang Timah), listed their shares either in New York or London. No single *pribumi* company has done the same. As these foreign exchanges generally impose more stringent regulations and disclosure requirements, it can be expected that those companies will be more disciplined than the others.

Generally speaking, the Indonesian financial sector has been characterised by a weak regulatory framework and supervision. Even if prudential measures are already in place, enforcement is problematic. The concentration of bank ownership is well known, which might have led to concentration of lending and to breaches of legal lending limits. External disciplines from such a weak sector, therefore, can hardly be expected.

FUTURE DIRECTIONS

As Indonesia moves towards a more open and liberalised economy, its corporations are also increasingly required to adjust accordingly, including making the necessary fundamental changes in their corporate governance. Indonesian corporations – be they Indonesian Chinese, *pribumi* or SOEs – are all induced to transform themselves, from family-owned and traditionally managed entities to professionally run corporations. At the same time, the Indonesian financial market has also become increasingly integrated into global markets, resulting in increasing requirements for quality disclosures. Fund managers, analysts, creditors and investment houses will be more demanding, and Indonesian corporations will have to learn to cope with their scrutiny.

At the business level, Indonesian companies have also started to transform themselves into major regional players, albeit at a very slow pace. The case of the Sinar Mas Group is instructive, as this is one of the success stories. The Group has been systematically professionalising its family business. At all levels of the organisation, expatriates are hired to work together with locals. Two of its subsidiaries went public in 1994 and its Asia Pulp and Paper (APP) Group, headquartered in Singapore, was listed in the New York Stock Exchange. Since 1994, the Group has aggressively entered into the US and other international bond markets and , in 1997, it issued a 30-year bond – one of the longest maturity from Asian issuers. The Sinar Mas Group has expanded into Asia, Europe and the United States, supported by production mills in Indonesia, China, India and Malaysia, each of which is supplied from huge forest resources. In terms of governance structure, the Group eclectically employs internal expansion (the India case), joint venture (Malaysia) and acquisition (China and Indonesia). During the process, it builds up engineering and management skills and deploys them to new projects, as necessary. In summary, the Sinar Mas Group has been able to successfully transform itself from family business to true regional player, with strong doses of market discipline.

Other Indonesian Chinese corporations have also undergone a similar transformation, with varying degrees of success. Astra is one of the most advanced in terms of professionalising its management and of distributing widely its ownership through the capital market. Its product market, though, is still largely domestic-oriented, although very competitive. Similarly, the Raja Garud Mas Group and its Inti Indorayon subsidiary have followed the path of the Sinar Mas Group by entering and investing in international markets, listing its shares in New York, and actively engaging in international bond markets. It still lags behind, however. The Salim Group has attempted to professionalise its management and enter global markets. As its main funding has come from bank loans (including syndicated ones) and not from capital markets, little is really known about the Group generally.

The *pribumi* businesses have so far been slow in transforming themselves by way of entering into global markets, be they product, debt or capital markets. To date, their efforts have been confined to attempts to professionalise management (Bakrie Group, Bimantara) and to listing in the Jakarta Stock Exchange (Bakrie, Bimantara, Semen Cibinong). Otherwise, little is known about what is taking place within *pribumi* enterprises.

Since 1995, the government has been actively pursuing privatisation programs to improve the efficiency of SOEs. A new ministry (without portfolio) was established in early 1998 to manage the privatisation program and, at the same time, to consolidate SOEs by way of improving efficiency and of closing the weakest ones. In the future, this privatisation is expected to generate much-needed cash to support the state budget and to eliminate incentive distortion and instil market discipline in SOEs.

Banking and capital market reforms are also underway. Under new draft banking laws, prudential measures and their enforcement will be strengthened significantly, while the administrative capacity of the oversight institution will also be improved. Banking secrecy will be limited to the liability side of the balance sheet of banks, improving disclosures on corporate lending. In general, more quality disclosures have been required from the banking and capital market supervisory agencies. As alluded to earlier, though, the real challenge is in the enforcement of the regulations. In essence, a better legal framework is still needed to discipline Indonesian corporations. A credible threat of effective bankruptcy proceedings, for example, will provide a strong check on corporate behaviour.

REFERENCES

Booth, A. (1989) 'Repilita V and Indonesia's medium-term economic strategy', *Bulletin of Indonesian Economic Studies* 25(2), August.

—— (1994) 'Repilita VI and the second long-term development plan', *Bulletin of Indonesian Economic Studies* 30(3), December.

Hill, H. (1996) *The Indonesian Economy Since 1966: Southeast Asia's Emerging Giant*, Hong Kong: Cambridge University Press.

Pangestu, M. and F. Harianto (1998) 'Corporate governance in Indonesia: prognosis and way ahead', paper presented at 23rd Federation of ASEAN Economic Associations conference, Kuala Lumpur, 15–17 October.

Pusat Data Business Indonesia (1993) Anatomy of Indonesian Business, Jakarta.

Stone, A., K. Hurley and R.S. Khemani (1998) 'The business environment and corporate governance: strengthening incentives for private sector performance', discussion paper, Washington DC: Business Environment Group, World Bank, October.

8 Development in Chinese corporate finance and its implication for ownership reform

Weiying Zhang

INTRODUCTION

Chinese economic reform, first introduced in 1979, has resulted in many significant changes in the organisational structure of economic activities and resource allocation. One such change has been taking place in corporate finance. In the pre-reform period, the whole non-agricultural sector was dominated by state-owned enterprises (SOEs), which were almost completely state budget financed with few debts. Since reform started, on the one hand, the share of the state sector has gradually shrunk and that of the non-state sector has gradually expanded, in terms of both employment and output; on the other hand, although SOEs are still tightly controlled by governments at various levels, debt finance from state banks has gradually taken over from state budget (equity) finance as the major financial instrument of SOEs. For instance, in the period 1978–97, the state share of urban employment fell from 78.3 per cent to 54.7 per cent and its share of industrial output declined from 77.6 per cent to 26.5 per cent. The average debt–asset ratio of all industrial SOEs has increased from 18.7 per cent in 1980 to 65.1 per cent in 1997 (*A Statistical Survey of China* 1998).

This change has mainly resulted from the fact that the distribution of national income has altered and households have taken over from the state as the major financiers of investment capital. Also, because direct financing markets have been very tightly restricted and underdeveloped, the state banks have become the dominant channel for funds flowing from households to enterprises (Zhang W. 1995).

The problem is that, although corporate finance has changed a lot, corporate governance has changed little: SOEs may be financed by households (through the banks) but they are still owned by the government. The government continues not only to hold full authority over the selection of SOE management but also to intervene considerably in SOE business. Since they do not bear financial risks, neither government officials nor management have adequate incentives to make enterprises under their control efficient. Because bank deposits are fully insured by the state and the state banks are fully controlled by the government, households as ultimate financial investors have neither interest in nor access to the monitoring of banks and SOEs. Similarly, it is impossible for the state banks as direct creditors to play any active role in the corporate governance of SOEs. This mismatch between the financial investors in the firm and the ownership of the firm has turned debt finance into a debt crisis.

The change in SOE financing has generated enormous impacts on the Chinese economy, both negative and positive. From the negative point of view, debt finance has driven almost all SOEs into financial distress. Many of them are unable to repay their due debts. As a result of SOE defaults, state banks as the major creditors are suffering because of substantial bad loans. A common estimate is that 20–25 per cent of their total outstanding loans are unrecoverable. This not only hinders commercialisation of the state banks but also potentially threatens the stability of the macro economy, unless the debt problem can be solved within a reasonable period. On the positive side, the debt crisis has unveiled the deep-seated flaws of the state ownership system. It shows that more fundamental changes in corporate governance are necessary, and it has made privatisation of the SOEs more acceptable and feasible than otherwise.

FROM STATE BUDGET FINANCING TO BANK LOAN FINANCING

In a market economy, a firm faces two basic financial problems. First, how much should it invest and what specific assets should it invest in? Second, how should the cash required for its investment and operation be raised? The answer to the first question is the firm's investment, or capital budget, decision. The answer to the second question is the firm's financial decision. Corporate finance is about these two decisions.

In the pre-reform Chinese economy, both investment and financial decisions were made by the state (government), instead of by individual firms themselves. Capital budgeting was centralised. The state treasurer and the State Planning Commission played the dominant role in deciding how much a SOE invested and what specific assets it invested in, and also how those investments were financed. Accordingly, the corporate finance of SOEs was actually state finance (Zhang C. 1997). Furthermore, state budget funds were almost the only source of a firm's fixed asset investments as well as of its working capital, only a fraction of which (known as 'extra-budget working capital') was financed by loans from state-owned banks. In the period 1950–79, state appropriations accounted for 84.1 per cent, on average, of annual total investment in the capital construction of state-owned units (mainly SOEs).

The reform of SOEs has been characterised by a continuously evolutionary process of shifting decision rights and residual claims from the central government to local governments, and from there to firm level (Zhang W. 1997). This has had a substantial impact on SOE corporate finance. First, although investment decisions constitute one of the rights that the central government has been very reluctant to give up, both state enterprises and local governments have acquired considerable autonomy in regard to such decisions as reform has proceeded. A recent study, by China Entrepreneur Survey System, indicates that the realisation of autonomy in investment decisions in 1993, 1994 and 1995 was, respectively, 38.9 per cent, 61.2 per cent and 72.8 per cent (see Table 8.1 for 1995 details).

Table 8.1 Realisation of autonomy in investment decisions, 1995

Control of firms	%	Size of firms	%
Central government	61.8	Large	73.0
Provincial government	67.5	Middle-sized	71.8
Prefecture/city	76.8	Small	75.2
County	76.4	87 experimental firms	72.9

Note: Survey covered 2,752 firms, 72.9 per cent of which were SOEs
Source: Almanac of China's Economy 1996

Table 8.2 shows the change between 1985 and 1997 in the proportions of total capital construction investment by the state-owned sector in central government projects and local projects. Investment decisions on central projects are generally made by the line ministries and the State Planning Commission, and on local projects by local governments and enterprises. It can be seen that, after 1992, local project investment exceeded central government project investment. It is clear that SOE investment decisions are now shared between governments at various levels and enterprises.

Table 8.2 Proportion of state investment in capital construction projects, 1985–97

Year	(1) Total investment (100m yuan)	(2) Central govt projects (100m yuan)	(3) Local govt projects (100m yuan)	(4)=(2)/(1)(%)	(5)=(3)/(1)(%)
1985	1,074.37	575.24	499.13	53.54	46.46
1986	1,176.11	632.52	543.59	53.78	46.22
1987	1,343.10	761.66	581.44	56.71	43.29
1988	1,574.31	873.71	700.60	55.50	44.50
1989	1,551.74	837.71	714.03	53.98	46.01
1990	1,703.81	919.15	784.67	53.95	46.05
1991	2,115.80	1,060.40	1,055.37	50.12	49.88
1992	3,012.65	1,341.69	1,670.96	44.54	55.46
1993	4,615.50	1,834.90	2,780.60	39.76	60.24
1994	6,436.74	2,430.75	4,005.99	37.76	62.24
1995	7,403.62	2,970.67	4,432.95	40.12	59.88
1996	8,610.84	3,379.33	5,231.50	39.25	60.75
1997	9,862.80	3,916.90	5,945.80	39.71	60.29

Sources: China Statistical Yearbook 1997; *A Statistical Survey of China* 1998

Second, parallelling this downshifting of investment decisions, financial decisions have been gradually separated from investment decisions and sources of investment funds have been dispersed. Roughly speaking, state bank loans have taken over from state budget funds as the dominant financial source of SOE investment, regardless of the investment decisions being made by governments or enterprises. Retained profits and non-bank debts are also used by SOEs to finance their investments and operations. State budget funds now account for only a tiny part of the total investment. Furthermore, even these funds have been taken as 'loan-for-grant', channelled from government through the state banks rather than directly appropriated to enterprises (that is, in SOE balance sheets, they are recorded as special debts rather than as equity). Many of the SOEs established since the 1980s have been purely debt-financed, without any equity funds.

Figure 8.1 shows the change in financial sources of the fixed asset investment of the state sector. The proportion of state budget funds declined from 79 per cent in 1979 to only 4.6 per cent in 1996; domestic loans, virtually zero in 1979, represented 16.2 per cent in 1982 and had increased to 23.6 per cent by 1996. Most foreign funds were injected into enterprises as investment loans rather than as government-equity investment; and, although official sources cannot identify the details of 'fundraising' and 'others', some informed researchers suggest that about half actually came from bank loans (Wu 1997) and a roughly equal part from retained profits, retained depreciation funds, extra-budget local government funds and other sources (e.g. bonds and shares issued to employees and other institutions). It is typical that enterprises financed their long-term fixed investments from short-term bank loans.[1] If 50 per cent of fundraising and 'others' were assumed to be bank loans, total bank loans would account for about 56 per cent of the financial sources of fixed investments in 1996.

Figure 8.1 Pattern of financial sources of fixed asset investment, 1979–96 (%)

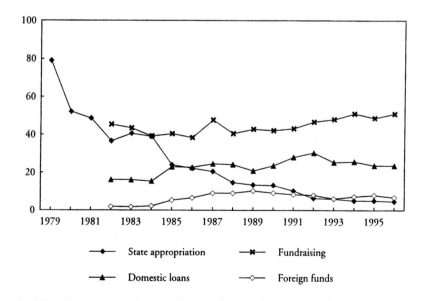

Apart from fixed asset investment, a firm also needs funds to finance its operation and inventory. From 1980 on, the government stopped appropriating working capital, and SOEs have had to rely on retained profits and bank loans. Since retained profits are very limited, working capital has largely been financed by loans.[2] As a result, the average ratio of current liabilities to current assets of industrial SOEs as a whole reached 103.4 per cent by the end of 1996. The financing of Chinese SOEs has fundamentally and substantially shifted, therefore, from state budget appropriations to bank loans. This conclusion is consistent with the results of various surveys. For instance, according to the study conducted by the Social Survey System of the State Commission for Restructuring the Economic System, 91.6 per cent of respondents (managers), when asked what the primary financial source of their enterprises was, answered 'bank loans' (*Almanac of China's Economy* 1996: 966).

However, although bank loans are the dominant source, more and more SOEs are seeking equity financing through emerging stock markets. After a few years of experimental corporatisation of SOEs through internal placement, two local stock exchanges were established in 1991, in Shanghai and Shenzhen, both of which were later endorsed by the central government and have now become national stock exchanges. Between 1992 and 1997, there were 739 IPOs (initial public offers, mostly SOEs), with total fundraising of 143.238 billion yuan (equivalent to about US$18.08 billion at the exchange rate of 8.2 yuan per US dollar; not including second issuing) (Table 8.3). By the end of 1997, the total number of listed companies reached 745, with a total market capitalisation of 1,752.9 billion yuan (US$213.7 billion). In addition, there are dozens of SOEs listed on the Hong Kong and foreign stock exchanges. The stock market is not expected to play a major role in the corporate finance of SOEs in the near future, however.

Table 8.3 Equity finance through stock exchanges, 1992–7

Year	IPOs	Funds raised (100m yuan)	Average funds raised per firm (100m yuan)	Equity capital of IPO firms (100m shares)	Average equity capital per firm (100m shares)
1992	86	230.0	2.67	36	0.42
1993	115	293.2	2.55	224	1.95
1994	108	107.84	1.00	30	0.27
1995	21	22.68	1.08	5.32	0.25
1996	203	220.0	1.4	244	1.2
1997	206	608.7	3.24	427.33	2.08

Note: Book value per share is one yuan for all listed companies
Source: Data collected by author from various sources

SOE FINANCIAL STRUCTURE CHANGE AND THE OVER-INDEBTED PROBLEM

As a direct consequence of debt finance, the financial structure of SOEs has gradually changed. According to a survey by the State Asset Administration, the debt–asset ratio of state industrial enterprises as a whole was only 18.7 per cent in 1980 and had increased to 67.9 per cent by 1994 (Wu 1997). According to the 1997 *China Statistical Yearbook*, the average debt–asset ratio of 86,982 state industrial enterprises at the end of 1996 was 65.1 per cent (61.1 per cent for large enterprises, 72.4 per cent for middle-sized ones and 72.4 per cent for small ones).

The distribution of sources of debt reconfirms that state bank loans indeed play a dominant role (Figure 8.2). According to Lu and Shen (1997), such loans accounted for about 60 per cent of total SOE debts at the end of 1995, with the remainder distributed as follows: 17.4 per cent were interfirm debts, 5.7 per cent were debts from other financial institutions, 5.9 per cent were from governments and 3.7 per cent from employees, and 7.2 per cent were company bonds.

Figure 8.2 Distribution of sources of debt, 1995 (%)

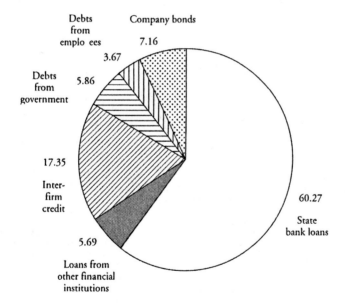

Source: Lu and Shen 1997

While the debt–asset ratio of 65 per cent is already considerably high by international standards, official statistics seem to have underreported SOEs' real debt burdens. Numerous case studies show that actual average debt–asset ratios are much higher and that, in fact, many SOEs are 'zero-equity firms'. For instance, a survey of four industrial cities by the Debt Restructuring Research Group indicated that average ratios in 1994 were 77.5 per cent (Chanchun), 81.3 per cent (Xi'an), 74.4 per cent (Ningbo) and 89 per cent (Tanshan). In total, this means about two-thirds of SOEs with debt–asset ratios over 80 per cent and more than a quarter with ratios over 100 per cent (Table 8.4). In other words, a considerable proportion of SOEs is technically bankrupt. This is the so-called 'over-indebted problem'.

Table 8.4 Distribution of debt–asset ratios across enterprises, 1994

	Chanchun	Xi'an	Ningbo	Tanshan
Total number of SOEs	2952	599	369	196
Sample SOEs	231	120	54	51
Average ratio	77.5%	81.3%	74.4%	89%
<60%	32 (13.7%)	6 (5%)	15 (27.8%)	4 (7.84%)
60–79%	59 (25.43%)	22 (18.3%)	20 (37.0%)	0
80–100%	72 (31.03%)	45 (37.5%)	14 (25.9%)	41 (80.39%)
>100%	68 (29.74%)	47 (39.2%)	5 (9.2%)	6 (11.76%)

Source: Wu Xiaolin et al. 1997

An important indicator of this problem is the ratio of short-term debt to total debt. In a study of 302,000 SOEs, at the end of 1995, short-term and long-term debt accounted, respectively, for 65.6 per cent and 34.4 per cent of total debt (Lu and Shen 1997). Since much of the short-term debt has been used to finance long-term fixed asset investment, most SOEs are illiquid in paying their due debts. The ratio of current assets to current debts in the state industrial sector was only 92.4 per cent in 1996, much lower than the international standard of 200 per cent. Massive default on debts is inevitable. In other words, debt finance has evolved into a debt crisis.

As SOEs are more and more debt-financed, the bad loans of their major creditors (the state banks) have mounted dramatically and become a serious problem. A common estimate is that more than 20 per cent of total outstanding bank loans are non-performing and unrecoverable. One rigorous study suggests that the figure in 1995 was 23 per cent (Lu and Shen 1997), which means that the absolute value of these bad loans reached 1,162.7 billion yuan (US$141.8 billion), equivalent to 20 per cent of the gross national product (GNP) of that year. It must be pointed out that bad loans are not normally written off; typically, they are recapitalised by the issuing of new loans. Even this accounting practice cannot completely hide the increasing worsening of bank balance sheets. The capital adequacy of the state banks in 1995 was estimated at only 6.49 per cent, much lower than the Bank for International Settlements (BIS) ratio of 8 per cent.

Another important indicator of the debt crisis is interfirm debts. In China, they are commonly referred to as 'triangular debts', since most of them involve an interlocking debt chain.[3] By 1990, triangular debts had become an economic headache which pushed the State Council to try a nationwide resolution by injecting more bank loans into SOEs. However, the problem seems not to have been really resolved. Incomplete statistics show that triangular debts have been growing steadily since 1993. The State Statistics Bureau estimates that, by the end of 1994, total uncollectable receivables among SOEs, as an indicator of triangular debts, stood at 648 billion yuan, roughly equal to one-sixth of China's 1994 gross domestic product (GDP). By June 1995, the figure had grown by 13.8 per cent to 737.6 billion yuan (Bank of East Asia 1995). According to a People's Bank of China survey of 248 representative SOEs in eight provinces, net receivables increased by 310 per cent between June 1992 and June 1995 (Lu and Shen 1997). However, the problem is not the interfirm credits themselves. In a mature market economy, enterprises voluntarily provide commercial credit to each other for transaction purposes, to economise on the cost of capital when the price of bank credit is high. The problem is that, in China, most interfirm credits are involuntary, in the sense that they originate from buyers' defaulting on payment, rather than voluntary. Because of this, interfirm debts have hindered rather than facilitated normal transactions between enterprises.

NATIONAL INCOME DISTRIBUTION CHANGE AND THE CAUSES OF DEBT FINANCE

Why are SOEs mainly debt-financed? What has produced the debt crisis? These questions have drawn much attention among Chinese economists as well as policymakers. The most popular answers are as follows:

- SOEs are inefficient and most of them are loss-makers rather than profit-makers. A common estimate is that a third of SOEs makes an explicit loss and another third, an implicit loss; only one-third is slightly profitable.

- SOEs are burdened with too many social obligations, such as the provision of medical care and housing to employees, and with too many retired people. One estimate suggests that total payments for these obligations account for about 34.8 per cent of administrative costs. Typically, retired workers account for about 25–30 per cent of total employees on the payroll. In 1995, the wage bill for retired workers paid by SOEs amounted to more than 54.4 billion yuan, equal to 81.7 per cent of total profit for that year. In addition, SOEs are also burdened with too many redundant workers, who produce nothing but must be paid something. They are estimated to account for about 25–30 per cent of total workers (Lu and Shen 1997).

- There are too many excessive investments and unproductive assets, a result partly of government intervention in investment decisions and partly of SOEs' soft budget constraint.

- SOEs have borne too many of the reform-related costs, including policy-generated losses, high taxation, various forms of prorations and so on.

- The government, as the owner, has failed to inject equity funds as it should.

All of these reasons are acceptable and plausible in some sense. However, they cannot be the whole story, or even a major part of it. The inefficiency of SOEs is not a new phenomenon; they were inefficient even before reform.[4] The social obligations are actually labour costs and should be paid by enterprises in any economy.[5] Waste and excessive investments are also not new problems.

To properly understand the debt problem, a distinction must be made between debt finance and the debt crisis. Debt finance is a necessary but not a sufficient condition for the debt crisis. That the government has failed to inject equity funds is an important clue to understanding China's debt finance situation, although a private enterprise under a well-functioning market economy does not have to be financed continuously by its initial owners to survive and grow. One needs to look at the changes in the distribution of national income and the flow of funds between enterprises and ultimate investors. My basic argument is that debt-dominated finance has mainly resulted from the fact that households have taken over as the principal source of investment capital and state banks have become the major channel for funds flowing from households to enterprises (Zhang W. 1995).

As economic textbooks tell us, investment decisions and financial decisions are fundamentally a question of intertemporal choice between current and future consumption of national income. In a market economy, this choice is mainly a consequence of decisions made by households. When householders decide to save part of their income for financing their future consumption, they become investors. Equity and debt are two instruments which an enterprise uses to raise funds from investors to finance its investment and operation. Equity and debt differ in both cash flows and control rights. Equity-holders claim the residual and hold the ultimate control over the firm in normal times; debt-holders claim the contractual return and take over control only when the firm is in insolvency. Banks and other financial institutions are nothing but intermediaries between investors and enterprises; they help to channel the available funds. Although banks are important, it is households who decide whether to invest as debt-holders through these intermediaries or to invest directly as equity-holders (or bond-holders). Similarly, it is enterprises who decide whether to issue equity or bonds directly to investors or to raise funds through these intermediaries. The financial structure of the firm is determined by householders' and enterprises' decisions through capital markets in which financial intermediaries are important players.

In pre-reform China, as in other socialist economies, the government not only deprived state enterprises of the capacity to make investment and financial decisions, but also deprived households of choice between current and future consumption (and thereafter of their financial decisions). It did this by directly controlling the distribution of national income in various ways. It was the government that determined how much a household should earn. Zhang Chunlin (1997), a well-known Chinese economist, has identified 'taxation' and 'administrative pricing' as the two basic instruments that the state employed to control national income distribution and to finance state enterprises. Administrative pricing was particularly effective in controlling rural household income. By underpricing agricultural products and compulsorily purchasing them, the government transferred to the state sector much of the income that could otherwise have been saved by rural households, in the form of lower living costs for state employees and lower production costs. Through the underpricing of state employees' labour services, much of the income that could otherwise have been saved by urban households appeared in accounting statements as SOE profits, which were then completely handed over to the state treasurer. The government then used budget revenue to finance state enterprises and capital formation.

By directly controlling national income distribution, the government left households with only minimum income for subsistence. In Chinese official language, household income was commonly called 'consumption funds'; household savings, if any, were called 'unmaterialised purchasing power', meaning that households did not spend this money because the supply of goods could not meet household demand. Any increase in savings was interpreted as a signal of an 'overdistribution of national income' and of an 'imbalance of supply and demand', which worried policymakers and economists. Not surprisingly, households played a trivial role in national saving and capital formation. In 1978, the total household savings deposit was only 21.06 billion yuan, equal to 5.8 per cent of GDP; the amount per capita was only 21.88 yuan, equal to 3.56 per cent of the average annual wage of a state employee (*China Statistical Yearbook* 1996). State banks, the only financial institutions before reform, were nothing more than a state accountant.

The economic reform begun in the late 1970s has fundamentally changed the distribution of national income by liberalising both prices and entries of non-state enterprises. In rural areas, as agricultural prices were raised in the late 1970s and eventually liberalised in the early 1980s, household incomes increased dramatically. For instance, per capita household income in rural areas from 1978 to 1985 increased by 137.6 per cent, in contrast to 75.4 per cent growth in per capita GDP (*China Statistical Yearbook* 1996). This, together with the entry of non-state enterprises, eroded much of the profits previously earned by SOEs, by raising labour costs and reducing profit margins. In urban areas, as SOEs enjoyed greater autonomy over decision-making and retained profits, government administrative control of wages and bonuses was undermined, and more and more SOE revenue was distributed to employees. As a result, urban household incomes have also quickly increased, although not as fast as rural household incomes in the earlier stages of reform.[6]

At the same time as these rapid increases in household income, the profit margins of state enterprises have fallen and the share of government revenue in GDP has shrunk sharply. According to official statistics, the ratio of pre-tax profits to sales revenue in the state industrial sector fell from 24 per cent in 1978 to only 9.2 per cent in 1995. The proportion of government revenue (budget revenue plus extra-budgetary revenue) in GDP dropped from 40.82 per cent in 1978 to 14.79 per cent in 1995 (*China Statistical Yearbook* 1997) (Figure 8.3). The government has failed to inject funds into SOEs simply because it has had no funds to inject.

Figure 8.3 Government share of GDP, 1978–97 (%)

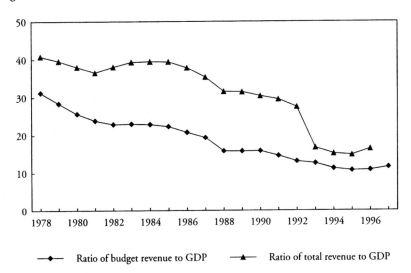

Source: *A Statistical Survey of China* 1998

The fundamental change in national income distribution and its far-reaching impact on corporate finance was not noticed until the early 1990s, when the accumulated debt had become a serious burden. A very sophisticated and informative study of the change in income distribution in China between 1979 and 1988 showed that households' share of national income increased from 64.4 per cent to 77.5 per cent in that period, up by 13.1 percentage points (Guo and Han 1991). At the same time and in contrast, the total share of government and enterprises declined from 35.6 per cent to 22.5 per cent (Figure 8.4).

As the distribution of national income changed, the pattern of national savings also changed. As their income increased, households began to make their own choices about their current and future consumption, just as households in a market economy normally do. Household income no longer represents just 'consumption funds'. Households save a considerable part of their income for future consumption; in other words, they become financial investors. According to Guo and Han (1991), households' share of national savings increased from 23.55 per cent in 1979 to 62.7 per cent in 1988, while the government's share dropped from 42.8 per cent to 7.25 per cent (Figure 8.5). Since 1983, household savings have been the largest source of investment funds; since 1985, households have provided more than half of total national savings. While households have taken over as the main financial investors, the enterprise sector has, since 1983, become the dominant physical investor (Figure 8.6). Both the enterprise sector and the government have increasingly relied on household savings to finance investment, that is, they have become the net debtors and households the net creditors (Figure 8.7).

Figure 8.4 Distribution of national income, 1979–88 (%)

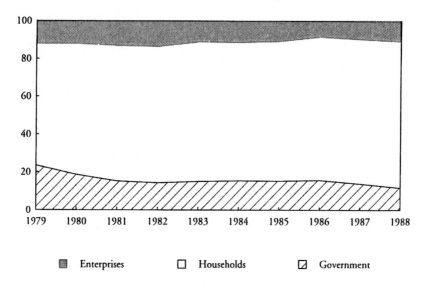

Source: Guo and Han 1991: 169

Figure 8.5 Pattern of national savings, 1979 and 1988 (%)

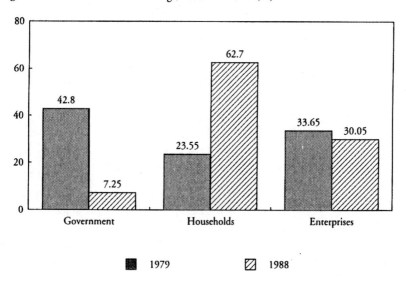

Source: Guo and Han 1991: 187

Figure 8.6 Pattern of investment, 1979 and 1988 (%)

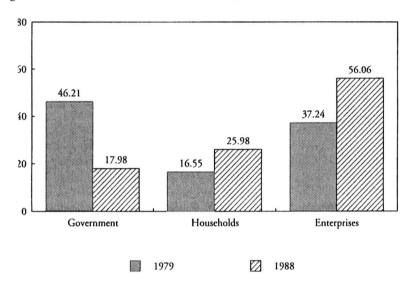

Source: Guo and Han 1991: 225

Figure 8.7 Gap between savings and investment in each sector, 1988 (%)

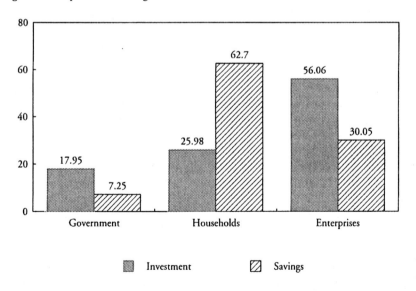

Source: Figures 8.5 and 8.6

The problem is not that enterprises should not use household savings for investment; it is normal in every modern economy. The problem is that the government failed to open capital markets to allow both households and enterprises to make their own choices among different financial instruments such as equity, bonds and mutual funds. Nor did the government try to privatise SOEs, as it should have, in response to the change in the savings pattern. Before the early 1990s, there was no stock market on which enterprises could raise funds. Enterprises were, and still are, tightly restricted in issuing bonds. Although rural area households can directly invest in township and village enterprises (TVEs) and private enterprises, urban households can only deposit their savings in state-owned banks, apart from buying treasurer bonds. As a result, banks have become almost the only channel for capital flow from households to SOEs. This can be seen from the fact that urban savings deposited in the state banks accounted for 93.4 per cent of total urban savings at the end of 1995. The ratio of household savings deposit to total funds in the national banking system increased from 18.79 per cent at the end of 1979 to 48.74 per cent at the end of 1996 (Figure 8.8). This is the fundamental reason why the corporate finance of SOEs has become dominated by state bank loan finance.

Figure 8.8 Ratio of household savings deposits to total funds in national banking system, 1979–96

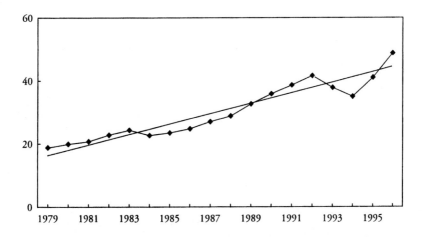

Source: China Statistical Yearbook, 1981–97

CORPORATE GOVERNANCE AND THE DEBT CRISIS

The debt crisis cannot be blamed solely on the shift to debt financing. If corporate governance were effective and efficient, debt financing might be good for a firm's value maximisation through disciplining management.

Corporate governance is an institution governing contractual relationships among equity-holders, management and creditors. For it to be effective and efficient, the following conditions must hold: first, equity-holders as the owners of the firm must have adequate incentives to select highly competent managers and to discipline them when necessary. Second, managers must have sufficient autonomy and incentive to make well-judged business decisions and be well-motivated to work hard. Third, creditors must have adequate incentives as well as effective measures to enforce debt contracts through bankruptcy procedures. None of these conditions holds in Chinese SOEs. The debt crisis in China has occurred because, although corporate finance has changed a lot, corporate governance has changed little.[7]

First, the government as the only equity-holder has malfunctioned in both selecting and disciplining management because of agency problems on the bureaucrats' side. The feature of SOEs that most distinguishes them from capitalist firms is that, by definition, the role of principals in SOEs is played by the 'state' (government) rather than by natural capitalists: it is the government who appoints, motivates and disciplines the managers. This fundamental feature remains intact after reform. In particular, the government still holds full authority over appointments. As Zhang (1994) has pointed out, because of the adverse selection problem, selecting good management is hard work. Selectors must have adequate incentives to obtain information about applicants' abilities and to install high-quality candidates. Adverse selection is most serious in China because, with no personal stake to signal ability, too many people pretend that they are qualified for management. Worse is that bureaucrats have the right to select but, unlike their capitalist counterparts, do not bear the consequences of their decisions. This means that not only would-be managers, but also bureaucrats themselves, have an adverse selection problem. There is no incentive to search for good managers or, even if found, to install them. Observation suggests that bureaucrats too often base their selections on personal connections (*guanxi*), rather than on merit, because of the rent-seeking benefits. For all these reasons, the management pool of SOEs is full of lemons.

Second, although reform has gradually shifted considerable autonomy to management in various ways, government can still intervene arbitrarily in SOE business. Separating the government from enterprise business has been assumed to be the basic purpose of reform since it was inaugurated. Nevertheless, this has so far never materialised. This is true even after state enterprises are corporatised, in which case the government is formally and legally defined as the 'equity-holder' and bureaucrats are appointed as 'board directors'. The fundamental reason for this is that, when the state is the owner, bureaucrats are given the right to control the firm but bear no financial risk for their intervention. By definition, any owner has to supervise management through control rights. The state as an (and, in most cases, *the only*) equity-holder will naturally intervene. The key problem is how to determine the boundaries of such intervention. Many economists have a misconception that there is a well-defined division of rights between equity-holders, the board of directors and management, and thus it is clear to everyone who should do what. This is definitely not true. Of course, part of the relationship among the three parties is well defined, but much of it is not. There exists a public domain in control rights where there is a tacit understanding as to who should move one step forwards and who should move one step backwards. For true stockholders or board members who bear financial risk, the decision whether to intervene depends on how much trust is placed in the manager. The problem is that this situation cannot be duplicated between bureaucrats and the management of SOEs. Bureaucrats do not bear the consequences of their intervention and, as a result of intervention, management has little accountability.

SOEs suffer not only from this intervention but also from inadequate managerial incentives. Although reform has increased the incentive to make short-term profits through both explicit and implicit profit-sharing (Zhang W. 1998), the long-term incentive problem has yet to be solved. Casual observation suggests that SOE managers prefer to distribute retained profits to employees, or to invest in quick revenue-generating projects rather than in long-term productivity-enhancing projects and R&D (Huang et al. 1998). They have too much incentive to expand their empires by borrowing from banks and to keep insolvent enterprises as going concerns, but not enough to make efficient use of the borrowed money or to repay. In many cases, abnormal short-term profits are made at the large expense of long-term productivity (Broadman and Xiao 1997). The reason for this management myopia is that, given that there is no personal capital stake, managers' enjoyment of benefits cannot extend beyond their tenure with a firm. There is always uncertainty as to whether they will still be in position even in the following year.[8] This is because tenure is mainly dependent upon bureaucratic preferences, which bear little relationship to a firm's performance; good performers are just as likely to be removed as bad performers, if not more. Once a firm becomes highly profitable, bureaucrats have every incentive to collect rents by replacing the incumbent with their favourite. Thus, the best way for incumbents to secure their positions is to make the firm look not too good and not too bad, which also partly explains why SOE managers typically underreport their profits.

Third, the state bank as the major creditor has failed to enforce the debt contract. In a market economy, debts play an important role in corporate governance through the threat of bankruptcy. China enacted a Bankruptcy Law in 1986, which became effective in late 1988.[9] Theoretically, when enterprises become insolvent, the creditors take control and the threat of bankruptcy disciplines the management. However, this is not the case in China. Rather, bankruptcy has been widely used by enterprises and local governments as a way to write off debts, instead of disciplining managers (ICBC 1997). After bankruptcy procedures, either through reorganisation or through liquidation, most incumbent managers still run the firms as going concerns and probably the only major difference is that considerable debts have been cancelled (and, in some cases, the enterprises renamed). Because of this, managers are more than willing to file for bankruptcy. In contrast, state banks, as dominant creditors, have neither access nor incentive to execute their creditor rights. They have been very passive in dealing with distressed firms. Typically, when debtor firms default, creditor banks accommodate them by, for instance, extending the loan payment period or capitalising unpaid interest, rather than pursuing their claims through bankruptcy or other active means.[10] Indeed, the banks have filed very few bankruptcies.

The fundamental reason for creditor failure is that, when the government acts as the owner of both debtor-firms and creditor-banks, the debt is not a real debt in the legal sense, that is, a contract between debtor and creditor. When a debtor borrows from a creditor, the debtor fully understands the obligation to repay in due time or else face a bankruptcy penalty and the creditor fully realises that there is some risk of default by the debtor. The terms of the contract negotiated between the debtor and the creditor take into account all these foreseen considerations. Bankruptcy is a procedure that enforces the debt contract. In China, however, debts between the banks and the SOEs are very different. In the 1980s, when SOEs borrowed from the banks, they just took it as a new way of getting funds from the government and had little sense that the borrowed money would have to be repaid, and the banks simply understood it as allocating funds to state firms on behalf of the government and had little sense of risk of possible default. In fact, many bank loans were decided by the government through an administrative procedure, rather than negotiated between the firm and the bank. In this sense, the 'debts' of SOEs were more like equity than debts. Perhaps the only difference between debts and budget funds was a change of items in the balance sheets. Not until the 1990s, when the state banks had become burdened with enormous overdue bad debts and when both they and the SOEs had become relatively independent entities with their own interests, was it recognised that bank money was different from budget funds. For this reason, I call the SOEs' debts 'ex post debts'.[11] Because of this ex post nature, the bankruptcy of SOEs is more like a bargaining process over the terms of new debt contracts rather than an enforcement of the existing debt contracts.

The second reason for creditor failure is that the incentive system of state banks is mis-structured. Managers of state banks in China care only for accounting numbers, rather than for the real value of the bank asset. This is because their careers and private benefits (e.g. perks) all depend only on the former and not the latter. They have every incentive to cover up rather than signal non-performing claims, which might result in dismissal or reduced bonuses. In contrast, by engaging in accounting tricks to disguise non-performing debts, a bank can overstate its profits and may therefore maintain the ability to pay higher bonuses to its employees and continue a level of loan quotas that would not be possible at lower reported profit levels. Incumbent managers would rather have any bad debts eventually show up in their successors' time than during their own tenure. This may explain why state banks are so passive in solving the SOEs' bad debt problem.[12]

The third reason for creditor failure is that bankruptcy procedures in China are dominated by local governments (Zhang C. 1998). While the state banks are owned by the central government, most SOEs are de facto owned by local governments. With decentralisation, local governments have acquired considerable autonomy and self-interest. They have every incentive to make use of bank passivity to write off the debts of the firms they control, even if these debts are recoverable. Although the Bankruptcy Law requires that reorganisation or liquidation schemes be discussed at and approved by a creditors' meeting with a simple majority of creditors and of an amount of unsecured debt claim, in practice, local judges and bank branch managers can hardly go against the local government's decision, because their careers and welfare are virtually determined by the local government. It is very difficult and costly for the central authorities and the bank's headquarters to verify the true financial state of a firm. Even worse is that some central government agencies (e.g. the State Economic and Trade Commission and the State Commission for Restructuring the Economic System) have a bias towards debtors, rather than creditors, because their delegated task is to 'invigorate SOEs' rather than 'take care of SOBs (state-owned banks)'.[13]

Finally, although households have become the ultimate financial investors of SOEs and the direct creditors of state banks, they do not have any interest in monitoring either, since their bank deposits are fully insured by the government and therefore they bear no risk at all. In summary, it is the mismatch between a firm's financial investors and its ownership that has led debt finance into a debt crisis (Li and Li 1997; Zhang W. 1997).

PRIVATISATION AS A WAY OUT OF THE DEBT CRISIS

If the debt crisis cannot be solved within a reasonable period, the whole economic reform process will be jeopardised and a financial crisis might be unavoidable. In recognition of this, the central government initiated in 1994 the 'capital structure optimisation' experiment. Special policies were designed to reduce the debt burden, to enforce the 1988 Bankruptcy Law, including:

• converting the treasurer-granted loans into government equity;

• converting tax arrears into equity (subject to the willingness of concerned governments);

• reinvesting part of paid corporate tax into the firm as equity;

• converting interfirm debts and debts to non-bank financial institutions into equity if agreement is reached between debtors and creditors;

• using bank debt provision to write off bad debts;

• listing selected large SOEs on stock exchanges; and

• writing off bank debts when an ailing or bankrupt debtor SOE is taken over by another SOE.

This experiment was first applied to eighteen major industrial cities. It was then expanded to 58 cities in 1996, and to a further 111 cities in 1997. The favoured policies are also applicable to some selected SOEs outside the 111 experimental cities, including 100 experimental SOEs in the modern enterprise system.

While both central and local governments have tried hard to deal with the debt problem, the achievement so far has been very limited. For instance, the average debt–asset ratio of state industrial enterprises fell by only 0.4 per cent, from 65.5 per cent in 1995 to 65.1 per cent in 1996, superficially because 'too much fire, too little water'. A more fundamental reason is that there is no good incentive structure for the relevant parties to do much. With the banks owned by the central government and the enterprises owned by local governments, fewer payments to banks is equivalent to more subsidies from the central budget (Zhang C. 1997). In some cases, asset prices were set by 'reverse calculation' (i.e. first calculate the total expenditure in compensation payment to workers and in legal fees, then set the price roughly equal to that level). As a result, in most cases, banks' recovery rates were much lower than they could have been if assets had been truly evaluated. For instance, it has been estimated that 30 per cent of bank debts in bankrupt firms should be recoverable, while actual average recovery rates were only 16.4 per cent and 14.9 per cent in 1995 and 1996, respectively (ICBC 1997).

The debt crisis calls for more basic changes in the relationship among enterprises, governments, banks and household investors. Chinese economists have proposed many alternatives. One proposal was for banks to take control of financially distressed state enterprises through debt–equity swaps (Research Group on China's Economic Reform Design 1993), but this idea, based on the Japanese and German bank finance-dominated model, posed a legal problem in that current Chinese commercial bank law (enacted in 1995) does not allow commercial banks to hold equity in enterprises. The more fundamental problem, however, is that, given that the banks are also owned by the state and they themselves suffer from inadequate governance, it cannot be expected that their control over enterprises will be any better. Being an equity-holder requires more managerial and monitoring skill than being a debt-holder. If state banks cannot manage their debts well, how can they manage equity better? The recent Asian financial crisis also revealed that government-controlled banks can generate serious moral hazard problems. This is a lesson China should learn.

For any proposal to be successful, therefore, it must simultaneously address both the over-indebted problem and the corporate governance problem. From this point of view, the privatisation of SOEs is not only desirable but also inevitable. Given that most of them need new equity funds and the state as the incumbent owner has none for injection, the problem can only be solved by introducing new, non-state shareholders. Privatisation is also more feasible now in China. Roughly speaking, with households the major suppliers of investment funds, the financial claims of SOEs have already been privatised. Now it is time to privatise SOE control rights. This can easily be done by transforming household investors from debt-holders of state banks into equity-holders of enterprises. In other words, China does not need to follow the Eastern European style of voucher privatisation; it can go its own way. This kind of privatisation will not only change the financial structure of SOEs but also restructure their corporate governance.

Privatisation has already begun. Observation suggests that the debt crisis has indeed been a powerful driving force behind this process. Many local governments are eager to sell the firms under their control, simply because they do not have the funds to ensure these firms' survival.[14] A recent survey estimates that more than 70 per cent of small SOEs in Shangdong and a few other provinces have been fully or partially privatised (China Reform Foundation 1997: 35). The process has been further speeded up since the Chinese Communist Party's 15th Congress. Now, newspapers in China frequently carry a list of the large and middle-sized SOEs selected by local governments for sale. Three northeastern provinces are most noticeable for their recent public offer of SOEs for sale.

Privatisation takes various forms. For small enterprises, 'management (or employee) buy-outs' are a popular solution. For instance, 77.2 per cent of Zhucheng municipality's enterprises were bought out by managers and employees between 1992 and 1994 (Wang and Xu 1996). A similar type of privatisation has also been undertaken in many other areas, such as Shunde of Guangdong province, Yibin and Deyang of Sichuan province, Shuzhou of Shanxi province, and Xishui and Xianfan of Hubei province. For large and medium-sized enterprises, 'forming joint ventures' and 'going public' are the two most attractive ways to privatise. Joint ventures with domestic or foreign private enterprises allow local governments to partially privatise their SOEs with minimum disruption to operations. In order to attract foreign investors, local governments compete to set up 'development zones' and to offer substantial tax concessions and other favourable treatment. Some have even sold their SOEs wholesale to overseas buyers. For instance, in 1992, Quanzhou municipal government of Fujian province sold all 41 of its SOEs to a Hong Kong businessman, who also bought dozens more in other regions and successfully packaged them for public offering on the Hong Kong and New York stock exchanges (Hu 1994).

As for going public, the central government has recognised that the two official stock exchanges in Shanghai and Shenzhen can play an important role in solving the debt crisis. All local governments are eager to get listing quotas.[15] Although the government often holds an absolute majority of shares when they are initially issued, typically its stake increasingly shrinks (and private shares expand) after the listing (Xu and Wang 1996). More recently, 'privatisation through Hong Kong' has become fashionable: Shanghai and Beijing have packaged their SOEs for listing on the Hong Kong stock exchange, and other regions are following in their footsteps.[16] In many cases, state-owned shares have been taken over by non-state owners through the stock market.

Observation also suggests that the privatisation of state enterprises has been and will continue to be a process of 'capitalistisation' of (some) incumbent bureaucrats. As reform proceeds, these bureaucrats find it more and more difficult to capture rents in their current positions because of the disappearance of monopolistic profits and managerial discretion. Experience teaches them that they can do much better by directly doing business with their remaining political capital of 'connections' (before it fully depreciates). They have to make up their minds to *xia hai* (go into business). By doing so, they lose little because the rents they used to enjoy can be embedded into profits which may legally accrue to them in various forms. They have no risk to bear because start-up capital has come from the state (which, initially, 'owned' the firm). Before they leave office, they grant full autonomy to the firms with which they will work. They appoint themselves chairmen of the board, directors or executives. Once they have pocketed some profits, they will buy into the firms. They can do this quietly because, once the firms are corporatised, they can easily be sold piecemeal instead of as a whole. This process may be further speeded up by the ongoing government restructuring launched by the new prime minister, Zhu Ronji. In addition, the central government may have to sell its stocks because of its budget deficit. The state-owned enterprises gradually evolve into private joint-stock companies. At this stage, it is possible for the government to become a bond-holder who can be protected by private shareholders. Once incumbent bureaucrats become capitalists, they will have an incentive to select high-ability people for management; they themselves will voluntarily step down if unqualified. The separation of government from enterprises will be achieved accordingly.

CONCLUSION

It should be pointed out that, while the privatisation of SOEs is very promising, privatisation of the state banks is yet to come. There may be good reasons for this delay but, unless banks are privatised, they cannot be expected to play a constructive role in the corporate governance of enterprises. This is because only private banks have adequate incentives to select good managers and good projects for financing, and to enforce debt contracts through the bankruptcy mechanism. As long as banks are owned by the state and run by bureaucrats, and thus the state remains the ultimate rescuer of losing concerns, enterprises, even if privately owned, cannot be financially well disciplined by the banks, and the fundamental problems of moral hazard and adverse selection cannot be solved as well as in a capitalist firm. This is the lesson China should learn not only from itself but also from Korea and other countries.

NOTES

I thank Ralph W. Huenemann and other conference participants for their helpful comments.

1   This can be inferred from the fact that the average current ratio – the ratio of short-term assets to short-term liabilities – of the state industrial sector was 96.7 per cent in 1996, far below the international standard of 200 per cent.
2   Unofficial estimates suggest that SOEs financed 80 per cent of their working capital through bank loans (Bank of East Asia, *China Analysis*, November 1995).
3   For example, a steel company fails to pay its supplier (e.g. a coal mine) because its customer (e.g. an auto company) has not paid on time. At the same time, the coal mine also owes money to the auto company.

204 Patterns of corporate governance, finance and reform

4   Of course, competition from non-SOEs after reform has made the situation worse.
5   However, it should be pointed out that, under the planning system, explicit labour costs did not include pensions. For those now-retired people, this part of the labour cost was collected by the government as 'profit'. Now, enterprises have to pay this cost, which is truly an extra burden for SOEs.
6   Before reform, state employees were underpriced. Now, it is more likely that they are overpriced. Since much of the earnings of state employees is 'grey income', statistical figures typically underestimate urban household income.
7   For further discussion of the corporate governance of Chinese SOEs, see Zhang (1998).
8   Although a contract is for three to four years, the government is not bound by it in replacing the manager.
9   Until the early 1990s, filed bankruptcy cases were few in comparison with the tens of thousands of financially distressed firms but have dramatically increased since 1994: a total of 6,753 between 1994 and 1996 (ICBC Bankruptcy Research Group 1997). In addition, there have been many out-of-court workouts.
10   A similar problem is also found in other transitional economies (see Mitchell 1993).
11   Liu (1996) calls it 'pseudo-debt'.
12   In 1997, the central bank inaugurated a risk management program, under which state bank managers face considerable non-pecuniary penalties such as dismissal. Since then, managers have been very reluctant to make any new loans to SOEs.
13. This is a typical 'multi-principal' problem in public enterprises (see Dixit 1996).
14. An alternative explanation is that cross-regional competition has driven privatisation (see Li et al. 1998).
15   Because the demand from local governments wanting to list on stock exchanges is so great, the central government's security regulatory commission has had to set provincial quotas.
16   There are two types of SOEs listed on the stock exchange. One type is H-share companies, registered on the mainland but listed in Hong Kong. The other is 'red chip' companies, registered and listed in Hong Kong, but the largest shareholder is the government(s) or the parent SOEs in mainland China. By September 1997, H shares and red chips accounted for about 15 per cent of market capitalisation, and 40 per cent of the daily volume, on the Hong Kong stock exchange (*Hong Kong Economic Journal* 16 September 1997).

REFERENCES

Almanac of China's Economy (1996) Beijing: China's Economic Almanac Press.
Bank of East Asia (1995) *China Analysis*, November.
Broadman, H. and Xiao Geng (1997) 'The coincidence of material incentives and moral hazard in Chinese enterprises', *Development Discussion Paper 606*, Cambridge, Mass.: Harvard Institute for International Development.
China Reform Foundation (1997) *Reality's Choice: Reforming Small State-owned Enterprises* [Xianshi de xuanze: Guoyou xiao qiye gaige shijian de chubu zongjie], Shanghai: Shanghai Yuandong Press.
China Statistical Yearbook 1981, 1983, 1985, 1991, 1994, 1996 and 1997, Beijing: China Statistics Press.
Dixit, A. (1996) *The Making of Economic Policy*, Cambridge, Mass.: MIT Press.
Guo Shuqing and Han Wenxiu (1991) *Distribution and Use of GNP in China*, Beijing: China People's University Press [in Chinese].
Hu Shuli (1994) 'The phenomenon of "China strategy": analysis and thinking of restructuring state enterprises through foreign investors' [Zhongce xianxiang: Guanyu yinzi gaizhao de jiexi he sikao], *Reform Journal* [Gaige] 3: 74–85.

Huang Yipping, Wing Thye Woo, K.P. Kalirajan and R. Duncan (1998) 'Enterprise reform, technological progress and technical efficiency in China's state industry', mimeo, Canberra: National Centre for Development Studies, Australian National University.

ICBC Bankruptcy Research Group (1997) 'A survey report on bankruptcy problems' [Guanyu qiyi pochan wenti de diaocha baogao], *Economic Research Journal* [Jingji Yanjiu] 4: 15–39.

Li, D. and Li Shan (1997) 'The corporate debt crisis in China: analysis and policy proposal', in D. Xu and J. Wen (eds) *The Reformability of China's State Sector*, Singapore: World Scientific Press, 79–98.

Li Shaomin, Li Shuhe and Zhang Weiying (1998) 'Competition and institutional changes: privatization in China', *Working Paper 1998E002*, Beijing: Institute of Business Research, Peking University.

Liu Li (1996) 'An analysis of the capital structure of SOEs', *Economic Science* 2: 40–5.

Lu Lilin and Shen Ying (1997) *Dealing with Debts in Restructuring SOEs* [Guoyou qiye gaizuzhongde zhaiwuchli], Beijing: Economic Science Press.

Mitchell, J. (1993) 'Creditor passivity and bankruptcy: implications for economic reform', in C. Mayer and X. Vives (eds) *Capital Markets and Financial Intermediation*, Cambridge University Press, 197–224.

Research Group on China's Economics Reform Design (1993) 'Restructuring the enterprise–bank relation', *Reform Journal* 6: 16–24.

A Statistical Survey of China (1998) Beijing: China Statistics Press.

Wang Yanzhong and Xu Heping (1996) *Studies of Zhucheng's Enterprise Reform* [Zhucheng qiye gaige tantao], Beijing: Economics and Management Press [Jingji guanli chubanshe].

Wu Xiaolin et al. (eds) (1997) *Research Reports on Debt Restructuring of China's State Sector* [Zhongguo guoyou jinji zaiwi chongzu yanjiu baogao], Beijing: China Financial Press.

Xu Xiaonian and Wang Yan (1996) 'Ownership structure, corporate governance, and firms' performance: the case of Chinese stock companies', mimeo, Washington DC: World Bank.

Zhang Chunlin (1997) 'State enterprise reform and state financing' [Guoyou qiyi gaige yu guojia rongzi], *Economic Research Journal* [Jingji Yanjiu] 4: 3–15.

—— (1998) 'Debt reduction, bankruptcy and enterprise restructuring in Chinese state-owned sector', mimeo, Department of Enterprises, State Economic and Trade Commission.

Zhang Weiying (1994) 'Entrepreneurial ability, personal wealth and assignment of principalship: an entrepreneurial/contractual theory of the firm', DPhil thesis, Oxford University.

—— (1995) 'Rational thinking of China's SOE reform', *China Business Time*, 13 January.

—— (1997) 'Decision rights, residual claims and performance: a theory of how Chinese state enterprise reform works', *China Economic Review* 8(1): 67–82.

—— (1998) 'China's SOE reform: a corporate governance perspective', *Working Paper 1998E004*, Beijing: Institute of Business Research, Peking University.

9 Financial reform and its impact on corporate organisation in Korea

Sang Yong Park

INTRODUCTION

The Korean economy stands today at a crossroads, as do some of the other economies in East and Southeast Asia. It was an economy envied and imitated by other developing economies for the past 30 years. It was described as one of the best examples of the East Asian 'miracle'. Korea's success was indeed impressive. Real gross domestic product (GDP) per capita in purchasing power parity (PPP) terms increased from US$2,500 in 1970 to US$12,600 in 1995, representing an annual real growth rate of 7 per cent. 'In just 25 years Korea accomplished what had taken the Western economies nearly one hundred years' (McKinsey Global Institute 1998: 1). Moreover, unemployment, hovering around 2 per cent, was never a problem. High growth and low unemployment were the key words summarising the path of the Korean economy. However, it suddenly spiralled into a currency-induced liquidity crisis in late 1997. Without the International Monetary Fund (IMF) bailout package of US$58 billion, a moratorium would have been declared in December 1997. As corporate defaults rise and bad debts mount, unemployment is soaring. A severe insolvency-induced economic crisis may still have to be faced.

A sudden collapse was, however, not accidental. Indeed, since the early 1990s, some economists had predicted an eventual breakdown of the economy unless there was fundamental market and corporate governance reform.[1] Market reforms were necessary for the product, financial and labour markets. In 1993, the President of Korea, Kim Young Sam, pushed for reform in the early stages of his administration. However, for various reasons that are beyond the scope of this chapter, no major reform measures were implemented. Even the 'real name financial transaction' system, which Kim Young Sam pioneered rather boldly in the summer of 1993 and which was the only serious reform to speak of under his administration, was by 1996 under severe attack from Korean establishments which considered it responsible for the declining international competitiveness of Korean firms.[2]

In 1996, the Korean economic problem, manifested by growing current account deficits and falling corporate profitability, was labelled in political circles and the popular media as a structural problem of high cost and low efficiency. On the one hand, the high factor cost included wages (labour), interest (capital), rent (land) and logistics. High wage and interest costs were a major focus of attention. On the other hand, it was not clear what 'low efficiency' meant. Since it was often brought up in the context of the fact that wage rates grew faster than labour productivity from 1987, it was apparent that low efficiency implied low labour productivity.

In late 1996, the government and ruling party decided to tackle the problem on the labour front. Labour market regulations and union-negotiated work rules were so rigid that not only was it nearly impossible to lay off excess workers but it was also very difficult to use part-time workers or institute more flexible working hours. These inflexible labour practices were largely adopted in 1987 when the democratisation process began in Korea. By 1996, however, it was very clear that the pendulum had moved too much in the opposite direction. In any case, the government came to the conclusion that, without labour reform, Korean industries would not maintain international competitiveness. The labour reform bill was sent to the National Assembly in December 1996. The opposition parties, though in agreement with the ruling party on the major elements of the bill, requested a delay of a couple of months. The ruling party, however, passed the bill early in the morning of 26 December, without opposition members present, in an Entebbe-like military operation style.

Massive and numerous labour strikes followed. The public was so furious that many white collar workers also participated in street demonstrations. The way the labour law was passed was also to be challenged in the Constitutional Court. The administration then belatedly realised that pushing the law through, without even weak consent from the labour unions and opposition parties, had been a grave mistake. It was also quite apparent that labour reform was unlikely to happen during the remaining one-year term of Kim Young Sam's administration.[3]

In early January of 1997, the President announced initiatives that set the stage for financial reform. These initiatives were intended, partly, to dissipate the problem arising from the new labour law fiasco. More importantly, however, now that labour reform was unlikely, the need for financial reform was much greater in order to improve what was often called the 'national competitiveness' of Korea.[4]

This chapter reviews the process and major elements of financial reform in Korea and the potential impact on the country's corporate organisations. Although the process started in early 1997, it was the currency crisis later in the year that provided the strong impetus to push real and painful reform. It should therefore be noted at the outset that financial reform is still ongoing and thus incomplete at this stage. The urgent need to restore the confidence of the international investor community is forcing Korea to speed up the process. This has two effects: on the one hand, the crisis provided a once-in-a-lifetime opportunity to implement various reform measures which would otherwise have been extremely difficult to introduce because of political resistance. On the other hand, however, sweeping reform creates an enormous amount of uncertainty about the new 'rules of the game'. This is due to the sheer magnitude, as well as the scope, of the necessary reform and to the lack of skills needed to manage the process on the part of the new administration led by Kim Dae Jung.

FINANCIAL SYSTEM AND CORPORATE ORGANISATION

Various characteristics of the Korean financial system have shaped corporate organisations and dictated their financial behaviour. The following discussion focuses mainly on those characteristics that have a close bearing on corporate finance and organisation.

A credit-based and administered-finance system

The first characteristic of the financial system is that it is largely credit-based as opposed to capital market-based. The major funding source for Korean firms has been credits from banks and non-bank financial institutions. Up until 1985, the proportion of indirect financing in the total domestic external financing of firms was about 60–70 per cent (Bank of Korea 1994). The remaining proportion, of 30–40 per cent, came from direct financing (i.e. bonds, stocks, commercial papers). From the second half of the 1980s, however, securities became a more important source of corporate funds, their proportion reaching 50–60 per cent of domestic external financing. Thus, although it appears that the financial system has been in the process of being transformed into one more akin to a capital market-based system, there is a caveat: the bulk of bonds and commercial papers, a much more significant source of securities financing in Korea than stocks, are *guaranteed* by financial institutions. For example, out of 34.3 trillion won of new corporate bonds issued in 1997, only 15 per cent were pure debentures; the remaining 85 per cent were bonds guaranteed by financial institutions such as banks, securities companies, merchant banks and a few specialised guarantee companies.[5] Since most corporate bonds, and commercial paper as well, for that matter, are backed by financial institutions, it could be argued that credits rather than securities are still the predominant source of corporate financing in Korea.

Korea's financial system is closer to the credit-based systems of Japan and France than to the capital market-based systems of the United States and the United Kingdom. It has other related features that are generally associated with a credit-based financial system:[6]

- the pricing mechanism is influenced more by administrative guidance than by competitive market forces;

- an important objective of monetary policy is resource allocation rather than the stability of the financial system;

- the major tools of monetary policy are financial regulation and administrative guidance, instead of monetary aggregates;

- an industrial adjustment is often government-led rather than company-led;

- the relationships between government, banks and firms are dependent rather than arm's-length ones; and

- the major suppliers of long-term funds are specialised banks, instead of investment institutions.

As will be seen, other characteristics and their bearing upon corporate finance can be partly attributed to the fact that Korea has maintained a credit-based financial system.

'Administered finance' is a derogatory expression in Korea for chronic and heavy intervention in the financial sector by bureaucrats and politicians. The practice of so-called administered finance originated when the former president, Park Jung Hee, launched a series of five-year economic development plans, beginning in the early 1960s. Since domestic savings were insufficient alone to meet the strong demand for investment funds, the savings and external borrowing were allocated by the government not only to industries but to individual firms that it selected.[7] In order to use finance as a major tool of industrial policy, the military government nationalised all commercial banks and usurped the independence of the central bank in the early 1960s.

What followed was familiar to both financial and development economists: Korea Inc. was born. Korea Inc. had similar features to Japan Inc. – a combination of political monopoly by a ruling party, the industrial policies of a commerce ministry, and the detailed micro-management of the financial markets by a finance ministry. Industries and firms in export sectors were given preferential treatment in terms of the availability of credit and low interest rates. During the 1960s and 1970s, when the economy was small and its structure rather simple, the Korean strategy of pursuing an export-driven growth path with finance as a major tool of industrial policy was largely successful and contributed to spectacular growth.

Financial regulation of prices, entries and products

As in any developing economy today, or for that matter as in most developed economies until the late 1970s, the Korean government heavily regulated the interest rates, entries and products of financial institutions. These regulations contributed to the shape of the financial landscape observed today.

Interest rates for both deposits and loans were tightly controlled until 1990.[8] Similarly, underwriting and brokerage fees, insurance premia and the prices of almost all other financial products were also regulated. Interest rate control, which was introduced to provide cheap funds to industrial firms, resulted in a few interesting financial conventions. First, since the maximum rate banks could charge to borrowers was often much lower than not only the market rate but also the risk-adjusted minimum rate, banks demanded either collateral or third party guarantees on loans. Also, the downward control of loan rates, combined with direct intervention by the government in banks' loan allocations, obviated the need for careful evaluation of each borrower's creditworthiness. In other words, the dual control of price and allocation resulted in rendering collateralised/guaranteed loans rather than pure credit loans, the norm in banking, and in making credit skills underdeveloped and/or underutilised. For example, of the commercial bank loans of 115 trillion won outstanding at the end of 1996, collateralised loans comprised 43 per cent, guaranteed loans 8 per cent and pure credit loans 49 per cent (Bank of Korea 1997: 189). If analysis is confined only to loans to small and medium-sized companies, the proportion based on collateral/guarantee exceeds 90 per cent! (Presidential Commission for Financial Reform 1997: 403).

Interest rate regulation in an economy with entry barriers and also with chronic excess demand for funds resulted in another interesting pattern of bank managerial behaviour: explicit pursuit of deposit maximisation as the primary objective. When the government sets both the deposit rate and the loan rate, it more or less guarantees the net interest margin. This tends to have three effects: first, banks tend to maintain inefficient cost structures. Second, and more importantly, since the volume of deposits has a crucial impact on operating profits, banks compete in taking deposits but not in making sound loans. In other words, they become very good at mobilising savings but rather poor at allocating funds. Third, banks lack an effective system of performance measurement and evaluation, an important element of the internal control system. In fact, the lack of an effective cost accounting system is one of the common characteristics of firms in any industry subject to government regulation of prices and entries.

Banks maintained their old management practices, however, even in the new business environment of the 1990s. In a regulated environment, they could survive and even prosper despite these poor practices. But, even after interest rates started to be liberalised and entry barriers were lowered mainly by opening the market to foreigners, banks continued to pursue deposit maximisation and neglected developing credit skills, for reasons explained shortly. The wrong objectives and poor skills, combined with inadequate incentives, were the critical factors that contributed to the economic crisis Korea faced in 1997.

Also, the so-called administered-finance practice continued even in the 1980s and 1990s, when the size and the complexity of the economy could no longer absorb the negative side effects of heavy government intervention in the financial sector. It was also the government-led development strategy and administered-finance practice that stifled not only market mechanisms but also, as a result, the entrepreneurial spirit of financial institutions, and that gave birth to the uniquely Korean corporate organisational structure known as *chaebol*, a business group consisting of many large firms that are owned and managed by family members in diverse business areas.

The ineffective corporate governance of banks

The government has been involved in the internal management of financial institutions, in general, and banks, in particular. The popular mechanism through which it exerted control was its strong influence on the appointment of the top managers. This practice continued even after all commercial banks, which had been nationalised in the early 1960s, were privatised in the early 1980s. Although the practice of direct appointment was discontinued from 1993, indirect influence remained until recently. With this unwarranted power to exert influence over the top management of private banks, bureaucrats, and sometimes politicians as well, could dictate what banks did. Most significantly, banks followed various explicit and implicit directives 'from above' to allocate credit to specific companies. When politicians were involved, the loans allocated were often linked to bribes or political contributions.[9]

Because the government exercised the power to change managers, it could also interfere in internal bank management. According to one study, the average tenure of bank CEOs during the period 1961–94 was merely 2.3 years (see Park 1994 for details). In such an environment, the manager's decision-making horizon would undoubtedly be very short. Bank managers thus lacked both managerial freedom and incentive to pursue the painstaking organisational changes that are necessary in adapting to new business environments.

Another unique feature of the Korean banking system was that the government imposed tight restrictions on the ownership of commercial banks, mainly to prevent *chaebols* from controlling them. The maximum fraction of shareholding by an 'identical person' was restricted to 8 per cent until 1993, when it was lowered to 4 per cent.[10] The government thereby forced ownership dispersion and prevented banks from being controlled by large shareholders. Although a few large shareholders (i.e. *chaebols*), each with a large block of shares, say 4 per cent each, potentially could have formed a coalition to exercise control, this was never attempted because it was clearly against the policy, albeit unwritten, of the government. Thus, Korean banks operated in a corporate governance vacuum, which in turn allowed further room for government interference.

One of the recurring debates in the Korean banking community has been about the lack of managerial freedom and accountability. On the one hand, managers argued that, since they did not have the necessary freedom, they could not be held accountable for their bank's poor performance. The bureaucrats, on the other hand, argued that the managers could not be given full freedom because it was ultimately the government that had to take entire responsibility for bank failures, in the absence of 'true owners' and safety mechanisms such as deposit insurance or orderly exit procedures. Because of this unproductive chicken-and-egg debate, entrepreneurial spirit in the financial industry was stifled and eventually vanished.

A *chaebol*-dominated economic structure

It is well known that Korea has a *chaebol*-dominated economic structure, rather intentionally set up by former president Park Jung Hee. President Park had a grand vision to modernise Korea, with a notion of Japan as a model on the one hand and as a competitive rival on the other. So Korea imitated Japan, which pursued an export-driven growth strategy and supported firms competing in world export markets. Having virtually nothing to start with in the early 1960s, the Korean government intentionally cultivated a handful of 'star player' firms so that they could reach a certain level of scales necessary to compete in the world market. The bulk of the support took the form of hard foreign currency, cheap loans and various business licences. In order to encourage these star player firms to go public and thereby to diversify their financing sources without worrying about the potential dilution of control rights, the government also protected the control rights of listed firms through various legal measures. The most notable measures included an extremely lax law for minority shareholder rights and a very restrictive legal provision for hostile takeovers. In fact, before 1997, there was not even a single incident of either a minority shareholder protest or a hostile takeover attempt.

The internal corporate governance mechanism has never functioned in Korea. The commercial code stipulates that there be checks and balances among the three legal institutions of corporation: the shareholders' meeting, the board of directors and the internal auditor. As in other countries, the shareholders' meeting has not been an effective governance mechanism. But the board system in Korea has not functioned either, because the board of directors, almost always composed only of insider executives, has been a puppet institution.[11] The internal auditor, although formally a non-employee of the corporation, has usually been an insider appointed by the largest shareholder and seen as a position between senior managing director and senior vice-president. Thus, both directors and auditors have had no independence whatsoever from the controlling shareholders.

These practices, although potentially very serious, did not create insurmountable problems, at least not until the early 1980s. The economy was growing fast and there were abundant business opportunities to be exploited. The star player firms that eventually evolved into today's *chaebols* were managed by founders who had great entrepreneurial spirit. The major businesses of most of the firms were in light manufacturing industries which required neither massive investment nor complex managerial or technological skills. Since the government's incentive scheme was designed to render export performance the most important factor in corporate success, a general trading company as the flagship of each *chaebol* could and did coordinate internal business transactions among affiliated or member firms.

The stakes increased substantially, however, in the mid-1970s when President Park pushed to promote heavy and chemical industries as an engine of fast growth, again following the Japanese model. The more important motive for the 'Big Push', though, was the political and security factor facing Korea at that time. As the administrations of presidents Ford and Carter tried to withdraw US ground forces from South Korea while the military threat from North Korea was increasing, from the late 1960s, Korea wanted to build up a self-sufficient defence system. Such a system required the capability to produce weapons, which in turn depended upon industrial capability and the capacity to produce steel, machinery, large ships and the like. This important security consideration led Korea to venture into heavy industry.[12] The underlying logic was indeed unique to Korea because it had neither the financial and technological resources at that time nor a large domestic market to develop and support such industries.[13] In fact, many characteristics of the Korean economy can partly be attributed to this intense focus, of a comparatively small and underdeveloped economy, on heavy industry.

At any rate, *chaebols*, relatively small until then, were given support again in the form of hard foreign currency, cheap bank loans and business licences. But this time the stakes were much greater, not only to the nation but also to each *chaebol*, because the required scale of heavy and chemical industries was of an order of magnitude much higher than that of light industries such as textiles, plywood and footwear. Every *chaebol* wanted to participate in these new ventures in order to preempt the market; in a monopolistic economy, there is always a first-mover advantage. The net result was overinvestment, the bulk of which went sour during the second oil shock in the late 1970s.

In the early 1980s, many large companies were on the brink of bankruptcy. Since *chaebols* had by then become large relative to the size of the economy, the principle of 'too big to fail' (TBTF) was invoked. The government initiated the massive restructuring and consolidation of firms in numerous capital-intensive industries. Each case involved a large amount of bailout money to firms in trouble or to firms taking over troubled ones. The bailout subsidy was offered through reductions in various taxes and the favourable rescheduling of bank loans. The banks involved were in turn subsidised through the central bank's low rate special loans. The seed of moral hazard was thus planted, which has since plagued the Korean economy in a fundamental way. After this experience, *chaebols* came to be perceived as seemingly invulnerable and grew faster than the economy itself.

The characteristics of chaebols

There are 30 *chaebols* in Korea, according to the legal definition. Among the various regulations they are subject to, the most prominent are the Fair Trade Act and the Credit Restraint Provisions administered by the central bank's Office of Bank Supervision. Each year, 30 of the largest conglomerates, in terms of the aggregate assets of affiliated companies under the control of an 'identical person', are designated as 'large company groups', which are then subject to *chaebol*-related regulations.

The first characteristic of a *chaebol* is that it controls a number of diversified firms and a large proportion of national wealth. As of the end of 1997, the average number of member firms in a *chaebol* was 27 (*Joongang Ilbo* 10 January 1998). The five largest *chaebols*, which are much more significant than the other 25 combined, had on average 41 firms each in late 1995. Hyundai, the largest one, had 46 member firms and its famous slogan has been 'From Chips to Ships'. *Chaebols* therefore command a large proportion of national resources, and the degree of concentration of their economic power has been increasing. For instance, the ratio of their total factory sales to GDP, a simple but informative measure of concentration, was 41 per cent in 1995 and has been increasing over the years.

Another important characteristic of the *chaebol* is its ownership and governance structure. Twenty-nine of the 30 are still family-controlled. The only exception is the eighth largest group, Kia, which has been under court receivership since March 1998. As of late 1995, the inside ownership of the ten largest *chaebols* was on average 44 per cent: a sum of founding family ownership of 8 per cent and member firms' cross ownership of 36 per cent.[14] The founding family, represented by the chairman of each group, thus has absolute control of each *chaebol*. Each group's major decisions are made by an operating committee that consists of about ten of the most powerful executives of the group, many of whom are family members. Each group has an 'office of the chairman' which carries out the central planning, coordination and auditing of member firms. Neither the operating committee nor the office of the chairman is a legally recognised institution. Nonetheless, their role is that of a parent holding company, which is prohibited by Korean commercial law.

What about governance? Note that, in practice, a *chaebol's* legally unrecognised headquarters performs the functions of board of directors and internal auditor. Thus, the latter have been totally ineffective mechanisms, even in corporations with a not insignificant minority shareholder ownership. In addition, as discussed earlier, external pressure for good governance was lacking. In a nutshell, the chairman of each *chaebol* exercised absolute control and his capability became the limit of the organisation's capability.

The 'cross guarantee' of credits has been a uniquely Korean practice, one of the many types of complex internal transactions among member firms. Of cross ownership and cross debt guarantee, it is the latter which has more powerfully bound member firms together. It has in fact been the primary tool that made *chaebols* appear so invulnerable, leading to the TBTF principle, and that made the Korean public a hostage of the *chaebols*. Recognising in the early 1990s the harmful effects of this practice, the government revised the Fair Trade Act and ordered *chaebols* to reduce the size of their cross guarantees over the next four years. As of April 1993, the outstanding amount in cross guarantees was 470 per cent of total equity. This was reduced to 91 per cent in April 1997, the deadline by which *chaebols* had been mandated to reduce their cross guarantees below 100 per cent of equity in order to avoid a penalty fine (Presidential Commission for Financial Reform 1997: 469). The 91 per cent was, alas, an aggregate size. A handful of *chaebols*, with cross guarantees ranging from 200 per cent to 800 per cent of equity, unravelled during the 1997 financial crisis, imposing an enormous strain on the entire economy.[15]

Another notorious characteristic of the *chaebol* has been its lack of accounting transparency, which became a focus of intense concern by the IMF and international investors during the recent financial crisis. Although a consolidation of financial statements is mandated for *chaebols*, its requirement by Korean accounting standards has been so loose as to cover only a fraction of *chaebol* member firms. Moreover, the Korean accounting profession cannot be praised for its professionalism. The lack of transparency was often driven by tax reasons. More importantly, however, it was driven to provide member firms with cross subsidies by circumventing various restrictions on intragroup transactions. Notable examples were questionable transactions at prices deviating substantially from market prices, and the roundabout infusion of equity or other types of funds either to subsidise a member firm or to transfer wealth from one member firm to another. As a result, it was extremely difficult to evaluate the creditworthiness or investment worth of member firms on an individual basis. In recent years, some *chaebols* have set up offshore paper companies that are at the centre of complex transactions among the parent company, a subsidiary company, foreign investors and domestic banks that provide credit guarantees. Often, derivative securities are used to create synthetic securities. These kinds of transactions are very difficult to identify, putting outsiders at a disadvantage.[16]

The managerial focus of *chaebols* can be characterised as 'size maximisation', as an explicit objective, with a tendency to overinvestment and overleverage. The size or sales focus was a direct result of the government's regulation of prices and entries in product markets. When the government regulates prices, it tends to follow a 'cost plus pricing' rule. This in turn results in more or less guaranteeing the operating profit margin, which can be maintained in the presence of entry barriers. Moreover, the Korean economy was largely in a state of excess demand for manufactured goods until the late 1980s. Thus, production meant sales which, given the more or less guaranteed margin, led to assured operating profits. The resulting volume orientation was directly responsible for overinvestment. From the early 1990s, many capital-intensive manufacturing industries (e.g. steel, automobiles, semiconductors) started to experience overcapacity in both domestic and world markets. And yet *chaebols* continued expanding, even when domestic markets were due to be opened to foreigners under the new World Trade Organisation (WTO) order. As a result, the capital productivity of capital-intensive manufacturing industries was, on average, only 50 per cent of the US level in 1995 and the return on capital fell short of its cost, a clear evidence of overinvestment and destruction of value.[17]

Overinvestment was made possible because of easy access to cheap credit. This in turn was made feasible due to a combination of several factors: cross guarantees, lack of transparency, the ineffective governance mechanism of banks, and business–politics cronyism. Easy money was in the form of debt, esspecially short-term debt. As of the end of 1996, the debt–equity ratio of the manufacturing sector was 336 per cent and that of the 30 *chaebols* was 389 per cent which, due to severe financial distress, went up to 519 per cent by the end of 1997 (*Joongang Ilbo* 10 January 1998). For troubled groups, a debt–equity ratio of over 1,000 per cent has not been uncommon! Moreover, the debt consists largely of short-term debt, representing about 60 per cent of the total. The current ratio, that of short-term assets to short-term liabilities, illustrates the picture more dramatically. The current ratio of a typical manufacturing company in Korea is about 95 per cent, whereas it is over 150 per cent in the United States. The current ratio of less than 100 per cent implies that firms finance investment in fixed assets partly from short-term borrowing. This practice violates one of the sound financing principles for corporate safety, namely the principle of financing at least part of short-term assets as well as long-term assets from long-term sources in order to maintain a liquidity cushion.

An antiquated regulatory and supervisory system

Prior to April 1998, there were four financial sectors for regulatory classification: banks, securities firms, insurance companies, and others. The Monetary Board of the Bank of Korea (the highest policymaking body of the central bank) set policy and the bank's Office of Bank Supervision supervised compliance, in regard to the bank accounts of the commercial banking industry.[18] For securities firms and publicly traded companies, the Securities and Exchange Commission set policy and the Securities Supervisory Board had supervisory authority. For the insurance industry, the Ministry of Finance and Economy (MOFE) set the policies and the Insurance Supervisory Board checked compliance. Those financial institutions not covered by these three groups came under the jurisdiction of the MOFE.[19] Those under direct MOFE control were the non-bank financial institutions, which included the trust accounts of commercial banks; development institutions such as long-term credit banks; investment institutions such as merchant banks and investment trust companies; leasing companies; credit card companies; and other savings institutions such as credit unions. Since the MOFE did not have the necessary infrastructure for detailed surveillance, this function was in large part delegated to the Office of Bank Supervision.

Although regulatory power appears to have been somewhat fragmented, the MOFE in reality enjoyed monopoly power. In this regard, the Korean MOFE was exactly like the Japanese Ministry of Finance. Essentially, it selected the heads of all the regulatory agencies, who more often than not were former high-ranking MOFE bureaucrats. The same was true for self-regulatory agencies such as the Korea stock exchange and the trade associations for each type of financial institution.[20] Moreover, the CEOs of the three largest investment trust companies with diffuse ownership structures were also appointed by the MOFE. Investment trust companies were the major vehicles for the government's price-keeping operations in the stock market, operations again similar to those frequently observed in Japan. The MOFE also dominated the Monetary Board, whose chairman was also minister for the MOFE, and essentially selected its members.[21] This is why the independence of the central bank from political considerations could not be assured.

The rationale for the absolute power of the MOFE was that, at least in a developing economy, monetary policy needed to be tightly coordinated with fiscal policy, and that, in the absence of a deposit insurance scheme and effective bankruptcy procedures, the government would have to bear full and ultimate responsibility for the failures of private financial institutions.[22] This reasoning may have had some validity in the past. As the 1990s approached, however, the size and complexity of the Korean economy had outgrown the old rationale. The government could not prevent the concentration of assets into specific sectors or borrowers, the dealings of financial institutions with related companies, the wild speculation in risky investments, the non-transparent and dubious accounting practices, and, most importantly, the enormous amount of bad debt.[23] The financial crisis of 1997 was clear evidence.

SWEEPING REFORM IN THE FINANCIAL SECTOR AND IN CORPORATE ORGANISATIONS

Korea had a golden opportunity to reform in the boom years of the late 1980s. It was, unfortunately, lost completely. The economy, in serious trouble from the late 1970s to the early 1980s, began to turn around dramatically and rapidly. Over the period 1986–8, as exports doubled, the balance of payments turned from chronic deficit into huge surplus; as corporate profits soared, stock prices quadrupled; and, as new issues of stock jumped, the corporate debt–equity ratio dropped from 340 per cent to 230 per cent. This unprecedented economic boom was created by three blessings: a low dollar (strong yen and mark), a low dollar interest rate and low oil prices. The dramatic appreciation of both the yen and the deutschmark after the September 1985 Plaza Accord created equally dramatic improvements in the price competitiveness of Korean export industries in general, and heavy industries in particular, which competed directly with Japanese and German firms in world export markets. The fall in the dollar interest rate also helped Korean firms which had borrowed heavily in the floating rate eurodollar markets. Low commodity prices, especially on oil, also helped Korea, which depended heavily on imports of primary commodities. The successful 1988 Seoul Olympics was, in a sense, a symbol of the arrival of this 'second take-off', engineered by the economic wind of the three blessings. However, this temporary boom, largely driven by external factors and thus good luck, made Korea Inc. blind to its structural weaknesses and urgent need of the reform necessary to meet the challenge of global competition in the next decade.

The economic boom came to a halt in 1989 and, by the early 1990s, the necessity of reform was being widely recognised. The challenging question Korea then struggled with was how to adopt market liberalisation without suffering significant macroeconomic dislocations and without undermining the competitiveness of its industries. As the consultancy Booz Allen & Hamilton (1997) found, there had been many good ideas but no action. This was because, as they accurately pointed out, most calls to action had run into a number of insurmountable transition issues, which included the concentration of economic power in *chaebols,* systemic risk in the financial sector and widespread bankruptcies in the manufacturing sector.

However, the IMF's bailout and the election of reform-minded President Kim Dae Jung–watershed events for Korea–have provided the necessary spur to action. As a result, revolutionary changes are taking place.[24] At a higher level of abstraction, these changes embody a belated recognition of two philosophies: first, the crony system of the past can no longer support fast economic growth and the welfare of the people. In the words of the new president, democracy and a market economy must advance hand in hand. Second, an unfriendly attitude towards foreigners does not have a place in a globalised world. Various regulations, intended or otherwise, which have made doing business in Korea rather difficult, are being rapidly removed, which will also have a profound impact on the regulatory landscape for domestic economic agents as well.[25]

The consolidation of regulatory agencies

In April 1998, the Financial Supervisory Commission (FSC) was established. This powerful new agency was placed under the jurisdiction of the prime minister instead of the MOFE. The new commission will be responsible for setting all regulatory policies for the financial industry. The MOFE will retain authority for setting major financial policies, granting business licences to new entrants and changing the business boundaries of each type of financial institution. The FSC will, however, set the regulatory policies necessary to ensure the safety and soundness of the financial system.

Under the commission, two new boards were created. The Financial Supervisory Board has supervisory and surveillance authority over the entire financial industry. This board, headed by the chairman of the FSC, will consolidate over a two-year period the three separate supervisory agencies (banking, securities and insurance). The Deposit Insurance Board will consolidate the two-year-old Korea Deposit Insurance Corporation and the other fragmented insurance facilities. This board will be directly involved in the restructuring and reorganisation of financial institutions in trouble.

The revised Bank of Korea Act has given the Bank of Korea independence and autonomy, the status for which it fought for over 30 years against the finance ministry. The governor of the bank is now also the chairman of the Monetary Board instead of the minister of the MOFE. The central bank's primary mission is unequivocally stated as ensuring price stability. In other words, maintaining a sound banking system is not one of its primary missions under the revised law. In turn, the bank has had to transfer to the new commission its supervisory functions, including the Office of Bank Supervision.

There has been consensus in Korea about the need for the central bank's independence. About the consolidation of the regulatory and supervisory agencies, however, there has been hot debate, even intense bickering. To discuss in detail, however, the pros and cons of consolidation is beyond the scope of this chapter. Suffice it to say that, under a consolidated structure, information about all financial institutions will be centralised in one agency which will then be able to check whether the diversification requirements of financial institutions have been properly set and enforced. As Capiro and Vittas have noted, 'officials intent on reforming their financial system should keep in mind that most banks – and banking systems – encounter solvency problems (or bank crisis) because they fail to diversify' (1997: 8). Thus, the centralisation of information is a great advantage of the consolidated regulatory structure.[26]

Deregulation/restructuring of the financial industry

It is widely recognised in Korea today that, unless there is a well-functioning financial industry, the efficient allocation of resources and ensuring corporate accountability are not possible. The same has been said many times before. The recent economic crisis, however, not only reinforces this thought, it also forces various reform measures into implementation. Financial reform measures in this regard can be classified into two types: long-term deregulation and short-term restructuring of financial institutions.

With a consolidated regulatory structure, which it is hoped will be more effective in ensuring safety and soundness, the financial system is shifting from a repressed regime to a market-oriented one. The overall direction for greater efficiency is to enhance competition and improve the incentives of owners and managers. More concretely, the old regulatory practices are being abandoned. First, any remaining price regulation on financial products, such as brokerage commission, has been virtually eliminated. Foreign exchange control was also removed in mid-1998. Thus, capital inflows and outflows will be fully liberalised. Second, entry barriers are much lower than a year ago. The capital requirements for establishing a new brokerage firm or an investment trust company have been made more realistic (i.e. much smaller). In addition, the ownership restriction for commercial banks has been relaxed from 4 per cent to 10 per cent, subject to approval from the FSC. Also, compartmentalisation among banking, securities and insurance will be loosened to move towards a universal banking system in the long run. The impact of deregulation will be long-term because essentially it involves changes in the financial infrastructure and the business culture as well.

The more immediate issue in financial reform is restructuring, because there are a number of very weak financial institutions. Since November 1997, 14 out of 30 merchant banks have been closed, and 2 out of 35 securities firms were already closed. Two of the largest commercial banks, nationalised in 1997, were due to be sold off in the latter part of 1998 to investors, foreign as well as domestic. Any financial institution that could not meet the capital adequacy requirements, like the Bank for International Settlements (BIS) ratio or its variant, by June 1998 had to make a painful choice: new equity infusion, merger or closure.[27] Many of the leasing, life insurance and investment trust companies are not expected to survive 1998. The Presidential Council for Economic Policy Coordination estimated the size of non-performing assets at the end of March 1998 at 118 trillion won (US$84.3 billion, at the early June exchange rate of 1,400 won per US dollar), representing 22.9 per cent of total credits.[28] This estimate did not include the non-performing assets of investment trust companies and regional financial institutions.[29] The size of the bad assets to be restructured was estimated at about 100 trillion won, approximately 25 per cent of GDP, and the amount of public money needed to clean up the books at around half the size of the non-performing assets. The government plans to issue bonds of 50 trillion won (US$35.7 billion): 25 trillion won to finance the purchase of bad assets by the Korea Asset Management Corporation, the state-owned entity similar to the Resolution Trust Corporation in the United States; 16 trillion won to finance viable banks' equity build-up to meet the BIS capital adequacy requirements, and 9 trillion won to finance payment on the insured deposits of non-viable banks to be reorganised.[30] Since there is a tremendous shortage of resources in the domestic economy, both public and private, the bulk of the necessary funding will have to come from a combination of foreign investors and the central bank.[31]

The current restructuring is undoubtedly happening on an ad hoc basis. This is because the bad asset problem is huge and Korea has never developed an effective exit mechanism for weak financial institutions. A vicious cycle has been developing since the onset of the crisis and the financial intermediation process has virtually broken down. The central bank increased the money supply. Money, however, does not flow into firms. As Mark Twain once put it, a cat once burnt will not sit on the stove again, even a cold one. Financial institutions do not have credit evaluation skills and thus do not know to whom to lend. Even *chaebols* are not invulnerable any more. Also, assets need to be shrunk in order to meet the BIS requirements. All this leads to a contraction of credits to firms, which combined with the extremely high level of interest rates leads to rising corporate defaults. This in turn aggravates the bad asset problems of financial institutions. Restructuring under such dire circumstances is bound to be ad hoc and subject to error.

Chaebol reform

Soon after the election in December 1997, President-elect Kim Dae Jung met with the chairmen of the five largest *chaebols* to discuss the need for and the direction of *chaebol* reform. The meeting, held on 13 January 1998, resulted in an agreement on the five reform agenda, later also agreed to by other *chaebols*.[32]

- From 1998, the 30 *chaebols* will prepare 'integrated financial statements' and make every effort to enhance management transparency.
- By March 2000, cross debt guarantees among member firms will be entirely eliminated and the practice of cross subsidies will be stopped.
- By the end of 1999, the debt–equity ratio will be reduced to 200 per cent.
- *Chaebols* will focus only on core businesses and will strengthen cooperation with small and medium-sized companies.
- *Chaebols* will ensure the accountability of the large owner-managers.

This agreement, if fully implemented, will lead to the de facto dissolution of *chaebols*. First, an integrated accounting system is the most important tool for bringing about transparency in corporate management. An integrated financial statement will include *all* member firms in a *chaebol* group, where membership is defined by the Fair Trade Act to be any firm under the control of an 'identical person'. All intragroup transactions will be disclosed and also netted out to reveal the true picture of each group.

Without cross debt guarantees, member firms will have to be evaluated in the financial markets on a stand-alone basis. If the practice of giving cross subsidies in other forms is also stopped, which could be enforced with a new integrated accounting system, each member firm will become independent in the market place.[33] A weak firm will not be able to obtain capital just because (or even if) it is a *chaebol* affiliate. This way, overinvestment is less likely to take place and thus more efficient allocation of capital can be ensured.

Another mandate forced upon *chaebols* is a dramatic improvement in capital structure. Reducing the debt–equity ratio from 5:1 to 2:1 in times of sluggish stock markets and falling profitability is the extremely difficult challenge facing the 30 *chaebols*.[34] In fact, the government is forcing them into dramatic business restructuring because, without it, Korea is less likely to overcome the current crisis or prevent a future one.

The requirement to focus only on core businesses, however defined, also forces *chaebols* into downsizing and restructuring. In fact, each *chaebol* has been required to submit a restructuring plan to its principal transaction bank.[35] The plan is finalised through an agreement with the bank, which will then monitor its implementation every six months. In a sense, banks are now expected to play a prominent role in ensuring effective corporate governance, as they do in Japan and Germany. It is very doubtful, however, whether Korean banks can play such a role effectively in the foreseeable future.[36]

The government is introducing various measures to facilitate *chaebol* restructuring and to also restore foreign investors' confidence. To focus on core businesses and to reduce financial leverage, many *chaebols* are trying to sell their real estate and to divest non-core member firms or divisions. Very few have been successful, however, because virtually all are trying to do so at the same time. To encourage restructuring, the government has taken two avenues of approach: one is to attract foreign capital and the other is to pour in public money. To bring in foreign capital, the limit on foreign ownership of listed companies was raised from 26 per cent to 55 per cent in December 1997 and, on 25 May 1998, was entirely removed. Hostile takeovers by foreigners were also allowed from May 1998. In addition, various regulations, implicit as well as explicit, inhibiting foreign direct investment are being dismantled. The government has announced that most state-owned enterprises will be privatised. Even significant ones, such as the giant Korea Telecom or the Korea Electricity and Power Corporation, will be allowed to be partially controlled by foreign investors. All these measures will contribute to restoring the confidence of international investors. More importantly, they will help and/or force *chaebol* restructuring.

Another avenue to help firms restructure has been the establishment of the Corporate Restructuring Fund, which was launched in June 1998 with an initial capital of 10 trillion won. The International Finance Corporation (IFC), a World Bank sister organisation, will be asked to manage the fund. It will consist of two sub-funds: an American-style mutual fund for securities investment, mainly in large firms; and an equity investment and debt restructuring fund to provide equity and long-term loans, mainly to small and medium-sized groups. In addition, the government is planning to change the tax law to eliminate any tax disadvantage from restructuring, for example by allowing tax exemptions on capital gains from selling real estate or divisions.

The government is twisting the arms of banks and *chaebols* to force them into 'voluntary' corporate restructuring. There were two interesting events in June 1998. One was the 'death list' of 55 troubled firms, released by the FSC on 18 June (*Korea*

Times 18 June 1998). The list included 20 firms of the five largest *chaebols*. Banks will no longer provide new credits to or extend the existing loans of firms on the list, which will result in their liquidation. Banks were forced to come up with this list because they and the *chaebols* were throwing good money after bad into non-viable firms: banks, to disguise the extent of their bad debt problems, and *chaebols*, to delay the painful restructuring of non-viable affiliates. The government took this drastic action because the cost of preserving non-viable firms would have been mostly and ultimately borne by taxpayers. It was widely speculated that this was only the beginning of the massive restructuring orchestrated by the government. The other event was public discussion of the so-called 'Big Deal', the swapping among a few of the largest *chaebols* of capital-intensive businesses (e.g. auto, semiconductor, electronics, petrochemical) which are in a state of global glut. President Kim is very forcefully encouraging this and it is highly likely to be consummated before the end of 1998.[37]

Ensuring accountability, along with the other reforms, is also a near-revolutionary concept in Korea. Three fundamental measures are being implemented in this regard. The first is corporate board reform. The Korea stock exchange has changed its listing requirements so that, from 1998, there should be at least one outside director.[38] From 1999, at least one-quarter of directors have to be outsiders. The chairmen of many *chaebols* used not to hold any legal position (i.e. directorship) in member firms. Without even being directors, they exercised absolute control. Now, they have all become directors of the main firms in their groups and they are legitimate board chairmen.

The second, and related, measure is the voluntary dismantling of group headquarters, namely the illegal 'office of the chairman'. Its coordination function has now to be performed either by a planning and coordination office or by a chairman's office in the parent company. This practice, inevitable in the absence of a legally legitimate holding company structure, is temporary. The third reform measure is to institutionalise the measures necessary for the legal protection of minority shareholders. For example, the minimum ownership requirement to initiate a collective action suit has been lowered from 1 per cent to 0.01 per cent. As a result, shareholder activism gained ground in 1998.[39] All these reform measures will take time to have a full impact. What is important, however, is that owner-managers, inside directors and minority shareholders are all awakened now.

THE POLITICAL ECONOMY OF DELEVERAGING

One of the most distinctive characteristics of the Korean economy has been the extremely high leverage of corporations. In an environment of low profitability, this contributed to the financial crisis. The current restructuring effort is therefore focused mainly on how to deleverage the corporate sector. The reasons for and ways to reduce leverage, although crucial, are not well understood either by foreign observers or by economists and finance specialists in Korea. This issue therefore deserves special discussion.

As already mentioned, debt–equity ratios of 300–400 per cent have not been uncommon, even in normal times. This high leverage resulted from the combination of several factors. First, Korea's manufacturing-oriented economy, dominated since the mid-1970s by heavy and chemical industries, required massive investment, most of which had to come from external sources (i.e. sources other than retained earnings).[40] Second, Korea does not have a well-developed stock market, essential if external equity financing is to be a significant source of funds. These two factors meant that a strong demand for 'bulky' investment financing could only be satisfied by bank credits. Third, Korea has maintained a high national savings ratio largely because of its high household savings rate, the bulk of which had to be intermediated by banks because of Korea's credit-based system.[41] Thus, domestic savings supplied a significant portion of the required investment funds, again in the form of bank credits.

These three elements, contributing to high leverage in the corporate sector,[42] are common in Japan as well, which also has a highly leveraged corporate sector.[43] Since such high leverage gives rise to enormous vulnerability in an economic downturn, there must be an additional factor that allows the sustainability of a highly leveraged economy with a heavy industry focus, a weak stock market and high domestic household savings.[44] This fourth factor is conjectured to have been cross debt guarantees in the case of Korea, and cross shareholdings in the case of Japan. The Korean cross debt guarantee has been a more powerful tool for avoiding bankruptcy, however, than the Japanese cross shareholding. This is because the former involved multilateral debt guarantees among member firms of a *chaebol*, while the latter, although multilateral among member firms of a *keiretsu*, involved as far as credit was concerned a bilateral contract between a main bank and non-bank member firms.

Both the cross debt guarantees in Korea and the cross shareholdings in Japan tended to render the risk of private corporations a social risk.[45] In Korea, however, the transfer of corporate risk to society in general, and to taxpayers in particular, was much more pronounced than in Japan. In Korea, a member firm in financial distress was initially bailed out by other *chaebol* member firms and later by the lending banks through the central bank. The cross debt guarantees demanded by financial institutions and supplied by *chaebols* therefore created the moral hazard behaviour of the two counterparties, which led to the even higher leverage of the corporate sector. The highly leveraged economic system thus established could be sustained when only a few industries were experiencing declining profitability and financial distress. It could not, however, when many were performing poorly and an external shock affecting the entire economy was taking place, as was evident in 1997.

Means of deleveraging

Whether and how drastic and speedy economy-wide deleveraging can be achieved is not quite clear. In principle, it can be done in four different ways.[46] First, highly leveraged firms can improve profitability and repay debt with internally generated funds, an avenue that is unlikely to be feasible for most firms in the near future.

Second, non-viable firms with high leverage can be allowed to go bankrupt, to be either liquidated or reorganised. There are three problems with relying on the bankruptcy route for economy-wide deleveraging. It is financial institutions that make a judgment on the viability of each corporate client, but they do not have adequate credit skills to do so. Moreover, such a judgment is particularly difficult in times of crisis because many firms are in a grey zone, rather than in a clear zone of either black or white. In addition, because the Korean economy is dominated by large *chaebols* to each of which numerous small and medium-sized firms are bilaterally linked, bankruptcies of even a few *chaebols* would bring down many potentially viable small and medium-sized companies. This high degree of interconnectedness therefore makes the contagion risk more severe than it would be otherwise. Given the heavy industrial structure and the poor financial infrastructure, rapid deleveraging may not be structurally feasible because bank credits would continue for the foreseeable future to be the dominant source of corporate funding. Even if wholesale bankruptcy is a feasible and efficient means of deleveraging, however, it may not be politically acceptable because Korea has no social safety net.[47] These considerations mean that economy-wide deleveraging through wholesale bankruptcies would be highly limited in scope and scale.

The third way is to convert bank loans into equity: a debt–equity swap. Although it is certainly a feasible method, it may be subject to a severe political problem. Once a non-performing bank loan is converted into the client firm's equity, the banks can keep holding the equity positions or sell them to third parties. Holding an equity position for a long period of time is not feasible, not only because the banks' profitability will then deteriorate even further but because the banks do not have the skills to adequately monitor and discipline corporations in the manner of a large shareholder, skills that German banks possess to a large extent. Therefore, the banks need to liquidate a significant portion of the new equity. The question is: who would have enough cash resources to purchase them? Practically speaking, only foreign investors and foreign companies. Thus, the debt–equity swap would eventually lead to the sale of many firms' shares to foreigners, probably at fire-sale prices. Given that such swaps and sales would also involve massive restructuring and, as a result, would not be very helpful in containing rising unemployment, this action would not be politically acceptable.[48] Thus, the debt–equity swap alone would not be able to bring about deleveraging in a manner both economically feasible and politically acceptable.

The fourth avenue to deleveraging is inflation. High inflation reduces a real burden of debt because inflation reduces the value of the fixed principal payment and also the real interest rate on the existing debt if the nominal interest rate is also fixed. Therefore, high inflation helps firms to lower their financial leverage. This method also has merits and demerits. On the one hand, the cost of deleveraging through an inflationary route is borne not just by a limited number of groups in a concentrated manner but by the entire people in the economy. The pain of deleveraging can thus be diluted,[49] the pace controlled and wholesale bankruptcies avoided. On the other hand, inflation would destabilise the exchange rate and further devaluation of the won would increase the burden of external debt obligation.

Given the magnitude of the debt problem, no single method would be sufficient to rapidly and substantially deleverage the corporate sector. For two reasons, however, Korea should rely more heavily on the inflation route. One, it would invite a less severe political backlash because the cost would be widely spread and the pain diluted. Two, it would also help the government to finance a social safety net and bank restructuring. Currently, the fear of inflation constrains the government's options for financing unemployment benefits and the public funds for restructuring financial institutions.

CONCLUSION

Korea is waking up from a long but unsustainable prosperity based on crony capitalism and the protection of domestic markets. There is another growing consensus: productivity is now the only source of future sustainable growth and international competitiveness. In order to transform the economy into a more productive one, urgent reform is necessary so that financial institutions can compete to allocate resources to efficient firms without impairing the safety and soundness of the financial system. Reform is also necessary to change corporate organisation and governance structures that no longer serve *chaebols* themselves, let alone the national welfare.

The main focus of the reforms is to eliminate moral hazard and to create an incentive-compatible business environment. The *chaebol*-dominated economic structure is being dismantled. Corporate reform is thus moving in the right direction. Financial reform, however, a precondition for successful corporate reform, is still in the infant stage for several reasons. First, the amount of bad debt is so large that the financial intermediation process is breaking down, which constrains policy options. Also, various ways for a badly needed deleveraging of the corporate sector are subject to a potential political backlash. Second, although the banks have an important role in ensuring the efficient and effective governance of industrial companies, it is not clear yet how to improve the governance of banks themselves. Another factor that renders the current financial reform quite incomplete is the lack of an efficient bankruptcy mechanism, not only for financial firms but also for industrial firms. Unless such a mechanism is developed, moral hazard problems might persist because Korea would continue to rely on the large (relative to the size of the economy) financial and industrial firms. Lastly, Korea needs to evaluate the feasibility of introducing a holding company structure, as Japan did recently. One of the reasons that *chaebols* maintained an awkward organisational structure for central planning and coordination was the fact that holding company structures were not legally allowed. Now that *chaebols'* moral hazard behaviour can be institutionally controlled, perhaps they should be allowed to conduct central planning and coordination through holding companies.

What are the implications of and lessons from the Korean case for other developing economies? First of all, the industrial structure and the financial structure of a nation should be congruent. If an economy does not have a well-functioning stock market, its financial system is likely to be a credit-based one. If such an economy promotes heavy industries and large enterprises as a matter of policy, corporate leverage is bound to be very high, which may create severe moral hazard problems including overinvestment. It is important for such economies, therefore, to promote less capital-intensive light manufacturing industries and also small and medium-sized enterprises in order to pursue a balanced economic growth path.

Second, until a modern financial infrastructure is set up, capital account convertibility should be delayed and the government should control short-term capital flows. As the IMF admits unequivocally, for Korea, 'capital account liberalisation . . . was not well sequenced nor accompanied by the reforms and strong prudential supervision of the financial system' (IMF 1998: 1). It is tempting for economists to argue that capital account liberalisation will facilitate the necessary reform process. Although true in principle, it is nonetheless a naïve argument that underestimates what is involved in implementing institutional reform. Even with a strong political will, reform will take at least a decade. But in a country with capital account liberalisation adopted already and thus exposed to a new global capital system, a decade is a 'long run', during which, according to Keynes, we could all be dead. Therefore, a recommendation for the proper sequencing and control of short-term capital flows cannot be overemphasised.[50]

NOTES

1 Of the two views about the origin of the Asian crisis, financial panic versus structural weakness, which are not necessarily mutually exclusive, the author tends to subscribe to the latter as far as Korea is concerned. For a comprehensive analysis of the Asian crisis, see Corsetti et al. (1998).
2 Kim Young Sam decreed an end to the use of street names on personal financial accounts, a commonly used means of hiding ownership and concealing cash generated from questionable practice. The real name financial transaction system was weakened in early 1998. In order to attract money from the wealthy who prefer anonymity in financial transactions, the government issued bonds of bearer form with tax benefits but lower yields.
3 In February 1998, a new labour law making layoffs and labour rules more flexible was passed in the midst of the IMF bailout and the worsening economic crisis. This time, however, the new law was based on consensus among the government, business, labour and all political parties.
4 As Paul Krugman has forcefully argued, there may not be such a thing as 'national competitiveness'. To be precise, it means the international competitiveness of firms.
5 The Korea Stock Exchange, *Stock*, January 1998. The fact that securities firms, which have neither credit skills nor comparative advantage in the guarantee business, have been very active guarantor institutions of corporate bonds is one of many anomalies in the Korean financial system.
6 For an excellent discussion about the two types of financial systems, see Zysman (1983).
7 Although Korea and Japan are similar in that both used finance to promote export-driven growth, there is an important distinction. While the Japanese government tried to direct funds to the industries it selected, Korea attempted to direct funds both to selected industries and to specific companies within each industry selected for promotion.

8   Interest rates were liberalised over four phases in seven years, the first starting in 1991. In mid-1997, the last phase was completed and now all rates, including the demand deposit rate, have been liberalised.

9   In fact, what is often called 'politics–business cronyism' in Korea, an expression for the give-and-take or crony relationship between politicians and businessmen, involved the granting of scarce bank loans or business licences by politicians.

10   An 'identical person' is a legal term that includes all individuals or firms that are under the control of one person, often the largest owner and manager of a *chaebol*. Also, the rule limiting ownership is subject to some exceptions. Notably, the limit for regional commercial banks has been 15 per cent.

11   For an excellent survey of the role of the corporate board in ensuring good governance, see John and Senbet (1998).

12   For a lucid discussion about the political economy of Korea in the 1970s, see Clifford (1998).

13   For the impacts of regional and global politics on the Korean financial structure and liberalisation, see Woo-Cumings (1997).

14   Kia's 25.9 per cent inside shareholding consisted of family shareholding of 0.3 per cent and member firms' 25.6 per cent (see Lim 1997 for details).

15   The three *chaebols* that went virtually bankrupt in 1997 had very high ratios of cross guarantee to equity: Halla 891 per cent, Jinro 473 per cent, and Daelim 256 per cent. A ratio lower than the legally mandated 100 per cent level does not ensure safety either, because the Haitai Group with a ratio of 57 per cent also defaulted (see *Joongang Ilbo* 13 January 1998).

16   As the legally pending derivatives deals between J.P. Morgan and Korean financial institutions demonstrate, the opaqueness of over-the-counter derivatives could indeed invite very serious agency problems and devastating results.

17   For example, the Korean semiconductor industry, compared with that of the United States in 1995, had a comparable capital intensity level of 96 per cent, but only 54 per cent in capital productivity and 64 per cent in the production rate of return (see McKinsey Global Institute 1998).

18   Commercial banks in Korea have two types of operations: commercial and trust. Bank accounts refer to traditional commercial banking operations. The two types of business are separated only on the books; that is, operation-wise, the two types of accounts are integrated. The assets of trust accounts exceeded those of bank accounts from the mid-1990s, an anomaly in the Korean commercial banking industry. And yet the Bank of Korea was given authority to regulate and supervise only bank account activities.

19   The Ministry of Finance and the Economic Planning Board were merged in 1993 to become the MOFE (a powerful 'monster', according to its critics), with tax, treasury and budget under its jurisdiction.

20   Although trade associations are private organisations, they have been operating as quasi-governmental entities through which the government controlled private industries with more convenience and less transparency.

21   Although the minister was legally the chairman, the minister rarely attended Monetary Board meetings, in order to avoid the often-physical protests of the central bank's labour union, and thus the governor of the central bank presided over the meetings, another anomaly of the Korean banking system.

22   The Korea Deposit Insurance Corporation was set up in 1995 but will need at least ten years in which to accumulate minimum reserves from the insurance premiums it collects from member banks.

23   The statistics for commercial banks' non-performing loans by the international standard (loans in arrears for more than three months) were released for the first time in Korea in 1997. The figure for 1996 was 14.3 per cent. Previously, the government disclosed only

the statistics for loans in arrears for more than six months: 5.1 per cent in 1996 (see Presidential Commission for Financial Reform 1997: 582).

24 Although the financial reform process launched in January 1997 brought about positive changes, implementation of the major measures recommended by the Presidential Commission for Financial Reform, and additional reforms of a 'big bang' nature, were possible only after the financial crisis took place.

25 It is interesting to note that, observing the troubles Korea was going through as of May 1997, Clifford (1998) wrote, 'a wholesale reorientation of the economy to focus more on productivity and profitability is not likely to happen until Korea gets closer to the brink of a major financial crisis than it is to date'. Many Korean intellectuals would agree that the 'IMF crisis', as it is called in Korea, provided a once-in-a-lifetime opportunity to embark on a fundamental transformation of the society and the economy.

26 For example, for all practical purposes, bank loans and trust loans have been nearly perfect substitutes. Large firms often therefore obtained loans from trust accounts when the loan limit on bank accounts was almost exhausted. Since the MOFE and the Bank of Korea were not on amicable terms, the necessary flow of information between the two agencies was hampered. In other words, there was a built-in failure mechanism in the old system.

27 The full-fledged 'big bang' for the restructuring of financial institutions started on 29 June 1998, when the five weakest commercial banks were closed. These were the banks that could not meet the 8 per cent BIS ratio by the end of 1997. Each was taken over by the five strongest commercial banks under the 'purchase and assumption (P&A)' formula. The remaining seven of the twelve weak banks were allowed to keep operating on the following conditions: adopt drastic restructuring measures, including mergers with sound banks and/or infusion of foreign equity capital; and replace all incumbent executives responsible for mismanagement.

28 Out of 118 trillion won of non-performing assets, the bad loans that are in arrears for more than six months represent 57.6 per cent (US$48.6 billion), which is 13.2 per cent of the total credits. The restructuring plans and related statistics in this section are from Presidential Council for Economic Policy Coordination (1998).

29 Another anomalous feature of Korean financial markets is that investment trust companies have huge security portfolios of proprietary accounts. When the stock market slumped in late 1989, the finance ministry forced the Bank of Korea into lending three trillion won to the three largest investment trust companies, which was then poured into the stock market to support the level of stock prices. This operation was an utter failure, from which the investment trust companies are still suffering.

30 Since payment on the purchase of bad assets and the infusion of equity into banks could be made in government bonds, the actual cash to be raised is 9 trillion won for insured deposits. There has been intense debate, for obvious reasons, between the finance ministry and the central bank about sources for the 9 trillion won, the former wanting the central bank to purchase the bonds and the latter preferring that they be sold to investors in the market.

31 Both will create political difficulties because funding by foreign investors will involve the eventual sale of many firms at fire-sale prices and funding by the central bank will bring about high inflation.

32 The broad directions were agreed on at that meeting, but the actual deadlines and other figures for implementation were later picked by the government.

33 New cross debt guarantees have been prohibited since 1 April 1998. Also, approximately 10 trillion won, about 30 per cent of the outstanding volume of cross guarantees of the 30 *chaebols*, had been defeased by March 1998 (see Presidential Council for Economic Policy Coordination 1998).

34   The actual mechanism to induce firms to lower the debt–equity ratio to 200 per cent is the corporate income tax law. From the year 2000, interest expenses for those debts exceeding 200 per cent leverage will not be tax-deductible.

35   The principal transaction bank system is a very weak version of the Japanese main bank system, which ties firms and banks through cross ownership and board members. The Korean system originated from a need to constrain credits to *chaebols*. The Office of Bank Supervision officially designates one commercial bank to each *chaebol*.

36   Anyone claiming that the German–Japanese model of a bank-based governance system could work, or be superior to the Anglo-Saxon model of a securities market-based one, should be able first to show how effectively bank governance itself works in Germany and Japan. Korean banks lacking a good governance structure would not be able to play a watchdog role for corporate wealth.

37   It appears ironic that these events are being orchestrated by President Kim who is a strong advocate of the free market system. These examples therefore illustrate how difficult it is for a country to shift from a state-controlled economy to a free market economy in times of crisis, when market mechanisms, poor in the first place, are even more shaky and moral hazard behaviours are more likely to be rampant.

38   As of March 1998, 505 listed companies whose fiscal year ends in December elected a total of 667 outside directors (see Presidential Council for Economic Policy Coordination 1998).

39   In March 1998, the Samsung Electronics annual shareholders meeting lasted for over thirteen hours, a world record, because of shareholders' protests over the firm's dubious transactions hurting minority shareholders' rights. In the case of SK Telecom, the top management gave in to the demands of minority shareholders by, among other things, appointing three outside directors and one auditor recommended by a coalition of minority shareholders.

40   In a mature economy (e.g. the United States), or in a small economy where small and medium-sized family businesses dominate economic activities (e.g. Taiwan), the majority of funding comes from internal equity, that is, retained earnings.

41   Unlike Latin American countries, Asian countries have a high savings ratio. Korea's gross domestic savings ratio during the period 1991–6 was, on average, 35.4 per cent (Bank of Korea, *Monthly Bulletin*, January 1998). Important reasons for the high ratio include a high household savings rate, an increase in per capita income and a change in the demographics (see Park and Rhee 1997 for details).

42   Wade and Veneroso (1998) also emphasise high savings ratios and 'major world industries' to explain the high debt model of Asian economies.

43   The debt–equity ratio of Japanese manufacturing firms 1986–95 was, on average, 228 per cent, a high leverage by global standards (Bank of Korea 1997). Of course, the market value-based leverage ratio would be lower than 228 per cent, a book value-based ratio.

44   A high debt–equity ratio and a capital-intensive business with a large investment in fixed assets make a deadly combination because both operating and financing costs have a high proportion of *fixed* costs, resulting in a large elasticity of net profits with respect to sales revenue. This is referred to, in corporate finance parlance, as a high total leverage arising from the combination of a high operating leverage and a high financial leverage.

45   In such economies, therefore, the leverage provides tax benefits without countervailing bankruptcy costs, which should put a lower limit on the maximum leverage.

46   This subsection draws partly from Wade and Veneroso (1998) who discuss various means of reducing debt burden.

47   Because efficient economic arrangements sometimes generate a political backlash, seemingly inefficient arrangements that increase political stability may turn out to be more efficient in the long run. Roe (1998) makes this point lucidly, with the example of Argentina.

48 For an analysis of the consequences of the foreign purchase of Asian assets, see Krugman (1998).
49 For this reason, large firms demanded that the central bank increase the money supply whenever a debt burden increased for various reasons. This demand was rejected most of the time because the resulting inflation would have transferred the debt burden from firms to the general public.
50 For one of the best arguments against premature capital account liberalisation, see Rodrik (1998).

REFERENCES

Bank of Korea (1994) *Understanding the Capital Flows in Korea.*
—— (1997) *Financial Statement Analysis for 1996,* July.
Booz Allen & Hamilton (1997) *Revitalizing the Korean Economy toward the 21st Century,* Seoul: Booz Allen & Hamilton.
Capiro, G. and D. Vittas (1997) 'Financial history: lessons of the past for reformers of the present', in G. Capiro, Jr. and D. Vittas (eds) *Reforming Financial Systems: Historical Implications for Policy,* Cambridge University Press.
Clifford, M.L. (1998) *Troubled Tiger: Businessmen, Bureaucrats, and Generals in South Korea,* New York: Sharpe.
Corsetti, G., P. Pesente and N. Roubini (1998) 'What caused the Asian currency and financial crisis?', unpublished manuscript, New York University, March.
International Monetary Fund (1998) 'IMF concludes Article IV consultation with Korea', Press Information Notice (PIN) No. 98/39, 19 June.
John, K. and L. Senbet (1998) 'Corporate governance and board effectiveness', *Journal of Banking and Finance* (forthcoming).
Krugman, P. (1998) 'Fire-sale FDI', unpublished manuscript, MIT, Mass.
Lim, Ungki (1997) 'Ownership structure and family control in Korean conglomerates: with cases of the 10 largest Chaebols', unpublished manuscript, Yonsei University, November.
McKinsey Global Institute (1998) *Productivity-led Growth for Korea,* Washington DC, March.
Park, Daekeun and Changyong Rhee (1997) 'A study of the savings rates in Korea: synthetic cohort analysis', *Research Report 97-06,* Seoul: Korea Institute of Public Finance.
Park, Sang Yong (1994) 'Scale, scope and ownership structure of financial institutions', *Finance Research,* Korea Institute of Finance, vol. 8.
Presidential Commission for Financial Reform (1997) *Financial Reform in Korea: The Final Report,* December.
Presidential Council for Economic Policy Coordination (1998) *Comprehensive Measures for Korea's Economic Restructuring,* 20 May.
Rodrik, D. (1998) 'Who needs capital-account convertibility?', unpublished manuscript, Harvard University, February.
Roe, M. (1998) 'Backlash', *Columbia Law Review* 98, 217–41.
Wade, R. and F. Veneroso (1998) 'Asian crisis: the high debt model vs. the Wall Street–Treasury–IMF complex', working paper, New York: Russell Sage Foundation, March.
Woo-Cumings, M. (1997) 'Slouching toward the market: the politics of financial liberalization in South Korea', in Loriaux et al. (eds) *Capital Ungoverned,* Ithaca, NY: Cornell University Press, 57–91.
Zysman, J. (1983) *Governments, Markets, and Growth: Financial Systems and the Politics of Industrial Change,* Ithaca, NY: Cornell University Press.

Part IV

Case studies in financial reform

10 Financial fragility in Japan

Akiyoshi Horiuchi

INTRODUCTION

The 1980s and the early 1990s saw bank crises in many countries. Many industrialised countries, most developing countries and economies moving from central planning to market-oriented systems experienced some degree of bank crisis. Of the 181 such countries reviewed by Lindgren and others in 1996, 133 had experienced significant banking sector problems at some stage during the past fifteen years (Lindgren et al. 1996: 20).

However, the Japanese bank crisis seems to have been unique in its long duration and in the seriousness of its influence on economic performance. Japan has taken half a decade to deal with the bad loan problem in its banking sector, without remarkable success – the problem had grown serious enough to endanger the viability of the financial system by late 1997.

This chapter tries to explain the Japanese bank crisis from the perspective of corporate governance. Any bank is a corporation of managers who must be monitored and disciplined by some means. However, in Japan, bank management has not been effectively controlled, and that deficiency led to the current bank crisis.

This chapter first describes the current banking crisis in Japan, and argues that there is still a danger of undermining the capital base of the banks. It examines the governance structure of Japanese banks, and explains how the comprehensive safety net implemented by the government undermined the capital market mechanism of monitoring bank management. It argues that the Japanese government rigidly controlled financial markets to the extent that market competition was unable to exert a disciplinary influence on bank management. It examines the regulatory authority's monitoring of bank management, and argues that the pervasive relationship between the regulatory authority and private banks (*amakudari*) increased the fragility of the banking industry. A key problem is that the management of the Japanese banks is 'entrenched', in the sense that managers are immune from external disciplinary influences. Entrenched management delayed necessary structural readjustments in the banking industry. The chapter concludes by drawing out policy implications.

DETERIORATION OF BANK BALANCE SHEETS

Table 10.1 summarises the official semi-annual figures on non-performing loans from March 1996 to September 1997 in the Japanese banking sector. The average ratio of non-performing to total loans was around 4 per cent as of September 1997. This is more than 0.8 per cent lower than the figure for March 1996. More than half of the non-performing loans were covered by provisions for loan losses (the provision ratio was 2.4 per cent at September 1997). Table 10.1 appears to show that the problem of non-performing loans has already been reduced to a minor policy problem in Japan.

A series of financial upheavals late in autumn 1997 made it clear that the banking problem was still considerable. Figure 10.1 shows recent changes in the Bank for International Settlements (BIS) capital ratios for the major banks, revealing that most major banks had been able gradually to increase their capital ratios until March 1997. The turmoil of 1997 retarded this improvement, precipitating a government injection of public funds into their capital bases in March 1998.[1] There is still a rather serious problem of capital inadequacy in the Japanese banking industry.

The cooperative credit banks have not recovered from their serious difficulties with non-performing loans (Table 10.1). Their non-performing loan ratio has stayed higher than 10 per cent, with no signs of significant reduction. The provision for losses is still very small. Thus, the cooperative credit banks are a weak point in the Japanese banking sector. As for *shinkin* banks – which are non-profit financial institutions – it was reported that, if they were to subtract non-performing loans from their equity capital, almost 90 per cent of these banks would be unable to satisfy the domestic standard of capital adequacy requirement (4 per cent) imposed on commercial banks in Japan (*Nihon Keizai Shimbun* 16 May 1996). The same newspaper report suggested that non-performing loans represent a serious problem for the cooperative banks.

Some people suspect the published figures underestimate the actual situation facing Japanese banks. This suspicion was reinforced by a tentative report about the amount of problematic loans in the banking sector published by the Ministry of Finance (MOF) in January 1998. The report made a survey of the loans that banks themselves recognised as 'problematic' during the period from March to September 1997, following the supervision criteria adopted by the MOF. According to this report, the total loans which were either impossible or very difficult to collect amounted to ¥11.4 trillion for the major and the regional banks (i.e. just 1.8 per cent of the total loans of these banks). However, in addition to this they held ¥65.3 trillion in loans which were likely to be more or less difficult to collect. In total, the proportion of problematic loans was higher than 12 per cent of the total outstanding loans for these banks. This figure is substantially higher than the non-performing loans ratio estimated in the published figures (i.e. around 3.8 per cent). The MOF's tentative figures are based on different criteria to those utilised to calculate the official figures presented in Table 10.1.[2]

Table 10.1 Non-performing loans in the Japanese banking sector (¥100 billion)

		March 1996	September 1996	March 1997	September 1997
Major banks					
a	Total loans	3,918.5	3,868.0	3,953.1	3,804.0
b	Non-performing loans	218.7	174.1	164.4	161.3
	b/a: %	(5.58)	(4.50)	(4.16)	(4.24)
c	Provision for losses	103.5	82.4	93.9	103.3
	c/a: %	(2.64)	(2.13)	(2.38)	(2.72)
Regional banks					
a	Total loans	1,896.8	1,876.5	1,902.9	1,900.0
b	Non-performing loans	66.4	55.8	53.5	56.0
	b/a: %	(3.50)	(2.97)	(2.81)	(2.95)
c	Provision for losses	29.5	24.7	29.5	33.6
	c/a: %	(1.56)	(1.32)	(1.55)	(1.77)
Total cooperatives					
a	Total loans	1,312.1	1,299.3	1,285.4	1,270.7
b	Non-performing loans	63.0	62.3	61.1	63.5
	b/a: %	(4.80)	(4.79)	(4.75)	(5.00)
c	Provision for losses	17.6	18.6	26.6	28.1
	c/a: %	(1.34)	(1.43)	(2.07)	(2.21)
***Shinkin* banks**					
a	Total loans	696.0	696.7	702.0	701.3
b	Non-performing loans	32.0	33.7	32.4	33.8
	b/a: %	(4.60)	(4.84)	(4.62)	(4.82)
c	Provision for losses	10.3	11.3	16.2	16.7
	c/a: %	(1.48)	(1.62)	(2.31)	(2.38)
Credit cooperatives					
a	Total loans	173.7	172.8	172.1	165.1
b	Non-performing loans	20.5	21.3	21.2	20.0
	b/a: %	(11.80)	(12.33)	(12.32)	(12.11)
c	Provision for losses	1.8	1.8	3.0	2.6
	c/a: %	(1.04)	(1.04)	(1.74)	(1.57)
Total					
a	Total loans	7,127.4	7043.8	7,141.4	6,974.7
b	Non-performing loans	348.0	292.3	279.0	280.8
	b/a: %	(4.88)	(4.15)	(3.91)	(4.03)
c	Provision for losses	150.5	125.7	149.9	165.0
	c/a: %	(2.11)	(1.78)	(2.10)	(2.37)

Note: Those banks which collapsed during the sample period are excluded from the table
Source: Federation of Bankers Associations of Japan, *Analysis of Financial Statements of All Banks*

Figure 10.1 Recent changes in BIS capital ratios of major banks

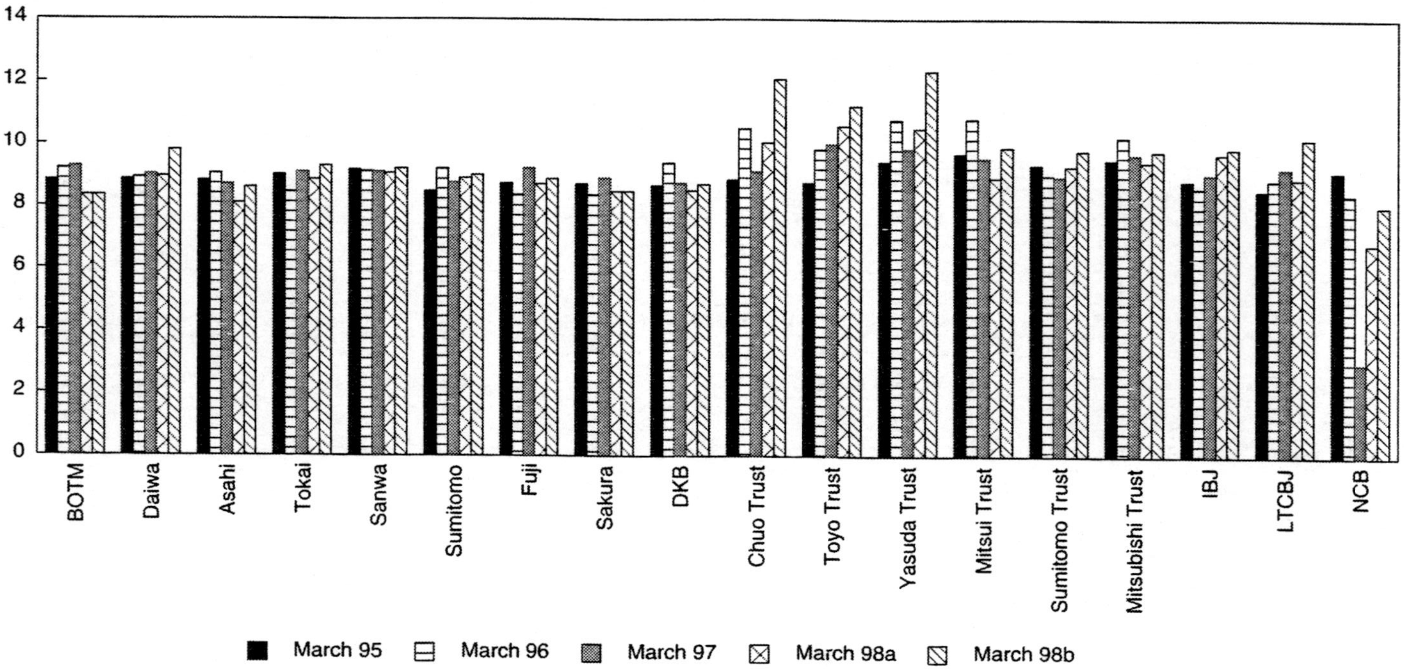

Notes: Figures for March 98a are the ratios expected if no public funds were injected. Figures for March 98b are the ratios attained with the help of capital injection
Source: Deposit Insurance Corporation

Danger of a vicious circle

After the 'bubble' burst in 1990, the Japanese banks faced 'the Japan premium' (defined as the difference between the yen London interbank offered rate on Japanese banks and the average on US and UK banks) for the first time since the first oil crisis of 1974. This was apparent in the international money market immediately after mid-summer 1995, when some Japanese financial institutions failed. After rapidly rising to higher than 30 basis points, the Japan premium remained at around 10 basis points until the beginning of November 1997. In late November, the Japan premium jumped to 90 basis points, reflecting the turmoil in the domestic money market.[3]

The development of the Japan premium suggests that the international money market was already starting to send an alarm signal about the Japanese banking system in the summer of 1995. The Japanese government belatedly started to force bank recapitalisation by announcing that new rules would be introduced in April 1998. This announcement, and the prolonged sluggishness of stock prices, led to a 'credit crunch' in 1997.

The requirement for more comprehensive disclosure of non-performing loans seems to have intensified the credit crunch. Combined with the impact of the tax increases which occurred in the first half of 1997, the credit crunch has contributed to increased non-performing loans in the banking sector. Obviously, this represents a vicious circle between the deficiency of bank capital and the macroeconomic slowdown.

GOVERNANCE STRUCTURE IN THE BANKING SECTOR

The bank crisis in Japan arose from failings in governance. A disciplinary influence could be exerted on bank management through three channels: capital market forces, whereby either investors including depositors monitor bank performance or the threat of hostile takeovers disciplines bank managers; competition in the banking industry, which weeds out inefficient banks; and supervision by the regulatory authorities, which should prevent banks from taking excessive risks and force managers to restructure their businesses in the case of crisis. These disciplinary mechanisms have not worked effectively in the Japanese banking industry, for reasons that are now explained.

Government safety net

The most important reason why the capital market has not effectively monitored and disciplined Japanese bank management is that the government has kept in place a comprehensive safety net – a social system for dealing with distressed banks and distributing any social costs associated with financial institution failures among related parties. Such a safety net has important implications for risk sharing. By taking control of the distribution of costs associated with bank failures, the safety net decreases the monitoring incentives of depositors and other investors in bank debt, who are either explicitly or implicitly protected from bank failure losses.[4]

The MOF has programs to rescue distressed financial institutions, in collaboration with both the Bank of Japan (BOJ) and private financial institutions, particularly major banks. Before 1990 there were some bank failures, though the number was quite small, and in all cases the MOF pressured private banks to rescue their distressed peers.[5]

In addition, the MOF often placed its officers on the board of the distressed bank, with a view to reorganising management. Dispatching MOF officials to a distressed bank may be an effective signal that the government has made a commitment to rescue the bank at any cost, which helps to persuade other banks to collaborate with the bailing out program. However, this signalling is not always successful.[6]

Since the actions taken by the authorities in rescuing troubled banks have been covert, it is difficult to estimate the social costs of the safety net and the exact distribution of the burden among various agents. Not only depositors but also almost all other debt holders (except a few major banks) have been exempted from the burdens of bailing out distressed banks. Even the shareholders of failed banks seem to have been rescued from bank failures. For example, in the case of credit cooperative banks, their failures did not require equity holders to share the costs of failures. Until the early 1990s, the financial authorities rarely paid the costs of the bailout procedure themselves, confining their role to coordinating the rescue programs. Thus, the costs of preserving financial stability have fallen disproportionately on sound private banks, particularly major banks.

In some cases, the BOJ may have extended loans to distressed banks at the official discount rate, which was substantially lower than money market interest rates, but it is impossible to obtain any information about these unofficial rescue programs. The BOJ utilised emergency loans (authorised by Article 25 of the BOJ Act) for the first time since 1965 to support the Tokyo Kyodo Bank, newly established in 1995, to take over two failed credit cooperatives in the Tokyo prefecture. The BOJ's emergency loans increased sharply during 1995, due to managerial crises in several small and medium-scale banks (including Hyogo Bank), reportedly to a little more than ¥1.0 trillion.

Deposit insurance

Deposit insurance has not been an element of the Japanese financial safety net. A system of deposit insurance was introduced in 1971, but it was not actually utilised in Japan until 1992. The MOF continued to implement the traditional safety net to avoid the bankruptcy of deposit-taking institutions. It gave priority to the protection of weak (and therefore inefficient) banks over the promotion of competition in the financial industry, even after the introduction of deposit insurance. The Deposit Insurance Corporation (DIC) remained nominal for a long time, and its functions were limited to paying out insured deposits in cases of bank failure (although the DIC never did any paying out). In 1986, the Law of Deposit Insurance was amended to extend the DIC's powers. The amended law allows the DIC to support the rescue or disposal of distressed banks by subsidising private agents. In April 1992, the DIC supplied ¥8.0 billion to help a medium-sized regional bank absorb another small bank in distress.

In December 1997 the government made a commitment to protect all deposits and other debts, such as bank debentures, issued by banks and financial institutions participating in the deposit insurance system, in order to calm people's anxiety about bank failures following the bankruptcy of the Hokkaido-Takushoku Bank and the failures of a few major securities companies, including Yamaichi.

The government's commitment is likely to increase moral hazard by weakening the incentives for depositors and investors to monitor bank management. However, the long-standing implementation of the comprehensive safety net has produced among depositors and other investors a perception that they will never be required to share the burden if their banks go bankrupt. Because of this widespread perception, the government's paying off insured deposits without rescuing investors in bank debts other than insured deposits would result in an unexpected shock to the financial system. Thus, at the end of 1997, the Japanese government felt that it had to support the widespread perception about the safety net.

The comprehensive safety deprived investors of incentives to monitor the performance of individual banks and hindered the development of capital market mechanisms to discipline bank management. The lack of market mechanisms, in turn, has made it quite difficult for the government to abandon the traditional safety net.

Disciplinary influence of market competition

What about the disciplinary influence of market competition on bank management? Nickell et al. (1997) show with regard to manufacturing industries that full-scale market competition exerts a strong disciplinary influence on corporate management by weeding out inefficiently managed firms. Regardless of a corporation's specific ownership or governance structure, corporate managers are disciplined by fierce market competition. Firms disappear if they have inefficient management.

Japanese manufacturing firms have performed excellently because they have long faced fierce competition in the global market. In contrast, the Japanese financial services industries have been protected from full-scale competition by regulation. Thus, market competition has not worked to discipline management in the banking and other financial services industries in Japan.

Role of regulation in restricting competition

Various restrictive regulations – such as controls on interest rates, new entries into banking and other financial services, and new branches – conferred handsome rents on existing banks and other financial institutions during the high-growth era of the 1960s and 1970s. The primary purpose of the MOF's administrative guidance was to suppress full-scale competition in each of the compartmentalised financial businesses, thereby protecting the less competitive small-scale banks such as *sogo* banks, *shinkin* banks and credit cooperatives. The MOF's policy stance was often called the 'convoy administration'.

Economic theory shows that the existence of rents can provide private banks with incentives to refrain from excessive risk-taking without effective prudential regulations, in order to continue enjoying handsome rents (Hellman et al. 1997).[7] In addition, the regulatory authority was able to utilise the rents accumulated in the banking sector as a means of dealing with banks in financial distress. Specifically, the regulator relied on private banks' collaboration in implementing the safety net, and major banks faithfully bore a disproportionate share of the costs involved. This mechanism would not have worked had the major banks not enjoyed the rents stemming from the restrictive regulations. The MOF also utilised the restrictive regulations to give private banks an incentive to accept its initiatives in the process of dealing with bank failures. The MOF manipulated the regulatory framework to favour banks which toed the line and to penalise banks which failed to heed their guidance.[8]

Delayed deregulation of the financial markets

Since the mid-1970s the competition-restricting regulations have gradually weakened the ability of Japanese banks and other financial institutions to adapt to environmental changes. The Japanese government adopted a policy of gradual deregulation for the purpose of preventing 'undue destabilisation'. In reality, this gradualism was synonymous with the policy of protecting established vested interests in the financial industries, thereby suppressing the disciplinary effects the financial deregulation was expected to exert.

Japanese financial deregulation was prompted by pressures from abroad, particularly from the United States, rather than a Japanese government initiative. For example, the yen/dollar agreement between Japan and the United States in 1984 compelled the Japanese government to provide an explicit timetable for liberalising financial markets (Frankel 1984; Takeda and Turner 1992). Compared with the international capital market generally, the Japanese financial markets have been belatedly deregulated. The 'big bang' proposed by Prime Minister Ryutaro Hashimoto in November 1996 was the government's commitment to abandoning the policy of gradualism. This is a sort of shock therapy to make up for lost time.

We should not totally deny the impact of financial deregulation on domestic financial markets during the 1980s. In particular, major companies reduced their dependence on bank borrowing by issuing a large amount of corporate bonds in international markets. This 'internationalisation' of corporate finance has induced deregulation in domestic corporate bond markets since the mid-1980s (Horiuchi 1996). However, generally speaking, the Japanese banks and other financial institutions have been able to base their business on the huge amount of wealth accumulated by households.

The role of government in bank managerial governance

The fact that official regulation led to neither the capital market nor market competition disciplining bank management in Japan is to some extent a natural outcome of the assignment of responsibility for monitoring bank management to the MOF and the BOJ. The Banking Law authorises the MOF to intervene in the management of banks for purposes of prudential regulation. The BOJ is also in charge of monitoring bank management, particularly from the viewpoint of money market adjustment. In the following section, we first examine how the Japanese government has implemented prudential regulations, then show how the weakness of regulatory monitoring contributed to the fragility of the banking industry, by examining the '*amakudari*' relationships between the regulator and the private banks.

Capital adequacy regulations

During the period of economic reconstruction immediately after World War II, the MOF was seriously concerned about the prudence of bank management, because banks' equity capital per deposit had fallen sharply from 29.9 per cent in 1930 to only 5.6 per cent by 1953. With a view to strengthening banks' capital bases, in 1953 the MOF started instructing banks to reduce current expenses to 78 per cent or less of current revenues. This administrative guidance continued until 1973.

In 1954, the MOF introduced capital adequacy regulation, which required banks to increase 'broadly defined capital' to more than 10 per cent of total deposits.[9] However, some depository financial institutions were not covered by this capital adequacy regulation – for example, the *sogo* banks. When the *sogo* banks converted to regional banks in February 1989, the MOF imposed the same minimum capital adequacy ratio on them as on city banks and other regional banks. *Shinkin* banks were free of the capital adequacy regulation until May 1986, when the MOF introduced administrative guidance in the form of a minimum capital adequacy ratio.

Figure 10.2 Capital–deposits ratios of commercial banks (%)

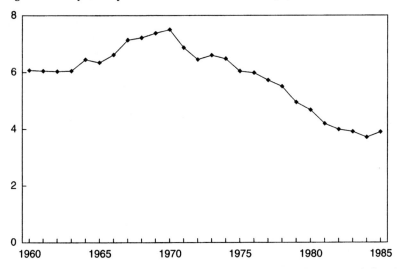

Source: Federation of Bankers Associations of Japan, *Analysis of Financial Statements of All Banks*

Thus, until the late 1980s, the capital adequacy regulation did not cover the whole range of deposit-taking institutions. Moreover, the regulation seemed to be ineffective. Figure 10.2 shows that, from 1960 to the mid-1970s, the average capital adequacy ratio for the banking sector (city banks and regional banks) remained almost constant at 6 per cent, far below the MOF's requirement of 10 per cent. Furthermore, the average capital:deposits ratio dropped abruptly, to below 4 per cent, during the 1980s.[10]

Bank capital and *amakudari*

If the prudential regulation implemented by the MOF was ineffective in making bank's management sound, it was not the only tool at the MOF's disposal. Aoki et al. (1994) argue that the financial authority effectively monitors bank management through the *amakudari* system – the system prevailing among private banks (and other firms) whereby state officials are granted positions on corporate managerial boards after retirement. According to this argument, this system has given regulatory officers ample incentives to rigorously monitor bank management because, if they fail as regulators, they will lose chances to obtain good jobs in private banks on retirement. Therefore bank performance will be positively influenced by, or at worst be independent from, *amakudari*.

However, this *amakudari* system is accompanied by an agency problem, because the bureaucrats assigned the role of monitoring banks' management expect to be employed by the same banks. If the financial authorities and private banks were to bargain with each other, the *amakudari* system might undermine the effectiveness of the regulators and allow banks to engage in unsound management (Horiuchi and Shimizu 1998). This hypothesis predicts that the banks accepting *amakudari* officials from the financial authority will show poor performance in terms of soundness.

These hypotheses can be tentatively tested using Table 10.2, taking the 125 regional banks operating in March 1996 as a sample. The 125 regional banks are categorised according to which *amakudari* officers, if any, they accept. Category 'MOF & BOJ' contains the banks which accept *amakudari* officers from both the MOF and the BOJ. Category 'MOF' consists of the banks which accept officers only from the MOF, and category 'BOJ' consists of the banks which accept them only from the BOJ. Finally, category 'NON' consists of the banks that do not accept *amakudari* officers at all.

Each panel of Table 10.2 shows performance averages over a five-year period. In all three of the panels, the capital:asset ratio (EQT) is significantly lower for both categories MOF & BOJ and MOF than for category NON. For example, during the first half of the 1980s, the capital:asset ratio (EQT) for category MOF & BOJ banks was on average 0.927 per cent lower than that of category NON banks. The differences are statistically significant at the 1 per cent level. As Keeley (1990) argues, the lower capital:asset ratio implies a higher level of risk. As for asset growth (GAS) and profitability (PRO), we find no significant difference between the banks belonging to either category MOF & BOJ or MOF, and the banks of category NON. Thus, Table 10.2 suggests that the banks accepting *amakudari* officials from the MOF tend to embrace higher levels of risk.

Table 10.2 *Amakudari* and performance of regional banks

	MOF & BOJ	MOF	BOJ	NON
Panel A: Period 1980–4				
	(42)	(48)	(19)	(16)
EQT	2.648***	2.739***	3.484	3.575
BRN	3.388	3.325	3.047	3.006
GAS	8.736	7.908	7.953	7.984
PRO	8.001	8.096	8.456	7.604
Panel B: Period 1985–9				
	(41)	(43)	(21)	(20)
EQT	2.849***	3.008***	3.390	3.411
BRN	2.513	2.430	2.777	2.206
GAS	10.945	9.927	10.526	9.815
PRO	8.913	9.087	8.641	8.610
BAD	4.145***	4.145***	2.205	2.200
Panel C: Period 1990–4				
	(40)	(43)	(20)	(22)
EQT	3.427***	3.698**	3.696*	4.046
BRN	1.877	1.853	1.795	1.698
GAS	1.985	2.570	2.359	2.405
PRO	4.054	4.148	4.809	4.950
BAD	4.225***	3.843**	2.761	2.159

Note: The symbols ***, **, and * indicate the figures are different from those of 'NON' significantly at 1%, 2.5%, and 5% levels respectively. Panels A and B exclude Daiko Bank because of its abnormal performances during the 1980s, and Panel C deletes Kumamoto Family Bank because of a merger with regional financial institutions at the beginning of the 1990s. The figures in parentheses are the numbers of banks belonging to the respective categories.

The bad loan ratio (the amount of non-performing loans per total loan) is another useful measure of bank risk. In March 1996, Japanese banks started to comprehensively disclose the amount of non-performing loans they held for the first time.

The rows of BAD in Panels B and C of Table 10.2 present the bad loan ratios for each category of bank. Panel B shows that the two groups of banks accepting *amakudari* officials from the MOF had almost double the bad loan ratios (4.145 as of 1985) of the banks totally independent from the *amakudari* relationship. These differences are statistically significant at the 1 per cent level. In contrast, the average level of bad loan ratios for the banks accepting *amakudari* from the BOJ is not significantly different from that of the NON. The same is true in Panel C, which classifies sample banks according to their *amakudari* status as of 1990. Thus, if we measure (ex post) risk by the bad loan ratio, the results are consistent with the hypothesis that the *amakudari* relationship undermines monitoring by the MOF.

Our examination of the influence of the *amakudari* relationship suggests that, rather than closely monitoring bank management, the financial authorities tend to help incumbent bank managers to continue their operations.

Thus, we conclude that a lack of effective monitoring by the regulators is a conspicuous feature of the governance of Japanese bank management.[11]

It would be an exaggeration to say that the MOF has totally neglected prudential regulation. Table 10.3 provides a list of prudential regulations for commercial banks – the city banks and the regional banks – as of 1974. The MOF has kept almost all of the prudential guidance listed in this table intact. However, on the whole, bankers did not consider that these official guidelines were to be met at any cost, and the MOF generously permitted some divergence between the required and the actual figures for individual banks.

VACUUM OF GOVERNANCE

This chapter has stressed that the Japanese bank management has enjoyed independence from outsiders' disciplinary influence. This is the 'entrenched management' phenomenon. Entrenched bank managers tended to take excessive risks under the comprehensive safety net during the latter half of 1980s. At the same time, entrenched managers tended to delay structural changes after recognising their failure in risk-taking (Boot 1992). This is particularly significant to the extent that the Japanese bank crisis was exacerbated by delayed responses on the part of bank management, rather than the absolute amount of non-performing loans. The Japanese banks hesitated to undertake the necessary drastic restructuring, and the MOF's forbearance policy supported the reluctance of banks to restructure, making the situation worse.

Table 10.3 Prudential regulations as of 1974

---

1   Loans/deposits ratio is to be no higher than 80%.

2   (a) Liquid assets/deposits ratio is to be higher than 30%.

    (b) For banks that do not satisfy (a), increment of liquid asset/increment of total deposits ratio is to be higher than 30%.

3   Ratio of current expenses (excluding tax) to current revenue is to be constantly decreased. (Until 1973, the MOF indicated a maximum level of 78% for this ratio.)

4   Annual dividend per share is to be less than 12.5% of the face value of the share.

5   Broadly defined capital/deposits ratio should be higher than 10%.

6   The amount of loan to a single borrower is to be less than

    (a) 20% of the bank's equity capital for city banks and regional banks;

    (b) 30% of the bank's equity capital for long-term credit banks and the trust banks;

    (c) 40% of the bank's equity capital for foreign exchange banks.

Notes: The MOF designated the above items as the desirable standards under administrative guidance. It has since altered the regulations to some extent. For example, ceilings on credit to individual borrowers were introduced in the revised Banking Law in 1982; the total amount of credit to any individual borrower should not exceed 20% of the bank's equity capital.
Source: The Banking Bureau of the MOF

Delayed restructuring in Japanese banking

As Lindgren et al. (1996) show, the bank crisis is not peculiar to Japan. However, Japan has taken too long to deal with this problem, without any remarkable success. Figure 10.3 presents an international comparison of banking restructuring during the first half of the 1990s, based on the BIS *Annual Report* (1996). This figure shows that, except in the United States, the profitability of commercial banks decreased in the first half of the 1990s, compared with the latter half of the 1980s, in all of the major industrial countries including Japan. In terms of the growth rate in the number of bank branches, the growth rate in the total number of employees, and the changes in wage index, Japan was unique in the sense that none of these measures decreased during the 1990s compared with the latter half of the 1980s. In other words, the commercial banks in all the other major industrialised countries downsized or reduced their scale of business after recognising a fall in profitability during the 1990s. Thus, Figure 10.3 confirms that the Japanese banks were hesitant to restructure their business in spite of decreasing profitability after 1990.

Figure 10.3 Restructuring in the banking industry: international comparisons

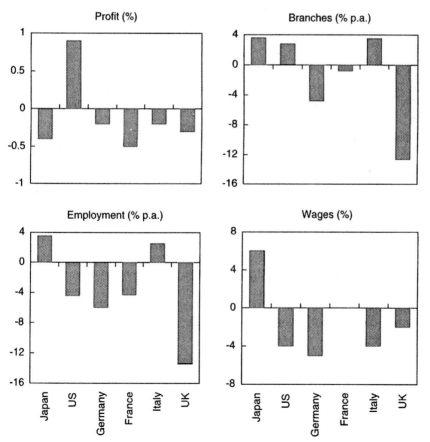

Notes: Profit (return on assets) is the difference between the average for 1986–8 and 1992–4; branches is the growth rate in the total number of branches from 1990 to 1995; employment is the growth rate in total employees from 1990 to 1994; wages (ratio of wage payments to total revenue) is the difference between the average for 1986–8 and 1992–4.
Source: BIS 1996

Limitation of the traditional rescue method

Since the 'bubble' burst at the beginning of the 1990s, it has become increasingly difficult for the MOF to maintain its traditional procedure of bailing out bank failures. In fact, the MOF has utilised the deposit insurance system extensively to deal with banks in distress. The scale of the DIC is still limited, but its increasing use marks a significant change in the operation of the Japanese safety net. Between April 1992 – when the DIC played a role in bailing out a distressed bank for the first time – and January 1998, the DIC has intervened in 22 cases of bailing out troubled banks, to the extent of more than ¥2.4 trillion.

One of the reasons for this shift is that structural changes in financial markets have decreased the rent accruing to major banks, so that the MOF has been unable to depend totally on the collaboration of those banks in implementing the safety net. Financial deregulation has made it difficult for the MOF to compensate major banks for their participation in rescue programs. The traditional methods of dealing with bank failures have not yet disappeared, and many private banks are still playing an important role through collaboration with the regulators. However, it is likely that the deposit insurance system will be utilised substantially in the future.

Use of the deposit insurance system to facilitate reorganisation does not, however, imply that banks will undergo formal bankruptcy procedures. The MOF has continued to avoid explicit bank failures, by using the deposit insurance system to provide sound banks with incentives to merge with insolvent ones or to collaborate with the authorities in restructuring troubled banks. This implies a slow reorganisation of the financial system and a marked increase in the burden borne by the DIC.

This policy stance adopted by the MOF reached a dead end when the principle of 'too big to fail' was abandoned and the Hokkaido-Takushoku Bank was allowed to go bankrupt in November 1997. Both domestic and international financial markets recognised that the Japanese traditional safety net was no longer sustainable. This market perception caused turmoil in Japanese money markets, as well as a sharp jump in the Japan premium in the international money market, at the end of 1997.

CONCLUSION

Bank management has been largely independent of outside control. More specifically, the comprehensive safety net has prevented the capital market from exercising discipline over bank management, and there have been no significant disciplinary pressures from market competition because of the deliberately controlled deregulation of financial services industries. In such circumstances, the regulatory authority should have actively monitored bank management in order to keep soundness in the banking sector. However, the regulatory authority (the MOF) was more concerned with preserving the viability of existing banks and other financial institutions than with effective monitoring from the viewpoint of managerial soundness. In addition, the traditional human ties between the MOF and private banks seem to have undermined the effectiveness of regulatory monitoring, thereby making the banking industry more fragile. Obviously, we have not resolved the issue of 'who monitors the monitor' in the Japanese financial system.

The vacuum of governance in the banking sector was responsible for the delayed restructuring of the banking industry, which has been suffering from the bad loan problem since the beginning of the 1990s. As recently as April 1998, the Japanese government adopted a policy of introducing the prompt corrective action rule. Also, in March 1998, the government ordered banks to submit explicit time schedules for managerial restructuring, as a condition for government injection of public funds into banks' capital. These policy measures seem to have at last induced hesitant banks to start restructuring their businesses. This fact in itself tells us that Japanese banks have no strong intention to drastically reform their businesses on their own initiative.

The recent government policy of strengthening both bank supervision and prudential regulations make sense from the long-term perspective of building a stable financial system. However, we need to note two issues related to strengthening bank supervision.

First, the supervision of bank management by the government has its own agency costs, as the examination of *amakudari* in this chapter suggests. Market competition and the capital market must also play a role in disciplining bank management. The Japanese 'big bang' advocated by the government is expected to enhance the capability of such market mechanisms.

Second, strengthening prudential regulation during the crisis situation has at least temporarily weakened the banks' intermediary capability even more. The strengthening of prudential regulations has led to a 'credit crunch' since 1997, exacerbating the slowdown of the Japanese economy. This side effect of strengthening prudential regulations might hinder the full-scale strengthening of government supervision. Thus, we need to prepare supplementary measures to mitigate the side effects of strengthening prudential regulations. What are those supplementary measures? They should be purely temporary ones which would not hinder the implementation of prudential regulation based on long-term perspectives. The government could help bank restructuring by injecting public funds. However, this policy should not allow the survival of moribund banks, but promote the necessary downsizing of the banking industry. At the beginning of this year, the Japanese government decided to inject capital into all existing banks, regardless of their performance, to overcome the current bank crisis. We doubt whether this policy is compatible with the long-term objective of strengthening the soundness of banks and, therefore, the banking system's contribution to Japan's economic growth.

NOTES

This paper has been published previously, in *East Asia in Crisis* (eds McLeod and Garnaut), Routledge, 1998.

1   In March 1998, the government injected a little more than ¥1.8 trillion into 21 major banks (nine city banks, three long-term credit banks, six trust banks, and three big

regional banks) by buying either preferred stocks or perpetual subordinated debt. This injection is estimated to have increased the equity capital of those banks by 5.1 per cent.

2   The definition of non-performing loans in Table 10.1 consists of: 'non-accrual loans'; loans over 180 days overdue; and some 'restructured loans'. This is a much narrower definition than that adopted by the Securities Exchange Commission (SEC) in the United States, which includes loans over 90 days overdue and more comprehensive 'restructured loans'. In addition to the non-performing loans defined above, the Japanese banks have disclosed loans for the purpose of rescuing borrowers since March 1997. These 'rescue loans' are also contained in the SEC's 'restructured loans'. (The total amount of rescue loans held by the major and regional banks amounted to ¥3.4 trillion and ¥3.1 trillion in March and September 1997 respectively.) On the advice of the MOF, the Federation of Bankers Associations of Japan decided to bring its definition of non-performing loans into line with the SEC definition in March 1998. The amount of 'non-performing loans' defined by the SEC criteria is close to the amount of 'problematic loans' reported by the MOF.

3   See 'The Japan Premium: Work in Progress', a paper submitted by Joe Peek and Eric S. Rosengren to the NBER–Japan Project on 17–18 April 1998.

4   Since most depositors are small-size wealth-holders enjoying no economies of scale in collecting and analysing information about bank management, and since there is a 'free-rider' problem to hinder efficient information production, it would be unrealistic to depend totally on market discipline to maintain the stability of the banking system. As Dewatripont and Tirole (1994) argue, we need to have a financial safety net in order to protect small investors in the banking sector.

5   Until the end of the 1980s, the number of banks that had come close to failing was small, with the largest rescue program involving not a bank but Yamaichi Securities Company in 1965. In this rescue, coordinated by the MOF, the BOJ provided emergency loans of ¥28.2 billion to Fuji Bank and two other banks which functioned as conduits supplying financial support to Yamaichi. Probably, the most important rescue program implemented by the MOF before 1990 was the merger of Heiwa–Sogo Bank into Sumitomo Bank in October 1986. Heiwa–Sogo got into managerial difficulty during the first half of the 1980s. Despite de facto bankruptcy, the closure of Heiwa–Sogo did not cause damage to depositors and other holders of debt issued by this bank. Sumitomo bore the costs of dealing with the distressed bank, and was able to expand its branch network at once by absorbing Heiwa–Sogo's branches.

6   One of the most recent cases was Hyogo Bank, to which the late chief of the Banking Bureau was sent to reorganise its management. Despite this intervention, Hyogo finally went bankrupt in October 1995.

7   Aoki (1994) argues, by assuming asymmetric information about banks' monitoring activities, that the rent was necessary to motivate private banks to faithfully and efficiently monitor their borrowers. He suggests that the long-term relationship between major banks and borrower firms – called the 'main bank relationship' – in Japan was crucially dependent on the competition-restricting regulations. However, restricting full-scale competition is not always necessary to motivate banks to supply a 'high quality' level of monitoring. A competitive market would be able to motivate banks to conduct good monitoring. See Klein and Leffler (1981).

8   In 1994, for example, Mitsubishi Bank obtained preferential treatment from the MOF in exchange for rescuing Nippon Trust Bank, which had been seriously damaged by the accumulation of a huge amount of bad loans since the early 1990s. Mitsubishi Bank was 'rewarded' by being allowed to pursue a full complement of trust banking business through Nippon Trust, which is now its subsidiary. Other banks are prohibited by the MOF from engaging in full-line trust banking business through their trust bank subsidiaries. The same story applied when Daiwa Bank financially supported Cosmo

Securities Company, which was seriously damaged by the depression in the securities market after the 'bubble' burst at the beginning of the 1990s. Cosmo became a subsidiary of Daiwa Bank yet retained its stock brokerage business, which the securities subsidiaries of other banks are not yet permitted to do.

9 Equity capital (net assets) and some reserve items.

10 The MOF amended the capital adequacy regulation in 1986, to at least 4 per cent of total assets – hardly a stringent requirement. Since 1987, banks with branches or offices in foreign countries have been subject to the BIS capital adequacy rule, but other banks continue to face only this domestic capital adequacy requirement of 4 per cent.

11 Unfortunately, we have observed a number of cases which suggest a weakness of regulatory authority during the early 1990s. The failure of Musashino Shinkin Bank in 1996 gives an example. Musashino Shinkin had been in trouble since 1993 and the MOF was in charge of examining the bank's account statements before publication. The MOF reportedly allowed the bank to engage in window dressing to record positive profits even as of March 1996, when the estimated amount of problem loans was nearly 70 per cent of total loans. In September 1996, the MOF decided to introduce an explicit ordering banks in trouble to improve their management based upon officially announced criteria (*Nihon Keizai Shimbun* 11 October 1996). According to the National Federation of Credit Cooperatives, nearly 40 per cent of credit cooperatives had violated the regulation limiting loans to a single party (to 20 per cent of capital in the broad sense) as of September 1994.

REFERENCES

Aoki, M. (1994) 'Monitoring the characteristics of the main bank system: an analytical and developmental view', in M. Aoki and H. Patrick (eds) *The Japanese Main Bank System: Its Relevancy for Developing and Transforming Economies*, New York: Oxford University Press, 109–41.

Aoki, M., H. Patrick and P. Sheard (1994) 'The Japanese main bank system: an introductory overvew', in M. Aoki and H. Patrick (eds) *The Japanese Main Bank System: Its Relevancy for Developing and Transforming Economies*, New York: Oxford University Press, 3–50.

Bank for International Settlements (BIS) (1996) *Annual Report*, Basle: H. Boehm.

Boot, A.W.A. (1992) 'Why hang on to losers?: divestitures and takeovers', *Journal of Finance* 47: 1401–23.

Dewatripont, M. and J. Tirole (1994) *The Prudential Regulation of Banks*, Cambridge, Mass.: Massachusetts Institute of Technology Press.

Frankel, J.A. (1984) 'The yen–dollar agreement: liberalizing Japanese capital markets', *Policy Analyses in International Economics 9*, Washington DC: Institute for International Economics.

Hellman, T., K. Murdock and J.E. Stiglitz (1997) 'Financial restraint: toward a new paradigm', in M. Aoki, H.-K. Kim and M. Okuno-Fujiwara (eds) *The Role of Government in East Asian Economic Development: Comparative Institutional Analysis*, New York: Oxford University Press, 163–207.

Horiuchi, A. (1996) 'An evaluation of Japanese financial liberalization: a case study of corporate bond markets', in T. Ito and A.O. Krueger (eds) *Financial Deregulation and Integration in East Asia*, Chicago: University of Chicago Press, 167–91.

Horiuchi, A. and K. Shimizu (1998) 'Did *amakudari* undermine the effectiveness of regulatory monitoring in Japan?', *Discussion Paper 98F-10*, April, Tokyo: Research Institute for the Japanese Economy.

Klein, B. and K.B. Leffler (1981) 'The role of market forces in assuring contractual performance', *Journal of Political Economy* 89: 615–41.

Lindgren, C.-J., G. Garcia and M.I. Saal (1996) *Bank Soundness and Macroeconomic Policy*, Washington DC: International Monetary Fund.

Nickell, S., D. Nicolitsas and N. Dryden (1997) 'What makes firms perform well?', *European Economic Review* 41: 783–96.

Takeda, M. and P. Turner (1992) 'The liberalization of Japan's financial markets: some major themes', *BIS Economic Papers* 34.

11 Reform of Australian and New Zealand financial markets

Kevin Davis

INTRODUCTION

In surveying recent international trends in financial market regulation, the Bank for International Settlements (BIS) commented that 'the last 25 years have been an eventful time for central banking' (1997a: 140), and pointed to the stagflation of the 1970s and the radical transformation of the financial environment in the 1980s as key factors in driving change. Central banks (and governments), internationally, have made dramatic changes to the modus operandi of monetary policy, to the techniques used for prudential regulation and supervision, and in their oversight of payments and settlement systems in attempting to achieve monetary and financial stability. While these changes have occurred partially in response to the changing nature of financial systems, policies of financial deregulation, adopted by governments searching for more efficient financial systems and responding to inconsistencies in previous regulatory structures exposed by financial innovation, have also been a key ingredient in the process.

The experiences of Australia and New Zealand match this template, although the regulatory frameworks developed by each government have some key differences.[1] This analysis of those experiences endeavours to draw out common themes and significant differences. While the approaches to monetary policy have now largely converged after following different paths during the second half of the 1980s, approaches to prudential regulation remain quite different.

ANTIPODEAN FINANCIAL REFORM: AN OVERVIEW

There are a number of parallels between the history of financial reform in Australia and that in New Zealand, although the paths traversed have differed significantly at certain key junctures. Twenty years ago, both countries had heavily regulated financial systems, with an emphasis on direct controls applied primarily to the banking sector. Monetary control and prudential regulation were inexplicably intertwined in both countries under regulatory frameworks developed largely as ad hoc adjustments to historical experience. This led to the growth of less regulated financial institutions and financing practices which weakened monetary control mechanisms. Both countries responded with varying changes to the regulatory structure. In the Australian case, the rhetoric favoured market-oriented techniques of monetary control, but reality involved occasional extensive use and extensions of direct controls. In the New Zealand case, there was an abortive flirtation with financial deregulation from 1976 to 1981. It was not, however, until the first half of the 1980s that financial deregulation became entrenched in both countries and financial sector supervision started to become divorced from monetary control issues.[2]

Driving these changes were a number of similar forces. The stagflationary experience of both countries from the mid-1970s, and the inconsistency between budgetary and monetary strategies, helped to undermine the feasibility of monetary policies based around direct control techniques. Financial innovation, prompted in part as a response to regulation, further diminished the effectiveness of direct control techniques. Also important was the emergence of a free market ideology as the dominant political paradigm, which favoured financial deregulation. More broadly focused policy initiatives, including privatisation agendas and significant changes to superannuation arrangements for private provision for retirement in both countries,[3] have had important consequences for financial markets, by altering flow of funds patterns. In both countries, significant changes to the taxation system occurred in the mid-1980s with the introduction of dividend imputation tax systems, and this has also affected financing patterns (by reducing the tax disincentive to equity finance previously arising from the 'double taxation of dividends' under the classical tax system). In both countries, there has been a significant increase in the relative importance of managed funds and direct equity investments relative to depository institutions.

Australia proceeded down the path of financial deregulation slightly earlier than New Zealand, but the speed and strength of the latter's embrace of financial deregulation has seen that nation reach a 'minimalist' regulatory structure unlikely to be achieved in Australia in the foreseeable future. While the outcome could be independent of the process followed, intuition would suggest not. Australian deregulation has occurred under the guidance of a number of large-scale government inquiries into the financial system,[4] providing opportunity for a variety of views and interests to find expression and possibly influence the set of reform outcomes seen as politically feasible. The New Zealand developments have been driven from within the political and public sector arenas, with less in the way of formal public discussion and input (although proposals developed within the official sector were distributed to interested parties for comment). In that respect, it might be asked whether the ability of the New Zealand government to introduce a relatively unique supervisory regime based on a clearly articulated and apparently simple view of the financial system owes something to the nature of this process. Also relevant, however, is the fact that the parlous state of the New Zealand economy in the early 1980s provided a unique opportunity for radical changes which might not normally be politically feasible. Whether the New Zealand model is a superior one to the more complex approach of Australia, or whether it could be adopted in other nations with different institutional characteristics, is a question considered later.

Whether financial systems and their regulatory structures can be viewed as tending towards some 'steady state' is a moot point. Kane (1981) has popularised the notion of a regulatory dialectic in which financial innovation and regulation are continually reacting to each other and external forces, suggesting that an equilibrium regulatory structure is unlikely. Given the 'minimalist' nature of the New Zealand regulation, it might be argued that it has reached something of a steady state, although the question arises (and is considered later) of whether the supervisory structure will induce changes in the structure and operations of the financial sector which are subsequently seen to have undesirable consequences necessitating regulatory revision. In contrast, the Australian financial system is still undergoing significant changes as the recommendations of the Wallis Inquiry (Wallis 1997) are gradually implemented. And although those recommendations will, in some areas, see the differences between the two regulatory systems diminish, there remain other areas in which there are significant divergences.

One important area of similarity can be found in the approaches to depositor/investor protection, with both countries eschewing any form of depositor insurance scheme or government guarantees of deposits. (The associated supervisory approaches do, however, differ dramatically, as explained later.) Both have also accepted the BIS risk-based capital adequacy requirements (although the enthusiasm of the New Zealand supervisors for regulatory prescription of such standards appears muted[5] and they have not followed Australia in adopting the amendments to capital requirements based on market risk). Other than such capital adequacy requirements, there are few restrictions imposed in either country on bank activities, and monetary control operates essentially independently of supervision of financial institutions and markets, and without reliance upon direct controls over financial prices. Indeed, under the Australian reforms post-Wallis, the two activities (of monetary control and prudential supervision) are being placed with separate institutions.

The approaches to monetary policy have largely converged. Both central banks now operate under a form of inflation targeting, although the New Zealand approach, premised on a strict assignment of monetary policy to an explicit target inflation rate established in a 'policy targets agreement' (PTA) between the government and the Reserve Bank, appears somewhat less flexible than the Australian approach. While the precise organisational and accountability structure for the Australian supervisory authorities under the Wallis proposals is still emerging, the greater accountability and independence of the Reserve Bank was affirmed with the appointment of the current governor in 1996. Again, the Australian arrangements appear to be somewhat more flexible than those enshrined in the Reserve Bank of New Zealand Act (1989). Whether, in both cases, flexibility is a virtue or a vice is discussed later.

There are significant differences in the regulatory structures of the two nations. While both explicitly distinguish between 'banks' and other financial institutions, the Australian approach does not involve such a clear-cut distinction. The New Zealand approach also places no restrictions on the foreign ownership of banks or other financial institutions. In Australia, the government has retained some restrictions on foreign ownership of major extant financial institutions, while otherwise allowing freedom of entry. The New Zealand approach places prime emphasis on the disclosure of information by banks to the public and gives no role to separate supervisory oversight, whereas the Australian approach gives the prudential regulator a key role in monitoring and supervising financial institutions. These differences reflect alternative approaches to attempting to ensure that incentive and accountability structures are such as to avoid moral hazard problems and to ensure that good corporate governance practices and effective market discipline are in place.

While both countries reject the notion of depositor insurance, or de jure or de facto government guarantees of deposits, there is a fundamental difference in the thinking that underpins the approach to deposit safety. Whereas official Australian committees of inquiry into the financial system have asserted the merits of the existence of a risk-free 'safety haven' for depositors, enabling them to avoid risk assessment issues, the New Zealand model gives no credence to such a view.[6] This finds reflection in an Australian approach which involves the authorities monitoring individual bank safety, in contrast to a New Zealand approach which perceives a role for the authorities only in the case of systemic crisis.

Rather than differences of principle between the two approaches, perhaps the most significant difference is the practical consideration that the Reserve Bank of New Zealand is largely a 'host' supervisor, reflecting the fact that virtually all of the New Zealand banking sector (and thus financial sector) is foreign owned (see Appendix 11.4). In contrast, the Australian financial system is still dominated by Australian-owned financial institutions (see Appendix 11.2). Whether a New Zealand 'minimalist' model of supervision can effectively operate in a system where institutions are largely domestic entities, or whether freedom of entry and ownership can be expected to lead to a situation in which overseas entities dominate (facilitating such a supervisory model), are questions which warrant attention. For, while the New Zealand model is sometimes held up as an example of how a deregulated financial system can be achieved and be viable, there is de facto regulation through home country supervision of the parent banks. Since the New Zealand banking sector can be interpreted (perhaps unfairly) as largely a part of the branch and subsidiary network of the Australian banking system, the success of the New Zealand supervisory model could be argued to be largely dependent on the success of the Australian approach.

THE AUSTRALIAN REFORM PROCESS

The pre-reform environment

The Australian regulatory structure until the late 1970s was one of direct controls, largely focused upon the banking sector,[7] and reflected largely ad hoc responses to various events since and during World War II. The variable reserve requirement (statutory reserve deposit (SRD) ratio), central bank power to impose limits on bank lending, and controls on bank interest rates can all be traced to wartime initiatives. The secondary liquid and government securities (LGS) reserve ratio on trading bank asset portfolios emerged during the 1950s as attempts by the central bank to control bank lending were found to be thwarted by the policy of pegging bond yields and subsequent elasticity of the supply of primary reserve assets. The (generally constant) minimum LGS requirement was seen as the fulcrum upon which changes in the SRD ratio (the main policy weapon) operated to affect bank lending.

Trading banks were also precluded from paying interest on chequing accounts, and maturity restrictions limited (interest-bearing) deposits to maturities in excess of 30 days. Indeed, until 1980, the only market-determined bank interest rates were those on 'large' overdrafts and negotiable certificates of deposit. In return for these regulations, many of which had prudential overtones (holding safe assets, preventing destructive interest rate competition), the trading banks had access to lender-of-last-resort facilities at the central bank and were generally perceived to have de facto guarantees of deposit safety. The banks also were the only authorised foreign exchange operatives and helped to administer the exchange control system which limited official forward cover, under the fixed (but adjustable) rate system and subsequent crawling peg system from 1976 to 1983, to a limited set of trade transactions.

The savings banks also faced quite restrictive regulation. Deposit raisings were restricted to the personal sector and subject to interest rate ceilings, and asset portfolios were restricted essentially to government paper and household mortgage debt. Mortgage interest rates were also subject to ceilings. On the deposit side, only at-call and notice-of-withdrawal accounts were permitted, although the state (government-owned) savings banks were permitted to offer chequing accounts. Other 'thrift' institutions such as building societies and credit unions came under state government legislation and were generally subject to similar, but slightly less restrictive, regulation.

From this brief review of banking regulation operating until the late 1970s, three features warrant emphasis. First, even in those markets open to them, banks were heavily constrained via interest rate controls and the 'tax' effects of various regulations. In the inflationary 1970s, these constraints had much greater bite and innovative ways of avoiding them were developed.[8] Second, bank involvement in a number of important markets (such as wholesale funds and consumer loan markets) was restricted. Innovation (naturally) occurred: banks developed finance company subsidiaries; the merchant banking sector grew as subsidiaries of overseas banks entered (and domestic banks took equity stakes to the extent regulations permitted); other non-bank financial institutions (NBFIs) grew rapidly.

A third feature was the structure of the government paper market. The enforced holdings of government debt by trading and savings banks have already been noted, but the 'captive' market extended much further to official money market dealers and (via tax concessions) to life offices and pension funds. Around 70 per cent of non-official holdings of government debt were in captive portfolios, creating significant distortions to the demand side of the market. On the supply side, the primary market arrangements were not conducive to the conduct of market operations, with both treasury note and bond issues being largely demand-determined at institutionally determined and relatively inflexible yields. In this environment, it was not surprising that, despite an expressed preference for 'market-oriented' measures, monetary policy operated until the 1980s mainly by the use of direct controls.

Structural change and reform

The Australian financial system has been profoundly changed by the process of financial deregulation since the late 1970s.[9] At that time, the banking sector was heavily regulated; foreign (and, it was believed, other) entry into banking was prohibited; banking and securities markets activities were segmented; public sector security markets were rudimentary; and financial market prices (exchange rates and interest rates) were subject to government regulation. NBFIs, which were subject to less regulation, had grown more rapidly than banks over the previous decade (although some of the institutions involved were bank subsidiaries).

1979 was a turning point. The Campbell Committee of Inquiry was formed in January 1979 and, although it did not report until November 1981, its existence focused attention upon ongoing developments in the financial markets. Moreover, the government did not (often could not) wait for its committee's report to alter the face of the financial system. The Campbell Inquiry was established by a Liberal government with a strong free market philosophy (if not record) and was directed to focus upon the efficient operation of the financial system. This it did from a perspective which emphasised the benefits of free markets and took as fundamental the propositions that: competitive neutrality should apply; social and sectoral objectives should be tackled through fiscal measures rather than through interference with financial markets; and some risk-free deposit-type asset should be available to unsophisticated investors. With the exception of its proposals regarding prudential regulation, the report advocated minimal government intervention. Monetary policy considerations received little attention.

While the Campbell Inquiry was in progress, changes in the financial system happened apace. The federal government began to experiment with new methods of issuing government debt, leading quickly to adoption of a tender system. Changes in the procedures for state (and federal) authorities' loan raising began, ultimately leading to a significant market in state government debt by the late 1980s. In February 1981 a new banking licence was issued, signalling that entry to banking was, in fact, possible and a few months later two bank mergers were approved, reducing the number of major banks to four. Consolidation was occurring in other areas (building societies, credit unions) as well and December 1980 saw the introduction of cash management trusts (money market mutual funds).

Apparently by chance, the entry of such trusts coincided with the removal of all controls on bank deposit interest rates (except that on cheque accounts), although continued regulation of some asset interest rates (on housing loans for savings banks and 'small' loans for trading banks) limited the ability of banks to vary deposit rates. The removal of bank deposit restrictions in December 1980 marks the start of a massive process of deregulation commenced by the Fraser Liberal government and surprisingly accelerated by the Hawke Labor government, elected in March 1983, whose party platform had until recently contained a call for bank nationalisation. Given that party's traditional stance, the process was remarkably uncontentious, due in part to the general support for deregulation given by a second inquiry (the Martin group), set up by Labor to review the findings of the Campbell Inquiry in the light of Labor's objectives.

Appendix 11.1 presents a summary of major events and indicates four major phases in the transition from a regulated to a less regulated system in the 1980s. The first phase, in December 1980, has already been discussed. The second, in mid-1982, saw a further step in the deregulation of banks and their ability to compete with other sectors: remaining interest rate ceilings were raised; banks were allowed to enter short-term deposit markets not previously permitted to them; the 'tax' effect of reserve requirements was reduced; Reserve Bank guidelines limiting bank lending growth were removed (and ended as a technique of monetary management); and lending opportunities for savings banks were expanded by the reduction in their LGS ratio.

The third phase in the deregulatory process was that of deregulation of the foreign exchange market, culminating in the floating of the exchange rate and the removal of most exchange control regulations in December 1983 and authorisation of 40 new foreign exchange dealers in June 1984. The fourth phase commenced in late 1984, although partly foreshadowed earlier. Banks were given freedom to pay interest on cheque accounts and compete freely in short-term deposit markets. All remaining loan rate ceilings, other than those on housing mortgages, were scrapped and captive market requirements on banks reduced and abolished for life offices and pension funds.

In addition to these changes, late 1984 also saw applications invited for foreign bank licences, of which sixteen were announced as successful in early 1985. Concurrently, freedom of entry into merchant banking was announced (as a temporary, later continuing, measure) enabling foreign banks to enter or rationalise existing Australian interests. Additionally, Australian banks were allowed to obtain full interests in merchant banking subsidiaries, while the deregulation of the stock market in 1984 allowed banks a 50 per cent shareholding in stockbrokers. Completing this catalogue of changes was the scrapping, in April 1986, of interest rate ceilings on new home mortgage lending by savings banks.

Subsequently, policies towards supervision or regulation of the financial system have followed a process which some have referred to as 'reregulation', although such a description ignores the reduction in barriers to financial conglomerates operating across the entire spectrum of financial markets (including banking, insurance, funds management and securities markets) which continued to occur. In accordance with international agreements, banks (and other depository NBFIs) have been subject to capital requirements, through the imposition of minimum capital requirements linked initially to counterparty or credit risk (since 1987 for banks) and more recently to market risk arising from trading activities. Risk-based capital standards are also applied to life offices and stockbroking firms. Greater supervision of banks' internal risk management systems has also been put in place.

Rather than a process of reregulation, it is perhaps more appropriate to see these developments as the prudent response of a government widely perceived to be a de facto insurer of the liabilities of certain financial institutions, endeavouring to prevent the moral hazard inherent in any insurance-type arrangement. As part of the supervisory process, marked changes have also been made in the supervisory structure. The Insurance and Superannuation Commission (ISC) was established in 1987 to supervise the insurance and superannuation industries. State-based powers over securities regulation and supervision of NBFIs, which impeded a nationwide policy, have been standardised and the Australian Securities Commission (ASC) established (in 1991) to supervise companies and the securities industry, and the Australian Financial Institutions Commission (AFIC) (established in 1992) to supervise NBFIs. Concerns over the possibility of inconsistent regulation led to the formation of a Council of Financial Supervisors in 1992, comprising the Reserve Bank (RBA) and the ISC.

It is widely accepted that the 1980s process of financial deregulation was not ideally handled in Australia. Newly deregulated institutions in an unfamiliar competitive environment expanded credit rapidly, contributing to asset price inflation and a minor financial crisis in the late 1980s. With the aid of hindsight, two deficiencies in the process were apparent, both reflecting gaps in the analysis of the Campbell and Martin Committees. One was the lack of attention paid to the operation of monetary policy in a deregulated financial system. In particular, the RBA was unable to determine the extent to which credit growth was a natural consequence of reintermediation (based on prudent lending by deregulated institutions), rather than a relaxation of credit standards. The other deficiency was the lack of attention paid, in the analysis of deregulation, to agency problems inherent in financial institutions. As a result, there was no coherent strategy to enhance corporate governance, accountability and market discipline or to develop appropriate techniques of prudential supervision and suitable capital standards to accompany the removal of a plethora of regulatory constraints on managerial freedom.[10]

Under the Wallis Committee proposals, a further round of regulatory restructuring is currently underway, involving the establishment of a prudential regulator of all financial institutions, separate from the RBA which retains responsibility for monetary control.[11] At one level, this aggregation of prudential regulatory responsibilities can be seen as a rationalisation of the prudential supervisory process. At another level, however, the separation of monetary control and supervisory responsibilities can be seen as an attempt to minimise the perception of de facto government guarantees – since the prudential regulator has no significant asset base which could be used to compensate depositors in a failed institution.

The current Australian framework

Australian monetary control and prudential supervision are now effectively independent activities. Both the techniques used are, and the responsible bodies will soon be, effectively separated – a quite different situation to that prevailing prior to the 1980s.

Monetary control is effected by RBA market activities aimed at achieving a level of liquidity which ensures that the short-term interest rate target announced by the RBA is achieved. The development of a monetary policy based on the announcement of a target short-term interest rate dates from January 1990 and has involved over 20 changes in the target level since that date. Unlike its counterpart in New Zealand, the RBA has not been made explicitly accountable for achieving a target short-term outcome for a single ultimate goal of policy (inflation), but adjusts its policy stance as it sees fit in the light of general economic conditions. Inflationary factors are, however, a very important determinant of those decisions, with an agreed medium-term inflation target of 2–3 per cent having been adopted since 1996 as an objective of policy and as an anchor for the formation of private sector expectations. MacFarlane (1997) dates the start of an 'inflation targeting regime' for monetary policy as 1993 (following a monetary targeting regime between 1976 and 1985, and a 'checklist' approach in the interim years), although formalisation of this approach occurred with the 1996 Statement on the Conduct of Monetary Policy (RBA 1996).

The adoption of this approach to policy has been facilitated by an explicit debt management policy framework and by the introduction at the start of the 1980s of effective tender systems for the primary market for government debt. More recently, changes to the operations of exchange settlement accounts have facilitated a more transparent means of liquidity management (and seen the demise of the authorised short-term money market dealers).

Policy transparency has been increased with the production of a semi-annual statement on monetary policy and six-monthly appearances by the governor of the Reserve Bank before a parliamentary committee. Changes in policy are announced publicly and are well documented. These developments, formalised in 1996, were also accompanied by an affirmation of the independence of the RBA in its conduct of monetary policy. Although the Reserve Bank Act (1959) established the power of the RBA board to act in an independent manner, in practice the ability of the Treasurer to veto decisions (and the necessity to obtain the Treasurer's explicit approval to use many direct control techniques in the earlier years where these were in vogue) had limited effective independence. While there has been no formal change in arrangements, the explicit affirmation of the RBA's independence and the necessity of public mechanisms for a government override of policy provides evidence of an acceptance of central bank independence. However, it would still seem to be the case, as Davis and Lewis noted, that 'the authority of the Bank rests on the personality and style of the Reserve Bank Governor and his officials' (1988: 251).

The prudential supervision of financial institutions is, under changes currently in process, to be the responsibility of the Australian Prudential Regulation Authority (APRA), which will have responsibility for supervising deposit-taking institutions (including banks), life and general insurance companies, and superannuation schemes. The prudential regulator is to be empowered to establish prudential regulations on relevant licensed entities, and non-licensed entities are generally to be precluded from offering key products such as deposits, insurance and retirement income products. The key plank in the prudential supervision process is the implementation of risk-based capital adequacy requirements. The Australian approach sees 'disclosure . . . as supportive of prudential regulation, not an alternative to it' (Wallis 1997: 336). Disclosure and market conduct matters impacting upon financial institutions and providers of financial services (including exchanges and OTC markets), the regulation of corporations, and finance sector consumer protection are to be the province of the Australian Securities and Investment Commission (ASIC, successor to the Australian Securities Commission). Notably, the Wallis Report recommended that finance companies and merchant banks not be supervised by the APRA but come under the purview of the ASIC.

THE NEW ZEALAND REFORM PROCESS

The pre-reform environment

In reaching the current 'minimalist' regulatory structure, financial reform in New Zealand has traversed a somewhat volatile path, although since 1984 there has been a consistency of purpose and direction limited only by the demands of international harmonisation.[12]

Prior to the election of a Labour government in 1984, the New Zealand financial system was heavily regulated, although over the previous two decades there had been bouts of financial liberalisation which were quickly reversed as macroeconomic conditions threatened economic stability.

In the 1960s, the regulatory framework was one based on direct controls on banks (reserve ratios, controls on bank advances, interest rate controls), accompanied by the growth of non-bank institutions which thwarted low interest rate policies and induced moves to regulate such institutions. The easing of some direct controls in the 1969 Budget (including the abolition of capital issues controls, deposit interest rate flexibility), unaccompanied by more general changes to the conduct of monetary policy, led to the expected effect of rapid monetary expansion and a return to regulation. Over the first half of the 1970s, the myriad of regulations created incentives for innovation by less regulated institutions and constrained banks' adaptability, and weakened monetary control. Leung (1991) notes that the trading bank share of private sector credit fell from over 62 per cent at the end of the 1960s to below 54 per cent by 1984.

A renewed attempt at financial deregulation was made in 1976, with a relaxation of bank interest rate controls and a move towards more market-related interest rates on government debt. However, the incomplete nature of this adjustment meant that monetary control was still found wanting and direct controls were strengthened in the early 1980s (and some interest rates frozen in line with the wage and price freeze introduced in mid-1982). Indeed, in surveying financial deregulation in New Zealand, the OECD commented that, 'by 1982, financial markets were as heavily regulated as they had been in the early 1960s – a movement in stark contrast to the trend seen in most other OECD countries' (1989: 42).

Structural change and reform

A fundamental change in the approach to financial regulation in New Zealand followed the Labour government election in July 1984. Liberalisation commenced virtually immediately (with the revoking of interest rate controls), and by the end of 1984 changes to the structure of government securities markets had been made, other interest rate regulations on banks which inhibited their competing in certain markets were removed, credit growth limits were abolished and restrictions on international capital flows relaxed. In early 1985, all compulsory ratios on financial institutions were removed[13] and the exchange rate floated. Among private sector initiatives, the New Zealand Futures Exchange was established and the first cash management trust appeared in 1985.

The flurry of deregulatory activity was formalised and extended in the Reserve Bank of New Zealand Amendment Act (1986). Underpinning the approach were principles of achieving competitive neutrality, increasing contestability, and development of a prudential supervision policy consistent with economic efficiency. Significant changes included: a licensing regime for banks (rather than a legislative entry barrier), with entry conditional on meeting general prudential criteria (e.g. capital, expertise, good standing); the ability of foreign-owned institutions to become licensed banks; the introduction of a disclosure regime; the explicit rejection of de jure or de facto deposit insurance; freedom for other institutions to undertake 'banking business', but prohibition on their use of the term 'bank'; the recognition of a failure management role for the Reserve Bank (RBNZ); and the introduction of the PTA approach to monetary management. Also in June 1986, the stock exchange was deregulated, with fixed commissions abolished and the incorporation of stockbrokers allowed. By 1987, the OECD was able to comment that 'reform of monetary management and of the financial system has possibly been more profound than in any other area of the economy or for that matter elsewhere in the OECD' (1987: 39).

A second phase of financial reform occurred in the 1990s, 'concerned with re-engineering some of the basic legal infrastructure for banking and commerce and overhauling supervision arrangements' (OECD 1998), particularly with regard to reliance upon public disclosure and minimal supervision. In 1996, significant changes were introduced to bank supervision arrangements which involved a further increase in public disclosure requirements, the increased accountability of managers and directors, and a reduction in the prudential regulation of banks (such as removal of limits on particular exposures and requirements to provide additional information to the RBNZ). In essence, reliance upon disclosure and market discipline of individual banks has become a replacement for, rather than a complement to, official prudential supervision. Underpinning these changes have been the objectives of: increasing the role of market discipline; minimising compliance costs; removing taxpayer risk (associated with bailouts of failed institutions); and improving the corporate governance structures of banks by strengthening incentives and accountability for bank management and directors.

The current position

The New Zealand supervisory system, as at the start of 1998, is premised on a clearly articulated simple model of the workings of a market system, albeit one with which many might take issue.[14] Fundamental to the approach is reliance on the public disclosure of information and an appropriate incentive structure (for customers of, and decision makers within, financial institutions) to ensure that 'important' financial institutions behave prudently and will not undermine financial system stability.

A distinction is made in the supervisory structure between banks and other financial institutions, whereby institutions wishing to use the label of 'bank' must be registered by the RBNZ and must meet certain prudential requirements. Such requirements involve meeting registration standards (e.g. minimum capital of NZ$15 million, good standing, prudential management) and adhering to a public disclosure regime (and BIS-style minimum capital requirements) once registered. There are no limitations on the ownership structure of a registered bank, other than that the owners (entities or individuals) will have incentives to appropriately monitor activities. Prudential rules are essentially limited to capital requirements based on risk-weighted assets and limits on exposures to connected parties. Capital requirements for market risk have not been adopted and 'there are no prudential rules applying to asset quality, large exposures (except connected person exposures), country risk, liquidity, or market risk' (RBNZ 1997a: section 6: 3).

The disclosure regime involves quarterly publication of a detailed general disclosure statement, together with a key information statement directed at the non-expert investor, which provide relevant financial information (e.g. credit ratings, guarantees, capital position, impaired assets, exposures, profitability, size) to enable investors to assess the institution's financial health. The general disclosure statement relates to the bank and banking group as a whole, whereas the key information statement relates to the banking group (the registered bank and its subsidiaries). While it is accepted that the typical bank customer will not study or fully understand these disclosures, 'we expect that journalists, financial analysts, investment advisers and other professionals will, and that any significant "news" about changes in a bank's financial condition will spread quickly' (RBNZ 1997b: section 3: 2).

There is no system of depositor preference (vis-à-vis other creditors), nor is there any form of deposit insurance, and a key element of the approach is to avoid any impression or prospect of contingent taxpayer liability should a bank fail. Public provision of information and an incentive structure for depositors to monitor banks and thus deposit riskiness is one part of the total approach. The other element is the establishment of an accountability structure which gives bank management and directors strong incentives to ensure that 'correct' information is disclosed and that banks have systems and procedures in place to ensure prudent operation. The outcome, it is hoped, is an efficient financial system not hamstrung by costly compliance and regulation, in which the possibility of bank failure is minimal and non-contagious. As Brash (1997) notes, the effectiveness of such an approach will depend upon the 'infrastructure' which supports disclosure (corporate law, accounting and auditing standards, the ability of external accountants and auditors, and the expertise of financial analysts).

Should a registered bank run into problems, the RBNZ has specific crisis management powers aimed at avoiding significant damage to the financial system. These range from its ability to place banks under direction or management, to its ability to provide liquidity support and lender-of-last-resort facilities (to both banks and other institutions) in case of systemic crisis. The RBNZ has outlined the broad principles which it will apply, emphasising that it will only intervene in the affairs of a failed bank where systemic issues assume importance, and in doing so will avoid placing taxpayer funds at risk rather than losses being borne by shareholders and creditors (including depositors).

Other financial institutions fall outside of the RBNZ registration and disclosure regime, even though they are able to undertake exactly the same activities as registered banks. Such financial institutions (which include life offices, managed funds, finance companies, merchant banks, building societies and credit unions) are subject to the provision of the Companies Act (1993) and the Securities Act (1978). Under the latter Act, the New Zealand Securities Commission oversees the activities of securities markets, deposit-taking institutions (other than banks) and managed funds, and imposes prospectus requirements, public provision of investment product statements, and trustee and trust deed requirements on institutions issuing public debt instruments. Following changes to the relevant Acts in 1996, offers to the public no longer need to be accompanied by the registered prospectus but only by an 'Investment Statement' (which can be provided electronically). Where banks have subsidiaries engaged in 'non-banking' business, such as insurance or funds management, these activities are supervised by other regulatory bodies.

One outcome of the New Zealand approach has been the transformation of the structure of the financial sector into one dominated by registered banks, which are virtually 100 per cent foreign owned. As at mid-1997, there were nineteen banks (of which eighteen were foreign owned), accounting for 73 per cent of the assets of the

New Zealand financial system. A further 16 per cent of total assets were under the control of managed funds, and a relatively small number of other types of institutions were in existence. In such an environment, it might be argued that the significance of regulation applying to other institutions is minor. However, such institutions are able to offer the same set of products as registered banks (should they so wish). They can thus look like, feel like, be like banks – but cannot use the 'bank' label. Should such an institution get into difficulties, the obvious question is whether the delineating of banks from non-banks by the labelling process will be sufficient to prevent the possibility of contagion occurring and spilling over to banks. Likewise, it should be asked why the use of the term should be restricted to registered institutions, since alternative labels such as 'disclosing institution' could be used. Most likely, there are safety overtones associated with the bank label and public perceptions of government backing, which give such labelled institutions a competitive advantage. However, until the situation is put to the test and depositors lose money from a registered bank failure, this hypothesis remains untested.

The New Zealand approach to financial sector regulation is also characterised by a rigidly specified monetary policy role for the RBNZ, involving a high degree of independence and accountability (see Brash 1993 for more detail). In conjunction with the deregulation of 1984, the focus of monetary policy was shifted to a single goal of price stability. This was formalised under the Reserve Bank Act of 1989, where the specific target for inflation is agreed and documented in PTAs between the government and the RBNZ. The Governor of the Reserve Bank is accountable for achieving that target, although certain caveats are provided for events (such as significant tax increases or oil price increases) where continued commitment to short-term price stability would involve excessive economic costs. Moreover, the RBNZ is given a high degree of autonomy in pursuing that target, with any government wishing to deviate from the inflation target having to publicly override the PTA and renegotiate it. As part of the RBNZ's accountability, public documentation of policy is required through a 'monetary policy statement', published at least every six months. In mid-1997, as part of this process, the RBNZ commenced publication of (both current values of and its forecasts for) the monetary conditions indicator, which attempts to capture in a single index the impact of interest rates and exchange rates on economic activity. With seigniorage from the note issue formally returned to the government, financial autonomy is achieved through formal five-year funding agreements negotiated with the government.

ALTERNATIVE VISIONS

In reviewing international developments in central banking over the past 25 years, the BIS noted that 'this process has led to a greater emphasis on transparency, market incentives and the credibility of policies' (1997a: 143), with the last of these factors inducing greater central bank autonomy and accountability and the specification of clearer goals for policy. The experiences of both Australia and New Zealand conform to this broad picture, but with some significant differences in the approaches adopted.

Notably, the New Zealand approach involves apparently simple answers to the complex questions of how to ensure monetary and financial stability. Whether such simple answers work or whether, echoing Kane's (1981) regulatory dialectic perspective, this will change the financial environment in such a way as to reduce the complexity of the questions or vitiate the effectiveness of those simple answers is an important issue.

In the realm of monetary policy, both countries have converged upon apparently similar approaches. Both work with established inflation targets which provide the nominal anchor for private sector expectations and act as a benchmark against which credibility can be judged. Both provide semi-annual statements of monetary policy and other relevant information, aimed at achieving policy transparency. Both provide for central bank autonomy, subject to a public political 'override' process.

Despite those similarities, there are a number of subtle differences which suggest a more 'hard line' approach by New Zealand. The inflation targets in Australia are set with a medium-term focus and allow the RBA to operate by 'taking account of the implications of monetary policy for activity and therefore employment in the short term' (RBA 1996: 2). In New Zealand, the inflation targets are short-term, albeit with specified caveats to allow for variation due to certain real sector or fiscal events. In both cases, the commitment to a specific inflation target value is thus 'conditional'. Which, if either, approach provides greater credibility and which is more compatible with overall effectiveness of macroeconomic policy are debatable issues.

While both countries have adopted freely floating exchange rates, there appears to be a greater willingness on the part of the Australian authorities to countenance intervention in the foreign exchange market if market trends seem at variance with market fundamentals. In essence, the RBA appears willing to accept that 'market psychology' may sometimes go awry.

It is in the area of central bank autonomy that the differences are potentially the greatest. In Australia, the RBA board includes the Secretary of the Treasury and is responsible for the formulation of monetary policy. While the governor, as chairman of the board, can presumably drive the policy process, the potential exists for policy to be influenced at board level by Treasury and government views. In New Zealand, the 'Board has no involvement in directing Reserve Bank policy, monetary or otherwise, and Board members do not receive market-sensitive information ahead of the markets. The Board's primary function is to monitor the Reserve Bank's performance, reporting to the Treasurer' (RBNZ 1997c: 6). A second difference concerns funding. The RBNZ operates effectively as a 'cost centre', relying upon five-yearly agreed allocations from the government to meet its operating costs. The RBA, on the other hand, receives the seigniorage from the note issue, out of which it can meet operating costs and remit a dividend to the government.

Both countries now provide for a degree of separation between monetary policy and prudential supervision. In the New Zealand case, this arises from the central bank largely eschewing responsibility for prudential supervision, except at a minimal level associated with bank registration requirements. Other (non-bank) financial institutions and financial markets are supervised by the ASC. In Australia, the APRA is to be the separate prudential supervisor of depositor institutions and life offices, while the supervision of securities markets and other financial institutions (finance companies and merchant banks) is to be undertaken by the ASIC. In both countries, the Reserve Bank is responsible for supervision of payments systems.

In designing the supervisory structures, each country has identified a class of institutions as banks, which are treated specially, but neither has effectively answered the longstanding question: 'Are banks special?' In New Zealand, anyone is able to undertake 'banking activities' (although compliance with the Securities Act is required), but use of the bank label is restricted to registered institutions. Registration is, however, open to all who meet the minimum requirements. In Australia, use of the label is similarly restricted, but a separate classification of institutions undertaking similar activities is made and these are also supervised by the APRA. However, activities such as deposit taking and life insurance are not permitted unless the institution is supervised. In both cases, the issue is, in effect, whether there is a regulatory case for whether certain financial products should only be allowed to be offered by a set of licensed/supervised institutions.

Regulatory restrictions on the use of the bank label suggest that the term has some information content and it must be asked from whence that arises. An obvious answer is that public perceptions are that institutions called banks are different in some way, and that allowing unlimited use of the label would lead to some form of market failure involving customers not adequately discriminating between institutions. If so, reliance upon disclosure to achieve market discipline seems inadequate.

The approaches adopted towards supervision are where the greatest variance arises. The New Zealand approach appears to be premised on a view that disclosure is a (perfect) substitute for prudential regulation, which is in distinct contrast to the Australian perspective. Consequent to the preceding difference, the New Zealand approach relies on the prudential supervisor having (virtually) no 'insider information' about the financial condition of registered banks, in contrast to the Australian approach where such information is obtained via regular reporting requirements and, in recent years, on-site inspections. Indeed, in this regard, the New Zealand approach appears to be one which involves a stance somewhat at variance to that generally accepted by central bankers and prudential supervisors. For example, it does not appear to meet a number of the 'core principles for effective banking supervision', released in 1997 by the BIS (1997b). Notable discrepancies involve: principle 7 (evaluation of bank policies, practices and procedures regarding loans and investments); principle 9 (prudential limits restricting bank exposures to single or groups of related borrowers); principle 16 (on-site and off-site inspection).

Do these differences matter? One important issue concerns the question of the credibility of the assertions that government will not bail out depositors or other creditors of failed banks or other institutions. The New Zealand model, by explicitly eschewing a role for central bank supervision, aims to distance the government from responsibility for deposit safety. The Australian model does not have that aura of distance. The issue is a complex one, made more complicated by the internationalisation of banking. The New Zealand approach relies on market discipline of banks and some (unknown) rate of bank failures could be expected to occur in such an environment. Whether that rate would be higher or lower than under a supervisory system is a moot point, although the Australian approach is premised on a view that it would be higher. The critical concerns are whether, when a failure occurs, one system is superior in enforcing the no-bailout policy under political realities and whether there are different likelihoods of contagion. Unfortunately, the New Zealand model does not provide a potentially useful testing ground for those questions because of the internationalisation of its banking industry. Ultimately, banks in New Zealand are subject to home country regulation, by virtue of their overseas parentage.

This raises the final area of difference warranting comment, that of competition and ownership policy in the financial services industry. The New Zealand approach is premised on the view that there should be no regulatory constraints on the ownership of financial institutions (except for the requirement to meet general 'acceptability' requirements), including freedom of entry and acquisition for foreign-based entities. While the Wallis Inquiry was of the view that current restrictions on foreign ownership of the largest Australian financial entities (the 'six pillars' policy) should be removed, it was of the view that 'a large scale transfer of ownership of the financial system to foreign hands should be considered contrary to the national interest' (Wallis 1997: 61). In New Zealand, such a transfer has occurred. To what extent this reflects the existence of efficiencies arising from the internationalisation of banking (with consequent messages for Australian policymakers), the ownership consequences of a 'workout' of a distressed banking sector, or the 'flight' of local bank directors from the legal risks or harshness of competition associated with operating purely domestic banks in the deregulated environment are important questions for the designers of regulatory structures in other nations.

In Australia, there is clearly still a perspective that 'banks are different' and that this is relevant to the design of regulatory policy. In New Zealand, policy is premised on there being no difference between banks and other institutions, but in practice the restricted use of the bank label induces such a difference.

CONCLUSION

The activities, and regulation, of financial institutions are replete with agency problems, and the Australian and New Zealand regulatory systems provide interesting contrasts in approach to the resolution of such problems.

The New Zealand model is premised on the view that adequate disclosure of information can resolve the standard owner–depositor conflict and obviate the need for government monitoring which can lead to the development of agency relationships involving government as a principal through (implicit or explicit) protection of depositors.[15] That alone would be inadequate, since the opaque nature of financial institutions gives an important role to agency relationships involving bank management. Here the New Zealand model pays particular attention to the legal responsibilities of, and possible penalties for, bank directors and management and aims to maximise the effect of market discipline through (virtually) no restrictions on ownership or takeover, and the possibility of enhanced product market competition through the information provision requirements.

In contrast, the Australian approach is less sanguine about reliance upon improved information and market forces to ensure a sound financial system. Government monitoring of the management of financial institutions is seen as a necessary complement to market discipline, a view consistent with the premise that governments may be able to obtain access to better information from financial institutions than can the private sector. However, once government takes on some responsibility for monitoring the management of financial institutions, the credibility of assertions that other stakeholders (e.g. depositors) will not be protected against loss is called into question by the nature of the political reality. While the Wallis reforms involve separation of the prudential supervisor from other agencies (such as the central bank) in an attempt to enhance the credibility of those assertions, that approach assumes (without any supporting evidence) that government administrative and organisational structures can alter the public perception of political realities.

From an international perspective, the decisions by both countries to adopt policies which eschew explicit depositor protection, but within quite different regulatory structures each aimed at providing credibility of a no-bailout policy, make for interesting case studies. Designing appropriate tests of the efficacy and efficiency of those national regulatory structures for financial system safety and efficiency, which take appropriate account of the internationalisation of financial systems, provides an exciting challenge for future research.

APPENDIX 11.1 FINANCIAL REFORM CALENDAR: AUSTRALIA

Date	Event
1947	Commonwealth government attempt to nationalise banks.
1960	Reserve (central) Bank separated from Commonwealth (trading) Bank.
1970	Bank (Shareholdings) Act (1972) applied restrictions to maximum ownership share in banks.
1971	A$ linked to US$ instead of to sterling.
1974	Financial Corporations Act passed, providing for direct controls on NBFIs, but those provisions not proclaimed.
December 1980	Interest rate ceilings on most bank deposits removed.
1981	Report of Australian Financial System Inquiry (Campbell Inquiry).
March 1982	Maturity controls on bank deposits relaxed, permitting increased competition in short-term markets.
May 1982	Interest rate on trading bank SRD accounts increased from 2.5 per cent to 5 per cent.
June 1982	Treasury bond tender introduced. Lending restrictions on trading banks abolished.
August 1982	Savings bank LGS-type requirement reduced from 40 per cent to 15 per cent. They are permitted to accept corporate deposits and are given greater asset flexibility.
December 1983	Australian dollar floated and exchange control regulations largely abolished.
December 1983	Martin Review Group Report.
June 1984	40 new foreign exchange dealers authorised.
August 1984	Interest rate prohibition on cheque accounts removed.
September 1984	Applications for bank licences from foreign banking interests invited. Temporary suspension of foreign investment guidelines regarding merchant banking. Abolition of 30/20 rule for life offices and pension funds.
April 1985	Interest rate ceiling on 'small' bank loans (under A$100,000) removed, leaving the housing interest rate the only one subject to control.
May 1985	Abolition of 18 per cent LGS convention and gradual phasing in of prime assets ratio (of 12 per cent) announced.
April 1986	Removal of interest rate ceiling on bank home mortgage lending announced.
1988	BIS risk-weighted capital adequacy requirements introduced.
1990	'Six pillars' policy introduced.
1991	Martin Committee Report.
1991	Australian Securities Commission (ASC) established as regulator of corporations, securities and futures markets.
1992	Foreign banks allowed to open branches and restrictions on new bank entry lifted.
1992	Australian Financial Institutions Commission established.
August 1996	Statement on the Conduct of Monetary Policy issued, outlining policy objectives, Reserve Bank accountability and independence.
1997	Report of the Wallis Inquiry into the Financial System.
1997	Adoption of BIS market risk capital adequacy requirements for banks.
1998	Government announces establishment of the APRA, as recommended by the Wallis Report.

APPENDIX 11.2   ASSETS OF AUSTRALIAN FINANCIAL INSTITUTIONS

Financial institution	Total assets (A$b)				Foreign controlled (%)*
	1978–9	1986–7	1995–6	1996–7	
Reserve Bank	10.3	26.1	37.0	50.9	n.a.
Banks	51.6	185.8	486.6	547.8	14.5
NBFIs					
Permanent building societies	8.8	18.3	13.1	10.6	0
Credit cooperatives	1.5	7.3	15.5	16.9	0
Authorised money market dealers	1.6	2.2	4.1	–	n.a.
Money market corporations	5.0	39.6	59.9	67.1	94
Pastoral finance companies	1.0	6.8	2.9	3.2	n.a.
Finance companies	15.9	29.5	34.8	36.2	37
General financiers	1.6	7.7	11.4	14.1	n.a.
Total	*35.4*	*111.4*	*141.7*	*148.1*	n.a.
Life offices and super funds					
Life insurance offices	12.3	46.3	127.3	145.7	35.5
Total	*23.1*	*100.0*	*282.2*	*335.0*	n.a.
Other managed funds					
Cash management trusts	–	3.4	7.0	10.7	n.a.
Common funds	–	4.2	4.6	5.8	0
Friendly societies	0.3	3.5	7.9	7.3	0
Public unit trusts	0.8	15.9	48.4	67.5	42
Total banks, NBFIs and managed funds	*111.2*	*424.2*	*978.4*	*1,122.2*	*n.a.*
Other financial institutions					
General insurance offices	8.4	22.6	60.4	n.a.	31
Intragroup financiers	0.4	4.4	n.a.	n.a.	n.a.
Other FCA financial corps	0.1	0.9	n.a.	n.a.	n.a.
Intragroup + other financial corps	0.5	5.2	7.2	8.0	30
Securitisation vehicles	–	–	14.3	20.9	30
Cooperative housing societies	1.4	2.0	1.6	n.a.	n.a.

Notes:
NBFI = non-bank financial institution
*Sector assets controlled by foreign-owned institutions (June 1996)
FCA = Financial Corporations Act
Sources: RBA Bulletin, December 1997; Wallis 1997, table 10.2

APPENDIX 11.3 FINANCIAL REFORM CALENDAR: NEW ZEALAND

Date	Change
1962	Deposit interest rate ceilings removed; controls on capital issues removed.
1965	Non-bank institutions voluntarily submit to 'captive market' requirements on holding of government debt, which are subsequently formalised as reserve requirements.
1967	Controls on capital issues reintroduced.
1969	Capital issues controls abolished; variable reserve ratio for trading banks replaced by fixed ratio; removal of interest rate limits on bank deposits over NZ$25,000.
1971	Exchange rate peg changed from sterling to US$.
1972	General controls on interest rates offered by deposit institutions introduced; variable secondary reserve asset ratio introduced; selective quantitative lending targets abolished.
1973	Exchange rate changed to peg against trade-weighted index (TWI).
1976	Interest on deposit regulations revoked; controls on overdraft lending rates abolished.
1978	Private sector lending guidelines set.
1978	Securities Act.
1979	Crawling peg exchange rate system introduced.
1981	Government threats to penalise excessive interest rate competition; extension of 1979 Financial Services Regulations to allow Reserve Bank control of lending rates.
1982	Freezing of some loan interest rates (reflecting wage and price freeze); controls on deposit interest rates; maximum credit growth guidelines issued by Reserve Bank; exchange rate regime returned to fixed rate (against TWI).
1983	Bond tender program introduced; deposit rate controls removed (but loan rates still constrained and adjustments made to ceiling rates).
1984	Reintroduction of deposit interest rate controls.
July 1984	New government elected, initiating deregulation; most interest rate controls revoked.
1984	Changes to Reserve Bank bond market dealings; removal of interest prohibition on short-term bank deposits and of ceiling on savings deposits; removal of credit growth guideline; liberalisation of international financing transactions and exchange controls.
March 1985	Floating of exchange rate.
1985	Abolition of all compulsory ratios on financial institutions.
1986	Reserve Bank of New Zealand Amendment Act 1986; liberalisation of entry into banking (based on registration rather than licensing); new supervisory framework not based on minimum capital or liquidity ratios but on improved information provision.
1988	Separation of cash and debt management activities from Reserve Bank central banking functions.
March 1989	Introduction of Basle risk-weighted capital adequacy requirements.
1989	Reserve Bank of New Zealand Act; introduced policy targets agreement.
1993	Companies Act 1993.
January 1996	Public disclosure regime for banks introduced; reduction in extent of prudential regulation on banks; accountability of bank directors increased.
October 1997	Legislative changes requiring simplified 'Investment Statement' to accompany offers of securities rather than registered prospectus.
January 1998	Reserve Bank releases proposals to refine disclosure arrangements.

APPENDIX 11.4   STRUCTURE OF NZ FINANCIAL SYSTEM, 1997

Type of institution	Number	Of which foreign owned	Share of total assets
Banks	19	18	73
Managed funds	n.a.	n.a.	16
Life offices	34	Majority	7
Finance companies	29	Minority (but majority by total assets)	2
Specialised mortgage providers	n.a.	n.a.	<1
Merchant banks	n.a.	n.a.	<1
Building societies	11	n.a.	<1
Credit unions	110	n.a.	<1

Source: RBNZ 1997a

NOTES

I am grateful to Rolf Cremer, Ross Garnaut and other conference participants for valuable comments.

1   Holmes (1994) provides an earlier comparison.
2   Davis and Lewis (1988) and Walsh (1988) provide concise overviews of developments in financial regulation and monetary policy in each country up until the mid-1980s.
3   Australian changes (Davis and Harper 1992; Covick and Lewis 1997) have encouraged growth in superannuation (despite some reductions in the tax advantages), whereas the New Zealand tax changes of 1987 stifled the growth of superannuation schemes (Bowden 1996).
4   Lewis (1997) provides an overview and comparison of the major financial system inquiries.
5   Brash notes that 'we believe that disclosure alone would ensure that banks would maintain capital at least equal to the 8 per cent minimum' (1997: 5).
6   Moreover, whereas in Australia bank depositors have the benefit of 'depositor preference' over other creditors in the event of liquidation, no such preference ranking exists under New Zealand legislation.
7   The Labor government passed the Financial Corporations Act in 1974 which provided for direct controls on non-bank financial institutions, but only those sections relating to the collection of statistics were proclaimed.
8   The dramatic growth in banks' commercial bill acceptances is one example. Another, prompted by foreign exchange market regulations, was the growth of the forward foreign exchange hedge market.
9   Appendix 11.1 provides an overview of major changes, while Appendix 11.2 illustrates the changes in the institutional structure which have occurred.
10   A more detailed analysis is presented in Davis (1995).
11   A Payments System Board is also to be housed within the Reserve Bank.
12   See OECD (1998) for a recent overview of financial reform in New Zealand.
13   See RBNZ (1986, ch. 5) for a detailed list of ratios which were abolished.
14   A brief overview can be found in New Zealand Treasury (1997).

15 The absence of depositor preference over other creditors is also relevant to incentives given to depositor monitoring.

REFERENCES

Bank for International Settlements (BIS) (1997a) *67th Annual Report, 1st April 1996–31st March 1997*, 9 June, <http://www.bis.org/publ/ar97h00.htm> (accessed 26 June 1998).

—— (1997b) *Core Principles for Effective Banking Supervision*, September, <http://www.bis.org/publ.bcbs30a.htm> (accessed 26 June 1998).

Bowden, R.J. (1996) *Kiwicap: An Introduction to New Zealand Capital Markets*, Palmerston North, NZ: Dunmore Press.

Brash, D.T. (1993) 'Reconciling central bank independence with political accountability: the New Zealand experience', 17 June, <http://www.rbnz.govt.nz/speeches/sp930617.htm> (accessed 26 June 1998).

—— (1997) 'Banking soundness and the role of the market', *Reserve Bank of New Zealand*, 30 January, <http://www.rbnz.govt.nz/speeches/sp970130.htm> (accessed 26 June 1998).

Covick, O.E. and M.K. Lewis (1997) 'Insurance, superannuation, and managed funds', in M.K. Lewis and R.H. Wallace (eds) *The Australian Financial System: Evolution and Practice*, Melbourne: Addison-Wesley Longman, 221–93.

Davis, K. (1995) 'Bank deregulation, supervision, and agency problems', *Australian Economic Review* 3: 17–28.

Davis, K. and I. Harper (1992) (eds) *Superannuation and the Australian Financial System*, Melbourne: Allen and Unwin.

Davis, K. and M. Lewis (1988) 'The new Australian monetary policy', in Hang-Sheng Cheng (ed.) *Monetary Policy in Pacific Basin Countries*, Boston: Kluwer, 247–78.

Holmes, F.W. (1994) *A New Approach to Central Banking: the New Zealand Experiment and Comparisons with Australia*, Wellington: Institute of Policy Studies, Victoria University of Wellington.

Kane, E.J. (1981) 'Accelerating inflation, technological innovation, and the decreasing effectiveness of banking regulation', *Journal of Finance* 36(2), May, 355–67.

Leung Suiwah (1991) 'Financial liberalization in Australia and New Zealand', in S. Ostry (ed.) *Authority and Academic Scribblers: The Role of Research in East Asian Policy Reform*, USA: International Centre for Economic Growth, 121–50.

Lewis, M.K. (1997) 'The Wallis Inquiry: its place in the evolution of the Australian financial system', *Accounting Forum* 21(2), September, 229–53.

MacFarlane, I. (1997) 'Monetary policy regimes: past and future', *Reserve Bank of Australia Bulletin*, October, 20–31.

New Zealand Treasury (1997) *Economic and Financial Overview: Supervision of the Financial Sector*, April, <http://www.treasury.govt.nz/pubs/nzdmo/efo_97/supervis.htm> (accessed 26 June 1998).

OECD (1987) 'Reform of the financial system', *Economic Survey: New Zealand*, May, 39–42.

—— (1989) 'Financial market reform', *Economic Survey: New Zealand*, 1988–89, 42–4.

—— (1998) 'Financial sector reform', *Economic Survey: New Zealand*, April, 101–46.

Reserve Bank of Australia (RBA) (1996) 'Statement on the conduct of monetary policy', *Statement by the Treasurer and the Governor (designate) of the Reserve Bank*, 14 August, <http://www.rba.gov.au/about/ab_scmp.html> (accessed 26 June 1998).

—— (1997) *About the Reserve Bank*, 16 December, <http://www.rba.gov.au/about/ab_ind.html> (accessed 26 June 1998).

Reserve Bank of New Zealand (RBNZ) (1986) *Financial Policy Reform*, Wellington: RBNZ.

—— (1997a) *The Role of the Reserve Bank of New Zealand in Supervising the Financial System*, November, <http://www.rbnz.govt.nz/fin/role.htm> (accessed 26 June 1998).

—— (1997b) *Briefing on the Reserve Bank of New Zealand,* October, <http://www.rbnz.govt.nz/briefing/sect3i.htm> (accessed 26 June 1998).

—— (1997c) Annual Report 1997, <http://www.rbnz.govt.nz/annrepor/97ar.pdf> (accessed 26 June 1998).

Wallis, S. (1997) *Financial System Inquiry Final Report,* Canberra: AGPS.

Walsh, C.E. (1988) 'Financial deregulation and monetary policy in New Zealand', in Hang-Sheng Cheng (ed.) *Monetary Policy in Pacific Basin Countries,* Boston: Kluwer, 279–302.

12 Thailand's financial reforms: problems and prospects

Chaipat Sahasakul

INTRODUCTION

Foreign currency turmoil in Asia since 1997 has cast some doubts on the benefits of financial system liberalisation. What went wrong with financial market management in Asian countries? Can they recover from the current crisis? Is an International Monetary Fund (IMF) package the best remedy? What are the prospects for these countries? Thailand has been cited as the originator of the currency turmoil. It might be useful, therefore, to consider its financial reforms in order to shed some light on these questions.

REFORM AND LIBERALISATION SINCE THE EARLY 1990s

The Bank of Thailand (BOT) has launched three comprehensive financial reform plans since 1990, each lasting three years. (For detailed coverage of the plans and their implications, see Wibulswasdi and Tanvanich 1992[1] and Hataiseree 1996.)

First reform plan

The first comprehensive financial reform plan, for 1990–2, was launched in 1989 with the following main objectives:
- to promote the efficiency of financial markets;
- to support restructuring and growth in the real economy;
- to keep up with global challenges; and
- to promote Thailand as a regional financial centre, the first of Indochina.

The plan had four broad components: deregulation of the financial system; improvement of the supervision and examination of financial institutions; development of financial instruments; and improvement of the payment system. The following discussion focuses on measures in the first component – deregulation of the financial system – and selected measures in other components that have had significant effects on Thailand's financial reform.

In June 1989, the ceiling on long-term deposits was removed. In March 1990, the ceiling on deposits of all maturity periods was abolished. In January 1992, the removal of the ceiling on savings deposit interest rates was announced, thereby completing interest rate liberalisation on the deposit side. In June 1992, the ceiling on lending interest rates was eliminated.

Measures providing greater flexibility in the management and operation of financial institutions were introduced in 1991: rural credit policy was streamlined, the ratio of government bond-holding as a branch-opening requirement was reduced, and the reserve requirement to the liquidity ratio was changed. The BOT lifted the regulation requiring commercial banks to maintain securities on branch-opening requirements, effective from 17 May 1993.

On 21 May 1990, Thailand announced official acceptance of the obligation under Article VIII of the IMF's Articles of Agreement, along with the launching of the first phase of exchange control deregulation. In fact, Thailand's exchange control practice had been in conformity with Article VIII requirements for many years – that is, there were no restrictions on payments for current account transactions and no discriminatory currency arrangements or multiple currency practices.

On 1 April 1991, the BOT announced the second phase of the exchange control deregulation, which allowed greater flexibility to private businesses and the general public in the purchase and sale of foreign exchange. No government approval was required, except for the outward transfer of foreign exchange for investment above a certain limit and for the acquisition of real estate and investment in the stock market abroad. Foreign funds, on the other hand, could move in and out rather freely. Moreover, residents and juristic persons were allowed to open foreign currency accounts in Thailand.

Subsequently, on 30 April 1992, further modification of the regulation was effected to provide more convenience for the public, particularly exporters. Exporters were allowed to transfer foreign currency deposits for overseas debt payments. Alternatively, they could also make payments in baht with their non-resident baht accounts. With regard to foreign currency accounts, commercial banks were free to approve the withdrawal of funds for payment overseas, provided that certain conditions were met, and the acceptance of foreign currency deposits from the government and state enterprises.

The Thai authorities also attempted to move towards the goal of a universal banking system in which financial institutions could compete more freely and fairly in the same line of business. To this end, steps were taken gradually from 1991. For example, commercial banks were allowed to conduct similar business to finance companies and other businesses related to financial instruments on a wider scale. Finance companies could undertake leasing business and act as selling agents for government bonds as well as providing financial advisory services in the securities market. However, equity business was still reserved for securities companies only.

On 18 September 1992, the BOT issued regulations allowing Thai commercial banks or branches of foreign banks to operate international banking facilities. Those in Bangkok are called the Bangkok International Banking Facility (BIBF) and those in other provinces, Provincial International Banking Facilities (PIBF). Adoption of the capital adequacy guidelines of the Bank for International Settlements (BIS) came into effect on 1 January 1993 for commercial banks.

Second reform plan

The second financial reform plan, for 1993–5, sought to develop financial and capital systems, to increase domestic savings and to develop Thailand into a regional financial centre. The first and third areas are mainly a continuation of the first plan; the second area is new. Since Thailand experienced current account deficits in most years of the past two to three decades, this implies that domestic savings were lower than domestic investment. Therefore, measures to increase domestic savings are also measures to reduce current account deficits.

Third reform plan

The third comprehensive financial reform plan, for 1996–8, is a continuation of the first and second plans, with more emphasis on economic stability. This plan concentrates on stability-oriented economic and monetary policies; development of the financial system and improvement of regulatory guidelines; improvement of the supervision and examination of financial institutions; and development of financial infrastructure and information technology. From this, one can conclude that the BOT is concerned about current account deficits. Interestingly, one of the measures in the first area of the plan is to expand international banking activity. Such expansion, coupled with a basket-pegging foreign exchange system, tends to be an economic destabiliser. Another measure is to increase the number of foreign commercial banks, which recently became more or less a reality.

The financial liberalisation and reform plans introduced by the BOT have been thorough, covering most areas except foreign exchange policy. However, the lack of change in the basket-pegging system in 1996 and the first half of 1997 significantly contributed to the currency crisis and caused economic recessions, if not depressions, in 1997 and 1998.

Brief overview of the foreign exchange system

In 1963, the Thai foreign exchange rate system was switched from the multiple exchange rate system to the par value system in which the value of the baht was fixed, in terms of gold and hence the US dollar, at the rate of 20.80 baht per US dollar. In preparation for the maintenance of the prescribed baht parity, the authorities had earlier established the exchange equalisation fund (EEF), with the aim of stabilising exchange rate movements within prescribed margins.

From 1963 to 1978, when the Bretton Woods system collapsed, Thai authorities twice devalued the baht versus gold (in 1972 and 1973) to maintain the dollar exchange rate, and revalued once. For a short period in 1978 after the abolition of the par value system, a system of pegging the baht to a basket of currencies was introduced. The exchange rate was determined solely by the EEF, until the daily fixing system was employed from late 1978 to mid-1981.

The system continued smoothly until 1981, when the value of the US dollar strongly appreciated relative to other currencies. To stabilise the baht value against other currencies, the Thai authorities devalued it twice in mid-1981. In July 1981, a decision to abolish the daily fixing was made; the EEF determined the exchange rate independently and provided swap arrangements for commercial banks to hedge against exchange rate risk. In November 1984, the authorities announced a baht devaluation of almost 15 per cent in order to prevent the external balance from deteriorating further as the value of the baht unrealistically rose with the US dollar. Moreover, dollar-pegging was replaced with a system of pegging against a basket of currencies. This exchange rate regime remained in place until 2 July 1997, when a managed float system replaced basket-pegging.

The reform plans and the 1997 currency crisis

The three comprehensive financial reform plans covering 1990–8 were, in general, quite timely and proceeded in gradual steps. To appreciate this, consider the period of economic recovery just before 1990 (Table 12.1). The Thai economy had begun to recover from the second oil shock and worldwide recessions in 1986, with a gross domestic product (GDP) growth rate of 5.5 per cent in real terms. Thereafter, real GDP growth continued to rise and peaked at a little over 13 per cent in 1988. Inflation was contained at a moderate rate. The current account was in surplus in 1986 but went into deficit in 1989, although still manageable at 3.5 per cent of GDP. International reserves were gaining momentum and the debt service ratio was dropping as a result of high export growth during 1986–9. Finally, the government balance switched from a deficit in 1986 to surplus during 1988–9.

Considering all these positive macroeconomic indicators, 1990 was the right time for the BOT to initiate its financial reform plans. The 1990–2 plan coincided with the period of still-high GDP growth rates, although they were showing signs of slowing down. Other macroeconomic indicators were also in an acceptable range. Therefore, it seemed that this first liberalisation plan did not put pressure on the Thai economy.

The situation was different for the 1993–5 plan. The economy, after appearing to slow in 1990–2, reversed this trend from 1993, with growing current account deficits. These deficits ended 1995 at approximately 8 per cent of GDP, despite the inclusion in this second plan of a measure to raise domestic savings. The BIBF, which commenced in 1993, contributed to this reverse trend in GDP growth and growing current account deficits. As Hataiseree (1996: Table 1) shows, the capital inflow of commercial banks through the BIBF grew from 193.2 billion baht in 1993, to 253.4

Table 12.1 Economic indicators, 1980–98

Year	GDP growth (%)	Inflation (%)	Current A/C (% of GDP)	External position Int'l reserves (months of import)	Debt service (% of export)	Government balance # (% of GDP)	Export growth (in mill. baht) Total goods (%)	Agriculture (%)	Manufacturing (%)
1980	4.8	19.7	-6.4	4.0	15.1	-3.6	23.1	20.7	26.8
1981	5.9	12.8	-7.4	3.3	15.9	-2.8	14.9	16.8	27.1
1982	5.4	5.2	-2.7	3.7	17.5	-5.2	4.4	0.2	15.5
1983	5.6	3.7	-7.2	3.0	19.9	-2.7	-8.3	-9.1	-2.9
1984	5.8	0.9	-5.0	3.1	20.0	-3.3	19.6	17.8	24.0
1985	4.7	2.4	-4.0	3.9	22.1	-4.0	10.3	-6.3	25.7
1986	5.5	1.8	0.6	4.9	20.2	-3.1	20.0	8.2	33.7
1987	9.5	2.5	-0.7	4.8	16.8	-0.6	29.2	4.9	47.1
1988	13.3	3.8	-2.6	4.2	12.6	2.4	34.6	25.5	41.3
1989	12.2	5.3	-3.5	4.9	11.0	3.4	29.2	15.0	34.6
1990	11.2	6.0	-8.5	5.2	9.3	4.9	13.1	-16.8	23.2
1991	8.6	5.7	-7.7	5.9	10.0	4.3	23.0	9.3	25.6
1992	8.1	4.1	-5.7	6.3	10.6	2.6	13.6	13.3	14.7
1993	8.4	3.3	-5.1	6.6	10.9	1.9	13.5	-10.6	18.6
1994	8.9	5.1	-5.6	6.7	11.8	2.7	21.6	17.0	22.6
1995	8.8	5.8	-8.1	6.3	11.6	3.0	23.6	23.7	24.8
1996	5.5	5.9	-7.9	6.6	12.1	2.4	-1.9*	4.3	0.0
1997e	-0.4	5.6	-2.0	5.3	15.8	-0.9	3.8*	10.1	29.4
1998e	-4 to -5.5	10.5	6.9	6.2–6.7	19.5	-2.4	1.4*	n.a.	n.a.

Notes:
# calendar years for 1980–95 and fiscal years for 1996–8
e = estimated
* in US$

Sources: Bank of Thailand; Custom Department; Comptroller-General's Department; Ministry of Finance; Wibulswasdi and Tanvanich 1992; and Royal Thai Government 26 May 1998

billion in 1994 and 202.4 billion in 1995. In addition, a majority of BIBF loans for 1994–5 were short-term (Table 12.2). This excess capital inflow was then used to finance many unproductive huge investment projects which, in turn, created high demand for imported raw materials, intermediate products, equipment and machinery, and also imported luxury goods. Unsurprisingly, Thailand ended up with alarmingly high current account deficits.

Another factor was monetary policy, keeping domestic interest rates high as a means of attracting more domestic savings and capital inflow, while leaving the foreign exchange regime unchanged. Since the baht value was near parity with the US dollar and interest rate differentials between international and domestic markets were substantial, blue-chip companies and financial institutions in Thailand could arbitrage these differentials with minimum foreign exchange risks between the baht and the US dollar for the period up to 1995.

The BOT was not unaware of the growing current account deficits, as it introduced its 1996–8 plan measures to stabilise the economy, increase domestic savings and reduce current account deficits. However, the economic situation deteriorated as the US dollar strengthened against other international currencies in mid-1995. With no changes in the foreign exchange regime in Thailand, the baht also strengthened against other international currencies (Figures 12.1 and 12.2). The export sector was the first to be affected, followed by growing current account deficits and a drop in real GDP growth. Thai exports registered a negative growth of 1.9 per cent in 1996 for the first time, after twelve years of positive growth rates following the previous baht devaluation in 1984.

It is interesting to note that the reform plans since 1990 cover all areas of financial liberalisation, including foreign exchange controls, but not the foreign exchange regime. It is also interesting to note that the Thai authorities have had experience in devaluation, from when the baht was overvalued in the 1970s and 1980s.

Figure 12.1 Exchange rate of selected major currencies, January 1985–June 1995

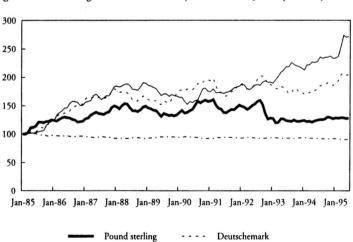

Note: Exchange rates expressed in baht/international currency were indexed to 100 in July 1995 for comparison purposes
Source: Raw data from Bank of Thailand

	1994	1995	1996	1997P	1997 Q2P	1997 Q3P	1997 Q4P	1998 Q1P	1998 MayP
tal debt stocks (end of period)									
blic sector	15,714	16,402	16,805	17,166	17,354	17,021	17,166	17,695	17,420
ong-term	15,534	16,317	16,751	17,146	17,334	17,001	17,146	17,675	17,400
hort-term[a]	180	85	54	20	20	20	20	20	20
vate sector	49,152	66,166	73,731	67,323	75,602	71,760	67,323	63,168	61,809
ong-term	20,153	25,155	36,172	37,410	39,066	39,296	37,410	37,017	36,892
hort-term	28,999	41,011	37,559	29,913	36,536	32,464	29,913	26,151	24,917
Commercial bank	9,865	14,436	10,682	8,164	11,762	9,886	8,164	8,923	9,025
Long-term	3,451	4,443	2,314	2,545	3,276	3,071	2,545	2,835	3,837
Short-term	6,414	9,993	8,368	5,619	8,486	6,815	5,619	6,088	5,188
BIBF[b]	18,111	27,503	31,187	30,079	32,568	31,166	30,079	27,819	26,544
Long-term	2,969	3,799	10,697	10,317	11,399	11,407	10,317	9,820	8,472
Short-term	15,142	23,704	20,490	19,762	21,169	19,759	19,762	17,999	18,072
Non-bank	21,176	24,227	31,862	29,080	31,272	30,708	29,080	26,426	26,240
Long-term	13,733	16,913	23,161	24,548	24,391	24,818	24,548	24,362	24,583
Short-term	7,443	7,314	8,701	4,532	6,881	5,890	4,532	2,064	1,657
onetary authorities	–	–	–	7,292	–	4,482	7,292	9,298	8,991
se of IMF credit	–	–	–	2,427	–	1,618	2,427	2,697	2,671
thers	–	–	–	4,865	–	2,864	4,865	6,601	6,320
tal	64,866	82,568	90,536	91,781	92,956	93,263	91,781	90,161	88,220
ong-term	35,687	41,472	52,923	61,848	56,400	60,779	61,848	63,990	63,283
hort-term[a]	29,179	41,096	37,613	29,933	36,556	32,484	29,933	26,171	24,937
nk foreign assets	6,856	9,672	4,745	6,369	4,500	5,085	6,369	6,902	7,896
oss official reserves	30,279	37,027	38,725	26,968	32,353	29,612	26,968	27,680	27,451
bt service payments	6,707	8,253	9,024	11,777	3,091	2,806	3,137	2,743	n.a.
rincipal	3,933	4,059	3,822	6,130	1,618	1,433	1,794	2,080	n.a.
terest	2,774	4,194	5,202	5,647	1,473	1,373	1,343	663	n.a.
Public sector	1,943	2,029	1,845	1,959	369	607	430	494	n.a.
Principal	1,106	1,125	987	1,077	195	366	216	210	n.a.
Interest	837	904	858	882	174	241	214	284	n.a.
Private sector	4,764	6,224	7,179	9,818	2,722	2,199	2,707	2,249	n.a.
Principal	2,827	2,934	2,835	5,053	1,423	1,067	1,578	1,870	n.a.
Interest	1,937	3,290	4,344	4,765	1,299	1,132	1,129	379	n.a.
port of goods and services	57,580	72,287	73,497	74,431	18,613	18,385	18,658	16,819	n.a.
bt service ratio	11.7	11.4	12.3	15.8	16.6	15.3	16.7	16.3	n.a.
ublic sector	3.4	2.8	2.5	2.6	2	3.3	2.2	2.9	n.a.
rivate sector	8.3	8.6	9.8	13.2	14.6	12	14.5	13.4	n.a.

tes:
hort-term external debt is defined as debt that has an original maturity of one year or less
IBF's debt, which was compiled according to maturity remaining since the establishment of BIBF activities in 1993,
been adjusted to original maturity basis since January 1996 consistent with other external debt items
rce: Bank of Thailand, *Quarterly Bulletin* 37(4), December 1997, p. 88, updated 17 August 1998

Figure 12.2 Exchange rate of selected major currencies, June 1995–July 1998

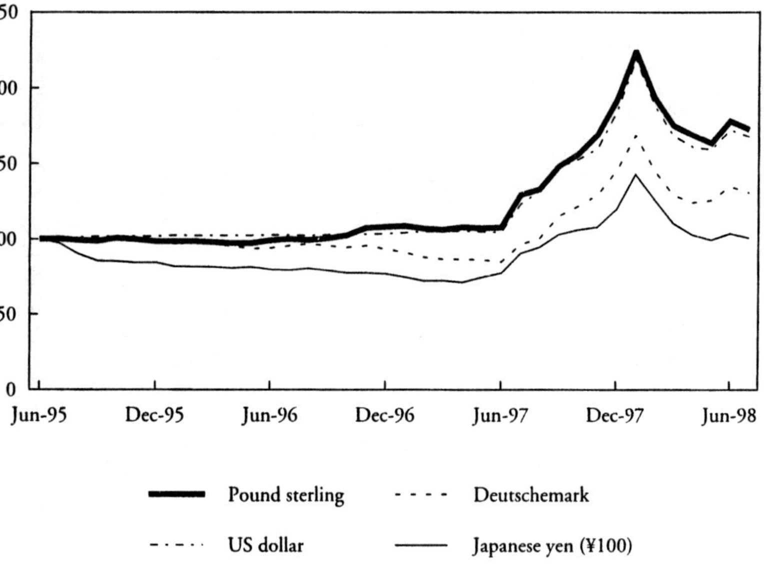

Note: Exchange rates expressed in baht/international currency were indexed to 100 in July 1995 for comparison purposes
Source: Raw data from Bank of Thailand

The 1997 foreign exchange crisis

Thailand's foreign exchange crisis in 1997 probably resulted from a combination of unexpected and unfortunate events.

The liberalisation of its financial markets, including the establishment of the BIBF, was one. As a result, international financial markets could be accessed easily at low cost, which led to overborrowing. Thai financial institutions and corporations consequently overinvested in their businesses and in unproductive investments such as speculation in property and stock markets. Another cause was the basket-pegging system. The baht had mostly (approximately 85 per cent) been tied to the US dollar since 1984, implying that most foreign exchange risks (basically from US dollars) were shouldered by the Thai government. There was also a maturity mismatch between source and use of the funds of Thai financial institutions and corporations since 1993. The maturity of many sources of funds was short-term but these funds were used to finance long-term loans and investment projects. Finally, the mismanagement of several financial institutions was certainly a factor.[2] The Thai economic boom between 1986 and 1995 caused the management of a number of institutions to overlook systemic and financial risks and to assume that economic growth of 7–8 per cent had become the norm for Thailand. As a result, they provided loans without proper credit analyses or in-depth feasibility studies. In many cases, they were clean loans, without collateral.

In this kind of business and economic environment, it made commercial sense for Thai financial institutions and corporations with good international credit standing to borrow from abroad in US dollars at low cost, while the government guaranteed near-parity between the baht and the dollar. During the period 1984–95, when the US dollar was weak compared with other international currencies, foreign borrowings were not subject to any foreign exchange risks. However, from mid-1995, as the US dollar appreciated, so did the baht. This baht appreciation made Thai exports uncompetitive in the world market and made imports look inexpensive, in baht terms. Export growth declined and import growth rose in the second half of 1995, throughout 1996 and in the first half of 1997. The current account deficit sharply increased and registered close to 8 per cent of GDP in 1996. This scenario led to speculative attacks on the baht in 1996 and, more forcefully, in the first half of 1997. The crisis intensified when foreign lenders did not roll over their, mostly short-term, loans when they matured or exercised put options, if available, to call their loans back. Instead of devaluing or floating the baht, Thai authorities defended it at the expense of losing international reserves, a domestic liquidity crunch and high domestic interest rates.

Eventually, however, like most governments in the world, the Thai government had no choice but to float the currency. It did so on 2 July 1997, with remaining international reserves, net of any swaps, estimated at approximately US$4–5 billion.

Effects on the economy

The effects of the crisis on the Thai economy have been detrimental. For the first time in the last 27 years, if not more, real GDP registered a negative growth rate of 0.4 per cent in 1997. Export growth, in US dollars, remained sluggish in 1996 (–1.9 per cent) and in the first half of 1997 (1.1 per cent yoy). However, after the float in July, the baht significantly depreciated against the dollar.

As expected, exports became price-competitive, when converted to US dollars, in the world market and export growth improved in the second half of 1997 (7 per cent yoy). On the other hand, the depreciation, coupled with a domestic credit crunch, dampened imports, the growth of which in US dollars had been negative since January 1997 (–7.7 per cent yoy in the first half and –19.5 per cent yoy in the second half, compared with a small growth rate of 0.6 per cent for all of 1996). As a result, Thailand's current account deficits shrank both in US dollar terms and relative to its GDP. In fact, the current account balance went into surplus in September–December 1997, registering US$1,179 million at the end of the year.

The float of the currency at a time of historically low international reserves left debtors, creditors, investors and speculators with an expectation of significant depreciation in the baht. Its average value in June 1997, before it was floated, was

25.78 baht per US dollar; afterwards, in July, it was 30.27 and it depreciated to 45.29 in December. In an attempt to deter speculation, the Thai authorities adopted a tight monetary policy which pushed the short-term interest rate upward. An interbank rate, perceived as a good indicator of short-term interest rates, increased significantly in the second half of 1997. The average rate, when annualised, was 15.1 per cent in June 1997, 18.66 per cent in July and 21.73 per cent in December. The inflation rate, if measured by the consumer price index (CPI) in December 1997, was not a problem, as it grew at approximately 7.7 per cent yoy, partly because of soft oil prices in the world market. However, when measured by the wholesale price index (WPI), it grew at approximately 11.7 per cent yoy.

The Thai banking sector also suffered from the economy slowdown. Bank deposit growth (yoy) softened in the first half of 1997 but increased sharply in the second half, since public deposits in the form of promissory notes with finance companies moved to commercial banks following the government's temporary suspension of the operations of 58 finance companies in late June and early August. However, when considering M2A growth, which includes notes in circulation, bank deposits and promissory notes with finance companies, one can see that it dropped significantly in the second half of the year in line with the slowdown in the economy. Banking credit growth, excluding the BIBF, also slowed throughout 1997. However, when the BIBF is included, the growth in baht rose sharply in the second half of the year because BIBF credit is generally in foreign currencies. If BIBF credit is converted to baht at the depreciating post-float value, there is an increase in the growth rate of banking credit.

The government cash balance in 1997 ended the year in deficit, at 15 billion baht. Real economic indicators represented by the manufacturing production index and the private investment index also confirm the slowdown in the Thai economy. Their yoy growth rates dropped over the year and registered negative growth from September and October 1997.

Restructuring measures and policies

In August 1997, the IMF put together a US$17.2 billion bailout package with a number of measures/conditions for Thailand. The Third and Fourth Letters of Intent, dated 24 February 1998 and 26 May 1998, respectively, from the Royal Thai Government to the IMF provide a good summary of the economic policies and measures planned and taken. On 14 August 1998, the government announced its Financial Sector Restructuring for Economic Recovery (FRER) package. Selected highlights from the Letters and the FRER follow.

Financial sector reform measures

Asset disposal of closed finance companies

- The BOT temporarily suspended the operations of 16 and 42 finance companies on 27 June and 5 August 1997, respectively. In October, the government introduced new laws governing the regulation and supervision of financial institutions – that is, amendments to and increases in BOT supervision of financial institutions, and establishment of the Financial Sector Restructuring Authority and the Asset Management Corporation. The Restructuring Authority closed all but two of the 58 suspended finance companies on 8 December 1997. It has completed the institutional structure for the disposal of their assets, which is scheduled to be concluded by the end of December 1998. In order to assure bids for each asset, two new government-owned institutions, the Radhanasin Bank and the Asset Management Corporation, will also participate in the auctions.

Strengthening the core financial system

- Since early 1998, Thai authorities have taken over four medium-sized commercial banks, two small commercial banks and a number of finance companies.

- The FRER resolved that: all assets, liabilities and staff of First Bangkok City Bank be acquired by the state-owned Krung Thai Bank; good assets, deposits, other liabilities, and branches of Bangkok Bank of Commerce be acquired by Krung Thai Bank; the rest of Bangkok Bank of Commerce be turned into a private asset management corporation; Bangkok Metropolitan Bank and Siam City Bank be recapitalised and be privatised by the end of 1998; Union Bank and a number of newly intervened finance companies be managed and eventually integrated with Krung Thai Thanakit Finance & Securities plc; and Laem Thong Bank be integrated with Radhanasin Bank.

- Krung Thai Bank and Krung Thai Thanakit will be restructured and recapitalised with the ultimate intention of privatisation, while Radhanasin Bank will seek a strategic partner.

- Financial institutions will be encouraged to set up, capitalise and fund private asset management corporations.

- Two capital support facilities for the tiers 1 and 2 capital adequacy ratio were introduced to provide funds to assist with the recapitalisation of viable financial institutions so that they can resume normal but prudent lending.

- A new regulation will be issued, regarding the composition of the tiers 1 and 2 capital adequacy ratio, in line with recommendations under the Basle Concordat.

- To strengthen the capital base of remaining domestic financial institutions, and particularly the core banking system, the stricter rules on loan classification and provisioning that came into effect on 31 December 1997 will be gradually upgraded to best practice internationally by the end of the year 2000. Where financial institutions choose to receive capital support facilities from the government, they are required to adopt upfront the end 2000 rules.

- Domestic and foreign private investment into existing domestic financial institutions will be encouraged.

- The liabilities of the Financial Institutions Development Fund have been restructured into government-guaranteed bonds, with medium- and long-term maturities and lower interest rates. The imputed interest costs of financial sector restructuring will be incorporated into the central government budget.

- An independent commission has been appointed to consider ways and means to restructure the BOT.

- The legal, regulatory and institutional frameworks for the supervision of financial institutions will be reviewed and reformed. The establishment of a self-financed and limited deposit insurance scheme to eventually replace the present general guarantee is also part of the plan.

Macroeconomic policies

- In the Third Letter of Intent (Royal Thai Government 24 February 1998), exchange rate stabilisation is the principal objective of monetary policy. Basically, when the exchange rate is under pressure, the repurchase rate will be adjusted upwards to support it. However, in the Fourth Letter (Royal Thai Government 26 May 1998), the stand is softened further, as there is room for further cautious reductions in interest rates and somewhat higher monetary growth rates in line with recovering money demand.

- The Third Letter states that the BOT will aim at maintaining reserve money growth at about 6.5 per cent during 1998.

- The government will allocate adequate credit to the priority non-bank corporate sector, especially exporters, agricultural producers and small borrowers.

- The consolidated public sector deficit is targeted in the Third Letter at about 2 per cent of GDP in FY 1997–8. With the current account in surplus in late 1997 and early 1998, the original target of 1 per cent budget surplus to GDP might slow down economic recovery. The 2 per cent target is increased to 3 per cent in the Fourth Letter.

- On 30 January 1998, the BOT ended the separation of onshore and offshore baht markets.

- The external targets of the program have been maintained for 1998 because: external current account adjustment has proceeded more quickly than envisaged, providing an important offset to larger-than-anticipated capital outflows; the BOT's outstanding forward and swap obligations are expected to unwind to about US$9 billion by end-1998; there has been considerable stability in the rollover of short-term credit lines; and, with the end to the baht market separation, there is reason to believe that capital account developments will evolve more favourably than anticipated.

Supporting and revitalising the real sector

This part of the package covers social plans, privatisation plans, corporate restructuring and legal reform. One of the measures that is directly related to financial reform is to amend the bankruptcy and foreclosure laws. The new Bankruptcy Law will permit corporate reorganisations (as opposed to liquidations), will increase the scope for out-of-court workouts and will ensure the fair treatment of creditors. Early administrative steps are also being taken to allow foreclosure. Another measure is to amend legislation to substantially liberalise ownership laws, including amendments to the Alien Business Law, in order to facilitate foreign investment and capital inflows.

CONCLUSION

Things will probably get worse for Thailand before they get better. The BOT, in the Fourth Letter, forecast real GDP in 1998 to contract by 4.0–5.5 per cent. Some international houses put it at around –10 per cent.

The value of the baht appreciated after January 1998 (when the BOT ended the onshore/offshore market separation), and stabilised at 40–42 baht per US dollar in June. Should Thailand be able to secure more capital inflows through external borrowings by the public sector, privatisation programs, asset auctions by the Restructuring Authority, and corporate recapitalisation, the baht is expected to become more stable. With less concern about baht instability, monetary policy will continue to be eased and domestic liquidity will improve, with lower interest rates.

Otherwise, the Thai economy will continue to experience tight liquidity, high interest rates and increasing non-performing loans, and will move deeper into depression. Inflation will easily hit double-digit rates due to the baht depreciation since mid-1997. Public external debt will rise, as the government needs to borrow from abroad for its international reserves. The BOT forecast public sector debt to increase from US$16.9 billion in 1996 to US$24.5 billion in 1997 and US$32.3 billion in 1998 (Royal Thai Government 26 May 1998: 16). For private external debt, the trend will, of course, be reversed.

The economic policies and measures proposed in the Third and Fourth Letters mainly conform to international standards and liberalisation policies, which are the key principles underlying the three comprehensive financial reforms launched by the BOT since 1990. The main differences are the speed, coverage and intensity of reform during the crisis. These policies and measures are generally on the right track. The fact that the fiscal target for budget surplus has been revised to deficit in the Third Letter reveals that both the Thai government and the IMF are flexible enough in their policy formation. The remaining issue in the Third Letter which requires change is the tight monetary policy and high interest rates. This has been relaxed in the Fourth Letter and, as discussed above, should Thailand be able to secure more capital inflows, there will be more room for easing monetary policy.

What can be learnt from this crisis? First, when making policies, a government should always balance economic growth and stability. Second, any liberalisation or reform plans should cover all key economic mechanisms. In Thailand's case, a foreign exchange regime was missing from its plans. Finally, both public and private sectors should understand the importance of risk management (i.e. foreign exchange risks and maturity mismatch between assets and liabilities), a good checks and balance system and good governance/practices. In spite of this painful experience, Thailand will be wiser and better in handling its economy and business for the year 2000 and beyond.

NOTES

The views expressed here are those of the author and do not represent those of the organisation with which the author is affiliated. Many thanks to Siriporn Nopwattanapong for collecting supporting data and plotting graphs, and to Sakuntala Chowsanitphan and Siripan Pliansakul for typing this paper.
1   Wibulswasdi and Tanvanich (1992) provide a good overview on the developments in the foreign exchange market and the series of measures to liberalise the system, as well as on the consequences of policy implementation for the period up to 1992. The discussion below for the period up to 1992 is mainly based on their paper.
2   Thanks to Hidenobu Okuda of Hitotsubashi University for suggesting this as one of the major causes of the Thai financial crisis.

REFERENCES

Hataiseree, R. (1996) 'Modern financial management and sources of funds: Thai experience during financial liberalization policy regime', *Monthly Bulletin*, Bank of Thailand, August, 13–60 [in Thai].
Ministry of Finance and Bank of Thailand (1998) 'Financial sector restructuring for economic recovery', joint statement, 14 August.
Royal Thai Government (24 February 1998) Third Letter of Intent to International Monetary Fund.
——— (26 May 1998) Fourth Letter of Intent to International Monetary Fund.
Wibulswasdi, C. and O. Tanvanich (1992) 'Liberalization of the foreign exchange market: Thailand's experience', *Quarterly Bulletin* 32(4), Bank of Thailand, December, 25–37.

Part V

Looking forward

13 Asia Pacific financial liberalisation and reform

Gordon de Brouwer

The chapters in this volume have concentrated on explaining the origins of the financial crisis that has wreaked havoc throughout much of East Asia, and how it has affected their economies and financial systems. This chapter draws these analyses together in two ways. It examines, first, the recovery and reform process underway in East Asia, examining the likely speed of recovery and what recent experience indicates is the appropriate speed, order and content of reform, especially given domestic political constraints. This also includes an assessment of the lessons for emerging East Asia from Japan's experience. It then examines three aspects of the way the public debate about the international architecture has evolved. It starts by reviewing the reports and outcomes of the G22 working groups on transparency, financial system reform and managing financial crises. Since the debate has also turned to the role or otherwise of capital controls, it also provides a summary of the arguments for and against capital controls. Finally, it assesses how the International Monetary Fund's position on capital controls has evolved in light of experiences with financial markets in 1998.

THE RECOVERY AND REFORM PROCESS

At the end of 1998, the widespread view was that the contraction in most of East Asia had reached its trough, supported by the expansion of exports and increasingly expansionary fiscal policies. Indeed, economic theory suggests that the recovery in share prices and exchange rates which the affected East Asian economies experienced in the last quarter of 1998 points to economic recovery in the future. The recovery phase, however, is likely to be uneven between the various economies and slow, with a number of affected countries likely to still be contracting slightly in 1999. Table 13.1 presents consensus forecasts at October 1998, which indicate that 1999 should be a better year for all regional economies than 1998, even if most will still be in recession.

Table 13.1 Consensus forecast for GDP growth, October 1998

	1998	1999
China	7.2	7.5
Hong Kong SAR	–4.6	–1.8
Indonesia	–16.5	–3.7
Japan	–2.5	–0.2
Korea	–6.7	–0.3
Malaysia	–4.8	–0.3
Philippines	–0.6	0.6
Singapore	0.0	–1.0
Taiwan	4.8	4.2
Thailand	–7.9	–0.4

The speed of recovery

There are several reasons to expect recovery in East Asia to be slow. In the first place, the economic expansions in these economies were associated with investment booms, resulting in an extensive widening of productive capacity which now mean substantial excess capacity. In Thailand, for example, estimates of excess capacity in manufacturing reach up to 50 per cent. Investment cannot be the engine of growth in these circumstances. Indeed, expectations are weak and domestic and foreign investors are more risk-averse in the current environment, which undercuts the willingness to spend on infrastructure.

One element of the crisis in the region was excessive borrowing, reflected in rapid rises in the ratio of credit to GDP, which left business and banks exposed to downturns in demand. This is a key feature in retarding recovery in East Asia: debt overhangs in the corporate and household sectors will take a number of years to be unwound, even if the countries clean up their banking systems fairly quickly. This is certainly the experience of other countries which have had debt overhang. Consider, for example, Australia's experience with the corporate debt overhang in the early 1990s (Figure 13.1), where the expansion of bank-intermediated credit following financial liberalisation took several years to unwind and also exerted a negative effect on investment activity for a few years. (The experience of the United Kingdom with a household-sector debt overhang and sluggish recovery in consumption over the same period is analogous to Australia's corporate sector experience.)

The final element is that the government and corporate policy framework is relatively weak. In general, the governmental process in the affected economies is not very adaptable and there are substantial constraints on the way policy is formed and what policy can do. This is evident in the lead-up to the crisis. For example, consider the Thai policy on the exchange rate prior to the crisis. Government officials have publicly stated that they in fact wanted to float the baht in 1996, to let the currency appreciate somewhat and take off some pressure from capital inflows, but that they

Figure 13.1 Business credit and investment in Australia

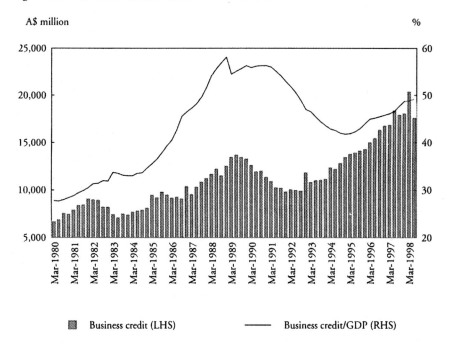

A$ million   %

▨ Business credit (LHS)   —— Business credit/GDP (RHS)

were unable to do so because of pressure from the export sector and the fragility of the political process after recent changes in government. Later, in the first half of 1997, the constraint changed, as pressures on the currency favoured depreciation, but by this stage the authorities felt constrained in adopting greater exchange rate flexibility because of large uncovered foreign currency borrowing in the financial sector.

These policy constraints are also evident in the way events have since played out. This can be seen in the willingness and ability of governments to stimulate their economies through fiscal policy. While the International Monetary Fund (IMF) policy response to the financial crisis in East Asia, until the first few months of 1998, required a fiscal tightening, this switched to a recommendation for some fiscal stimulus. But the initial focus on fiscal stringency, combined generally with a regional pride in not having large government debt and a desire to be seen to be 'dealing with the crisis', led officials and politicians to think that orthodox policy entails persistent fiscal surpluses. As a result, policymakers have tended to resist running fiscal deficits in line with the projections of the more recent IMF country programs, overperforming on the fiscal side at the cost of growth. This has been compounded by inflexibilities in the disbursement process, with spending programs taking time to be put in place. But deficit fetishism is in fact heterodox, with the orthodoxy being that policy stabilise the economic cycle, keeping inflation low and stable and debt at sustainable levels. (Indeed, most industrialised countries tend to run counter-cyclical fiscal policies and some countries which have experienced major banking crises, like Sweden and other Nordic countries in the early 1990s, temporarily ran more stimulatory fiscal policy at the time of the banking crisis in order to support their economies through the contraction.) The problem is that, once a view has taken hold and so much political capital has already been spent supporting it, it is hard to correct.

Moreover, the international economic environment is not particularly supportive, and Japan, in particular, is not in a position to play the locomotive role that the United States did to Mexico in 1994. Japan's economy contracted in 1998 and, fiscal stimulus packages notwithstanding, looks to be contracting or flat in 1999. Moreover, Japanese banks have been contracting their operations worldwide in order to reduce their assets and boost their capital ratios, and reduce the amount of capital they have to hold (since banks which only operate domestically are required to hold less capital than banks which operate internationally). This has put pressure on the rollover of Japanese funds in emerging East Asia. These two negative effects have been offset to some degree by the international financial packages made available to Indonesia, Korea and Thailand, of which Japan is a substantial contributor, but it does not follow that the two types of funds have been close substitutes.

There are also problems with policymaking at the corporate level. For example, while most industrialised countries have been making substantial preparations for the effect of the year 2000 on computer systems (the so-called millennium or Y2K bug), business in emerging East Asia has not. This means that, to the extent that computer systems are used, infrastructure and businesses in these economies are likely to be under pressure in 2000. While this could be a positive shock – since governments and firms will need to write off some capital and invest in new infrastructure – it is more likely that it will be a negative, with parts of the infrastructure failing to operate properly.

Overall, it is important not to place unrealistic expectations on the reform process. Reform is often a matter of three steps forward and two steps back. Onlookers to events can see all sorts of policies and institutions that need reform but they also need to accept that this is not a linear process. It is also one thing to change the laws of a country; it is another to change long-held business customs and practices. In Indonesia, for example, the law on bankruptcy has been changed, but expatriate lawyers have commented that there is strong resistance to using Western (particularly common law) forms of dispute resolution and actual bankruptcy proceedings are rare. Even in industrialised countries, reform needs testing and consensus, and it is rarely a smooth process – in the United States, for example, basic government decision making, such as the budget process, can be tortuous and delayed, even to the extent that government can 'close down'. It is important, then, not to have expectations about processes in developing countries that do not even exist in the major industrialised nations of the world.

Lessons from Japan

Japan, the leading economy in the East Asian region, has also experienced major problems in its banking and financial sector, but its problems stem not from a year or two ago but from a decade ago. It provides, therefore, an example of what emerging economies in East Asia should not do, showing what can go wrong with the financial system and the economy as a whole when problems in the banking sector are not addressed.

Japan's experience in the 1990s shows that banking system problems undermine growth, and that recovery depends on fixing the problem. What we know from the experiences of the past decade – and what has been brought home most forcefully in the past year in East Asia – is that having a healthy banking and financial system is crucial to maintaining stable economic growth. In short, the process of financial intermediation matters.

There are (at least) three ways in which failure to deal with problem loans in the banking system can affect economic growth. The first is that confidence in the banking system is weakened. This distorts the allocation of wealth between various assets and can destabilise the financial system by making it more prone to runs on institutions. In Japan, for example, there has been a shift of financial wealth to the postal savings system, foreign banks and currency (the latter associated with a strong rise in the sale of personal safes), away from domestic banks. The risk premium that Japanese banks have to pay when they borrow in the international money market has also risen, reaching one percentage point late in 1997 and again late in 1998 (Figure 13.2). Moreover, a general lack of confidence in the banking system can undermine consumer and investor confidence and hence weaken economic growth. It is difficult to argue that this has not been the case in Japan.

Failure to deal with the problem can also lead to a credit supply crunch, by which banks are unable to extend their loan book because they cannot get capital to underwrite it. This is unusual but it does seem to be evident in Japan. Figure 13.3 shows how large and small firms now perceive the willingness of financial institutions to provide finance. The availability of finance deteriorated sharply in 1998. While it is not as bad as the credit crunch after the first oil price shock, it does rival that following the second oil price shock. This is a supply constraint on the Japanese economy which has its origin in the banking crisis of that country.

The third effect of not dealing with non-performing loans in the banking system is that it makes the economy much more susceptible to adverse shocks, akin to the argument that being debt-heavy makes people/business/countries more vulnerable to falls in income. The implication of this is that the *marginal* effect of the Asian financial crisis will be greater in Japan than otherwise because it is harder for the banking system to absorb each yen lost. The upshot is that economic recovery depends on fixing the banking sector.

These problems in Japan are not just the outcome of benign neglect; they are also the result of a series of flawed policies. In its 1998 *Economic Outlook*, the OECD (1998) provides a summary of the features of successful bank restructuring programs,

Figure 13.2 The Japan risk premium (Japanese banks' 3-mth US$ LIBOR rate less 3-mth US$ LIBOR rate in basis points)

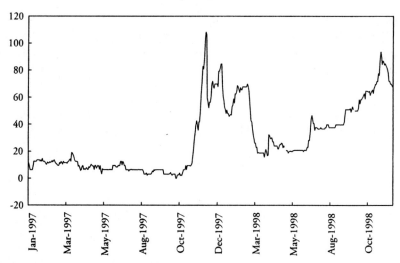

including identifying weak institutions, separating good assets from bad, closing institutions which were not viable, and ensuring that losses accrued first to shareholders, that managers responsible for bad decisions took responsibility and that adequate funding was provided to support the financial system as a whole.

Some of these features have been present in Japan, although only in recent years: the authorities liquidated insolvent housing loan corporations (*jusen*), banks have been encouraged to use operating profits to write off bad loans, insolvent institutions have been closed (e.g. Hokkaido Takushoku Bank and Yamaichi Securities in November 1997), the traditional 'convoy' system (whereby strong institutions were obliged to support their weaker competitors) has been broken down, and a special vehicle, the Cooperative Credit Purchasing Company (CCPC), was established in 1993 to take over banks' non-performing loans. In March 1998, 30 trillion yen (US$255 billion) was dedicated to support financial reform, of which 17 trillion yen is to protect depositors of insolvent banks and the remainder is to be used in recapitalising solvent banks by the purchase of subordinated debt and preference shares. In June this year, the government announced that the newly established Financial Supervisory Agency (FSA) will inspect and evaluate the books of the nineteen major banks and will have the power to close banks down over the next two (but possibly five) years. Performing loans of banks which fail will be transferred to temporary 'bridge banks'. The financial reform package was revised and upgraded in October 1998 with a 60 trillion yen (US$510 billion) plan, directing 17 trillion yen

Figure 13.3 Perceived lending attitude of financial institutions

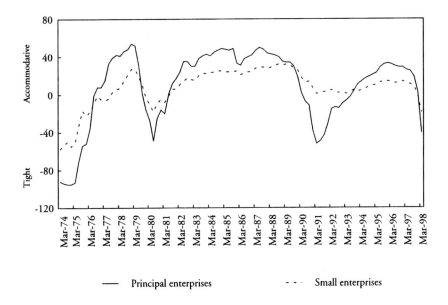

——— Principal enterprises   - - - Small enterprises

Note: Tankan Survey, net balance of respondents

to depositor protection, 18 trillion yen for bank nationalisation and 25 trillion yen for bank recapitalisation.

But there is still a sense that the authorities and bank management have not done all that they could. In its most recent *Economic Outlook*, the OECD again criticised business and government in Japan for their inaction. Even basic prerequisites for recovery are not in place. For example, asset recovery and foreclosure rates are low by international standards, and the authorities have not even got to first base by facing up to the extent of the problem. Information on the non-performing loans of credit cooperatives is not available. And information on banks understates the problem. In their own self-assessment in September 1997, for example, the banks said that about 77 trillion yen in loans, out of a total of about 620 trillion yen, were non-performing to varying degrees. They estimated that 11 trillion yen are uncollectable. The OECD (1998), however, has estimated that uncollectable loans are probably double this amount, at about 20 trillion yen, which is more than double the loan loss provisions of 9.4 trillion yen at March 1997. Some market estimates of non-performing loans reach up to 150 trillion yen, and Prime Minister Obuchi was reported in mid-October as saying that they were 100 trillion yen. If the figures that the authorities and the banks cite lack credibility, then there is also a lack of credibility in the policy prescribed and adopted by these institutions. We know that expectations matter to economic outcomes, which means that how information is transmitted also matters. Being open and giving the market full information, combined with a credible program to deal with bad debts and insolvent institutions, should be stabilising. It removes uncertainties and the source for speculation, and gives the impression of a willingness to deal with problems. Indeed, the experience of other countries indicates that the best way to support bank share prices is to be frank.

Nor have the public funds set aside for financial reform been used adequately. As pointed out by the OECD, of the 13 trillion yen (US$90 billion) set aside in the March 1998 package for recapitalising solvent banks, only 1.8 trillion yen was drawn down and funds were provided to all the 21 banks which applied in March 1998, since the authorities did not want to stigmatise weaker banks. This approach is self-defeating. In the first place, it provides scarce resources to relatively strong banks when these funds could have been used elsewhere. It is wasteful of public funds. Second, all institutions which applied for funds received them, but it is not clear that this should have been the case. Things look a little better with the second package, with banks seeking different amounts of funds for recapitalisation, but, as at the end of 1998, only about one-fifth of the recapitalisation funds had been called on. Finally, it serves no useful purpose to try to hide the fact that risk differs between institutions. Treating all institutions as having equal risk leaves the casual observer with the impression that the authorities are not yet willing to deal with the problems in the banking system. It also makes the authorities look silly, since the market generally has a good idea of which institutions are strong or otherwise. Indeed, bank share prices have remained weaker than the rest of the stock market in Japan and weaker banks have weaker share prices.

The slowness in the policy process can be related to a number of broader features of the policy process and structure in Japan. For example, it is partly a function of the 'main bank' structure and policy framework in Japan, with the emphasis throughout the decade being on private workouts of corporate debt within the main bank structure rather than through the use of open workout procedures.

It is also a result of inadequate basic infrastructure concerning the 'rules of the game': the judicial process is relatively slow, expensive and inaccessible, which limits foreclosure; accounting systems are not clear and not binding, letting banks hide their problem loans; and the tax system is unfriendly to clearing out bad debts in the banking system. Consider the last point in more detail. Packer (1998) argues that the tax system has not supported banks dealing with problem loans. For example, in order for a bank to be able to receive tax concessions in writing off non-performing loans, the company's liabilities must have exceeded its assets for at least two years or bankruptcy proceedings must have been commenced against the company. This may be good for government revenue but it is bad for prudential policy. Moreover, the Ministry of Finance has imputed interest earnings to banks for the purposes of determining their tax liability even if interest is not paid (the origin of which may lie in an attempt by the authorities to prevent 'transfer pricing' arrangements between a main bank and its client corporation). These conditions were initially eased with respect to losses from loans transferred to the CCPC in August 1992, but only eased more generally in fiscal 1994 when banks started to more extensively deduct loan losses associated with assisting related borrowers.

The slowness and seeming re-activeness, rather than pro-activeness, of the whole reform process itself generates a further problem: a pessimistic psychology which infects markets and the community more broadly. The months-long saga in the third quarter of 1998 in obtaining political agreement between the government and the Opposition about bank restructuring, for example, steadily bled the market and economy of confidence. There are many instances of this. But the problem goes deeper because a negative psychology distracts focus from the good things that policymakers have done over this period, including the fiscal, bank-reform and international-financing packages that the government announced in 1998.

THE INTERNATIONAL FINANCIAL ARCHITECTURE

The events in emerging East Asia and, subsequently, in other emerging and industrialised economies' financial•markets have excited a new discussion on the behaviour, structure and regulation of international financial markets.

The G22 process

In response to the evolving East Asian financial crisis, the US government called a meeting of finance ministers and central bank governors of 22 countries in April 1998 to examine issues related to the operation and stability of international financial markets. The countries comprised the world's seven largest industrialised economies – the United States, Japan, Germany, the United Kingdom, France, Italy and Canada (the G7) – as well as a mix of smaller industrialised and emerging economies, including Argentina, Australia, Brazil, China, Hong Kong SAR, India, Indonesia, Korea, Malaysia, Mexico, Poland, Russia, Singapore, South Africa and Thailand. This grouping of countries, known as the G22, was innovative in the sense that it included representatives of major regions and markets, affected and (what were at the time) unaffected economies, and developed and developing economies. By including such a broad set of countries, the grouping also increased the probability of widespread acceptance and adoption of its recommendations.

At this meeting, the finance ministers and central bank governors commissioned three working groups to report to them on particular topics related to the structure of the international financial system: enhancing transparency and accountability, strengthening domestic financial systems, and managing international financial crises. These working groups comprised senior staff of the ministries of finance and central banks of the G22 economies. The working groups also consulted widely with the private sector, countries not included in the grouping, and international financial organisations like the IMF, the Bank for International Settlements (BIS) and the World Bank.

The reports

Each of the reports deals with the three key issues in the international financial architecture: the need for transparency of governments and private financial institutions, particularly of hedge funds; the need to have strong domestic financial systems as a precondition for international financial stability; and, in a world where private capital flows dominate, the need for mechanisms to deal with financial crises that involve the private sector in their resolution.

Transparency and accountability

As a broad principle, accessible, visible and understandable information about existing conditions, decisions and actions is a prerequisite for good decision making and efficient allocation of resources. Moreover, decision makers should be in a position to explain and accept responsibility for their actions, since such discipline generally improves the quality of decision making. Thus, transparency and accountability of private and public decision making are key attributes of a stable economic system.

It was recognised that, even though transparency and accountability are important, they are not a panacea and do not guarantee economic and financial stability; it is unlikely that they would have prevented the Asian crisis from occurring. Nonetheless, greater transparency and accountability may have helped to ease the build-up of financial and economic imbalances in particular economies and may have induced an earlier response from the private sector and government.

There are also limits to the degree of transparency and accountability that is desirable for economic efficiency. For example, some types of information are costly and burdensome to acquire, which suggests less frequent disclosure. Some statistics collected over short time periods are also more volatile and hence contain 'noise' rather than information, which may confuse decision makers rather than help them. Moreover, confidentiality can be an important consideration in some cases, for both the private sector and government, which limits disclosure. In general, the benefits from more information must be weighed against the costs.

Transparency and accountability apply to all groups of decision makers in the economy: the private sector, the public sector and international financial institutions. The crisis in Asia – and its subsequent spread to emerging and developed economies – highlights the need to improve data on the operations of banks and international investors such as hedge funds. The working group recommended the establishment of a group to examine ways to compile and publish data on the international exposures of investment banks and hedge funds, as well as upgrading the BIS' data on international banking statistics.

The working group also examined corporate reporting and recommended that countries adopt key principles in company reporting: periodic and timely disclosure; comprehensive detail of on- and off-balance sheet transactions; standards which are consistent across time and jurisdictions; explaining strategies to manage risk; and effective internal control procedures subject to external independent audit. But it also recognised that, even if countries have the 'right' laws on the books, it is necessary that companies comply with them and that authorities enforce them. It recommended the International Accounting Standards Committee (IASC) work out a core set of accounting standards and that the International Organisation of Securities Commissions (IOSCO) review and endorse them.

The promotion of transparency and accountability of government centres on the provision of information about the state of the macroeconomy and macroeconomic policies. The working group recommended that national authorities publish timely and accurate information about foreign exchange reserves (including their forward book) and about the foreign exchange exposures of private financial institutions and the corporate sector. It also recommended that countries follow the IMF's code of good practices on fiscal transparency – advocating clarity of roles and responsibilities, public availability of information, open budget processes and independent assessment of integrity – and develop a similar code for monetary policy.

The third group of players in the evolving international financial crisis are the international financial institutions, such as the IMF, World Bank and regional development banks. These institutions have increased the transparency of their own operations in the past few years, and the working group argued that their advice and policies should be publicly available unless release would compromise confidentiality and the ability to obtain the information in the first place. There was wide support for publishing background papers, but not for individual country reports in the Article IV consultation process. The working group also recommended that the IMF should report on the extent to which an economy meets internationally recognised disclosure standards.

Strengthening financial systems

The international financial crisis that began in East Asia shows the fundamental importance of a robust, stable and efficient domestic financial system. Weak banking systems and poorly developed local capital markets increase the vulnerability of an economy to adverse developments in the international economy and financial system.

The starting point in strengthening financial systems is identifying the core principles and standards that should underpin the design of a system. In many areas of banking supervision and securities regulation, there is already an international consensus about best practice and standards. The working group endorsed the existing set of principles of the Basle Committee on Banking Supervision (BCBS) and of the IOSCO. It also backed recent OECD and BCBS work on corporate governance and foreign-exchange risk management structures. It recommended that the BCBS consider ways to reduce the potential for mismatches of foreign currency liabilities and assets in national banking systems. It also argued that local money and capital markets need to be strengthened and developed.

As the financial crisis unfolded, individual governments thought it necessary to offer support to financially troubled banks or companies to help them meet their obligations and stop panic from spreading through the financial and corporate system. Making policy 'on the run', however, can lead to other problems, with poorly designed or excessively generous arrangements dulling incentives to monitor risks – and even encouraging undesirable risk-taking – and encouraging enterprises which do not need support to seek assistance. Ideally, a well-designed set of explicit ex ante procedures with predetermined hierarchies of claims and loss-sharing reduces the need for ad hoc actions which are potentially inconsistent with reducing the risks of future crises. Hence, the working group recommended a system of early, structured and graduated intervention in the banking sector and outlined a set of mechanisms for this. It also recognised the importance of well-structured insolvency regimes and clear recognition of property rights.

The working group also recommended that countries adopt deposit insurance schemes as part of the financial safety net. A limited system of deposit insurance can enhance financial stability by reducing the risk of bank runs and contagion. It also enhances the efficiency and equity of the banking system by assisting small depositors who typically do not have the capacity to monitor the soundness of banks. The working group recognised that it is important that limits on deposit insurance be in place to preserve internal and external governance mechanisms in banks and to control the incentive of banks to lend for excessively risky projects.

Market discipline, the working group argued, is a crucial element in promoting sound banking practices but such discipline does not work without adequate transparency and incentives to price risk. The lack of international consensus on sound practices for loan valuation, loan-loss provisioning and credit-risk disclosure seriously impairs the ability of markets and regulators to understand and assess the risks in each financial institution's activities. The working group called for the relevant authorities to work further on these matters. It also recommended that governments work with private sector and professional organisations to develop and use information about institutional aspects of national financial systems.

International governance is a necessary part of ensuring that countries adopt and enforce rules and practices which support sound corporate and financial systems. The working group thought that the particular type and combination of oversight mechanism – be it through IMF conditionality, IMF or World Bank surveillance, peer review or technical assistance programs – that is most suitable for enhancing financial stability would vary from country to country. But it did have a strong view that all countries should go through some process of independent assessment, so long as the process adopted meets certain minimum standards and contains a core set of elements. It suggested that serious consideration should be given to forms of peer review.

While supervision is functionally and geographically fragmented, financial markets are becoming increasingly globalised and integrated. This implies that policies must be coordinated between governments and institutional regulatory agencies. While the working group did not regard the establishment of a new international supervisory agency as feasible, it thought advances in international supervisory policy coordination could be enhanced by establishing a financial sector policy forum in which finance ministries and central banks from a broad set of countries and representatives from international financial bodies could meet to discuss broad financial sector issues. The working group also saw value in greater exchange of information about regulatory systems and practices and in setting up a 'clearing house' to match demands for technical assistance with technical experts.

Managing international financial crises

International capital flows in the first half of the 1990s were predominantly private rather than official in nature, and they were large relative to the recent past. These flows also turned out to be volatile, rapidly exiting emerging markets once conditions deteriorated without due consideration of the differences in structure and prospects for these economies. This exacerbated the downturn in the various economies and spread it to others. It is critical that the international financial system strengthen its ability to limit and better manage international financial crisis.

The first step is for countries to have policies in place that reduce the scope for financial crises to occur in the first place and which limit their severity. These include, in the first instance, a limit on the range of economic and financial activity that the government guarantees, either explicitly or implicitly. While depositor protection is an important element in preserving stability and equity in the banking system, this in no way requires protecting individual banks, their managers or their owners. The policies also include the private sector developing and using more innovative financing techniques in advance, such as contingency credit lines, pre-negotiated options to allow a creditor to automatically extend the maturity of specified obligations, or debt instruments which reduce interest payments under specified conditions.

It is better to have predictable, clear and well-understood resolution mechanisms in place before a crisis occurs. For this purpose, the working group endorsed a set of principles and key features of effective solvency and debtor–creditor regimes. These are designed to maximise the value of firms affected by the crisis, to provide a fair and predictable regime for the distribution of assets recovered from debtors, and to ensure that credit continues to be provided to business during and after a crisis.

One feature of financial crises is that it can be difficult to coordinate the response of creditors. This can be difficult enough when finance has been intermediated through the banking system, but it is even more so when finance has been provided by a range of disparate entities such as bond-holders. While individual creditors seeking immediate redress and compensation through the legal system may be acting in their own self-interest, this may not be in the interests of the broader group of creditors or the country involved, since it reduces the value of domestic assets and undermines incentives for orderly adjustment. The working group recommended, therefore, that all countries in their sovereign debt issue adopt collective action clauses, allowing for collective representation of creditors, majority action and sharing arrangements between all creditors (rather than litigants only). They also emphasised that this should be accompanied by dialogue with financial markets on the usefulness of such clauses in maximising value to creditors and to the country involved.

Despite everyone's best efforts, financial crises will occur in the future and it is important to prepare for them. It is important that the IMF have the financial resources to deal with crises as they occur. It is also vital that countries act in advance of a crisis, seeking early resolution of the issues that place them at risk. This may mean seeking advance advice or assistance from the IMF. The working group also emphasised that simply suspending debt payments is not a viable alternative to dealing with problems and adjusting policy, and that it is important to meet the terms and conditions of debt contracts. However, an interruption in debt payments will be unavoidable sometimes, in which case it is vital that this be orderly and cooperative and be set in conjunction with a strong policy reform program. Obtaining the agreement of creditors to this process is important, as unilateral actions are more likely to destabilise the local, and other, economies. It may be that creditors will not agree to a debt suspension, even if it is accompanied by a reform program, and in these instances, as a last resort, it may be necessary to impose emergency temporary capital and exchange controls. The working group argued that this should not be done unilaterally, and only with the involvement of the IMF.

The working group also endorsed an IMF policy decision to consider providing financial support for policy adjustment even when the country has loans to the private sector which are in arrears. This is a powerful signal of the confidence of the IMF in the reform process under way in a country and, as such, would only be available under certain conditions. These include the country in crisis not interrupting debt payments as an alternative to reform and adjustment, implementing a strong reform program, working in good faith with creditors, and international support being necessary to the success of the adjustment program.

After the G22

The reports were subsequently endorsed at a meeting of the G22 finance ministers and central bank governors in Washington DC on 5 October. Given such approval, it is now a matter of how to put them into practice, a matter which is still evolving. There are two issues in this process.

One is the priority to be accorded to implementing the various recommendations, which involves balancing what needs to be done as quickly as possible with what should be done in the medium to longer term to improve efficiency and stability. For example, it is important to ensure that domestic financial systems, and the provision of trade credit in particular, start working as fast as possible. Similarly, the G7 has proposed that IMF emergency lending facilities be available in advance of a crisis, as a preventative rather than reactionary measure, and echoes of this were evident in the IMF-organised US$41.5 billion package for Brazil, which differed from other packages in that the vast bulk of funds is available for more or less immediate use, rather than in specified tranches over time, and the bilateral funds forming US$14.5 billion of the package are available at the same time as, rather than after, the disbursement of multilateral funds. But it is also important from a longer-term perspective that mechanisms, like collective action clauses and standstill procedures, be put in place to deal more quickly, efficiently and equitably with financial crises in the future.

The priority of the issues has also partly changed as the nature of the crisis itself widened, highlighting weaknesses in the international financial system, rather than simply deficiencies in the financial systems of particular countries. There is, for example, currently more attention now focused on the importance of understanding, and working out effective mechanisms to deal with, the behaviour and positions of large institutional investors like hedge funds. As shown in the response of the US Federal Reserve to the instability of financial markets in October 1998, most people would now believe that players which can take large positions in markets can adversely affect the stability of the international financial system. How this should be dealt with is a matter under scrutiny worldwide, with the debate ranging from requiring more disclosure from these funds, to limits on banks lending to them, to direct regulation of their activities.

The second issue is the appropriate forum in which to pursue the recommendations and subsequent analysis. The general view is that there needs to be some grouping of countries with sufficient authority, representation and support to put the more important of these recommendations in place, rather than some narrow set of countries. From where things currently stand, it is unlikely that the G22 will be this grouping, although some other similarly constituted grouping may be formed by the G7 to address such issues.

But the issues raised by the G22 are being addressed by a range of groups, many of them international, including various working groups or committees within the BIS, the IMF, the World Bank and the OECD. Regional groups have taken up the reform baton, with, for example, Asia Pacific Economic Cooperation (APEC) leaders agreeing to set up two working groups to assess the G22's proposals for transparency (particularly in relation to institutional investors) and the early resolution of financial crises.

The literature on capital controls

One thread that has emerged in the debate about the financial crisis in East Asia is the appropriateness or otherwise of capital controls. It is probably right to say that the paradigm has shifted somewhat in favour of selective controls, at least in regard to prudential regulation and restraints on some forms of capital inflow in emerging economies under certain conditions. There is also considerable passion in some of these arguments, given the desperate change in conditions of so many of the emerging East Asian economies. Given the strength of the debate, it is probably timely to revisit some of the key elements of the arguments for and against capital controls. This section summarises these basic arguments with the aim of giving some flavour of the richness and complexity of the debate; readers who want more detail are referred to Dooley (1996a) and Fischer et al. (1998) for excellent, more polemical accounts.

The arguments for capital account convertibility

The basic argument that a country should not have controls on its capital account is analogous to the argument for free trade in goods and services: basic economic efficiency. To quote Stanley Fischer (1998: 1–2): 'Free capital movements facilitate an efficient global allocation of savings and help channel resources into their most productive uses, thus increasing economic growth and welfare.' He goes on to explain what this means in more detail:

> From the individual country's perspective, the benefits take the form of increases in the pool of investible funds and in access of domestic residents to foreign capital markets. From the viewpoint of the international economy, open capital accounts support the multilateral trading system by broadening the channels through which countries can finance trade and investment and attain higher levels of income. International capital flows expand the opportunities for portfolio diversification and thereby provide investors in both industrial and developing countries with the potential to achieve higher risk-adjusted rates of return.

Cooper recognises the efficient allocation of resources as the most powerful argument but suggests three further reasons. The first is property rights: 'Individuals should be free to dispose of their income and wealth as they see fit, provided their doing so does not harm others' (1998: 12).

The second is that these controls do not work anyway. The basic point is that capital and financial instruments are highly fungible and markets are able to avoid controls when they have a sufficiently strong incentive to do so. Controls also only tend to be effective in the short term, since markets can move into substitutes or create avoidance mechanisms over time. Controls on foreign currency, for example, can be and are avoided by smuggling, corruption, internal transfer of funds by multinationals, the creation of black markets, or changing foreign trade invoices (Johnston and Ryan 1994; Mathieson and Rojas-Suarez 1993). Capital controls are also ineffective in the sense that they do not prevent speculative attacks and exchange rate adjustment from occurring, even if they buy time before this happens (Eichengreen et al. 1994).

The third argument set out by Cooper (1998) is that capital controls give rise to corruption and favouritism. The people who have access to these mechanisms are the rich and well connected. This is not fair. Controls can also generate collusion: firms which have invested in avoiding controls may want the controls kept in place because they serve to disadvantage and deter potential competitors who do not know the avoidance mechanisms (Dooley 1996a).

Hanson (1994), Dornbusch (1998) and others discuss another reason for an open capital account: high capital mobility limits discretionary policy and forces governments to adopt 'good' or market-conforming policies, including sound financial supervision policies. The basic point is that the market reacts negatively to inflationary or time-inconsistent policies. One echo is in the speculative attack models of Krugman (1979) and Flood and Garber (1984), whereby attacks on a currency arise precisely because of policy inconsistencies, and hence their occurrence serves to generate sustainable policies.

The arguments for capital controls

There is also a large literature which argues in favour of capital controls.

First-best arguments

The first argument for capital controls is that they can be a first-best policy response, and are valid in their own right, because of multiple equilibria (see Dooley 1996a). A policy regime that is otherwise viable becomes unviable because of self-fulfilling private expectations which generate a speculative attack on the currency. One equilibrium may be worse than another and controls may delay the change in private expectations which drives the market to challenge the system in the first place.

Some analysts cite ERM in 1992 as an example of where there were multiple equilibria consistent with a given set of fundamentals, and speculative attacks on certain currencies were validated by the subsequent policy actions of government (Eichengreen and Wyplosz 1993; Eichengreen et al. 1994; Portes 1993). In this view, the speculative attack on the ERM was justified because the governments that dropped out of ERM did so because they did not have sufficient commitment to the peg. Once the governments dropped out, they eased monetary policy, which was what the markets thought they would do in the first place.

Dooley (1996a) argues that the existence of multiple equilibria does not necessarily merit the use of capital controls, since they may destabilise expectations. For example, the imposition of controls may lead the market to reassess the stability of the system and hence challenge it. In addition, Obstfeld (1986) shows that controls themselves may generate multiple equilibria when none exists otherwise.

Second-best arguments

The other arguments in favour of capital controls are essentially second-best arguments: that the ideal world described by Fischer in the previous section does not exist, and that capital controls can offset some other existing distortion. There are basically four types of distortions: fiscal, legal, trade and financial. They are generally analysed with respect to developing or transitional economies and in relation to the sequencing and speed of reform; that is, most of the proponents of capital controls argue that they have a temporary role until other reforms are in place. They also tend to be raised with respect to fixed or pegged exchange rate regimes.

There are four arguments that capital controls can be used to offset an existing fiscal distortion. The first relates to the efficacy of fiscal policy in the basic sticky-price Mundell-Fleming model. Suppose an economy is at less than full capacity. Under fixed exchange rates and capital mobility, fiscal policy is effective but monetary policy is not. But if there are constraints on fiscal policy – typically meaning the tax system does not function well – it may be desirable to use monetary policy with controls on capital outflow. In this case, a monetary expansion does not lead to a capital outflow and self-correcting rise in interest rates. The capital controls give the authorities power to set interest rates independently of world rates.

The second fiscal argument is essentially a 'which tax works best?' argument. Capital controls often take the form of taxes on particular transactions. If the tax base is weak, as it often is in developing countries, capital controls may be less distortionary than some other tax. Similarly, as capital controls are removed, the government has to extend its tax base to maintain revenue (Giovanni and de Melo 1993). One option may be higher debt or monetisation of the fiscal deficit, but these may be more costly to economic efficiency than capital controls. In this context, the argument may be which type of capital control is most effective and efficient.

Third, capital mobility induces tax evasion when tax systems and rates differ between countries, which may be socially suboptimal (Cooper 1998). Fourth, if the government is less able to tax domestic-based capital income than foreign-based capital income, and if capital is mobile, then there may be domestic under-investment and hence lower growth. Controls on capital outflow may correct this distortion.

The second set of arguments relates to the legal system. If property rights are not well defined, domestic firms may prefer to invest overseas rather than locally, which may be socially or economically suboptimal (Tornell and Velasco 1992). Controls in this case may promote efficiency.

Capital mobility can also misallocate resources if there are significant distortions in trade. If capital flows to a country with a lot of labour and protected capital-intensive industries (like steel or cars), for example, the world capital stock is misallocated, national product is lower, and national income is reduced by the payment on foreign capital (Brecher and Diaz-Alejandro 1977). Edwards and van Wijnbergen (1986) also present a model in which capital controls are optimal if there are trade distortions. Edwards (1987) uses a model to show that opening the capital account in the presence of tariffs directs capital flows to the import-competing sector, expanding capital and output in that sector, thus complicating the political economy of trade reform.

Finally, there is a large literature on capital account liberalisation and domestic financial distortions. If the domestic financial sector is distorted, then the unimpeded entry of foreign capital may be costly. This has been explored in detail in relation to the Latin American debt crises of the early 1980s, where the problem was identified as various guarantees given to financial institutions and associated problems of moral hazard. Foreign capital may also engage in excessive risk-taking based on these implicit guarantees (see Dooley 1996a). There is also a concern about countries overborrowing in the early stages of openness, as may occur if the interest rate on debt increases with foreign borrowing and borrowers overextend themselves in anticipation of this (Edwards 1984). More recently, domestic financial distortions have been raised in relation to the East Asian financial crisis: the willingness of foreign capital to lend to these countries and misprice risk, and the willingness of banks and business to take on large unhedged and short-term foreign exposures.

A number of analysts have also questioned the basic efficiency of financial markets in general (Argy 1996; Cooper 1998; Rodrik 1998). They argue that the improved allocation of capital implied in the basic neoclassical model only occurs if information is adequate and reliable, which does not necessarily happen when markets 'herd', trade on noise and rumours, or overreact. Herding is not necessarily irrational, as, when, for example, traders are rewarded for where they stand in relation to the market as a whole. Garber (1998) also argues that herding can in fact be exaggerated by good risk management practices in open financial markets. For example, risk control mechanisms and margin calls based on the *international* variance–covariance of market prices can cause volatility in one market to spread to other, similar, markets.

Rodrik (1998) states the polemic most strongly. After referring to Kindleberger's observation that financial crises have occurred at roughly ten-year intervals for the past 400 years, he argues that 'boom and bust cycles are hardly a sideshow or a minor blemish in international capital flows; they are the main story' (Rodrik 1998: 56). He argues that markets may have the wrong model and send the wrong signals, and that capital mobility can pressure countries to adopt lowest-common-denominator prudential standards which may generate financial and macroeconomic instability.

This has led some to argue for a broader, internationally based set of controls (which can be applied to a floating exchange regime). Tobin (1978), for example, has argued for a broad-sweeping tax on international financial transactions aimed at slowing the adjustment speed of international capital. He argues that this would increase monetary autonomy and reduce destabilising capital flows. Dooley (1996a; 1996b) argues against this on four grounds: it may interfere with 'proper' – that is, trade-based – private commercial decisions; transactions taxes applied in other markets have not been shown to affect volatility; speculation can still occur with low-frequency trades; and such a tax must be enforced by most, if not all, countries if it is to be effective.

Putting the arguments in perspective

Controls are not, of course, an all-or-nothing proposition. Countries face a menu of different types of controls: controls on inflow or outflow, and applied to foreign direct investment (FDI), long-term capital (bank loans, bonds, equities) or short-term capital (money market instruments). This allows for a more sophisticated debate.

Consider, for example, the inflow and outflow argument. Polak (1998) argues that the current consensus among economists is that controls on outflows are ineffective, apart from the short run, and that controls on inflows of FDI and portfolio investment are harmful, reducing the supply of capital and managerial/technical innovation. But he also argues that controls on short-term capital inflows can in fact help prevent excess demand and prevent overshooting behaviour in developing countries. Chile is the oft-cited example; see Massad (1998) for the Chilean authorities' view.

But even here there is considerable debate about how meaningful these classifications are. Claessens et al. (1995), for example, present evidence that the classifications are uninformative about the durability or volatility of the particular type of capital flow, since they have similar predictability and variability properties. Also, long-term instruments, like bonds and equities, can be traded on short time horizons which, they argue, makes the short–long distinction meaningless.

Industrialised countries now generally regard open capital accounts as a basic element of their market structure. In their study on the effects of financial liberalisation on OECD economies, Edey and Hviding (1995) argue that liberalisation has provided three general benefits to industrialised countries. First, it has improved internal efficiency in banking firms, as shown by declining operating costs and some fall in interest margins. It has improved allocative efficiency by removing distortions in relative funding costs and providing greater opportunities for international portfolio diversification. Finally, it has reduced liquidity constraints and so enabled households to better smooth consumption over time. But the broad evidence on macroeconomic and microeconomic gains is mixed; de Brouwer (1999) provides a general review of the costs and benefits of financial openness applied to East Asia.

Even if an open capital account is the aim of policymakers, there is considerable debate about the speed with which controls should be removed. This is often tied to the country's stage of development. Massad (1998), for example, summarises one stream of the literature which argues that full openness can induce strong capital inflow which appreciates the nominal and real exchange rates, generates excess demand and inflation, and leads to a build-up of foreign debt which leaves the country vulnerable to changes in investor sentiment. McKinnon (1973; 1982) and Edwards (1989), for example, argue for gradual liberalisation. Others, such as Kreuger (1984), Hanson (1994) and Dornbusch (1998) argue for rapid reform. To quote Dornbusch: 'A persuasive case for gradualism has never been made' because that policy is liable to be 'hijacked by political pressures adverse to the best use of resources' (1998: 22). On this matter, there is no consensus.

The IMF's view of the world

The arguments for and against capital controls both have persuasive elements, and the cost of the failures in East Asia has led to some quite general modification of the standard paradigm that liberalisation of the capital account is always and everywhere a good thing. This is even evident in the views of the IMF. Without seeking to compromise its view that capital account liberalisation is an important and necessary part of ensuring full economic development, its position became more nuanced in 1998, with a greater emphasis on gradualism, the need for prudential regulation and the possible role of controls on short-term capital inflows in a transition phase.

The 1996 IMF annual report provides an example of its standard position on capital account liberalisation: 'The Board agreed that controls should not – and, in fact, could no longer – support inefficient policies and that capital account convertibility was intrinsically desirable. However, they emphasized that sustainable capital account liberalization required, in particular, a strong and well-supervised financial system in order to avoid costly reversals in the reform efforts' (p. 45). It is 'desirable to develop financial market instruments either before or concurrent with liberalizing the capital account'(p. 46).

This view has been modified but the IMF is particular about the type of control implemented. In June 1998, Manuel Guitian (Director, Monetary and Exchange Department) observed that

> in an effort to reduce inflows before the crisis and to staunch outflows during the crisis, Indonesia and Thailand resorted to capital controls. The controls not only failed to achieve the desired effect but also exacerbated the problem. They introduced new distortions and sent markets a negative signal during the crisis, discouraging new inflows at a critical juncture . . . In general, controls should not be included as a standard weapon in a country's policy arsenal. But they may play a limited and – if properly monitored – constructive role. For example, restrictions may be useful in providing the time needed for policy corrections to take effect . . . It is because controls are a double-edged sword and because of their externalities that international monitoring is necessary. Basic principles for such monitoring include evidence that controls are necessary to protect the balance of payments, that they are transitory and exceptional in character, and that policies are being put in place that will eventually eliminate the need for them.

At the 11 September press briefing for the 1998 annual report, Stanley Fischer said that amendment of the Articles of Agreement to make orderly liberalisation of capital flows one of the purposes of the IMF and to 'possibly' extend its jurisdiction is controversial at this time but is still justified. But he also stated that the debate over liberalisation has changed: 'We would not have recommended to countries to do what some of the countries now in crisis did, which is to open up their capital accounts at the short end while keeping them closed at the long end. It's the other way if you are going to go gradually. I think we need to develop an understanding of how to liberalise capital accounts and that is the way that we think of the amendment, not as a helter-skelter move to capital liberalisation but as a way of bringing order to this process.'

Perhaps the strongest statement of the new position was in the conclusion of the IMF's international capital markets report of September 1998:

> Countries in the process of undertaking . . . reforms may benefit from a temporary strengthening of prudential safeguards, such as stricter regulation and control of financial institutions' foreign currency and liquidity management, and closer monitoring of private capital flows. Some countries may, in addition, find it useful to complement the tightening of prudential controls with well-crafted temporary taxes on (short-term) capital inflows to lessen the vulnerabilities associated with short-term foreign currency exposures of the domestic financial and corporate sectors. In particular, a cross-border

Chilean-type 'tax' on short-term capital inflows would be a way of reducing external vulnerabilities while, at the same time, not discouraging desirable longer-term capital inflows and foreign direct investment. (p. 150)

There is merit in this more moderate view which still preserves the idea that international capital supports growth but that the domestic economy and financial system must be sufficiently robust. But it is also important to note that the 'appropriate sequencing' is much more difficult than just making sure that the domestic financial system is well established before it is opened up internationally. It is not that simple. Even if the focus is on developing domestic financial markets, countries may still need the expertise and experience of foreigners and foreign institutions to do so. That is, limiting international financial exposures is not the same thing as closing access to the system to foreign institutions, and this is particularly pertinent to troubled East Asia in the sense that foreign financial institutions are one of the key routes to recapitalising and reforming the sector.

REFERENCES

Argy, F. (1996) 'The integration of world capital markets: some economic and social implications', *Economic Papers* 15(2): 1–19.

Brecher, R. and C. Diaz-Alejandro (1977) 'Tariffs, foreign capital, and immiserizing growth', *Journal of International Economics* 7: 317–22.

Claessens, S., M. Dooley and A. Warner (1995) 'Portfolio capital flows: hot or cool?', *World Bank Economic Review* 9(1): 153–74.

Cooper, R.N. (1998) 'Should capital account convertibility be a world objective?', in S. Fischer et al. *Should the IMF Pursue Capital Account Convertibility?*, Princeton University, *Essays in International Finance* 207: 20–7.

de Brouwer, G. (1999) *Financial Integration in East Asia*, Cambridge University Press.

Dooley, M.P. (1996a) 'A survey of the literature on controls over international capital transactions', *IMF Staff Papers* 43(4): 639–87.

—— (1996b) 'The Tobin tax: good theory, weak evidence, questionable policy', in M. ul Haq, I. Kaul and I. Grunberg (eds) *The Tobin Tax: Coping with Financial Volatility*, New York: Oxford University Press, ch. 3: 83–106.

Dornbusch, R. (1998) 'Capital controls: an idea whose time is past', in S. Fischer et al. *Should the IMF Pursue Capital Account Convertibility?*, Princeton University, *Essays in International Finance* 207: 20–7.

Edey, M. and K. Hviding (1995) 'An assessment of financial reform in OECD countries', *Working Paper 154*, OECD Economics Department.

Edwards, S. (1984) 'The order of liberalization of the external sector in developing countries', Princeton University, *Essays in International Finance* 156.

—— (1987) 'The liberalization of the current and capital accounts and the real exchange rate', *NBER Working Paper 2162*.

—— (1989) 'On the sequencing of structural reform', *NBER Working Paper 3138*.

Edwards, S. and S. van Wijnbergen (1986) 'The welfare effects of trade and capital market liberalization', *International Economic Review* 27: 141–8.

Eichengreen, B., A.K. Rose and C. Wyplosz (1994) 'Is there a safe passage to EMU? Evidence on capital controls and a proposal', *CEPR Discussion Paper 1061*.

Eichengreen, B. and C. Wyplosz (1993) 'The unstable EMS', *Brookings Papers on Economic Activity 1*, Washington DC: Brookings Institution, 51–143.

Fischer, S. (1998) 'Capital account liberalization and the role of the IMF', in S. Fischer et al. *Should the IMF Pursue Capital Account Convertibility?*, Princeton University, *Essays in International Finance* 207: 1–19.

Fischer, S., R.N. Cooper, R. Dornbusch, P.M. Garber, C. Massad, J.J. Polak, D. Rodrik and S.S. Tarapore (1998) *Should the IMF Pursue Capital Account Convertibility?*, Princeton University, *Essays in International Finance* 207.

Flood, R.P. and P.M. Garber (1984) 'Gold monetization and gold discipline', *Journal of Political Economy* 92: 90–107.

Garber, P.M. (1998) 'Buttressing capital account liberalization with prudential regulation and foreign entry', in S. Fischer et al. *Should the IMF Pursue Capital Account Convertibility?*, Princeton University, *Essays in International Finance* 207: 28–33.

Giovanni, A. and M. de Melo (1993) 'Government revenue from financial repression', *American Economic Review* 83: 953–63.

Hanson, J.A. (1994) 'An open capital account: a brief survey of the issues and the results', in G. Caprio Jr., I. Atiyas and J.A. Hanson (eds) *Financial Reform: Theory and Experience*, Cambridge University Press, ch. 11: 323–56.

Johnston, R.B. and C. Ryan (1994) 'The impact of controls on capital movements on the private capital accounts of countries' balance of payments: empirical estimates and policy implications', *IMF Working Paper 94/78.*

Kreuger, A. (1984) 'Problems of liberalisation', in A. Harberger (ed) *World Economic Growth*, San Francisco: ICS Press.

Krugman, P. (1979) 'A model of balance-of-payments crises', *Journal of Money, Credit and Banking* 11: 311–25.

Massad, C. (1998) 'The liberalization of the capital account: Chile in the 1990s', in S. Fischer et al. *Should the IMF Pursue Capital Account Convertibility?*, Princeton University, *Essays in International Finance* 207: 34–46.

Mathieson, D.J. and L. Rojas-Suarez (1993) 'Liberalization of the capital account: experiences and issues', *IMF Occasional Paper 103.*

McKinnon, R.I. (1973) *Money and Capital in Economic Development*, Washington DC: Brookings Institution.

—— (1982) 'The order of economic liberalisation: lessons from Chile and Argentina', in K. Brunner and A. Meltzer (eds) *Economic Policy in a World of Change*, Carnegie-Rochester Conference Series, Amsterdam: North Holland, 159–86.

Obstfeld, M. (1986) 'Capital controls, the dual exchange rate, and devaluation', *Journal of International Economics* 20(1): 1–20.

OECD (1998) *Economic Outlook*, Paris.

Packer, F. (1998) 'The disposal of bad loans in Japan: the case of the CCPC', paper prepared for Financial Restructuring in Japan conference, Columbia University, New York, 1–2 October.

Polak, J.J. (1998) 'The Articles of Agreement of the IMF and the liberalization of the capital movements', in S. Fischer et al. *Should the IMF Pursue Capital Account Convertibility?*, Princeton University, *Essays in International Finance* 207: 47–54.

Portes, R. (1993) 'EMS and EMU after the fall', *World Economy* 16: 1–15.

Rodrik, D. (1998) 'Who needs capital account convertibility?', in S. Fischer et al. *Should the IMF Pursue Capital Account Convertibility?*, Princeton University, *Essays in International Finance* 207: 55–65.

Tobin, J. (1978) 'A proposal for international monetary reform', *Eastern Economic Journal* 4(3–4): 153–9.

Tornell, A. and A. Velasco (1992) 'The tragedy of the commons and economic growth: why does capital flow from poor to rich countries?', *Journal of Political Economy* 100: 1208–31.

Index

Printed in the United Kingdom
by Lightning Source UK Ltd.
110794UKS00002B/42